Romantic Revolutions

Romantic Revolutions

CRITICISM AND THEORY

EDITED BY
KENNETH R. JOHNSTON, GILBERT CHAITIN,
KAREN HANSON, AND HERBERT MARKS

INDIANA UNIVERSITY PRESS
BLOOMINGTON AND INDIANAPOLIS

The following essays have appeared previously in substantially similar form and are reprinted here with permission: Don Bialostosky, "Wordsworth, New Literary Histories, and the Constitution of Literature," in *The Wordsworth Cir cle* 11 (Autumn 1988), 194–99; Cynthia Chase, "Monument and Inscription: Wordsworth's Lines,'" in *Diacritics* 17 (Winter 1987), 65–77; John Irwin, "Back Home Again in Indiana: Hart Crane's *The Bridge*," in *Raritan* 8 (Spring and Summer 1989), 70–88, 99–113; Andrzej Warminski, "Facing Language: Wordsworth's First Poetic Spirits," in *Diacritics* 17 (Winter 1987), 18–31.

© 1990 by Indiana University Press

The paper used in this publication meets the minimum requirements of American National Standard for Information Sciences—Permanence of Paper for Printed Library Materials, ANSI Z39.48–1984.

⊗ ™

Manufactured in the United States of America

Library of Congress Cataloging-in-Publication Data

Romantic revolutions : criticism and theory / edited by Kenneth R. Johnston ... [et al.].
p.   cm.
ISBN 0–253–33132–3 (alk. paper). — ISBN 0–253–20562–X (pbk. : alk. paper)
1. English literature—19th century—History and criticism—Theory, etc.   2. American literature—19th century—History and criticism—Theory, etc.   3. English literature—19th century—History and criticism.   4. American literature—19th century—History and criticism.   5. Wordsworth, William, 1770–1850—Criticism and interpretation.   6. Romanticism—Great Britain.   7. Romanticism—United States.   I. Johnston, Kenneth R.
PR457.R644   1990
820.9′145—dc20   89–45355
CIP

1   2   3   4   5   94   93   92   91   90

C ONTENTS

III. *American Counterpoints*

IV. *Critical Reflections*

Romantic Revolutions
AN INTRODUCTION

> We, it seems, are critical; we are embarrassed
> with second thoughts; . . . Is it so bad then?
> . . . If there is any period one would desire to
> be born in, is it not the age of Revolution;
> when the old and the new stand side by side
> and admit of being compared?
>
> —EMERSON, "THE AMERICAN SCHOLAR"

Since there has never been a time when Romantic literature
was *not* critically and theoretically contentious, it may be disin-
genuous to present a collection of recent "revolutions" in Romantic criticism and theory as if there had ever been anything else,
as if there could be a calm, classical Romanticism. Yet, subject to
that historical proviso, and well aware that revolutions may be cy-
clical returns as well as epochal transformations, this is what the
present volume makes bold to introduce: a selection of current
critical and theoretical work on English and American Romantic
literature that allows both new and old voices to state their case
and engage each other in dialogue. It brings together some of the
major critics who have shaped our view of Romanticism over the
past generation, as well as younger scholars who have begun to
challenge this view—and who will undoubtedly be challenged in
turn by a coming, *fin de siècle* generation.

The critical animus of Romanticism was directed not only
against cultural works which it opposed, as in Wordsworth's biased but effective attack on Thomas Gray in the Preface to *Lyrical
Ballads* (1800), but also against cultural possibilities which it recognized as its own, as in Coleridge's biased but effective attack on
Wordsworth's Preface in the *Biographia Literaria* nearly a genera-

tion later (1817). The very concept of "generation" is contested in the Romantic dispensation. Its successive generations have consistently aimed to overthrow their own predecessors, denouncing their implication in a conservative status quo while reclaiming for themselves the oppositional role of true representatives of the "spirit of the age." This has been true since Byron and Shelley defined themselves against the "renegade" failures of nerve they saw in Wordsworth and Coleridge, and since Emerson challenged a third generation of Romantics, in America, to cease their retrospective deference to English models. In our own time, these generational revolutions continue in the efforts of Romantic critics like Harold Bloom to make anxiety rather than generosity of influence the motive power behind literary history.

This built-in yet unpredictable contentiousness has contributed much to the infamous difficulty of defining Romanticism, a task which has come to seem the Catch-22 of literary history, since with the advent of Romanticism literary history itself became a ground of contention, or was finally recognized as being always already contested. Definitions of Romanticism have been so numerous that any critical revolution, however progressive, can appear in historical perspective as a return, if not a reaction. The long lists of Romantic characteristics, which were the despair of scholars like A. O. Lovejoy and challenged the erudition of polymaths like René Wellek, kept proliferating in part because they had to embrace so many mirroring oppositions—leading others like Morse Peckham to create flexible or dialectical definitions, such as "positive" and "negative" Romanticism. In an (English) nutshell, this difficulty often comes down to the challenge of fitting Wordsworth and Byron (or Austen) into the same minimally coherent definition, course syllabus, or—as in the present instance—collection of essays. Few of the essays collected here offer to accept the definitional gambit—one sign of how times have changed in Romantic scholarship—yet none fails to address some key figure, or methodology, that has been important in previous descriptions of Romanticism. Perhaps we might better regard the question, What is Romanticism? as by now defining a minor genre of imaginative writing itself, to which many of the present essays contribute.

The seventeen essays were selected from more than thirty papers delivered at an international symposium on Romanticism held in Bloomington, Indiana, in 1988. The purpose of the conference, funded principally by Indiana University and the National Endowment for the Humanities, was to assess the current state of scholarship and criticism in Romantic literature, art, and philosophy. It provided not only a forum for the presentation of new directions in Romantic research, but also an occasion for established scholars to refine or reassert their views and to engage in debate with proponents of alternative approaches. The symposium was the major academic event marking the 1987–88 tour of *William Wordsworth and the Age of English Romanticism*, an extraordinary exhibition organized by The Wordsworth Trust and Rutgers University, containing more than three hundred paintings and manuscripts from over seventy museums and private collections in England and America. An exhibition of such scope and quality could hardly have been mounted so successfully a generation ago. Romantic art and literature were then just beginning to emerge from the cloud of neglect and disapproval under which they had lain since the 1920s, if not since the 1890s. The intervening decades had been devoted, by an unfashionable minority of scholars, to rescuing first Wordsworth and eventually the entire Romantic period from the damaging rhetorical effects of Matthew Arnold's sweeping claim (in 1864) that they "did not know enough." It now seems rather that it was Arnold who did not know enough, or dare enough, to face Romanticism's fearful symmetries. But the long Arnoldian and New Critical neglect of most Romantic literature left the field open for ambitious new interpretive work, much of which has now been accomplished. Indeed, Romantic studies, far from being devalued, have probably been the most active area of productive critical controversy during the past twenty-five years.

In this perspective, the exhibition and the many public events which it generated can be seen as a high water mark in the resurgent fortunes of Romanticism. But the "Romantic Revolutions" conference, and this volume of papers selected and edited from it, mark that resurgence and something more: an acknowledgment that revaluation and interpretation have not stopped, but continue to move in revisionary as well as revolutionary directions. These essays show how the syntheses of the past generation are breaking up, evolving, and coalescing in new forms. They also testify to the continuing vitality of the work of the past twenty-five years, which enlarged the boundaries of Romanticism as an object of critical reflection. For the critical ferment in Romantic studies today is not a sign that prevailing views are weak, but that they are being vigorously defended against challenges from several directions. Some of these challenges, like deconstruction and historicism, are often at odds with each other philosophically, but occasionally appear in strategic alliances against the cultural optimism and idealism of still-standard views of Romantic art. If the exhibition was a triumphant hailing of a fully recuperated Romanticism, some voices at the conference delivered their tributes in none-too-regretful tones of farewell. We certainly hope that this volume does not signal an end to the stature which Romantic art and literature have come to enjoy in modern culture. But then, the beginning of the end has always been a favored Romantic position, whether adopted in the calm anticipation of Wordsworth's "something evermore about to be," or assuming the keener aspects of Stevens's "great shadow's last embellishment."

Other collections of essays, in addition to individual landmark works of criticism like Bloom's *The Visionary Company* (1961), Hartman's *Wordsworth's Poetry, 1787–1814* (1964), and Abrams's *Natural Supernaturalism* (1971), have marked the progress of Romanticism's fortunes during the past generation. Abrams's collection *English Romantic Poets* (1960) exhibited Romantic poetry's acceptance by the New Critical establishment in the postwar American academy, and Harold Bloom's *Romanticism and Consciousness* (1965) announced some of the first demurrals from that acceptance by a phenomenological criticism more indebted to European traditions, as did Hartman's *New Perspectives on Coleridge and Wordsworth* (1972) and his and David Thorburn's *Romanticism: Vistas, Instances, Continuities* (1973). Since then, the post-structuralist movements of the past fifteen years also have begun to produce their own collections: the deconstructive voices in Arden Reed's *Romanticism and Language* (1984) and the New Historicists in Jerome McGann's *Historical Studies and Literary Criticism* (1985), to name but two. But we think it is safe to assert that no collection of Romantic critical essays has orchestrated (or at least corralled) as many diverse and polemically contrary voices as the present one.

A usual task of editorial collectives is to assert unities and common threads running through their volume; our task is more like a critical surgeon general's warning. Remembering that Emerson was content to apply the term *Romantic* to literature we usually call medieval while characterizing his own era as "the Reflective or Philosophical age" (and adding "age of Revolution" for good measure), it follows that such unity as this volume claims must be in a double sense Emersonian. First, respecting the sharp clash of its mutually opposing voices, the editors have from the outset eschewed all "foolish consistency." Second, perhaps the only conviction shared by all contributors is that critical reflection is integral to any definition of Romanticism. It is this common emphasis, more than any direct dissent from the judgments or readings of earlier volumes of Romantic criticism, whose unifying concerns were imagination and nature, the emergence of self-consciousness, or the secularization of romance, that distinguishes this collection. Recent critics have been drawn to Romantic writers precisely because theirs is *the* age of criticism: not only in the explicitly critical writings of Coleridge or the Jena circle, but also in the best-known works of the major poets themselves, in which self-consciousness often has an explicitly textual or hermeneutic dimension. Nor should this emphasis on critical reflection be understood as slighting the importance of social and political revolutions in the career vocations of many Romantic writers and critics: whether in ecstatic embrace or violent recoil, they are alike in their scorn for the middle of the road, for compromise and accommodation. Thus readers will find several critical "generations" alive and well herein, each signally different from the others: cultural idealism, agonistic phenomenology, deconstruction, New Historicism, psychoanalytic biography, Romantic anti-skepticism, and a "comparatist" approach to British and American Romanticism. But in their reflections on the relation of the aesthetic to the historical, on the limitations of mimesis, the specularity of inscription, and the primacy of interpretation, most of these essays are revisiting sites first explored by the Romantics themselves.

The collection thus also presents an occasion for reflection on the oft-noted coincidence between Romantic texts and advanced critical theory in our intensely self-conscious critical generation. Simply to name the leading Romanticists of the present generation is to recite some of its leading theoreticians: Abrams, Bloom, Hartman, de Man, Miller. The same is true for emerging younger generations, who continue to be preoccupied with Romantic texts, but often in an antagonistic relation to received theoretical accounts of them. This could hardly be otherwise, since much of the linguistic, immanentalist, or relational thrust of the leading new theories has been aimed most tellingly at conceptions of literature that are nothing if not Romantic: the presence of spirit (in both Text and World), the incarnation of the symbol, the plenitude of imaginative insight, the cult of genius and the individual, the primacy of mental over social revolution, and so on. Hence the combination of Romantic texts and post-structuralist theory creates a productive paradox for advanced theoretical work.

But this coincidence and tension between theory and practice is not a new one in Romantic history; rather, as we have already suggested, it is one of the most constant reference points in that history. And it is less a coinciding of two things than a continual metamorphosis of the one into the other: a refusal to accept clear lines of demarcation between critical "theory" and literary "practice," or to acknowledge either one as properly master of the other. Just as the mixture or recombination of classically defined genres has always been a characteristic of Romanticism (a characteristic flaw, for many), so the unsteady relation between *opera* and opera*tor* has always been part of it, whether we think of Schiller and the Schlegels, of Blake, Wordsworth, Coleridge, and Shelley, of Rousseau and Hugo—or of Emerson and Thoreau. Nevertheless, this perennial Romantic characteristic has come back into our consciousness with a vengeance in recent years, reminding us that "Romantic Revolutions" is not merely a handy alliterative tag, still less an oxymoron, but nearly a tautology, the usual state of the art: Romantic thinking "as it's most used to do"—to adapt Coleridge's self-vexing conclusion to *Christabel*. More than one essay in the present collection suggests that contemporary generations of Romantic critics in America and Britain are advancing this same strain of "creative criticism," inhabiting the rehabilitated forms of Romanticism only to render their status problematic once again, at a higher, if also more difficult, level of cultural discourse.

It should be noted that both the essays and the groupings in this collection are significantly different from those presented at the "Romantic Revolutions" conference: this is not a "proceedings" volume. Only half of the papers from the conference are printed here, most of them significantly revised from their original form, in light of discussions at the conference and the demands of their new context. Two essays (those by James K. Chandler and Charles Altieri) were written after the symposium, in response to issues raised there. We regret that reasons of economy prevented us from including several excellent papers on art and music history that indicate significant new directions in Romantic interdisciplinary criticism. The resulting four-part division of the volume does not correspond exactly to any of the nine panels of the conference, but forms a new configuration created by the editors, realigning the work of the conference in ways which seemed best to represent the central issues and directions of thought it pursued: (1) the question (pro and con) of Wordsworth's presence as the central representative figure of English Romanticism, (2) the importance of newly reconceived historical, political, and social considerations in the study of Romanticism, (3) the role of American literature as the dark interpreter of a continuing Romantic tradition, and (4) the mode of highly theoretical self-reflection so apparent at any gathering of Romantic scholars nowadays—a mode which, as some of the essays here make manifest, is perhaps Romanticism's most enduring legacy.

I

The Spell of Wordsworth

The Spell of Wordsworth

The four essays in this section set a challenging itinerary through the high defiles of Wordsworth criticism of the past generation, from the publication of Geoffrey Hartman's *The Unmediated Vision* (1954) to the present moment. If they seem to attest the presence of Hartman almost as much as of Wordsworth, that is appropriate to a volume of Romantic theory and criticism, for few would deny that Hartman has been *primus inter partes* of Wordsworth critics during this time—and one with few equals, at that. As Donald G. Marshall says, Hartman reopened the modern dialogue with Romanticism by addressing modern, or "existential," questions to a Wordsworth who had finally become, by mid-century, philosophically respectable, thanks to the work of two generations of twentieth-century scholars—from A. C. Bradley in the 1890s through Arthur Beatty in the 1920s to Newton Stallknecht's *Strange Seas of Thought* (1945). But Wordsworth's philosophic centrality had been purchased at the expense of his human interest: legions of students were indoctrinated in a poetry whose importance was too strongly underwritten in terms of its congruence with selected passages in Kant, Hartley, or Spinoza.

Yet this Wordsworth was important as a bulwark behind which important revisionary critical work could be mounted for a counterattack on the bastions of modernism. Hartman and David Ferry and John Jones began in the 1950s to reveal a Wordsworth who was every bit as interesting in his doubt and isolation as was T. S. Eliot in his wasteland or W. B. Yeats in his tower. The apparent solidity of the "philosophical" Wordsworth was in a way necessary to their project because it had been Wordsworth's Truth, along with Keats's Beauty, that had carried most of the cultural respectability Romantic literature retained during the first decades of high Modernism. Thus the revival of Romanticism's fortunes in our times has been, first and foremost, a revivification of Wordsworth, and of ways of reading him. Whether a new turn in the revolutions of Romanticism's fortunes will be accompanied by a displacement of Wordsworth's preeminence remains to be seen. Here we are concerned with Wordsworth's continuing presence, and certainly the young pioneer of that revolution was Geoffrey Hartman over thirty years ago—who now tries to maintain a certain critical *glasnost* in the face of challenges both from within the movements he helped get rolling in America (phenomenology and deconstruction), as well as from hard-liners in the New Historicist and neo-Marxist camps who were always fundamentally opposed to formalist and idealist assumptions like his.

In what follows, Hartman restates his case for Wordsworth in different terms than *The Unmediated Vision* of 1954 or *Wordsworth's Poetry, 1787–1814* of 1964, thus partly anticipating the deconstructive revisions of his insights which are presented by Andrzej Warminski and Cynthia Chase. Donald Marshall rounds out the sequence by assessing some of the features of Hartman's belated response to deconstruction, and by establishing a valuable perspective in which Hartman's project is viewed once again in the Romantic-to-Modern intellectual history initiated by Kant.

Hartman now argues not for the "apocalyptically" self-conscious imagination of his 1964 Wordsworth, but for a quieter apocalypse of *words*, as prior to and constitutive of the imperious imagination he had located in Wordsworth's Crossing of the Alps passage in Book 6 of *The Prelude*, written in 1804. Reflecting the impact of the new textual situation in Wordsworth studies, Hartman's attention is now directed primarily to the earlier Two-Part *Prelude* of 1798–99. He begins by suggesting parallels between ancient mythic theogonies and Wordsworth's perplexed account of the strange growth of his imagination. Yet he respects Wordsworth's enlightened, Protestant drawing back from his own divine suggestiveness and turns instead to consider something godlike in Wordsworth's words' birth, his turn "toward the semiotic." He thus anticipates the two deconstructive critiques which follow, but not wholly, for he continues to credit a substantive power to language, an Otherness neither referential nor transcendental, which he sees Wordsworth suggestively giving/gaining to/from Nature, that promises "something" (one of Wordsworth's most powerfully implicated philosophic words, as in "something far more deeply interfused") that Warminski and Chase want to keep in suspension.

Andrzej Warminski launches his essay from Hartman's assumptions about language to show that Hartman's phenomenological updating of the traditional Western topoi of Eden-Fall-Redemption (the paradigm of Abrams's *Natural Supernaturalism*) with a sequence running from nature through self-consciousness to imagination will not work, once we admit a linguistic rather than a simply psychological or even phenomenological self-consciousness. For language, deconstructively interpreted, allows no crossing beyond itself, no recuperative return from fallen experience to redemptive reinterpretation. The third stage, which in Kant's philosophy or Wordsworth's poetry is to achieve love and community with one's fellows (the "Human Life" of Wordsworth's own epic triad: Man, Nature, Human Life), is marked instead in Warminski's remodeling only by a neutral *difference*—that is, an awareness that the second stage has misfired, that no language can effect a "real" connection between Mind and Nature because the system of language can never be closed and thus completed *as* system, or statement. But, though Warminski's Wordsworth is definitely the kind of impish "counter-spirit" that Hartman tries to ward off, it turns out to be a figure full of fun. His punning etymological reflections on the "garments" of Wordsworth's Drowned Man of Esthwaite give that corpse a new life of its own, which Warminski disports with not just for the necro-phrill-of-it, but as a telling instance of "the first (murderous) poetic spirit of our not-so-human life," bearing little resemblance to any Wordsworthian babes we have known. Warminski's deconstruction of Wordsworth's and Hartman's assuring connections between mind and nature can only be countered, he argues, by arbitrarily positing an "aesthetic ideology" that will permit identifying (that is, confusing) linguistic reality with natural reality. For Warminski, Wordsworth's text knows better—for better or worse.

Cynthia Chase similarly bases her argument on the achievement of Hartman's revitalized modern Wordsworth, proposing an "alternative history" to the one Hartman offers, whereby Wordsworth was seen as creating a characteristically Romantic nature poetry out of classical tradition by inscribing the observing mind into his descriptive landscapes. Instead of following the organic or subjective possibilities of Wordsworthian "nature poetry," Chase tries to take more seriously the *inscriptive* quality of Wordsworth's writing: its very materiality as language. We do not go out from it, in her view, to a relation between the mind and nature, but, rather, remain within the "indeterminably meaningful." "The poetic text is one that leaves its *meaningfulness* (as distinct from its meaning) unknown"; while various possible meanings of a text can readily be constituted by interpretation, the question of which of its elements are meaningful and which contingent remains in principle undecidable. This claim becomes in her argument an interesting connection to history, in light of deconstruction's supposedly ahistorical ramifications. We are placed in history because of the contingency opened up by language, which cannot control or close off its relation to the extralinguistic. Chase reads Wordsworth as refusing any closure, any completed system "that treats as determined the difference between the meaning and its means." Hence she is not without hope, though to some it may appear as a most unWordsworthian hope, for it is based on language and its conditions of meaning rather than on Mind, Nature, and Society as knowable entities.

Marshall's essay usefully completes these passages of thought by locating Hartman's Wordsworth in the history of post-Kantian philosophy and then projecting him forward to his recent engagements with deconstruction. He situates Wordsworth on the Kantian launching pad of the self's reasoned autonomy (what it knows), contemplating its problematic journey outward to the world, history, or what Wordsworth called "the life of things" (what we can think, but not know)—a journey for which there is no infallible support, but only, at best, an assumption of the possibility of meaningful transfers. For Wordsworth as for Kant, the task by which the self legitimates itself is in finding a way to speak to others: "a man speaking to men." And indeed, as Kant called this way "God," so for Marshall "the decisive hint" of Hartman's intentions is provided by his increasing readiness to use religious terminology, not of dogma or mere spiritual emotion, but in that sense of subjectivity philosophically articulated by phenomenology. Though this "sense" still provides no necessary bridge across the gap from self-knowledge to other-knowledge, but only the exercise of a more or less persuasive eloquence along the way (in Charles Altieri's use of the term), it did permit Hartman to develop "a cultural herme-neutics that allows Wordsworth to speak a word to our time." Lat-terly, this strategy has forced Hartman to engage deconstruction, and to acknowledge his earlier naive emphases on nature and con-sciousness. Marshall portrays Hartman as trying to skirt the abyss of endless indeterminacy from which Chase and Warminski beckon seductively by keeping an openness to "something [that] has to be forgotten" that is the very condition of thoughtfulness.

Marshall ends, as do Chase and Warminski, with Hartman at one of Wordsworth's many gravesides, the Boy of Winander's. All four critics stand close together here, yet on opposite sides of a narrow but deep abyss, where Hartman's "persisting ambivalence" is not far from Chase's "indeterminable meaningfulness." In posit-ing a sequence of meanings, however unpredictable, in our trans-actions with Nature, echoing from the Boy to Wordsworth to Hartman, Marshall implicitly extends it to himself, and to other willing readers, proposing in these "infinite echoes" of language a sequence of possibility that avoids the all-too-ready decon-structive critique by not presupposing any continuity in sequence (as Kant warned). In placing Hartman between the austerities of deconstructive analysis and the more passionate commitments of consciousness represented by the New Historicism, he also ends this first section appropriately by advancing the argument to its next contemporary revolution, represented by the radically dif-ferent reactions to the spell of Wordsworth in part 2.

K.R.J.

"Was it for this . . . ?"
WORDSWORTH AND THE BIRTH OF THE GODS

GEOFFREY HARTMAN

> Was it for this
> That one, the fairest of all rivers, loved
> To blend his murmurs with my nurse's song,
> And from his alder shades and rocky falls,
> And from his fords and shallows, sent a voice
> That flowed along my dreams?
>
> —THE TWO-PART *PRELUDE* OF 1799, ll. 1–6

Wordsworth's contemporary American reception has been remarkable. For, in general, he is a poet who does not travel well. The Continent still does not recognize his poetry: only his early revolutionary sympathies and illegitimate daughter stir flurries of interest. In America, however, he is taken seriously, more seriously even than in England. Wordsworth seems finally to be creating the taste by which he may be enjoyed. The growth of the poetic mind, or of the sympathetic imagination—his greatest theme—is no longer mistaken as a retreat from otherness into Englishness.

And, as the concrete jungle looks for its ecological saint, Wordsworth's reputation should soar. A *New Yorker* cartoon shows two sixties-style hippies browsing through the outdoor shelves of a bookshop. A bearded youth holds up a slim volume and declaims to his companion: "'I wandered lonely as a cloud'— Hey, wild!" Yet how many of us respond to Wordsworth's kind of wildness rather than to Blake's or Whitman's? Our appreciation has increased, yet it is hard to pretend that his age or any age needed the story of Peter Bell the Potter or of Benjamin the Waggoner or other tales of mild idiocy, already ridiculed by Francis Jeffrey.[1] Something less than trumpets, moreover, announces Wordsworth's intended epic: can we really compare his uncertain "Was it for this" to Hölderlin's heroic-hopeful "What are poets for in a time of crisis?" Yet Hölderlin's question too betrays a doubt: it is a modified self-accusation, implying that the age demands Caesars, Napoleons, Nelsons—statesmen and prophets—not poets, and certainly not a Colin Clout "burring" verses in the Cumberland countryside.

Lewis Carroll's Wonderland parodies, placing Wordsworth into the only English tropics around, have not lost their point. They undercut his sentimental and simplistic reception, yet they confirm our sense that conformity has worsted nonconformity, until what's left are droll imaginative doodles. Even those who do not put extreme expectations on poetry have been troubled by Wordsworth's idiosyncrasy. David Ferry saw the precarious quality of his "love of man"; F. W. Bateson caught an unresolved tension between public and private, "Augustan" and "Romantic." Indeed, the charge of solipsism or egotism has never been totally laid to rest, and Jeffrey's comment remains telling. The school of Wordsworth, he said, in distinction from that of Crabbe, does not truly observe nature; its poets excite an interest for their subjects "more by an eloquent and refined analysis of their own capricious feelings, than by any obvious or intelligible ground of sympathy in their situation." All we hear of the Boy of Winander, he complained, is his pastoral game with the owls, "and for the sake of this one accomplishment, we are told that the author has frequently stood mute and gazed on his grave for half an hour altogether!"

Others too, including Coleridge, could not always discern the "intelligible ground of sympathy" that motivated Wordsworth. It may have been this disparity between object and feeling—the lack of a conventional fit between the b(l)eatings of his heart and the ordinary sight or thought, that kept his mind restless, unable to fix its "wavering balance," and obliged him to ask, anticipating Jeffrey, "Was it for this?"

* * *

Let me turn directly to that half line on which so many have commented. The absence of a clear antecedent endows the phrase with a certain independence and pathos. In MS JJ and the Two-Part *Prelude* it gets the narrative started (it is aptly called a launching pad by Kenneth Johnston), but its range of reference remains unclear. The famous verses in JJ on the "mild creative breeze" that becomes a "tempest," disturbing created things by a "redundant energy," indicate that inspiration itself, its duality, may be at issue. This early fragment, as Jonathan Wordsworth has argued, need not connect directly with "Was it for this," yet it is clear from all the versions that Wordsworth was puzzled by the twofold character—mild and wild—of nature's inspiring effect. It is also clear that he believed both types of inspiration had contributed to his growing up as a poet: he was "fostered alike by beauty and by fear" (1805 *Prelude* 1.306), and he finds it strange that so many "discordant elements" have harmonized and formed his "calm existence," one that is obviously not stable but continues to be buffetted by tempestlike motions:

> trances of thought
> And mountings of the mind compared to which
> The wind that drives along th[e] autumnal [?leaf]
> Is meekness.
>
> (JJ, 9–12)[2]

I am not confident that we can sort out, better than Wordsworth himself, who is an instinctive phenomenologist, the elements of his character that cohere so strangely. He was, like the Wanderer, a "being made of many beings." But the unsettled question of identity does merge in *The Prelude* with a question about the sources of inspiration: from what depth of otherness do they come, and what do they imply about the relation of mind to nature, even of human existence to other-than-human modes of being? These modes of the other are apostrophized rather than named, and generally they are not developed as pictures or personifications. If the early MSS use traces of the *genius loci* myth, it is because that kind of personification is ancient, allows the vocative, and does not merge beings into being. The later, more complete transformation of such genii into an entirely humanized perception is one of Wordsworth's achievements. But it would not be an achievement if it did not retain a sense that the person speaking is not the only or even major locus of being and that, conversely, the poet's mind is but a "haunt" analogous to the external world: a theater for actions and purposes of larger scope.

"Was it for this" points to this larger scope: sublime, obscure, frightening. The question responds to a demand, an incumbency. The nature of those other modes of being, of Powers and Presences, needs to be defined, together with the poet's own presence among them. He has to represent, even justify, himself. "Was it for this I came into the world?" Without falling back into a romance mode of representation, he inhabits a realm popularized by romance. These genii or Powers are ranged against the human being, who as an alien or interloper is to be admonished, conquered, seduced. "How is the 'I' to enter this scene which has no need for it and in which it has no place?"[3]

The first memory-image of the Two-Part *Prelude* counters that sense of human intrusion:

> Was it for this
> That one, the fairest of all rivers, loved
> To blend his murmurs with my Nurse's song,
> And from his alder shades, and rocky falls,
> And from his fords and shallows, sent a voice
> That flowed along my dreams?

To convey intimacy, there is a deft recomposition of the stream as a flowing voice and of the mind as penetrable. More remarkable still is a hint that we are witnessing the birth of a hero. The child who hears Derwent may be of mixed human and divine origin: his native stream, "fairest of all rivers," is like a nymph or tutelary presence or even genetrix. (Compare the heavier allegory of Romney's "Birth of Shakespeare".) The infant is surrounded from the beginning by other than purely human sounds and sights.

The doubt in "Was it for this" does not diminish, and even motivates, this depiction of a nativity, extended by *The Prelude*. Wordsworth multiplies the gifts of a magian countryside. If "sweetest Shakespeare," in Milton's phrase, was "fancy's child," Wordsworth is nature's child. And he is at pains to emphasize the softer aspects of this prolonged, generous, natural incubation. The euphemistic strain so marked and unsettling in the mature poetry is already in evidence. His native stream is "fairest" and "beauteous"; a "sweet birth-place" is evoked; the child's thoughts are "composed" "To more than infant softness"; the doublets "fords and shallows," "night and day," "fields and groves" evoke complementarity not contraries; and's and or's spring up in profusion; there is a subtle, expansive movement from "one" to "thou," from "Stream" (l. 8) to "streams" (l. 20);[4] and in "the frost and breath of frosty wind" (l. 29) something faintly adversative is at once energized and mellowed by a redundance which doubles the locus of what is later (and more philosophically) named an "active principle." The surplus rhetoric of

> Yes, I remember when the changeful earth
> And twice five seasons on my mind had stamped
> The faces of the changeful year   (JJ, 144–46)

is grounded in a natural surplus.

Redundance, classical periphrasis and euphemism combine to convey a multisourced principle of generosity. Sometimes even the locus of perception expands, as when Wordsworth stations the boy within a natural scenery that animatedly and eagerly offers itself. He sees, and is seen:

> The sands of Westmorland the creeks & bays
> Of Cumbria's rocky limits they can tell
> How when the sea threw off his evening shade
> And to the shepherds hut beneath the craggs
> Did send sweet notice of the rising moon
> How I have stood. . . .   (JJ, 152–57)

This is not the language of mystery, even if the poet does not know why he felt what he felt in moments that seemed primordial:

> How I have stood to images like this
> A stranger li[n]king with the spectacle
> No body of associated forms
> And bearing with [me] no peculiar sense
> Of quietness or peace yet I have stood
> Even while my eye has moved oer three long leagues
> Of shining water, gathering as it seemd

New pleasure like a bee among the flowers—
(JJ, 157–65)[5]

Such experiences allowed Wordsworth to record the phenomena themselves rather than what they meant. An intense outline remains; the rest, affect or meaning, has "Wearied itself out of the memory." This unintelligibility does not seem to be a burden. It is unlike "the heavy and the weary weight / Of all this unintelligible world" characterizing later experience.

Among archetypal moments more permanent than their meanings are the terrifying (wild) and calming (mild) incidents we have mentioned. Wordsworth refuses to see them as irreconcilable. He simply weathers them, and they continue to "work" on him as if he too were water, heath, or mountain. They did not resolve into, or become resolved by, thought. In that formative time the supplement of thought (an interest "unborrowed from the eye") was not there or was not needed. But at present they *are* mediated by thought, and the perplexity he expresses arises from a twofold source: (1) in the past, the fearful incidents outnumbered the calm; (2) at present, the fearful incidents have become an essential part of his "calm existence." He glimpses what the complete *Prelude* calls a "dark inscrutable workmanship" that coheres contrary experiences like music's concordant discord. Given the dominant emphasis on dissonance-resolution, the "this" could be metalinguistic and refer to a recurrent turbulence which has now taken the form of an incessant questioning. "Was it for this kind of questioning, this 'Was it for this.'"

Yet Wordsworth, as he writes on, so enhances the early moments of calm, and so euphemizes the moments of dread, that the opening question, with its hint of continuing turbulence—fretful interludes that threaten a desired equanimity—acts as if it referred to a threatening calm that borders on entropy or the grave. Already by the end of the first paragraph of the Two-Part *Prelude* we have traveled from birth to a composure that has a "rest-in-peace" quality about it. The boy's thoughts were "composed / To more than infant softness" and given "a dim earnest of the calm / Which Nature breathes among the fields and groves."

When Wordsworth later uses the formulaic title "Composed upon Westminster Bridge. . . ," "Composed by the side of Grasmere Lake. . . ," does "composed" carry an echo of "made calm" and refer to poet as well as poem? The scenes before him "compose" his thoughts by touching back to those early, calming moments. Yet the calm is not savored for its own sake alone, or because it soothes a fretful mind, but chiefly because in its remembered form it has power—or should I say, powers—in it. To summarize, then, several referents enrich the "this" of Wordsworth's question: fear, or terrible beauty, as a factor in a tempestuous poetic inspiration; the calm that alternates with fear and composes it, but may end by overcoming life itself; the turbulence created by this opposition between poetry's feeding-sources, splitting or unsettling the poet's identity; and the brooding on this, which becomes a "rigorous self-inquisition" in the longer, complete versions of *The Prelude*.

Despite such overdetermination, "Was it for this" potentially simplifies into an "it was for this" and even "it was". The question wants to be a statement about an "it" (nature) that "was" (acted in the past) "for this" (a poetry it calls to birth). Ranged against this affirmation are not only doubts about the tendency of the past but also about the poetry it fosters. While Wordsworth must claim his identity and emerge into major song (*majora canamus*), the very experience that moves him toward self-presentation (the "egotistical sublime") also magnifies a nature that makes the human appear as only one locus of being in an active universe. His privilege is less to say "I" than to identify with nature's purposive and impersonal mode, an "It was" that resembles the ballad's "It is," "There is," "There was"—a "sentiment of being" singled out by Lionel Trilling as the key to Wordsworth's poetic temperament. By the very act of writing *The Prelude*, "Was it for this" turns into "It was for me." The impersonal seems to address and justify Wordsworth's not inconsiderable poetic ego. But his claim to be "a Power like one of Nature's" only revives an ancient question, found in the most lyrical epic of them all. "What is man, that thou dost make so much of him, and set thy mind upon him. . . ?" (Job 7.17). *The Prelude*'s account of the birth of a poet as "the subject in question" is also a phenomenology of elemental feelings connecting that account with another story: the birth of the gods.

To think of the early versions of *The Prelude* as an embryonic theogony might seem just the wrong context. Such a context fits other Romantics better, especially Blake, Shelley, and Keats. Their revisionary mythic poems are linked to the French Revolution and a change fatal to old ideas about religion. Yet we underestimate Romanticism's connection with the Enlightenment (which it revises not abrogates) if we do not see that Wordsworth too, more radically perhaps, confronts the gods. He does so as part of the history of his development and he brings about a change—even revolution—in the language of representation. Indeed, he naturalizes natural religion so effectively that we barely think of Blake's outraged polemics against it or the psychological aspects of a methodism which Richard Brantley has shown is closest to Wordsworth.

The gorgeous mythopoeia of the other Romantics poses a question of appropriateness. What is special about Wordsworth is that he fashions a language for poetry that does not differ essentially from prose yet allows us to understand myth and religion. He describes their sources in the imaginative life from childhood on and their representational career—the way concepts arising from elemental feelings form and deform mental growth.

The beauty that has terror in it is predominant among those feelings. An old dictum runs that fear founded the gods. The eighteenth century produced a number of sophisticated genealogies expounding the idea. "It was fear," Vico remarks, "which created gods in the world, not fear awakened in men by other men, but fear awakened in men by themselves." That fear, interpreted as self-astonishment, is then connected with figurative language, or with the idiom of our ancestors the giants. Blake also linked fear to figuration, though of a distorted kind. His visionary poems show a continual theogony whose "big bang" is the self-astonishment of an imagination that shrinks from its own power and then abdicates it to the priests. By this recession it also produces the void described in the first lines of Genesis, and a God who has to create something from that nothing. Our present religiously reduced imagination continues to exnihilate creation, that is, to understand created nature as the product of a creator who has raised it from nothing (ex nihilo). The result is a flawed image of power that has inscribed itself in domestic, political, and religious institutions—it has become a second nature, and frozen the hierarchy of human and divine.

The separated gods, then, are forms of fear that terrify, check, and (in the hands of a priestly religion) exploit us. We astonish ourselves with our own conceptions and continue to alienate the modes of mental production by at once abstracting and realizing (reifying) these gods or genii: we forget that "All deities reside in the human breast" (*Marriage of Heaven and Hell*, plate 11). The English Reformation, for both Blake and Wordsworth, began to free the imagination from fears about itself, or "Mystery" in the shrouding and restrictive sense.

Yet the difference between the two poets is striking. Blake's attack on mystery, his redemptive theogony, is a lurid affair, with logos indistinguishable from pathos and with words and emotional states providing the weapons. We are inside some traumatic mental process, or a mock-up of it devised by an ingenious advertising company pushing a mind-altering drug. These decomposing and recomposing gods, these expanding and contracting metamorphs, display recognizable human emotions on a sublime stage that leaves nothing to the imagination because it is the imagination. Instead of mystery, there is too much illumination from Blake's will, burning up and leaving no trace of mystery-religion in any domain. What is missing, even after Yeats, Frye, and Bloom, are the coordinates that would allow reader or spectator to stand on firm ground and not suffer interpretive vertigo. Interpretation, ironically, is the only mysterious thing here, as all that light creates the very darkness Blake wanted to dispel.

In the natural theology that Blake combats, the light of nature goes out when revelation supervenes "dark with excessive bright." But in Wordsworth the light of nature is never totally extinguished by any shade thrown up from the soul. Sense and soul are primordially linked so that fear, whether attributed to nature or mind, is an "impressive agency," an elemental and numinous emotion, not a social construct resulting from age-long imaginative error. Yet no one depicted more sensitively, before Wordsworth, the color of fear and how it might stimulate a demonic religion. In Wordsworth too, fear reflects imagination awakening to a sense of power, though nature's power as well as its own.[6] The child, however, remains ignorant of its own part in this drama till time becomes an interpretant. Blake is all theogony and genealogy; he has nothing to teach about development in time or the growth of the poet's mind. Eternity, not time, is his milieu, even if "Eternity is in love with the productions of Time." But Wordsworth records how the impressive event, being temporalized, opens to interpretation without losing its sensuous hold. The basic shift that time brings about is referential: from nature to imagination, with nature remaining a heavenly agency.

> O heavens, how awful is the might of Souls
> And what they do within themselves while yet
> The yoke of earth is new to them, the world
> Nothing but a wild field where they were sown.
> (1850 *Prelude* 3.178–81)

The colloquial oath ironically displaces the heavens it evokes and recalls instead the wars of the imagination on earth. Yet Wordsworth can be nervous about his own discovery, so that a new fear, of interpretation itself, occasionally enters and tempts him to foreclose his insights through euphemism and didactic overlay.

To make these observations more concrete, let me comment briefly on the episode in which the youngster steals a boat and imagines a huge cliff striding after him. Demons are born of that moment of visionary dread, border-images of something alive yet not human. Nature is emptied of the comforts which its shapes and colors normally provide:

> after I had seen
> That spectacle, for many days my brain
> Worked with a dim and undetermined sense
> Of unknown modes of being: in my thoughts
> There was a darkness, call it solitude
> Or blank desertion: no familiar shapes
> Of hourly objects, images of trees,
> Of sea or sky, no colours of green fields:
> But huge and mighty forms, that do not live
> Like living men, moved slowly through my mind
> By day, and were the trouble of my dreams.
> (Two-Part *Prelude*, First Part, 120–29)

The light of sense goes out "with a flash that has revealed / The invisible world." Such moments turn nature into theater, a place of heightened action and demand. The poet describes that vividly enough, yet his impressions might have induced romance themes, and even a dramatic form of representation. We want to hear those beings speak "as if a voice were in them" and hear the response of the pursued boy. Can human voice answer to such pressure and remain human, rather than alienating itself and adopting a sublime rhetoric? Can one have a "conversation" in or about such circumstances? Wordsworth talks past the experience, shifting from narrative to apostrophe, from description to an interpretation that assumes a "fellowship" between nature and the developing poet:

> Ah! not in vain ye Beings of the hills!
> And ye that walk the woods and open heaths
> By moon or star-light, thus from my first dawn
> Of childhood did ye love to intertwine
> The passions that build up our human soul. . .
> (Two-Part *Prelude*, First Part, 130–34)

This shift, it seems to me, still does not recognize the awful power of imagination. The enumeration and pluralizing (he goes from the one huge cliff to "Beings of the hills" and associates them with "spirits" of the milder sort) take the edge off a singular event. The apostrophe functions as a sublime punctuation mark, a reflective breathing-out that fills the gap between incidents. That gap disturbs me, not so much because Wordsworth's narrative remains episodic but because the episodes that constitute it run off into apostrophe and didactic speech. "Was it for this?" also has no direct addressee: it is uttered, one might say, to the genii of the air. The mind is conversing with itself in the presence of an after-image that still "works" on the poet, who is never free of the impression it recalls. Solitary recall and reflection may be the best outcome, given the isolating force of imagination, yet Wordsworth continues to represent imagination as destined to become sociable and sympathetic.

The drama on both psychological and expressive levels is not all that different from what Coleridge records in a mountain experience of his own. First described in November 1799, it was reentered in Coleridge's notebooks shortly after his ascent of Scafell, at the time of composing the "Hymn Before Sunrise in the Valley of Chamouny" (September 1802). "Ghost of a Mountain—the forms seizing my Body as I passed and became realities—I, a Ghost, till I had reconquered my substance." Coleridge adopts a sublime or supernatural mode of representation for this kind of experience. The different poetries that emerge from the "dialogue" between the two poets are so absorbing precisely because they question the possibility of a purely human speech, of that conversational style which Coleridge enacts in his famous Conversation poems but then yields to Wordsworth's genius. In this light *The Prelude* is Coleridge's greatest Conversation poem, with "the giant Wordsworth, God bless him!" as the mountain that has "stolen" his substance. Reeve Parker has said a similar thing about the mock-sublime of the Chamouny hymn, and both Kenneth Johnston and Paul Magnuson have rightly called the Two-Part *Prelude* an extended conversation with Coleridge.[7] My main point would be, though I cannot develop it here, that the Romantic poets show us how problematic it is to reduce imagination to conversation, or to a dialogic mode, even as the political ideals they share move in that direction, that is, in the direction of a dismantling of hierarchy and a recovery of vernacular or conversational relationships.

As if inevitably, I have arrived at the political theme haunting contemporary reflections on literature. From the time of Vergil, when the relation of poetry and politics is explicitly raised and the theme of empire and the destiny of nations enters Western literature, poets have never lost sight of the exceptional character of their occupation in the greater world. I cannot say the same about recent commentators, who insist that the political content of literature has been neglected or must be our first if not exclusive concern. No pronouncement of this kind will change the fact that our own occupation as literary scholars working within a university context is as exceptional as poetry itself. The privilege that causes our concern will not be cancelled by mimic wars against the "aesthetic" element in art or art theory. Such attacks deny what is strong and peculiar about both art and art education, and so may be self-scuttling and politically the worst thing to do.

I want to return, therefore, to Wordsworth's self-scrutiny during an era in which, as Napoleon remarked, politics was fate. Poetry, sidelined by the Enlightenment and the beginnings of industry, as well as by the war, was passing again through an identity crisis. An early poem of Hölderlin's sees Napoleon as too transcendent a subject for poetry. "He cannot live or dwell in the poem: he lives and dwells in the world."

Wordsworth's turn to nature meant that an answer to his question had to come from that source. Experientially but also conceptually it was a necessary move. No heavenly voice was expected or even desired. Nature here is not simply the field of the poet's early hauntings; it is the birthplace of genius—"genius" understood as a force of nature, a force of destiny real as any other, including Napoleon's. We are not dealing with daily politics but with visions that ravaged Europe, of empire, revolutionary liberty, and national destiny. A poet gains his legitimacy from the fact that he too has a vision, or counter-vision, inspired by the genius of the place he embodies. "Was it for this?" embraces a doubt—that has to be resolved—about Wordsworth's "leading genius": is he destined to be a poet, and if so, what will be his poetical character? A temperament allied to terror and tempest is indicative of the heroic and suggests not simply an older type of sublimity but also a vocation that is military rather than museal.

What happens when Wordsworth turns to nature? In the "field of light" passage already quoted, he tries, unsuccessfully, to move from sight to insight. He remembers how he used to scan *visibilia*, or the Book of Nature, without understanding the pleasure received and without seeking to go beyond it. He emphasizes the very fact of not-knowing—which does not augur well for his initial question. In the midst of all this light there is opaqueness: why did such scenes hold him? He specifically rules out a psychological interest derived from the mechanism of association: the charm was more elemental than that. Yet his appeal to Cumbria and Westmorland, "they can tell . . . how I have stood," suggests an extreme, animistic development of the sympathetic imagination that places the young poet among other consciousnesses and evokes a sense of possible sublimity—enough, perhaps, to feed the feeling that he was Nature's child, and even perhaps the glorious imp whom Vergil celebrated in the *Fourth Eclogue*, his prophetic pastoral. Yet the transition from prelusive trials of strength to a "work of glory" eluded Wordsworth. His self-questioning and apologetic

strain impeded what the coda to Vergil's *Fourth Eclogue* called for:
"Incipe, parve puer," "Begin, little child. . . ."

Wordsworth refused to step fully into the light with a mythi-
cal beginning of this kind. (Even the Great Ode hesitates on the
threshold of myth.) Despite teleological breathings he did not
claim a manifest destiny but deferred the vision of First and Last,
painting nature and his relations to it by a negative knowledge that
was his honesty. A higher strain, Miltonic or Vergilian, cuts across
the pastoral narrative without transforming it. The deepest feeling
of calm, at the same time, though it may purify the quest for meaning, cannot dispel an apologetic or higher consciousness:

> Nor unsubservient even to noblest ends
> Are these primordial feeling[s] how serene
> How calm those seem amid the swell
> Of human passion even yet I feel
> Their tranquilizing power
>
> (JJ, 166–70)

The question of "ends" always intrudes. Yet here too we find a significant link to Vergil and the rival vocations of poet and leader.

At the conclusion of the *Georgics*, Vergil contrasts the poet's
activity with that of Octavius Caesar:

> These verses about the culture of the fields, cattle and trees, are
> what I sang, while great Caesar was unleashing the thunder of war
> against deep Euphrates and, victorious, imposed his laws on its
> consenting people, on his way to commanding a place on Olym-
> pus. At that very moment sweet Sicily nourished me, Vergil, pros-
> pering in the arts of ignoble leisure (*ignobilis oti*). . . .

This not entirely modest modesty-topos became a literary commonplace. "Inglorious" or "ignoble" in Wordsworth, whether applied to poetry or poetry's description of ordinary childhood, contrasts with the idea of a productive calling, with mature work or
"honorable toil." It is not surprising, then, that "Was it for this" is
prompted in the 1805 *Prelude* by the New Testament parable of
the unprofitable steward. The intensely experienced *otium* must
be defended in terms of *negotium*. Wordsworth calls himself "not
uselessly employed" in describing childhood activities, his shad-

owy moods are "not profitless," the pines murmur "not idly." The poet assures himself of the dignity of talking about his youth and its after-images by hinting that there is a noble end. His strong metaphorical use of "work" and "working" derives from the same apologetic vein. The unproductive life is not worth living: *The Prelude* reflects the oldest of bourgeois scruples.

Yet this Wordsworth, "prince of poetical idlers," as Hazlitt dubbed him, had his own way of breaking through to an astute visionariness and representing subliminal modes of action: "The influence of power gently used." Nature's agency in "There was a Boy" quietly counterpoints the exaltation of revolution in the greater world and Vergil's Roman promotion of Caesar to Olympus. A lyrical ballad in which nothing much seems to happen depicts instead the apotheosis of an ordinary child, cousin to Vergil's glorious *puer*. A life is summed up in a few traits that mainly show life taking place elsewhere—a displacement of "heroic argument" more striking than Milton's (compare *Paradise Lost* 9.25–29).

Speech itself, in fact, is almost displaced, so strong is the pressure of a concept of natural development on a concept of formal education. The boy is not given a name, and the opening words are interrupted by an apostrophe to Winander, "ye knew him well" (compare the "you can tell" addressed to Cumbria and Westmorland), which is a first pause in a deepening series. The apostrophe transfers permanent consciousness from man to landscape— subordinating even the poet who utters those words. The narrative almost ends in that first pause, as if "There was a Boy" were story enough, or keenest epitaph.

If Nature intended the youngster to mature into a poet by fostering intuitive rather than tutored speech, her plan is curiously aborted. For Wordsworth's elegiac "There was" refracts into strong and weak emphases that require an internal echoing or doubling, and so contrasts ironically with the boy's own "speech" that raises echoes yet remains primitive mimicry. "There was," as a narrative opening, is the weak form, though gesturing toward the more dramatic temporality of the traditional ballad. The strong form, "*There* was a Boy," locates him not only in place (time) but also in existence: the essence of childhood is adumbrated as a bond between place and mode of being. Thus the episode as a whole projects an archetype of natural being: the near-silent and inglorious *puer* merges with his birthplace rather than being enskied. He dies into the spot where he was born, becoming a Miltonic *genius loci* who haunts Winander's shore and halts the passer-by.

To juxtapose Milton's *Lycidas*, Vergil's *Eclogue*, and this episode reveals more than the apprenticeship of genre or the influence of the majors. Wordsworth aborts, as it were, the mentality of myth while still allowing access to myth's mode. A complex symmetry builds between the pathos-haunted death of a boy at the threshold of self-awareness and the myth-haunted liminality of Wordsworth's style. Can the force of nature—or vision—be carried over into the next developmental stage? The poet who stands mute, remembering the boy he had been, must save vision not only from the twilight of myth (that is, the Enlightenment), but also from myth itself. The episode poses a double question: Was it for this mythless, muted voice that intimations of immortality dowered childhood? Or, is there a more original form of imagination than myth?

It is far from adequate, then, to define Wordsworth's peculiar strength in terms of a displacement of myth, by internalization or secularization. It is true that he depicts a heroic action removed from its usual martial or worldly locus. Heart and mind, starting with childhood—and almost ending there—are the haunt and the main region of his song. But there is a further displacement, away from visibility, or phenomenality in general, and toward the semiotic.[8] After an eloquent assertion in the third book of *The Prelude*:

> Of Genius, Power
> Creation, and Divinity itself,
> I have been speaking
> (1805 *Prelude*, 3.171–73)

the poet goes on to declare:

> Not of outward things
> Done visibly for other minds—words, signs,
> Symbols or actions—but of my own heart
> Have I been speaking
> (1805 *Prelude*, 3.174–77)

Words and signs are compared to actions, because of their visible, outer-directed nature. It is as if Wordsworth wished to displace even words (the formal subject of *Prelude* 5 is Books) as too external. His argument is supported by the theme of inward (Christian as against Pagan) heroism; what is remarkable, however, is not his extension of the Protestant commonplace but a radical, antiphenomenal attitude that does not spare the spoken word. All the more understandable, then, that the Boy dies before speech makes him known to others. Wordsworth's "ye knew him well" is addressed to native cliffs and islands, not to human companions.

Through this rhetorical turn, however, the displacement that shifts heroic or mythic action inward aligns with a figural displacement that operates independently of the Protestant theme and even preempts it. By the speech act "ye knew him well" a knowledge without speech is evoked: the animating metaphor displaces knowledge, transfers it to a mute observer. Metaphor does "naturally" (that is, conventionally) what on the level of theme is tendentious or exceptional. The quiet(ed) boy and a quiet style go together. We are closer, in this episode, to the birth of words than to the birth of the gods, to verbal figures rather than to myth. It is as if phenomenality had been restored as a property of words rather than "outward things."

The entire episode can now be seen as metaphor writ large rather than myth writ small. Poetry does not compete with Nature as a counterspirit, or with the phenomenal world by a glittering sort of mimesis: it displays a phenomenality of its own that conspires with Nature's milder aspect of "power gently used" (1850 *Prelude* 12.15). We realize that Wordsworth's radical inwardness—so much more, I have suggested, than an extension of Christian or other kinds of internalization—does not disparage language. A poet's words too are "visibly for other minds." A magnification or landscape-enlargement of metaphor creates the subtlest sublimity on record. The point (which Jeffrey missed) is to catch, in poetry, a hint of that apostrophaic and transmuting power[9] Wordsworth ascribes to imaginative action. "Inward light alas," we read in Milton's *Samson*, "Puts forth no visual beam." Poetic words, ideally, overcome that defect: they endow a silent light with shape, sound, and being. If Derwent, Winander, and all the influences of Nature had raised Wordsworth only for this, it would have been enough.

NOTES

1. Don H. Bialostosky has made a case even for these. See *The Poetics of Wordsworth's Narrative Experiments* (Chicago, 1984).

2. My text is *The Prelude. 1798–1799*, edited by Stephen Parrish (Ithaca, 1977).

3. Thomas Weiskel on the third stanza of "Resolution and Independence," *The Romantic Sublime: Studies in the Structure and Psychology of Transcendence* (Baltimore, 1976), p. 61.

4. All references, unless otherwise indicated, are to the First Part of the Two-Part *Prelude* in Parrish's edition.

5. In the 1805 *Prelude*, 1.607, the leagues of shining water suggest the marvelous, near-Vergilian phrase, "field of light."

6. The role of fear or terror in moving the mind beyond "unregenerate perceiving," is the center of Weiskel's important analyses of Burke and Kant, as well as the Romantic poets.

7. Reeve Parker, *Coleridge's Meditative Art* (Ithaca, 1975); Kenneth R. Johnston, *Wordsworth and the Recluse* (New Haven, 1984); Paul Magnuson, *Coleridge and Wordsworth: A Lyrical Dialogue* (Princeton, 1988). Weiskel makes the interesting claim that when Wordsworth naturalized the archaic and demonic (or divine) sources of power, he discovered "a mode of conversation, now most easily recognized outside of poetry in the domains of the authentic psychoanalyst or a certain kind of expert teacher too tentative to know or say for sure what he 'really' means." Yet he admits, at once, "to describe *The Prelude* as any kind of conversation seems perverse. Its apparent form is closer to monolithic monologue...." (*Romantic Sublime*, p. 169).

8. For Wordsworth's understanding of the radical inwardness (non-phenomenality) of words, see Geoffrey Hartman, *The Unmediated Vision* (New Haven, 1954), the chapter "Pure Representation"; *Wordsworth's Poetry* (reprint, Cambridge, Mass., 1987), pp. 33–69 (these writings of 1954 and 1964 describe not a semiotic process but phenomenality turning against itself); Paul de Man, "Intentional Structure of the Romantic Image" and "Autobiography as Defacement" (now in *The Rhetoric of Romanticism*, [1984]); Thomas Weiskel, *The Romantic Sublime* [1976], esp. "Wordsworth and the Defile of the Word"; and Hartman, "Words, Wish, Worth," (now in *The Unremarkable Wordsworth* [Minneapolis, 1987]).

9. See 1805 *Prelude* 13.94: [higher minds] "Like transformations, for themselves create"; and 1850 *Prelude* 13.94: "Kindred mutations; for themselves create," "Mutation" suggests, as a word, a turning around of what was *mute*. To "silent light," on Snowdon, voices issue by a reversal or breakthrough that is said to be the express resemblance of imaginative action, human or divine.

Facing Language
WORDSWORTH'S FIRST POETIC SPIRITS

ANDRZEJ WARMINSKI

> It would be naive to believe that we could
> ever face Wordsworth, a poet of sheer lan-
> guage, outright. But it would be more naive
> still to think we can take shelter from what
> he knew by means of the very evasions
> which this knowledge renders impossible.
>
> —PAUL DE MAN, "WORDSWORTH AND THE
> VICTORIANS," *THE RHETORIC OF ROMANTICISM*

Among the institutionalized ways of *not* facing Wordsworth perhaps none continues to stand upright quite as solidly and fixedly—"as if sustained by its own spirit" (1805 *Prelude* 3.280–81), as it were—as the interpretation of the relationship between man and Nature, Imagination and Nature, as a dialectic of immediacy and mediation, consciousness and self-consciousness. A most suggestive global statement of this interpretation is offered by Geoffrey Hartman in "Romanticism and 'Anti-Self-Consciousness'" when he reminds us that "Romantic art has a function analogous to that of religion. The traditional scheme of Eden, fall, and redemption merges with the new triad of nature, self-consciousness, imagination; while the last term in both involves a kind of return to the first" (54). In other words, if self-consciousness marks a fall from nature, then the only kind of return that would not be a regression to the immediacy of mere self-consciousness would be the return by way of yet another turn of self-consciousness. "Anti-self-consciousness" is not *un*-self-consciousness but rather self-consciousness *of* self-consciousness, the (self-)negation of the negativity of self-consciousness. As Hegel puts it in his interpretation of the Fall quoted by Hartman: "the hand that inflicts the wound is also the hand that heals it" (49). In short, the mechanism involved in the last term's being, in the last term's *becoming*, a kind of return to the first, is Hegelian negation *of* negation, the determinate negation that, because it is always the negation *of* something, always has a content and thus is never *mere* (one-sided, abstract) negation. Without this mechanism, the return could go astray, as Hartman well knows: "Yet everything depends on whether it is the right and fruitful return. For the journey beyond self-consciousness is shadowed by cyclicity, by paralysis before the endlessness of introspection, and by the lure of false ultimates" (54). But as long as the negativity of these haltings on the way can be experienced as the negation *of* self-consciousness, it can be surmounted (sublated, *aufgehoben*, in Hegel's terms) and recovered for the unity of a higher synthesis: the paradise regained of reflected, mediated immediacy, the clarified, Self-conscious Nature of the Imagination. We know what kind of interpretation of Wordsworth this path leads to, and Hartman's *Wordsworth's Poetry, 1787–1814* continues to stand as its most eloquent monument.

But the shadows along the way beyond self-consciousness are not confined to the recoverable, sublatable negativity proper to (self-)consciousness. Another negative—for lack of a better word, a "linguistic negative," one proper to language—haunts the journey all along the way and brings with it its own snares, its own cyclicity, paralysis, and false ultimates. To introduce this other negative, all we need do is to ask a direct question: what happens when, what if, the second term of the triad Nature/Self-consciousness/Imagination is understood, is read, as a linguistic self-reflection, a linguistic self-consciousness, as it were, a linguistic turn of language on language? The question is not idle or perverse since at least in the case of Wordsworth's *Prelude* it is explicitly thematized throughout in a poem about poetry, about the relation of Books and Nature (for instance, Book 5), about the relation of reading and seeing (for instance, in the drowned man episode in Book 5). And, on an even more immediate level, the question is the first "textual" (in the sense of philological) fact of our "experience" of the text of *The Prelude*: that is, the re-visionary nature of the text, the fact of the many revisions, the many manuscripts of this autobiography. In other words, from one's first experience of the text, what one gets is not any neat division between, on the one hand, Wordsworth's life, his experience, and his memory of that experience and, on the other hand, Wordsworth's text, his manuscripts, and his writing. Since the writing and the reading, and the rereading and the rewriting, are very much a part of Wordsworth's life and experience, they become *events* in his life, what one gets from the first is texts on texts—not just a story of how experience becomes text but also always already how text becomes experience. But the question remains whether the text—its writing and its reading—can become "part of" a life, whether that which works according to its own laws, the laws proper to language, can be recovered and included in that which (the experience of life) works according to the laws of consciousness and self-consciousness, according to the laws of the dialectic of experience (in the Hegelian sense, *Erfahrung*). The question is, of course, a problem for all autobiographies—because despite being written from the point of view of death, as it were, all autobiography is nevertheless written during the author's lifetime—but it becomes particularly visible, particularly readable, whenever there are *two* autobiographies, for the one that comes second always has, in some sense, to include the first, the writing of the first, in its account of the life.[1]

Hartman is, of course, well aware of the disruption that something that happens during composition—"and which enters the poem as a new biographical event" (Hartman, *Wordsworth's Poetry*, 46)—can cause, as his interpretation of the uprising of Imagination before the eye and progress of Wordsworth's song in *Prelude* 6b demonstrates: "The way is the song. But the song often strives to become the way. And when this happens, when the song seems to capture the initiative, in such supreme moments of poetry as 6b or even 6c, the way is lost" (47). But the "interposition [of the Imagination] in the very moment of writing," as Hartman puts it, and the negativity of its disruptive power is recovered and crossed over precisely by being taken *as* a negative—as a negation *of* experience that therefore can in turn be experienced: in the case of 6b, a missed crossing (of the Alps) that can in turn be crossed over *as* missed, a negation *of* the crossing that is the crossing's own. It is a familiar dialectic whose Hegelian rigor, at least in the case of Hartman's interpretation of the crossing of the Alps, can be demonstrated point by point. What this means for our question—"What happens when, what if, the turn of self-consciousness is understood linguistically, as a linguistic turn?"—is, simply, *"Nothing* happens, nothing what if." For in such a recovery of the negative of writing, a negative peculiar to language, the understanding of language is, quite simply, *not linguistic enough.* That is, language and the text are being thought on the basis of phenomenological models. *Phenomenological* is meant here in the sense of Hegel's *Phenomenology of Spirit* as the logic of phenomena, as the logic of appearances—the logic that brings along with it a whole series of concepts: *experience* (*Erfahrung*—the process of going over from one object of knowing to another object of knowing by way of the inversion and negation of the knower—consciousness—by way of a turn of self-consciousness), *consciousness* (*Bewusstsein*—a knower as knower of an object and of itself, a subject, as knower of the *truth* of the object and the *certainty* of the subject), *subject* and *object*, and so on. These are concepts and terms whose meaning is modeled, at least initially (and ultimately), on sensory perception (the immediacy of presence/absence, inside/outside oppositions). If such is the linguistic model—that is, ultimately based on perception—then its resiliency in the face of any negativity that "language" can muster is not surprising. In order for our question—"What happens, what if. . . ?"—to make a difference, we need to think *language* and *linguistic* differently, otherwise, no longer in terms of a phenomenology of language (or a "phenomenalization" of language). In my work on *The Prelude*, I have come up with three linguistic models of the text (and of the poetic "I") that, for lack of better terms, I call: (1) "performative," (2) "tropological," and (3) "inscriptional." Each is a model that in setting itself up gets undone by becoming text and thus is not a model at all, and each is mutually intertwined with the other two in any single passage of *The Prelude*. Demonstrating this would take a book-length series of readings, but, for short-hand purposes, I can say that the performative model is provided by, for example, the "Blest the infant Babe" passage in Book 2, the tropological model by the drowned man passage in Book 5, and the inscriptional model by the Blind Beggar passage in Book 7. Here I propose to begin reading only the first two of these passages, "Blest the infant Babe" and the drowned man.

If we want to know what *language* and *linguistic* mean in Wordsworth's *Prelude*, we could do worse than to begin with Wordsworth's incredible baby, for it is a passage about the beginnings of language, a veritable "essay on the origins of language as poetic language," as Paul de Man puts it ("Wordsworth and the Victorians," 90). That this "essay" indeed takes its place among the eighteenth-century speculations on the origins of language is already clear from its rhetorical status, for like the stories of his predecessors, Wordsworth's myth of origins is a theoretical fiction. Whereas the lines directly preceding the passage tell us that analyzing a soul is a hard task because "Not only general habits and desires, / But each most obvious and particular thought [...] in the words of reason deeply weighed— / Hath no beginning" (1805 *Prelude* 2.233–35), the Blest Babe passage would not only "trace the progress of our being" but purports to tell us what the "first poetic spirit of our human life" is. Like Condillac's wild children, Rousseau's primitive man up against his "giant," or Herder and his sheep, Wordsworth's story is not a history that parcels out by geometric rules but an allegory. The fact that this allegory traces the origin of language not to some literal language of need but to the figural language of passion is also much in line with its eighteenth-century predecessors. Small wonder, then, that like its predecessors this (circular) allegory of the passions has been misread as, literalized into, a history of needs with a beginning, middle, and end. What is language at its origin according to Wordsworth?

According to the naturalistic, literalistic interpretation of Richard Onorato, language for Wordsworth is to be understood in terms of a most traditional scheme, indeed, virtually an application of Hartman's triad of Nature/Self-consciousness/Imagination. Childhood, infancy (as in *in-fans*, unable to speak), is a preconscious, prelinguistic state: "infantile appetite, the capacity for almost unlimited sensation and fantasy comes in a period that is rich and dumb" (Onorato, 622). In this state, the child's communication with Nature is perceptual, immediate even though it takes place "through the mother," for, as "the essential reality of the world," the mother here is a veritable "Mother Nature." Language, on the other hand, introduces self-consciousness: because it is ultimately utilitarian and reductive, "language gradually limits the wonder of experience, darkens the vision and recollection of pleasure" (623). The reality of the mother and the child's rich and dumb dialogues with her are absent. But, three, because her absent reality has been "traumatically introjected" and then this "preconscious sense of a lost relationship" has been projected into Nature, Wordsworth the poet, by listening to the "ghostly language of the ancient earth," can use the imagination to evoke in his poetry "lost objects of love and wonder," "the infantile and fantastic sense of alternatives to reality, of a prior and superior existence, perhaps as soul, from which the sense of self and time are a gradual estrangement" (623). In short, poetry, because it is "partially elusive of the limits of ordinary human speech," can "return through imagination to the past," may even in fact uncover and present "a knowledge of what has been lost in death" (624).

As traditional as this scheme may be, it leads Onorato into some symptomatic quandaries: for one, the curious conclusion that poetry is nonlinguistic—for him, poetry has a "'light divine' which suffuses objects and presents them 'in flashes', whereas there is a darkness in language" (625), a most anti-Romantic position, since from at least Vico to at least Heidegger poetry is what is *most* linguistic, what language is at its origin and in its essence. This is because Onorato confuses "language" with speaking, with its merely phenomenal nature, and thereby takes literally the "infancy" of the infant. In order to make this interpretation, Onorato needs to take all the terms referring to language in the Blest Babe passage as metaphors *for perception*. Thus in the lines "by intercourse of touch / I held mute dialogues with my Mother's heart," "mute dialogues" here is, for Onorato, a metaphor for the passage of passion from mother to child (and vice versa) by the communication of *touch*. That is, he reads the "muteness" of these dialogues as referring to the absence, the negation, of *sound*, when "mute dialogues" could rather be read as referring precisely to a communication, a language, *dia-logos*, deprived of *speech*: a speech deprived of speech, language deprived of speaking, *mute*. For this is indeed the kind of communication that takes place by *intercourse of touch* with the mother's *heart*. It has to be some kind of semiotic or tropological transfer of passion here: that is, *touch* is a figure for a figural process (and not language a figure for perception). How *touch* someone's *heart*? Unless *touch* is going to be understood as a rather gruesome surgical operation on the mother, it had *better* be a figure for a linguistic, semiotic process (for instance, the child's mute apprehension of the mother's heartbeat as a sign of the mother's love) or figural process (as in "Frank Sinatra touched our hearts"). In other words, unlike the Babe's reading of the Mother, Onorato's phenomenalizing, phenomenological interpretation cannot read "passion"—because it wants to think it in naturalistic, perceptual, preconscious, prelinguistic terms, that is, as a *need*—and hence cannot understand the origin of language. As Paul de Man puts it in a footnote on the erotic in "Hypogram and Inscription," "Rather than being a heightened version of sense experience, the erotic is a figure that makes such experience possible. We do not see what we love but we love in the hope of confirming the illusion that we are indeed seeing anything at all" ("Hypogram and Inscription," 53). This statement applies not only to the sense of touch in the child's mute dialogues with the mother's heart but also to its "gathering passion from [the] mother's eye." How read passion in the eye?

Considerably more subtle than Onorato, Frances Ferguson installs passion (or the affections) rather than perception as the focal point of her reading. In seeking to explain "the specific process through which nature—the visible world—becomes a substitute for the mother" (Ferguson, 133), Ferguson asks: "but how was that link established *before* that beloved presence [the mother] became an absence?" (134). It was established on the basis of an "affection between mother and child so strong as to preclude the possibility of the child's recognizing nature as something alien" (135). This affection is communicated in the passage of passion between the eye of the mother and the eye of the child—"the communion between the eyes of mother and child is so intense that it seems never to occur to him that he is external to her" (135–36)—in "a complicated projection—the projection of love from mother to child, the projection of love and absoluteness from child to mother, and the projection of the world from her eyes

to his" (136). But because this communication and its complicated series of projections—the passage of passion from mother
to child and back—is understood on the basis of the presence or
the absence of the object of the passion, the old scheme returns:
the communion that is so intense, so strong, is a prelinguistic (perceptual) condition; language is "essentially different in seeming to
be an institutional embodiment of the sudden perception of externality and separation" (137) and therefore is always second best,
"an attempt to communicate across difference where difference
was once never felt to exist" (137). And poetry winds up being
"an elegy, an attempt to reimagine the certainty which the affections once lent to all perception" (138). But one could argue that
in Wordsworth, as in Rousseau, passion has nothing to do with the
presence or absence of the object. As the Preface to *Julie* puts it:
"Love is mere illusion. It invents, so to speak, another universe;
it surrounds itself with objects that do not exist or to which only
love itself has given life. Since it expresses all its feelings by means
of images it speaks only in figures [*comme il rend tous ses sentiments en images, son langage est toujours figuré*]" (quoted by
de Man, *Blindness and Insight*, 135). In fact, to understand this
passionate scene of mother and child in terms of the presence or
absence of the object is to understand the scene that is to found
the subject/object relation *in terms of* that relation. Hence a trouble necessarily comes into Ferguson's reading, and one symptom
of it is the reading's inability to say *what* the prelinguistic link or
bond or communion—so strong, so intense—between mother
and child *is* except as an eye-to-eye "projection"—a projection
which, as in the case of Onorato, can only be some kind of linguistic process (semiotic or figural, a tropological substitution between inside and outside). How else read or write passion, the passion of love, into the mother's eye? The linguistic nature of the
communion between the eyes of the mother and the child is already hinted at, indeed *performed*, by Ferguson's reading, for the
real passage between eye and eye in her argument takes place not
as some perceptually based projection but on the back of a pun
on the word *pupil* (from Latin *pupilla*—little orphan girl): "The
pupil of the mother's eye in fact presents itself to her child, her
best *pupil*, as a charmed circle in which his own reflection seems
united with all the reflections of the visible world surrounding the

mother" (135, my emphasis). This slip of the pun can help us read the child's reading of passion as a linguistic act.

First of all, the act is linguistic because the child, despite being an infant, *in-fans, reads* passion in the mother's eye (or breast or heartbeat) by performing a metaphorical process of gathering (as in *lego, legere,* or *lesen*) the metonymical dispersal of the mother's parts (eye here, breast there) into an object, a face. This is not so much a process of *projection* as a process of *conjecture*—"For with my best conjectures I would trace / The progress of our being" [1805 *Prelude* 2.238–39]—virtually a translation of the Greek *sun-ballein*, throwing together, symbolization. It goes *from* the "elements and parts [...] else detached /And loth to coalesce" *to* "*one* appearance," "*one* beloved presence," and then *out, back,* to "all objects" (that is, Nature), which are irradiated by the "virtue" of this "combining" power—a synecdochal or metaphorical process of forming parts into wholes. But even before this reading of metaphor, there is the linguistic *act* of the child "when his soul, / Claims manifest kindred with an earthly soul, / Doth gather passion from his mother's eye" [1805 *Prelude* 2.241–43]. This is where the child constitutes himself as a subject, as a subject for a subject, and identifies himself as the child of its mother by making a *claim* to or shouting out (from *clamo, clamare*) the name of the mother, "Mommy," or, better, since this claim stakes out, appropriates, the mother as *his* mother—the kindred is *manifest* not just in the sense of "self-evident" or "visible" but in the sense of *mani-fest*, grasped by hand— "*My* Mommy!" In other words, the child is able to constitute itself as an I, a subject, thanks to the blind, arbitrary, and violent power of sheer linguistic positing. This act is blind and arbitrary because it is not based on anything that the child can see. Gathering passion from the mother's eye is rather an act of reading: the blind imposition of love in the mother's eye. A most arbitrary, unwarranted conclusion that runs something like: "I am seen, therefore I am loved, or therefore I am not a bastard." Again, he does not love what he sees but rather loves in the hope of confirming the illusion that he is seeing anything at all: not "I love my mommy because I see her" but "I love my mommy in the hope that there will be a mommy to see (and hence an 'I' to see her)." In other words, the child constitutes itself as an "I" by appropriating the "eye" of the mother (as *his* mother): "I see myself being seen by an eye." He inscribes the eye/I in the face of the mother. In the slippage of a pun or a pen (or a pen-knife?), the child "slashes" the eye of the mother. The act that constitutes the mother *as* the mother—that puts her face together out of metonymically dispersed parts and elements (like the eye)—is also the act that, in a sense, mutilates her by using that face as a stage or a surface on which to play or inscribe the "I." Linguistically speaking, there is as little (and as much) violence in this act as in the punctuation mark that "slashes" the eye/I.

This linguistic act could be called a "catachresis"—the imposition of a name and a sense where there is none—but it would have to be a catachresis that is an act, that has a *performative* power.[2] Hence, one could call it a performative, but it would be a performative that is illegitimate because the two necessary conditions of a successful performative—the conventional procedures and the proper persons (here mother and child)—do not exist before the "utterance" of this performative. In short, it would have to be a performative that would institute its own legitimacy, a self-legitimating performative. But as soon as one talks about the legitimacy of a performative, one is reinscribing it within cognitive constraints, questions of epistemological authority, truth and falsehood, and so on. To determine that a performative came off and did not misfire, it is necessary to verify (as in *make true*) that the conventional procedures were followed under the appropriate circumstances by the duly empowered legal subjects. But since in the case of the self-constitution of the "I," the only procedures, circumstances, and persons provided are those of language—a performative, tropological, or inscriptional "system" that cannot authorize or legitimate anything (and which is not a subject)—it is no wonder that the "I" needs to legitimate itself by recourse, reference, to something "outside" language, whether it be called "perception" or "passion" or "affection." But such recourse is always the story of a cover-up, an allegory of the disjunction between act and knowledge, position and reflection, performative and cognitive, a disjunction always already "within" language.

In the case of the Blest Babe passage, the cover-up covers the writing off of the mother—for the act that writes her into the text (in a celebratory tone) is also the act that writes her off, has always already written her off, *as* a text. In taking his mother as a stage, a stage *prop*[3] in fact, a scene on which to play his "I," the child kills her by reading her as already dead.[4] The narrative that follows the act—and within which this act is inscribed (not unlike the inscription of the eye in the face of the mother)—is an attempted legitimation and verification, an attempt by knowledge and reflection to catch up with the act, with what happened, the event. But this narrative can only be the story of a cover-up, covering up the illegitimacy of the blind act of self-positing by a story. And, as it turns out, it is the story of the disposal of the already dead mother's body: the "props" of the child's affections are removed, and yet the building stands (that is, the building of the I's passionate relation to the mother which he can then transfer by analogy, as it were, to Mother Nature). But the props *as* props (that is, the mother) were always already removed, their removal was the condition for the construction of the building. This means that if Wordsworth's mother dies in this passage, it is not because it "really happened" (Wordsworth's mother died ere he was eight years old) but because, textually speaking, she *had to*: it is a linguistic necessity, one of those "necessary accidents" of language (utterly random and utterly determined simultaneously—overdetermined). Or, to put it even more directly, Wordsworth's mother died so that the Wordsworth Baby could become an "I" and the Boy Wordsworth could become a poet. And this holds for all the other deaths and mutilations cluttering Wordsworth's poetry: dead Lucys, dead Boys, drowned schoolteachers, disfigured and maimed men and women. In its effort to catch up with its posited self, the self is rather *caught up with* by the death that made the self-positing possible: the death *performed* by the self on a stage—whether it be the marking or mutilation or murder of the mother or of Mother Nature[5] or, ultimately, the mutilation of the self for which all the other deaths are a figure. Such, verily, is the first (murderous) poetic spirit of our not-so-human life.

However sketchy, this reading of the "origin" of the self, of subjectivity, and of language may help us toward a new beginning, a new itinerary, and a new triad for the rereading of Wordsworth's *Prelude*. In brief, the new story would run something like this: (1) a blind act of self-positing—like the claim on the mother's eye or, for that matter, like the claim to blessing in the gentle breeze at the very outset ("O there is blessing in this gentle breeze" is the "opening" of *The Prelude*—an opening that is not at all the "glad preamble" it seems to be at first but rather a self-quotation, indeed a stutter of sorts); (2) the story of attempted legitimation of that claim by reflection, and reflection's inevitably coming up against an opacity, a self-opacity, a radical lack *of* knowledge that it cannot surmount (*aufheben*)—for knowledge can never *know* an act, it can only reflect on it *after the fact*—a lack of knowledge, then, that reflection cannot surmount without (3) reperforming the blind act of self-positing. Some compact examples of this itinerary would be, again, the much-deferred, stuttering opening of *The Prelude*; the recovery, by apostrophe, from the "dim and undetermined sense of unknown modes of being" after the rowboat-stealing episode in Book 2 ("Wisdom and Spirit of the Universe...") or the "recovery" from the missed crossing of the Alps in Book 6 by an apostrophe to Imagination which turns out to be a self-apostrophizing: "And now, recovering, to my soul I say / 'I recognise thy glory'..." The upshot in each of these passages is that the "first," blind act of self-positing is not totalized, recovered, recuperated by its "repetition" (in step 3) because it is separated from itself by reflection's attempt to *know* the act, by an impossible reading of an act of reading. "Claims manifest kindred," for example, is indeed an *act* ("claim") *of reading* ("kindred" *means* "reading [from *raedan*] of kinship"). Hence this story is not some teleologically oriented history that would allow the act finally to coincide with itself but is, rather, for lack of another word, an allegory, and an allegory of self-unreadability at that: the reading of unreadability is what comes between one act and another, one act and "itself" (just as the blind act comes between reading and reading). In other words, it makes little difference whether we conceive of this story, this allegory, as a sequence that goes from (1) blind act to (2) reflection and its opacity to (3) blind act *or* that goes from (1) reflection and its opacity to (2) blind act to (3) reflection and its opacity. What matters is the disjunction between language and "itself"—for instance, as knowledge and as action, cognitive and performative—and the hinging or articulation (or, better, *un*-hinging and *dis*-articulation) of that disjunction.

In order better to mark the (dis-)articulation of that disjunction—better than by phrases like "allegory of unreadability"—it would be good to know more precisely, on the level of language, what happens in step 2 (or 1 or 3), that is, in the story of reflection's attempt to catch up with and legitimate the blind, un-knowing act of self-positing and its being unable to do so. On the basis of a reading of the Blest Babe passage, we know a little better what happens in the blind act of self-positing: in linguistic terms, a performative misfires because it would be and cannot be self-legitimating (since it is not a self but rather the attempted institution of a self). And we also get a certain indication toward what happens in the story of reflection and its opacity: the setting up of a tropological system—a system of figure, a system of metaphor. Here it is the figure or metaphor of the mother's face which is then transferred, transported, carried over to the figure or metaphor of the face of Mother Nature. The illegitimate imposition of a face on the mother (*as* the face of the mother) is transferred in turn by illegitimate analogy to the face of Nature—a transfer that is as much a catachresis as "face of a mountain" or "head of lettuce." How do these illegitimate acts catch up with reflection and render it opaque to itself on the level of language? If the story of reflection is the story of the setting up of a tropological system, a system of metaphor, then the story of reflection's opacity will be the story of that system's inability to constitute itself *as* a system, its inability to close itself off: in short, it will be the story of the undoing of the system of metaphor, metaphor's self-undoing.

Book 5 of *The Prelude* (entitled "Books")—and in particular the famous episode of the drowned man—provides a good example of the undoing of a system of metaphor because it is explicitly about the figure of the face (the face of man and the face of Nature) and the unsettling opacities of its reading.[6] That it is a question of *reading* the figure of the face of Nature is clear from the beginning of Book 5, for its prologue sets up the basis of the book's tropological system as follows: "Hitherto / In progress through this verse my mind hath looked / Upon the speaking face of earth and heaven / As her prime teacher, intercourse with man / Established by the Sovereign Intellect, / Who through that bodily image hath diffused / A soul divine which we participate, / A deathless spirit" (1805 *Prelude* 5.10–17). As Timothy Bahti has pointed out, *looking* at a *speaking face* is quite clearly a reading—how else *look* at a *speaking?*—and equally clear that here it is the reading of a *book*. That is, the Sovereign Intellect or the deathless spirit—call it God—manifests itself to man, gives itself a face, in a book: the Book of Nature. This is a conventional enough topos, here made explicit in the analogy between the Sovereign Intellect's book and the bookmaking activities of man: "Thou also, man, hast wrought, / For commerce of thy nature with itself, / Things worthy of unconquerable life; / And yet we feel—we cannot chuse but feel— / That these must perish" (1805 *Prelude* 5.17–21). In other words, just like God, man makes himself a face—a face for his mind or his "immortal being"—in the form of books. Of course, there is an asymmetry between their respective books: whereas the Book of Nature's perishing is only the sign of its future return and revival ("presage sure, / Though slow perhaps, of a returning day"), man's books, it seems, perish utterly in a way qualitatively different from that of Nature. I have begun the reading of this asymmetry elsewhere (Warminski, "Missed Crossing"); its understanding is indeed crucial for a reading of the Dream of the Arab that follows directly on the prologue in Book 5. Here I am more concerned with the setting up of the tropological system of analogy and substitution—between God's Book and man's books, God's face and man's face—and its implications for a reading of the face of the drowned man. For despite the asymmetry between their different perishings, the analogy is clear and untroubling enough: the speaking face of earth and heaven or the bodily image is to the Sovereign Intellect or the deathless spirit as books are to the immortal being or mind of man:

speaking face of earth and heaven, bodily image	books
Sovereign Intellect or deathless spirit	immortal being

The analogy is untroubling and reassuring because it amounts to the statement of a phenomenological, incarnational model of language and the text: indeed, a veritable *phenomenology of spirit*— the logic of how spirit appears, the logic of its phenomenal appearance. And the closer man's books follow the phenomeno-logic of God's, the better their chances of being recovered and redeemed like the Book of Nature. Nevertheless, there is at least a hint of trouble here in God's Book's, the speaking face of earth and heaven's, being called a "bodily image." The trouble is not so much in the difference between God's Book and man's books as in the difference internal to God's. On the one hand, the meaning of calling Nature a "bodily image" is quite clear: Nature is the bodily, physical, phenomenal manifestation of something intellectual or spiritual—namely the Sovereign Intellect or the deathless spirit. But, on the other hand, "bodily image" also means that Nature is an image, a figure, taken from the (human) body: for instance, in the sense that giving Nature a "face" (as in "speaking face of earth and heaven") is very much a tropological transfer *from* the human body and *onto* Nature. Trees and fields do not have faces but people (especially mothers) do. (The possibility of this second reading of "bodily image" is certainly supported by the text's writing "*that* bodily image"—as though to confirm that the image is "bodily" in the sense that the figure of the speaking face is bodily). The second, other reading is potentially troubling because it introduces the possibility that the "speaking face" of Nature, God's Book, rather than being the incarnation of a deathless spirit—God's phenomenal figure, as it were—is rather a manmade face, man's book, man's image—a figural substitution and transfer not between spirit and body but merely between one (physical) body and another: from the face of man to the "face" of rocks and stones and trees. Rather than the image of God, the "speaking face" would be the "image" of man—in fact, worse than that, an image *of* language, an image created by man's language, by man's speech. For it is only insofar as man has a *speaking* face, insofar as he speaks, that he has a face at all, since his *having* a face is also the product of a figural, tropological, metaphorical linguistic process (as in the construction of the mother's face in the Blest Babe passage). In other words, as a "bodily image," the transfer or transport or metaphor of the "speaking face" would not be a transport to spiritual transcendence of any sort but, rather, a tropological substitution confined to the horizontal plane of exchanges between body and body—without any spirit's necessarily manifesting itself through it. Again, rather than being God's Book, Nature would be man's

book—or, rather, *language's book*, a product of the same tropological operations that *man's* bookmaking activity entails—and
thus perhaps subject to the same perishing. We give nature a per-
ishable face in order to say that it has an immortal spirit, just as
we give other human beings and ourselves faces in order to say
that they and we have immortal souls or spirits. On the level of
language, or as far as the rhetorical structure is concerned, the operation is the same. And insofar as he makes *books*, God—
whoever or whatever he may be—is also subject to their "human,"
that is, *linguistic*, conditions. The difference between the two
books—not God's Book and man's books but God's Book and language's book—that is, the difference between an incarnational, in-
spirited Book (a Book diffused with a spirit, "a soul divine") and
a dis-incarnate, dispirited book returns (and with a vengeance)
with the dead face of the drowned man and the word that links
it to the prologue and the ostensibly living face of Nature: *garment.*

   At first sight, it may appear more than a little perverse—as
in "turning the wrong way"—to see anything besides an incarnational textual model in this passage. The "ghastly face" of
the drowned man may be devoid of spirit, but, after all, the point
of the story is precisely the *re*-inspiriting of this "spectre shape":
the Boy Wordsworth is not possessed by "vulgar fear" because his
"inner eye had seen / Such sights before among the shining
streams / Of fairyland, the forests of romance" [1805 *Prelude*
5.475–77]. That is, he is not frightened by the spectacle of the
drowned man because he had read of such sights in *books*. It is
a spirit coming from books that now re-inspirits the corpse and
renders it an aesthetic object with ideal meaning, a veritable work
of art, as the (presumably very stiff) drowned man becomes sculp-
ture: "Thence [that is, from books] came a spirit hallowing what
I saw / With decoration and ideal grace, / A dignity, a
smoothness, like the works / Of Grecian art and purest poesy"
[1805 *Prelude* 5.478–81].[7] Although we may wonder at the haste
with which aesthetic education transforms a human, that is, material, fact into an edifying scene with an ideal meaning—in brief,
the drowned man is not just not terrible but positively beautiful
(if not downright sublime)—at least on the thematic level the text
is unequivocal in its being *for* an incarnational (sacrificial, resur-

rectional, aesthetic, dialectical) model of language and the text.

But to confine oneself to the thematic level is to *see* rather than to *read*, and this passage is precisely about the difference between seeing and reading or, rather, about the unbroken link, the possibility of passing relatively uncomplicatedly, between the two—from face to book, from book to face. Indeed, we can formulate what happens as follows: what he saw in reading allows him to read what he sees. That is, the sights he saw while reading books allow him now to take what he sees as a book to be read. What he *saw* in *reading* allows him to *read* what he *sees*—a neat chiasmic reversal between seeing and reading. But is the chiasmus symmetrical? Is there nothing left over or missing in the happy crossing between Nature and Books? Whatever this "nothing" may be, it is certainly not the corpse or the ghastly face of the drowned man. For being re-inspiritable as it is, the corpse participates in the Nature—the Book of Nature—through which the Sovereign Intellect has diffused a soul divine. In fact, the corpse's re-inspiriting here by a spirit coming from *man's* books can be taken as a figure, presage sure, of its re-inspiriting—its resurrection and transfiguration—by God on the last day. In short, the corpse remains very much within the tropological system—the speaking face of earth and heaven is to the Sovereign Intellect or the deathless spirit as man's books are to his immortal being—that the prologue had set up. The corpse is a figure for the literal, as it were, the dead letter in need of being redeemed by the living spirit, and, as such, within a tropological system where literal is to figurative *as* physical or sensuous is to spiritual or intelligible. (And one can see how the phenomenological, dialectical, aesthetic interpretation of this passage and all of Wordsworth [and all of poetry]—and the patristic model of allegorical reading that is part and parcel of this interpretation—follows ... follows, that is, as long as the corpse remains inscribed in this tropological system.)

But this tropological system and its analogies hold only as long as we keep turning toward the corpse—and turning *from* the corpse *to* books modeled on the incarnational body-is-to-soul relation. For what the incarnational, sacrificial interpretation has consistently to *turn away from*, what it always does not see and cannot read, are the garments of the drowned man, that "heap of garments" Wordsworth sees distinctly on the opposite shore "left as I supposed / By one who there was bathing" [1805 *Prelude* 5.460–62]. Wordsworth supposes that the garments have a supposer, a sub-ject, and awaits their re-sub-jection, "but no one owned them." What is the story with these garments? Although the passage quickly abandons the garments for the corpse and for the spirit coming from books—we never do find out what happened to them—this somewhat unsightly heap of "unclaimed garments" has quite a tale to tell. And it is very much a "plain tale"— "Those unclaimed garments telling a plain tale" [1805 *Prelude* 5.467]—not at all a pretty sight. For in telling a tale, the garments are books, and books that provide a textual model different from that of the fairy tales and romances whose spirit hallows the corpse. But the garments are also books, were already books, because the prologue had already called books garments, and abandoned garments at that: "Tremblings of the heart / It gives, to think that the immortal being / No more shall need such garments" [1805 *Prelude* 5.21–23]. As such, that is, as books, the garments are the hinge or articulation of the tropological system set up, in fact the articulation or jointing between man's books and God's Book, man's books and the Book of Nature. How? In brief: once books are called garments, it becomes clear that the analogy between God's Book and man's books—the speaking face of earth and heaven is to the Sovereign Intellect as books are to man's immortal being—is articulated on the analogy body is to soul as garments are to body. This is an old analogy, and it produces some old metaphors: for instance, one can say that the body is "the garment of the soul." And, indeed, one can also say something a little more weird like: the garment is "the body of the body" (or the soul is "the body of the garments"). Despite such possibilities, it is easy enough to see how books could be figured as garments: that is, books are garments because like them (and like the body in relation to the soul) they are the visible, external covering of an invisible, internal covered, they are the visible, carnal manifestation of an invisible, spiritual entity—here the "garments" of man's "immortal being." And it is equally easy to see how *God's* Book, the Book of Nature, as the "bodily image" of a Sovereign Intellect or a deathless spirit, could also be figured as a garment: just as the body is the garment of the soul, so the body of Nature, her speaking face, can be said to be the garment of the deathless spirit.

This is all well and good. The analogy body is to soul as garment is to body links, and verifies the link between, God's Book
on the one side and man's books on the other. This can be schema-
tized thus:

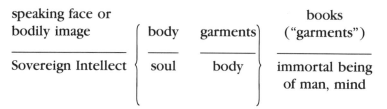

speaking face or bodily image	body	garments	books ("garments")
Sovereign Intellect	soul	body	immortal being of man, mind

Nevertheless, a trouble is introduced into this tropological system
of analogies by the surfacing of the drowned man's corpse. For
what happens is that the *corpse* is introduced into the slot in the
analogy occupied by the body. And the analogy now reads: the
corpse is to the soul as the garments are to the corpse. On the
one hand, this is as it should be and is not at all threatening: in
relation to the soul or the immortal being, the mortal body was,
in a sense (for instance, as fallen and unredeemed), dead all along,
and hence in need of hallowing by a spirit. In rhetorical terms, the
corpse, or the body as mortal, in relation to the soul is just the
figure for the literal, the dead letter in need of conversion to and
redemption by the living spirit. But the problem comes with the
introduction of the corpse in the slot of the body in the relation
garments are to body. For in occupying the slot of the body in this
relation—which now reads "garments are to *corpse*"—the corpse
occupies the slot that the spirit or the soul, analogously, occupies
in relation to the body or the corpse. This means that the corpse—
in the relation garments to corpse—can now be read, now *has*
to be read, as the figure for a *dead spirit* or a "deathful spirit," as
it were. And, on the other side, there is now nothing to stop us
from reading the soul or the spirit as the figure for a "living
corpse," let us say, a "spiritual corpse" or a "soulful corpse," a
"zombie" or the "living dead." In short, the relation "garments are
to corpse" introduces the possibility that the body, too, rather
than being the dead (because mortal), visible, physical covering
of a living (because immortal), invisible, spiritual cover*ed*, may be
the dead covering of a dead cover*ed*, the garment of a garment
that may "cover" or "manifest" or "incarnate" nothing but a dead

spirit or no spirit, that is, be a zombie. None of these latter is threatening in itself as long as we conceive of it as a garment (or a body) of something living or spiritual. The terror comes only with the possibility of a garment of a garment, a body of a body, or a corpse of a corpse. And it is instructive that the text itself, no matter how much it is *for* the incarnational model of books, of language and the text, inscribes such a figure in the phrases "spectre shape" and "ghastly face." In both of these formulations the tension between, on the one hand, the ghostly, the undefined, the undelimited, and undetermined and that which comes from the realm of defined and delimited determined surfaces is readable: *spectre / shape, ghastly* (which is the same thing as "ghostly") / *face*. The latter is particularly unsettling in the context of a poem about faces, about giving and making faces— whether they be those of man or of Nature, that is, God's face. For, as should be clear enough, just as man's face may "cover" or "manifest" or figure no spirit or a dead spirit, so the "speaking face" of Nature may "cover" or "manifest" or "figure" nothing but a deathful spirit or a dead God. As a garment, Nature too may be only the garment of a garment, the dead, visible covering of a dead, invisible covered. As soon as we give Nature a face, we inscribe it in the same tropological system that produces zombies and the living dead. In calling Nature a "speaking face," we also necessarily turn it into a "ghastly face."

In any case, the figures of dead spirits or living corpses—their specter shapes or ghastly faces—are not, as such, what is of theoretical, or rhetorical, interest here. Rather, it is the regular production of these figures and its necessity that we must interrogate. What does it mean on the level of language, in rhetorical terms, for the tropological system (of metaphor) that the prologue had set up? Summarily stated, it means this: once the corpse is introduced into this system of analogy—in garments are to corpse as corpse is to soul—the system is "opened up" radically and can no longer be closed off for regular metaphorical substitutions between literal and figurative in which the relation literal to figurative remains analogous to the relation physical to spiritual, sensuous to intelligible. But in order to understand how the tropological system cannot close itself off, it is necessary to notice, to see, better, *to read*, the heap of garments of the drowned man. Because only when we notice these garments are we also forced to notice that the corpse is not just the "figure for the literal" (the carnal, the mortal) but also (always already) the figure for the figural, the figure for figure—namely, in relation to the garments. (The moral is: a naked corpse is not so fearful. One can recover from the spectacle by re-inspiriting it or aestheticizing it. It is, rather, the garments *of the corpse* that are threatening, for they make readable the possibility that the body too, the corpse, is just a dead, material remainder rather than an incarnate spirit. Again: there is nothing to fear from naked corpses; it is only a corpse with clothes that will get you.) In short, once you create figures for the literal or, even more minimally, once you create figures, once you read figuratively—for instance, when you figure books as "garments"— you make it possible to read any term of any analogy—for instance, any term in the analogy garments are to body as body is to soul—either literally or figuratively, as either a figure for the literal or a figure for figure. And since this includes the terms of the relation literal/figurative, it means that the analogy between the relation physical/spiritual and literal/figurative no longer holds. (For the analogy to hold, it does not matter whether *literal* is aligned with *physical* or with *spiritual*, whether *figurative* is aligned with *spiritual* or with *physical*. What does matter, however, is that in a given tropological system each of these terms remain on the other side of *its other* term—*physical* [that is, dead] on one side and *spiritual* [that is, living] on the other—so that *physical* and *spiritual*, living and dead [and *literal* and *figurative*], do not, as it were, intercontaminate one another. Reading the garments as the garments of a corpse makes such contamination inevitable.) As soon as the (mortal, dead) body can be the figure for the (immortal, living) spirit—in garments are to body as body is to spirit—so can the immortal spirit be the figure for an immortal, living corpse, and the mortal body can be the figure for the dead spirit.

Perhaps a helpful way to summarize the reading of the garments and the trouble it brings is in terms of the differential relay system that travels on the back of the figure of garments. That is, the relay goes from *books* (that is, *garments*) in the prologue of Book 5 to the abandoned *garments* of the drowned man (which are also books) to the corpse (the abandoned *garment* of the soul), which latter is to be hallowed by a spirit coming from *books* (that is, *garments!*). This is a relay system that is supposed to produce the fiction of the *soul*, the living spirit (whether man's or God's) by postponing it, deferring it, displacing it. But once one traces, that is, reads, the relay from the abandoned garments that are books to the abandoned garments that are books, one notices that the text would have books hallow themselves, garments hallow garments, books bless books. The trouble is that the only "spirit" that can come from books, from reading books, to hallow books is a *dead* spirit, for it is precisely books, *reading* books—in a minimal sense, taking literally or figuratively, taking even literal and figurative literally or figuratively—that introduces an other, "linguistic" death into the tropological system and its relay of analogies in the first place. And this "dead" of the spirit is all the more deadly, for it is *not* dead in the way that a corpse is dead (that is, in comparison to the living spirit or soul that has presumably abandoned it). No, the dead spirit coming from books is dead in the way that the *garments of a corpse* are dead, as a garment of a garment. This is, again, a "linguistic death"—a death proper to language. How get this linguistic, tropological machine that produces nothing but garments of garments—dead souls and living corpses, figures for figure—to produce a garment of a body or a body of a soul, to produce a living spirit that will allow garments to hallow garments, books to bless books? (Or, as an ad for a horror movie put it: "How do you kill what isn't alive?")

One time-honored way—and it is the Boy Wordsworth's way in the drowned man episode—is to aestheticize it, turn it into a work of art with an ideal content and a dignified and edifying moral to teach. Such a turn is what Paul de Man in his last work called "aesthetic ideology," and the drowned man passage is a veritable model of it, aesthetic ideology incarnate, as it were. If "ideology is precisely the confusion of linguistic with natural reality, of reference with phenomenalism," as de Man puts it, then the boy Wordsworth's aestheticization of the corpse is a textbook example. For, ironically enough, the boy's turn from the corpse to books is not, as it would seem to be, a turn from the phenomenal to the linguistic, from *seeing* (the corpse) to *reading* (the books), but the reverse. In order to shield himself from the spectacle and the terror of natural death, the boy turns to books all right, but to books not *as read* but *as seen*. The text says so: "my inner *eye* had *seen* such *sights* before...." If what he saw in reading allows the boy to read what he sees, it is because books, reading, are conceived here on the basis of the phenomenological, incarnational (sacrificial, resurrectional), dialectical model of language and the text and the whole chain of metaphorical polarities that this model brings with it: outer eye/inner eye, physical sight/spiritual sight, and so on. In other words, turning to the corpse and away from the heap of garments allows the boy to remain within the tropological system of metaphor that has been set up, whereas turning to the garments would have disarticulated that system and its substitutions. Again: *seeing* books allows the "I" not to *read* the heap of garments. The turning to books is ironically a turning away from reading—away from truly linguistic models of language and the text back to phenomenological, incarnational models. If the Boy Wordsworth follows this logic, this ideo-logic—that of aesthetic ideology—the *text* Wordsworth knows, *does*, better in its rhetoric.

WORKS CITED

Bahti, Timothy. "Figures of Interpretation, The Interpretation of Figures: A Reading of Wordsworth's 'Dream of the Arab.'" *Studies in Romanticism* 18:4 (Winter 1979), 601–28.

Burt, E. S. *Rousseau's Autobiographics*. Baltimore: Johns Hopkins University Press, forthcoming.

Caruth, Cathy. "Past Recognition: Narrative Origins in Wordsworth and Freud." *MLN* 100:5 (December 1985), 935–48.

Chase, Cynthia. *Decomposing Figures*. Baltimore: Johns Hopkins University Press, 1986.

De Man, Paul. *Blindness and Insight*. Minneapolis: University of Minnesota Press, 1983.

———. "Hypogram and Inscription: Michael Riffaterre's Poetics of Reading." In *The Resistance to Theory*. Minneapolis: University of Minnesota Press, 1986.

———. *The Rhetoric of Romanticism*. New York: Columbia University Press, 1984.

Ferguson, Frances. *Wordsworth: Language as Counter-spirit.* New Haven: Yale University Press, 1977.

Hartman, Geoffrey. "Romanticism and 'Anti-Self-Consciousness.'" *Romanticism and Consciousness.* Edited by Harold Bloom. New York: Norton, 1970.

———. *Wordsworth's Poetry, 1787–1814.* New Haven: Yale University Press, 1971.

Onorato, Richard. "*The Prelude*: Metaphors of Beginning and Where They Lead." *The Prelude 1799, 1805, 1850.* Edited by Jonathan Wordsworth, M. H. Abrams, and Stephen Gill. New York: Norton, 1979.

Warminski, Andrzej. "Missed Crossing: Wordsworth's Apocalypses." *MLN* 99 (December 1984), 983–1006.

———. *Readings in Interpretation: Hölderlin, Hegel, Heidegger.* Minneapolis: University of Minnesota Press, 1987.

Wolfson, Susan. "The Illusion of Mastery: Wordsworth's Revisions of The Drowned Man of Esthwaite." *PMLA* 99:5 (October 1984), 917–35.

Wordsworth, William. *The Prelude 1799, 1805, 1850.* Edited by Jonathan Wordsworth, M. H. Abrams, and Stephen Gill. New York: Norton, 1979.

NOTES

1. On the question of autobiographies, see E. S. Burt, *Rousseau's Autobiographics.*

2. On catachresis and its mutilations, see the final pages of my "Prefatory Postscript: Interpretation and Reading" in *Readings in Interpretation.*

3. For a reading of "props" in the Blest Babe passage, see Cathy Caruth, "Past Recognition: Narrative Origins in Wordsworth and Freud."

4. On de Man's "killing the original by finding it already dead," see Cynthia Chase, "Primary Narcissism and the Giving of Figure," forthcoming in Warwick Studies in Philosophy and Literature.

5. Compare the Boy of Winander's *marking* of the owls' hooting. See my "Missed Crossing: Wordsworth's Apocalypses."

6. In my reading of the drowned man I am indebted to a running dialogue with Cynthia Chase and to her *Decomposing Figures.*

7. The Norton edition of the 1805 *Prelude* prints "words" rather than "works," but it seems that the reading should be "works." See Susan J. Wolfson, "The Illusion of Mastery: Wordsworth's Revisions of The Drowned Man of Esthwaite."

Monument and Inscription
WORDSWORTH'S "RUDE EMBRYO" AND THE REMAINING OF HISTORY

CYNTHIA CHASE

"It need scarcely be said, that an Epitaph presupposes a Monument, upon which it is to be engraven" (*Prose* 2:49). In this remark, the opening sentence of Wordsworth's longest critical text, the *Essays upon Epitaphs*, "Monument" has a flatly literal meaning: a material object, stationary and commemorative, that provides a surface for inscription. The word is devoid of any attribution of value, such as it carries in a usage like "monuments of Western art." It differs also from the usage whereby one describes literary texts as "monuments" because they have the "immanence and permanence" of the work of art or the symbol. A monument that exists as the support for an epitaph does not have its meaning immanent within it, and its permanence is subject to external conditions. Wordsworth makes "monument" mean the material element that is "presupposed" by a text; the term would cover the material dimension of language necessarily presupposed by language as meaning. The importance accorded to the materiality of language is a remarkable feature of Wordsworth's *Essays*, which will go on to discuss prosopopoeia of a certain kind—epitaphs written as if spoken by the dead—as justified because such a fictional voice evokes the intended permanence *of the inscription*, evokes "the slow and laborious hand" with which it "must have been engraven" (60). Thus, Wordsworth's specific restrictive sense of the word *Monument* is significant: it marks an attention to the *nonsemantic* elements of language and an insistence on their impingement on literary texts. This is a departure from the view that the literary nature of a text is the function whereby it becomes a "monument" in the sense of an immanent and permanent meaningful form, a semiotic structure that *determines* the boundary line between nonsemantic and semantic elements (Riffaterre, Interview, 13–14).

Wordsworth's *Essays upon Epitaphs* grants a priority to the material dimension of writing which may not be assimilable to an understanding of his poetry as a practice transforming the unremarkable and unmeaningful into forms worthy of remark. Geoffrey Hartman draws on Riffaterre's conception of the literary monument where he writes, in the stirring and subtle title essay of his new book *The Unremarkable Wordsworth*, of "two kinds of perceptibility": "Without the commonplace, or phrases from the sociolect"—"those clichés that pass us by in common usage"—"there could be no perceptibility; yet it is the literary intervention which moves the commonplace from indeterminate to determinate and meaningful status" (213). Wordsworth's reinscription of the commonplace lends it a second order of perceptibility, makes it meaningful, draws our response. Surely in our responsiveness to the unremarkable themes and phrases of his poems, Wordsworth's writing does function in this way. Yet an account that seems fully apt for the elements of Wordsworth's language seen as themes or commonplaces, as "semantic givens," in Riffaterre's expression (*Semiotics* 12, 19; *Text Production, passim*), will not suffice when those commonplaces include the topos of inscription. For inscription, in that circumstance, comes to include *them*: the re-marked commonplaces of ordinary language and perception returned to indeterminably significative and uncertainly perceptible marks, by their proximity with the nonsemantic elements that inscribe them, by their function as inscription. This is the occurrence I shall pursue by way of a reading of a poem in which a range of "unremarkable" elements comes into contact with the function of a mark. It is a poem Wordsworth designates an "Inscription" and identifies as inscribed on an entity the poem calls a "monument." In the poem the distinction between inscription and monument is undone, and that very *indetermination* of the distinction between semantic, determined, encoded elements and nonsemantic ones, I suggest, is what defines for Wordsworth the literary or poetic text. One could thus locate in Wordsworth's writing a "post-structuralist" undoing of the conception of language as coextensive with meaning. The irreducibility, in Wordsworth, of the material to the cognitive dimension of language, marks the shift from a cognitive to a performative model of the text—a shift that has the irreversible and nonintentional character of what one would not be far from the thematics of Wordsworth's inscriptions in calling "history."

"What Wordsworth did is clear: he transformed the inscription into an independent nature poem, and in so doing created a principal form of the Romantic and modern lyric. . . . When fugitive feelings are taken seriously, when every sight and sound calls to the passing poet—"Nay, Traveller! rest"; . . . —then the Romantic nature lyric is born" (Hartman 39–40). So Geoffrey Hartman's decisive essay of 1965, "Wordsworth, Inscriptions, and Romantic Nature Poetry," defines Wordsworth's achievement in literary history. Yet it can be argued, starting from the crucial focus of inquiry first identified by Hartman, that Wordsworth does something else: that in his writing, nature poetry is aborted, that in writing inscriptions, Wordsworth deliberately prevents such "beautiful conceptions," as he writes, from culminating in the birth of a new form. Hartman's elaboration of his claim is in fact the starting point for this alternative history. Wordsworth's poetry has a peculiar way, Hartman explains, of making "Nature herself [seem] a larger graveyard" (34). Wordsworth brings a new dimension to the deictic gesture of the "nature-inscription" genre: it will now not only "point to," but "evoke," the landscape in which it is inscribed. The crucial innovation Hartman locates in "Wordsworth's enlarged understanding of the setting to be incorporated. This is never landscape alone. . . . [he incorporates] in addition to a particular scene the very process of inscribing or interpreting it. . . . The poet *reads* the landscape as if it were a monument or grave" (40).

To re-pose the question of Wordsworth, literature, and history, I want to reconsider what it means that Wordsworth wrote inscriptions, and that he went on throughout his career writing poems designated as such by their titles. One of these is the following poem of 1800, from the second edition of *Lyrical Ballads*:

Lines

WRITTEN WITH A SLATE-PENCIL UPON A STONE,
THE LARGEST OF A HEAP
LYING NEAR A DESERTED QUARRY, UPON ONE OF THE
ISLANDS AT RYDALE.

Stranger! this hillock of misshapen stones
Is not a ruin of the ancient time,
Nor, as perchance thou rashly deem'st, the Cairn
Of some old British Chief: 'tis nothing more
Than the rude embryo of a little dome
Or pleasure-house, which was to have been built
Among the birch-trees of this rocky isle.
But, as it chanced, Sir William having learned   10
That from the shore a full-grown man might wade
And make himself a freeman of this spot
At any hour he chose, the Knight forthwith
Desisted, and the quarry and the mound
Are monuments of his unfinished task.————
The block on which these lines are traced, perhaps,
Was once selected as the corner-stone
Of the intended pile, which would have been
Some quaint odd play-thing of elaborate skill,
So that, I guess, the linnet and the thrush,   20
And other little builders who dwell here,
Had wondered at the work. But blame him not,
For old Sir William was a gentle Knight
Bred in this vale to which he appertained
With all his ancestry. Then peace to him
And for the outrage which he had devised
Entire forgiveness.————But if thou art one
On fire with thy impatience to become
An Inmate of these mountains, if disturbed
By beautiful conceptions, thou hast hewn
Out of the quiet rock the elements
Of thy trim mansion destined soon to blaze   30

In snow-white splendour, think again, and taught
By old Sir William and his quarry, leave
Thy fragments to the bramble and the rose,
There let the vernal slow-worm sun himself,
And let the red-breast hop from stone to stone.

In the 1815 edition of Wordsworth's collected poems this poem
appears under the heading "Inscriptions," with the title *"Written
with a Slate Pencil on a Stone...."* That word *written* in the title
is what is termed an "inscription" by Paul de Man in his 1981 essay
"Hypogram and Inscription: Michael Riffaterre's Poetics of Reading," in which he reads a poem of Hugo analyzed by Riffaterre as
an example of descriptive poetry, which bears the title *"Ecrit* sur
la vitre d'une fenêtre flamande."* What is special about the word
écrit or *written*—written down—is that it does not say or tell anything that the perceptible scribble does not already manifest. In
this sense it does not mean anything. It does not really function
as a sign. The word *written*, written, is an indeterminably significative sign or mark. The word has "the materiality of an inscription,"
writes de Man, a "here and now" which is "undeniable as well as
totally blank" (42). How does *inscription*, in this sense, relate to
the "inscription," in the literary-historical and the literal senses of
the word, in Wordsworth's poem? Hartman's thesis that Wordsworth's poetry "incorporates the very process of inscribing" enables one to move from "inscription" in the literary-historical meaning with which his essay richly endows it, toward "inscription" in
the literal and textual sense. De Man stresses the disparity between this element of the poem and all the rest: "Every detail as
well as every general proposition in [Hugo's] text is fantastic except for the assertion, in the title, that it is *écrit*, written" (53).
But it can be shown that Wordsworth's poem in fact both portrays
and performs "inscription," in that specific sense, such that the
poem takes on the status of an indeterminably significative sign,
while it thereby provides a figuration of the nonsemantic,
noncognitive dimension of language. I shall be interpreting, then,
how "Lines: Written with a Slate Pencil on a Stone..." indeed incorporates inscription—and arguing that what this implies is not,
finally, the development of inscription into nature lyric but, rather,

an engagement of the cognitive with the material dimensions of language that exceeds the conventional boundaries of the lyric, even as it makes up the poetic or the literary text. Wordsworth does not transform epitaphic inscription into nature poetry, he transforms lyric into epitaph, of a kind not representing life, but figuring the possibility of history.

"Lines: Written with a Slate Pencil on a Stone. . ." "incorporates the process of inscribing" by explaining (partly) how the lines come to be there. The heap of stones alluded to in the title is said to be the remnant of an unfinished building—like the unfinished sheepfold in "Michael," with the difference that this poem is not only "on" or about the heap of stones, but is supposedly literally *on* it. "The block on which these lines are traced, perhaps, /Was once selected as the corner-stone / Of the intended pile." But the "pile" was not constructed, and the poem was inscribed on the stone instead. In an unusually literal way, the existence of the poem depends on the particular facts the poem is relating. Does the text, then, *account for* the origin and status of the inscription? In a sense, yes. Starting with its title and its opening apostrophe and corrective negative assertion—"Stranger! this hillock of mis-shapen stones / Is not a ruin"—this poem is this poem's historiography or history. That history, however, will be the *in*determination of the text's limits and origin. For what it recounts is the *repeated* re-marking of a circumscribed site. The initially planned building of the "little dome or pleasure house" on the island and the "quarry and the mound" left by the building's interruption, as well as the lines "traced" on one of the stones, are marks, inscriptions—acts of marking, one might say, if that were not already to say too much, for the poem seeks to evoke an activity or process of uncertain agency[1]—not acts, but repetition and interruption. This is the import of the poem's careful distinctions between building and inscribing and among different kinds of building. The poem's history is its indetermination in another sense also: it is not primarily a narrative but, rather, an instruction, framed by an apostrophe, which tells the reader not how an inscription *did* come into being, but how it could or ought to. Although, on the one hand, the inscribing of the landscape had already happened, on the other hand, it is still to come—when the *reader* addressed by the poem obeys the injunction to "Leave *thy* fragments to the bramble and the rose." The reader is to leave a place where the red-breast may "hop from stone to stone," as on the gravestones of a country churchyard. It is as if not the writer but the reader is responsible for the effect Hartman describes in Wordsworth's poems, of making "Nature herself" seem "a larger graveyard." Rather than being simply narrated, recollected, the engraving, the inscribing, is instructed.

The poem instructs the reader not to build and records Wordsworth's appreciation of the traces of an interrupted building project; thus it poses an opposition between building and the suspension of building, in which suspension or interruption is associated with inscribing, with writing. One could construe this in terms of the Romantic conception of the sublimity of the fragment and interpret the poem's centering on the "monuments of his unfinished task"—the unfinished task of a "Sir William," no less—in light of the monumental stature of *The Prelude*, as a trace of the never completed "philosophical poem" *The Recluse*. It might seem as well that the *suspension* of construction, the "desisting" from building valued and invoked in Wordsworth's poem could be identified with the meaningful "*suspension of meaning* that defines literary form," to quote de Man evoking the formalist conception of the poetic text ("Hypogram" 39). But this would be a mistake, for the poem's statement consists more precisely in a condemnation of a certain *sort* of building and an association, not opposition, of building both with marking and with dwelling. Thus the poem alludes not only to the misguided would-be builders, Sir William and the tourist impatient to become an inhabitant of the Lake District, but also to "the linnet and the thrush, / And other little builders who dwell here," who if the pleasure-dome had been completed would have "wondered at the work." Not all "builders" are objectionable, then, and rather than a sharp opposition between building and inscription, the poem implies gradations. Sir William, "bred in this vale to which he appertained / With all his ancestry," is brought close to the "builders that dwell there," the thrushes and linnets and other "little builders," and may be absolved of any blame for his impulse to build, as though it were a natural concomitant of dwelling. The startling intensity of the unconditional pardon combined with the unconditional blame in these lines—

"Then peace to him, / And for the *outrage* which he had devised, / *Entire* forgiveness!"—suggests how crucial is the issue of building's accommodation to a site, with the tenuous, uncertain, or indeterminable agency that that implies.

The condemned buildings in this text are those that would violate their site. Their unfitness lies in a pretension to distinction that Wordsworth's text indicates with extra exactitude. Wordsworth's *Guide to the District of the Lakes* objects to whitewashed houses because their whitewash sets them sharply apart from their surroundings (*Prose* 2:216–17). The poem describes not one but two structures faulty in this way: Sir William wanted his pleasure-house to be set apart from the surrounding district and gave up his building project when he learned that the nature of the site prevents such isolation, that the water dividing the island from the shore provides no absolute boundary or barrier but permits access to any full-grown person inclined to wade through it. The poem's interest and satisfaction in this unenforceability of property rights suits with the fact that it owes its own existence to this situation— as if the inscription itself were a squatter. The block of stone on which it is inscribed, the inscription pointedly instructs the reader, owes its position to Sir William's inability to prevent his intended pleasure-house from serving as another man's destination or chance shelter. This is as if to affirm that Wordsworth's poetry owes its existence to the inseparability of poetic language from "the very language of men" (*Prose* 1:130). But that notoriously nontransparent assertion in the Preface to *Lyrical Ballads* simply opens every question; what sort of inseparability between poetry and ordinary language is being maintained?

The poem's geography provides a way of distinguishing a formalist and another, different, notion of that inseparability. The formulation of such a distinction is the crux of de Man's argument with Riffaterre in "Hypogram and Inscription," which contains the following provocative rendering of the literary text's status as a "monument." The formalist axiom drawing a borderline between literary and nonliterary language, writes de Man—and this is the borderline, or rather lack of a borderline, that is stressed as the decisive factor in the circumstances of Wordsworth's inscription—is most often thought to be a fastidious attempt to keep literature sheltered from the ... real world. But enclosures or borderlines function in at least two directions. One may indeed want to keep the rabble away from the sacred monument one is privileged to inhabit; monuments, however, are also highly public places, known to attract squatters and miscellaneous citizens not necessarily motivated by reverence, and *one might want to protect what lies beyond the realm of the poetic from the shameful goings on that occur within its boundaries.*" (30, emphasis added)

In the formalist gesture of monumentalization and separation of the literary, this passage is saying, the disturbances to be sealed off are felt as coming from poetic to ordinary language, rather than the other way round. For it is poetic texts—or language precisely *as* monuments—that "attract squatters," that incite the reclaiming for trivial or contingent uses structures distinguished by their forming the very landscape of a language. De Man differentiates, in this essay, between conceptions of the inseparability of literary and nonliterary language that can be distinguished as follows. According to the first (de Man's presentation of Riffaterre's view, as exemplary of a formalist poetics stretching to its limits), the literary text derives from and refers to pieces of ordinary language, elements of the "sociolect," clichés, which it disguises and elaborates. Such elements are themselves referential, representational; the text, however, takes *them*, the words, not the things they name, as its object and is a *nonreferential* construct. The inseparability of literary and nonliterary language, in this case, is that the literary text is the negation of reference, that it is "still derived from representation as its negation," writes de Man. It is still a model of language as cognition (of figure as trope) rather than as performative. According to another conception, ordinary language and poetic language are inseparable because the deictic, descriptive, and representational functions of both—the function, that is, of consciousness—derive from the illegitimate power without authority of a *figure*, the figure whereby the materiality of *inscription* gets confused with and conferred on meanings, on signifieds, and ultimately on things, which thereby acquire their phenomenality, their illusory presence. In the first conception, nonliterary and literary language are related through their symmetrically opposite positions with respect to representation, within the semantic and cognitive dimension of language. In the second, they are related through their uncertainly distinguishable positions with respect to materiality, with respect to the material element of language and the performative dimension of figure—figure, of course, being a component not solely of literary texts.

It is the second conception of the text that Wordsworth's text sustains, and the authority or status of such a "figure" that it gives a history. This takes place partly by way of the effects of signature and anagram that make "Sir William" the figure for such a founding and decomposing figure. The predicament of "Sir William" (unable to close off his monument, to make his work his own) alludes to the ineluctable referential and performative dimensions of language and is a way in which Wordsworth suggests their nonexclusion from poetic works. Recast by least abrupt gradations, the geographic details of the anecdote would give us the following: the would-be work of art, as poetic text, is not cut off from its site in ordinary language—neither by a special poetic diction (Wordsworth's quarrel with eighteenth-century verse) nor by a determinate negation of referential language, and, further, no *intention* determines how the work relates to what lies outside it.

No doubt the most accessible point, in this passage, is the very question of *access*: the fact is that an author cannot control who will have access to his work or prevent later comers from "camping" on it whether in discreet or irreverent fashion. But in the more abstract terms of the poem's geography (and in the terms of the figure's literal inscription: "Will I Am") Sir William is a figure here not only for a would-be creator of art-for-art's-sake, but also for *controlling intention*, as such. The inscription would remind us that this is, although a principal figure in the work's production, not a controlling agent. No intention can fully decide or discover the text's material conditions, can establish a fixed boundary between the work's essential elements and its contingent surroundings—between nonintentional, nonsignificant elements of the work such as the language's grammar, say, and possibly highly significant structures such as its syntactical structures. That the site of the inscription is a site that may always be a "common" place is both a statement of this situation of the work and a figure that links with this situation the status of the "commonplace," of thematic or verbal elements such as "semantic givens" or clichés, which are hereby figured as practically continuous with, inseparable from, the nonmeaningful and un*remark*able, in the sense of uncognizable, elements of language. "Semantic givens" are thereby figured as not given to cognition, but given by a *positing* of the significative status of the nonintentional elements of discourse, a mark.

Not that there is no difference between the semantic and the nonmeaningful. Rather, it is the *difference* between them that is imperceptible or indeterminable. Implicit in the poem's geography is the same relationship spelled out in *Essays upon Epitaphs*, in which "monument" and "inscription" are both distinguished and rendered inseparable and (but for their reinscription) indistinguishable. The nonsemantic or *material* dimension of a text—which would include, potentially, not only its letters but its punctuation and grammar as well—is both irreducible to and indistinguishable from its semantic or *cognitive* dimension. For although meaning is necessarily propped on mere devices of meaning not themselves meaningful, in the process of reading they are immediately confused with meaning.[2] Such a *specular* relation between the performative and cognitive dimensions of a text is allegorically figured, conceivably, in the watery surface that separates the island with its "monuments" from the remainder of the local terrain. Tellingly, though, the poem shows that in allowing the passage from locale to site—from nature to monument—that watery expanse operates not as a mirror, but as the interruption of a certain surface. The model here is not nature—say, the reflection of sky in lake—but "Resolution and Independence," for example, in which a figure is positioned by a pond not to gaze into it (the topos classically corresponding with such a scene) but to stir it up.[3] In that poem, the Old Man, muddying the waters, "gathers" his elusive and ambiguous resource, not an image or reflection, whether of himself or of nature, but tiny wriggling leeches (in Dorothy's account, his ware in fact was books).[4] "Lines: Written with a Slate-Pencil upon a Stone..." introduces a similarly unpoetic or unlikely figure, in the verse (inimitably or parodically Wordsworthian) "having learned / *That from the shore a full-grown man might wade.*" The difference between nature and monument, between nonsemantic and semantic elements, is not given to perception or reflection; it takes place in the nonperceptual act of reading, a figural gesture figured here, with a teasing metaphorical aptness, as "wading through."

As the boundary cannot be fixed between significative and nonsignificative textual elements, the literal or figural reference of a text—just *where* it touches on the world—is indeterminable, unenforceable, in the same way. Here the question of *colors* posed with the allusion to whitewash abuts on that allegorical commonplace, the "colors" of rhetoric. In Wordsworth's *Guide to the District of the Lakes*, white is what is *not* the color— is the negation of the colors—of the material of the site, of the "elements" of the structure. The work's materials are of the site, and the work is delusive if it presents itself as their negation. In the poem, such delusion is suggested to be the mode of error specific to a structure meant not for pure leisure but for use, the habitation rather than "the pleasure-house," according to the poem's distinctions. The would-be work—of history, of philosophy—delusively would appear set apart in the "snow-white splendour" of colorless truth—as knowledge, uncompounded by the colors of rhetoric or of allegiance to function. But the privilege accorded the *literary* text in a formalist poetics falls beneath the same Wordsworthian stricture against determinate negation of the matter by the form, of the site by the structure.

In this part of the inscription enjoining the reader against persistence in his wrong construction, the poem's wordings identify "to *blaze* / In snow-white splendour" and to be "*On fire* with thy impatience*." Impatience, then, is a kind of construction that violates the site, that denies the relationality, the materiality, of thought and of language, denies its condition as the site or occasion or possibility for a thing rather than a thing-in-itself, or a form-with-meaning—spirit, the determinate negation of mere matter. Fired with impatience that the mere mark be consumed by its meaning, with the impatience to cease existing as a marker, something "on fire" is about to be consumed as matter and to become hot air. Such is the nature of the referential historical interpretations of the poem's site that it begins by correcting. "This hillock of mis-shapen stones" is "not a ruin" or, at any rate, "not a ruin of the ancient time,"[5] not an artifact from a past definitively remote from our current period; "Nor, as perchance thou rashly deemst, the Cairn / Of some old British Chief." The poem not only reproves what Wordsworth evidently sees as his contemporaries' essentially antiquarian interest in relics of Britain's past; it would also check what it deems a "rash," an impatient and dangerous impulse to see a yet-to-be-examined site as a monument of past authority belonging to the history of political rule. *This* site is rather "nothing more or less / Than the *rude embryo* of a *little* dome or pleasure-house"—not the fragment of a large domed building (the Pantheon, St. Paul's) such as might figure in the macrohistory of monumentalized historical events, but the elements of a small structure for individual enjoyment. And the decisive fact about this building is that it was never built; Sir William "desisted" from his "task," checked his rash impulse to construct. This monument is "not a ruin" because it has never been a completed self-enclosing form.

Wordsworth's inscription is also an instruction in history. It instructs its reader in the identity or provenance of an ambiguous monument, which is (in the literal reading the poem solicits) a feature of the landscape—an object in the world, which ought to be identified correctly. This object is also the material support of the inscription. What its text would have the reader identify is that which makes its writing possible—and necessary. The entity that makes it possible—the object remarked by the "Stranger" or the reader, the entity that enables the inscription—is "not a ruin," we are instructed first of all. It is not, that is, a structure that has lasted continuously through time, through and beyond its completion and its use, a thing "matured" by time, acquiring value through its very passage. More is involved, in this poem's odd pedantic enthusiasm for its aesthetically and historically insignificant setting, than Wordsworth's presumable dissention from a certain Romantic sensibility that felt ruins to be more beautiful or more sublime than intact buildings. Wordsworth's writing finds its material support on a temporal entity: not an object acquiring value from time's passage, but something that *exists* as a temporal occurrence, an interruption, the interruption, precisely, of the continuous time of the project of erecting a building or of becoming or of contemplating a ruin. It is this which is "not a ruin" but a living agency—in the sense that it is itself an entity with the capacity to interrupt, an object with the capacity to be remarked.

Of course it is *rude* to interrupt, and the "hillock of misshapen stones" called a "rude embryo" is "rude" in this sense of "unmannerly" as well as in the sense that it is crude and unfinished, embryonic. For an instant, the hillock is personified as a rude child or, rather, foetus—rudely aborted to match its rude intrusiveness. This low-key lurid figure flickers into focus and out again like "the shadow of a babe" in the little pond beside the hill of moss in "The Thorn": "Whene'er you look on it, 'tis plain / The baby looks at you again." The similarly persistent specular figure in "Lines: Written with a Slate-Pencil on a Stone. . ." is that of an inscription. For as its being called "rude," with a hint of "rude to interrupt," brings out, the heap of stones functions of its own accord like a wayside inscription, *interrupting* the reader's journey or her contemplation of the landscape. The account of how this interrupting element was produced—by the interruption of a building project— gives a face again to the act of interruption, the textual performance of an inscription. Naming the heap of stones a "rude embryo" gives a face to its function with regard to language—to its having the rudeness to interrupt. That the heap of stones thus functions like a wayside inscription makes the inscription *on* the stone indeed a dubiously significant sign. The account of how the heap of stones was produced entails another redundancy, for like the incipient personification in "*rude* embryo," it evokes an interruption: this interrupting element, the "rude" "heap," was produced by the interruption of a building project. Thus the history of the poem gives a face again to the act of interruption, to the textual performance of an inscription.

The functioning of inscriptions is in fact being recalled in the poem's entire thematics of building and dwelling. As Debra Fried observes in her remarkable essay "Repetition, Refrain, and Epitaph," in written inscriptions or epitaphs, the pause to *read* the epitaph is often represented as "an emblem of the more permanent hiatus that will bring the reader back to the marked site," the grave (617). Wordsworth's inscription plainly draws on this pattern: Sir William's remnants—"the quarry and the mound," the "monuments of his unfinished task"—point a lesson to the reader, who is figured, in the poem's final lines, not only as letting his intended mansion rest, but also as reposing in a country churchyard, like those lovingly evoked in Wordsworth's *Essays upon Epitaphs*. It is as if the poem's concern with place and habitation—its allusions to "inmate," "Stranger," "corner-stone," "freeman of the spot"—were to culminate in implying "the prophecy that the passerby will soon no longer be a visitor to the graveyard, but a resident there" (Fried 626). It is as if it were to culminate in writing the reader's epitaph:

> ... if thou art one
> On fire with thy impatience to become
> An inmate of these mountains,—if, disturbed
> By beautiful conceptions, thou hast hewn
> Out of the quiet rock the elements
> Of thy trim mansion destined soon to blaze
> In snow-white splendour,—think again; and, taught
> By old Sir William and his quarry, leave
> Thy fragments to the bramble and the rose;
> There let the vernal slow-worm sun himself,
> And let the red-breast hop from stone to stone.

"Thy fragments," here, reads both as the fragments of the unfinished mansion, first, and, second, the fragments of the builder, of a body. It reads as the fragments of a text as well. "Leave /Thy fragments to the bramble and the rose"; this line says at the same time, "Desist from building, instead leave uncertain signs, an inscription" and, "Make your grave in a country churchyard." This is a variation on a conventional feature of epitaphic inscriptions, which compare and identify two aspects of the reader's situation: that he is reading (an inscription), and that he will die, and will compose, will constitute, an inscription. The resonance of "thy fragments" as both a body and a text as well as a building comes also from their linkage in Book 5 of *The Prelude* (via the "garments" of the Drowned Man and the "shell" of the Arab-Quixote) and in the *Essays upon Epitaphs*, where it constitutes the main figural system. "We respect the corporeal frame of Man," writes Wordsworth, "not merely because it is the *habitation* of a rational, but of an immortal Soul" (124, my emphasis). Wordsworth's accompanying emphasis on a metonymical, not only metaphorical, link between the dead body and language—the "record to preserve the memory of the dead" is "to be accomplished, not in a general manner, but, where it can, in *close connection with the bodily remains of the deceased*" (125, Wordsworth's emphasis)—

disrupts the identification of language with perception or cognition in the *Essays*, it could be shown, in ways similar to this inscription's interruption of the reader's act of understanding or construction.

Why does death come into the picture with monuments, with such objects as "the quarry and the mound," "monuments of his unfinished task"? Why do graves come into the picture with inscribing or engraving? Neither the logic of etymology nor the conventions of *epitaphic* inscription and *funerary* monument captures the significance of this figuration in Wordsworth's text. It lies rather in the function of the inscription that the poem's figures repeatedly bring forward: its performance as a material object rather than its meaning; its performance as the *interruption* of perception or cognition. According to Wordsworth's poem, that interruption, and not cognition or the negation of perception—neither the intention nor the act negating an intention of a perceiving subject—transmutes indeterminably significative marks into inscriptions, with their semantic as well as material dimension. This is a performative and figural, rather than a cognitive and phenomenal, model of language, and it is what assures the referentialization of language and its insertion in history.[6] A passage from Hans-Jost Frey's essay "Undecidability" can serve as a gloss for Wordsworth's figuration of inscription as an effect of interruption:

> Where discourse begins, it can—before diverting attention from itself to what it says—be known as an act of linguistic positing. This act cannot be derived. It is unconnected and *abrupt*. This means: it does not signify. Discourse as act is the presupposition for everything that can be said, but this act itself remains outside the range of language. It has no communicable meaning. . . .
>
> Where discourse ends, there is something else. Ending, discourse comes up against that which has neither entered, nor can it enter, discourse, yet which still helps to form what it borders on. (131–32)

These passages describe what follows from the figural nature of language, from the possibility, that is, that any word or text may be either literal or figurative, and that "the referentiality or nonreferentiality of language can only ever be asserted" (131), not determined or known. Rather than being a text that can be certainly known to be nonreferential and figurative—and thus meaningful, not in referring to real things, indeed, but in taking as its matter the meaning-units, the semantic elements, the signifiers, of ordinary language—the poetic text is one that *leaves its meaningfulness* (as distinct from its meaning) unknown. Evoking the implications of this involvement in language not simply of the nonreferential, but of the nonsemantic, Frey writes in terms that repeat the geography of Wordsworth's inscription: "although no construction can reach and integrate its own relation to whatever is outside it, neither can it avoid contact with it. Every construction, every system—that is, every text—has within itself the ignorance of its own exterior as the rupture of its coherence which it cannot account for. No text can remove itself from a relation to the extralinguistic, and none can determine that relation. This undecidable relation to what it is constantly related to, prevents the text from closing into a totality" (132). In this way the structure of the text assures its referentialization. (Or, as de Man writes, "every text generates a referent that subverts the grammatical principle to which it owed its constitution.")[7] Wordsworth's poem figures that impossibility of a construction's closing into a totality as the condition of the possibility of his text.[8]

That this figure is not another, subtler form of closure or totalization is borne out by the peculiarities of the poem's conformity to the genre of inscription. In taking on the character, at the end, of an epitaph for the reader, Wordsworth's poem operates just as epitaphs characteristically do. Epitaphs and inscriptions, as a genre, incorporate in their content a representation of how they perform as texts: of their interruption, their *stilling*, of the reader. It is not surprising that a Wordsworth poem that titles itself an inscription should perform in this way. But this is to say that a poem of Wordsworth may well "incorporate" in its evoked setting "the very process of inscribing," as Hartman wrote, without thereby developing from an inscription into the new "free-standing form," the Wordsworthian nature lyric. Rather, by incorporating the process of inscription, the poem *remains* an inscription, and I suggest that this is Wordsworth's distinctive transmutation of lyric poetry. For the function or performance of inscriptions is incorporated in Wordsworth's inscription in a peculiar way. The performance of the inscription, the situation of the reader, is not asserted as knowledge. Wordsworth's poem diverges in this significant respect from the characteristic gesture of epitaphic inscriptions, the assertion that the reader *is* reading, and *will be* dead, and read. In Wordsworth's text the reader's situation is instructed—put in the imperative mode. And it is at the same time being made indeterminate, made not in any simply recognizable sense the act of reading, the fact of death. "Think again"; "Leave," or, "Leave thy fragments": rather than being *pictured* as reading or writing, the reader is being *instructed* to do so. Like other epitaphic inscriptions, this one incorporates recognizable elements of the performative dimension of such an inscription, instantiated in the situation of a reader reading one: having interrupted his activity, having desisted from impatiently pursuing her journey or task, being not an inhabitant or "inmate" (yet) but only a visitor to the spot, one who is reading a stone rather than building with one. But *this* text commutes those elements into another performance—into a singularly indeterminate imperative. For if the poem says, "Read," "Put yourself in the situation of a reader," it implicitly denies that we are already reading, or that we know what that instruction means. The peculiar effect of a written imperative to read, of an inscribed injunction to constitute an inscription, is to make unintelligible either the text's figural system or its performance by implying a contradiction either of the figural logic whereby interruption of building implies inscription and reading, or of the presumption that we are reading an inscription now.

This irrepressible contradiction is Wordsworth's "rude embryo": a prosopopoeia or personification—as an imperative utterance—of inscription. If Wordsworth's poem gives a voice and a face to inscription, to the *performance* of a written text, it is not a face we necessarily know. The effect of this figure is to open, in the history of the poem as a place or point in the evolution of the lyric or in some other developmental pattern, a fissure which makes the work in another sense historical. It combines the historiographical with the unpredictability of a nonintentional act.

Another way of putting this would be to say that it is by dint of remaining an inscription or figural text that Wordsworth's writing opens the field of the social and of history. Neither history nor the social may be assimilated to an idea or an intentional action, to the cognition or representation of a performance or a process, or to the intention of a subject or an agency. The condition of history, as unpredictable and irreversible occurrence, and the condition of the social, as open, unsutured, a matter not of a nature or race, would be not the phenomenal world as such, neither time nor space, neither structure (as accessible to cognition) nor event (as available to intention), but only their reciprocal subversion: the interference of the structural, nonintentional, material conditions of discourse with its actualization as intentional meaning, and the interference of the arbitrary, formal character of structure, as signifying structure, with its transparency or predictability as mere objectivity or code. Such interference can be conceived as coming into play to the extent that grammar and rhetoric—or the performative and the cognitive dimensions of a system—can be conceived as in tension rather than as solidary with one another. For it is then that the force of the material conditions of discourse can be construed as other than the mere reflection (whether as matter or as manifestation) of an idea or intention.[9] These are the stakes of the shift from a conception of language as meaning to a performative model of language. A hermeneutic model does not bring the dimension of history or the social into play. For it is not merely the difference between manifest and hidden, between literal and figurative or figural and proper meaning, but the impossibility of deciding between them on linguistic grounds alone—and the necessity or inevitability of a decision occurring—that constitutes the social and historical dimension of discourse.[10]

In concluding I shall seek to explain how Wordsworth's text brings to light why any inscription has to incorporate its performance as an inscription, and how its performance remains indeterminable—persists as history. Another way of stating the contradiction or disjunction within the poem would be to stress the disjunction between the figure of dwelling or habitation (or the continuity between semantic and nonsemantic elements) and that of an inscription, "mound," or grave (or their disjunction). The forcing, in both senses, of their connection could be said to take place with the verse "Thy fragments...," insofar as it alludes both to the (abandoned) habitation, the dwelling for the body, and to the (abandoned) body, and at the same time its "dwelling," its grave. This "dwelling" for a "dwelling"—like the "unclaimed garments" of garments (of the body as the soul, which "no more shall need such garments," 5.23) in the drowned man passage in *The Prelude* (5.450–81)—is the no-place that disables the tropological, cognitive, phenomenal system of language, a material dimension that cannot be assigned certain location or perceptual status.[11] Building, then, the poem's foremost trope, associated both with marking and with dwelling, carries two disparate and finally incompatible registers: the possibility of place, and of placing, and the placelessness which is that of inscription or of (in Blanchot's words) "that which one calls mortal remains" (348).

This disparity comes through in the tension between the poem's precise or evocative renderings of place—the island, "thy fragments," "There"—and its disqualification of every precise location (temporal as well as spatial) of the inscription. The heap of stones on which Wordsworth's text is inscribed is, prior to that, *already* in some sense an inscription. It interrupts (or may or may not interrupt) a perceiver's gaze, and it records what may or may not be deemed an intentional act: the leaving behind of traces of an interruption, the interruption of a building process, an intervention in or interruption of the process of dwelling. In specifying that the hillock is *not* a cairn and *not* a ruin, the poem distinguishes it from entities that are decidedly markers or signs or intentional structures. The "hillock of misshapen stones" is of the order of the misshapen names, the anagrammatic patterns in Latin and Vedic poetry identified by Saussure: perceptibly they were there, but whether they were deliberately encoded meaningful signs or just effects of the laws of probability was impossible to determine. A short poem of 1830 placed next to this one as Inscription 8 in Wordsworth's final edition makes this point in an amusing way.[12]

> In these fair vales hath many a Tree
> At Wordsworth's suit been spared;
> And from the builder's hand this Stone,

> For some rude beauty of its own,
> 　　Was rescued by the Bard:
> So let it rest; and time will come
> 　　When here the tender-hearted
> May heave a gentle sigh for him,
> 　　As one of the departed.
> (*Poetical Works* 4:201)

Any stone, any *tree*, "In these fair vales," *may have* been "rescued" by Wordsworth "from the builder's hand," and so be a marker or inscription of that act, have the "rude beauty" not that of a finished structure nor of a natural object, but of an interruption, a possibly meaningful mark. The inscription, Wordsworth's text, would single out one such entity, which only becomes visible as an instance of his intervention: as the "rude embryo" of the poet's inscription. To be perceptible at all, the indeterminable significative status of the mark has to be *re*-marked, registered as a potential sign; its indeterminable mode of performance has to be incorporated as a particular imaginable act, as an imaginable agency. A poet's selection of a writing surface is only one such incorporation. Its peculiarity is to reveal the reception of the perceptual object—through the singling out for inscription of an entity already marked, already inscription—as a remarkably gratuitous activity.

Thus, Wordsworth's "Lines" is embryonic not only in its dependence on a future performance—on the future *leavings* of its reader—but also in its possibly superfluous repetition of a prior one. It happens that while the poem does not precisely say this, it can be made to say it, for owing to the way the sentences of the poem are interrupted by its line-endings, it says, in line 16, "these lines are traced perhaps." The lines are only *perhaps* traced, not certainly seen; or, the lines are perhaps merely traced, retracing a trace already there. That "lines" may mean just "lines" or lines of verse dwells on the material nature of the inscription in a way that just slightly intensifies the overdetermined semantic and syntactic indetermination of the text. But its burden is confirmed by the assertion that there existed already, as the poem instructs us, "monuments of his unfinished task": "The quarry and the mound," monuments even before their inscription. The phrase is a strange one, drawing on a meaning of the word *monuments* that here disqualifies, without effacing, the other. *Monuments* here means not the commemoration of an accomplished action, but the trace of an unfinished one, not architectural monuments, or works, but monuments in a more primary sense of the word: "record"—and under the same heading in the *OED*, "written document," as well as "indication, evidence, token"; "a mark." The synonymy of *monument* and *document* thus opens in another way the question of the action performed by inscription rather than giving an answer; I allude to the prior meaning not to say that texts are what those things in Wordsworth's poem are, but to pursue the contention that this text's own action is uncertain. For *is* it an action to inscribe, on a monument, *monument?* But this is the way in which—even in its figures, its apparent descriptions—this text remains an inscription: an *indeterminably meaningful* mark rather than a meaning or a sign. Wordsworth's poem seems to have found a way to inscribe—to perform, rather than represent, the process of inscription—through the very process of describing inscription.

The other sense of the word *monument* persists via its juxtaposition with *task*, which irresistibly suggests an *accomplished* task honored by a monument. It is as if the idea of the monument to a finished task is one the verse must negate, but which leaves remains. The verse "monuments of his unfinished task" is strange insofar as the existence of monuments implies the accomplishment of the task. Insofar, say, as it presupposes it. The line reinscribes the opening line of Wordsworth's *Essays*: "an Epitaph *presupposes* a Monument." Fragmented or interrupted thus, the sentence is a statement about the *hypothetical* status of positional language—that in fact it has to presuppose the structure or system which it would posit and in which it must find its support. It has to presuppose a structure of meaning. Inscribing, or the nonderivable, gratuitous, interruptive "act of linguistic positing," only fictionally and as a contradiction in terms, has the force of an act, one that *institutes* meaning. Rather, necessarily, all positing is *pre*positing, presupposing; "all *setzen* is *voraussetzen*": all positing is presupposing of already existent signification.[13] This conclusion of Nietzsche's analysis of performative force takes form in Wordsworth's text as what can look like "nature poetry": the affirmation of the *possibly* significative status of "nature," its evocation as a gathering of inscriptions, with the poem as their reinscription or citation. An inscription presupposes a monument in the sense that it necessarily and merely *presupposes* a to-be-accomplished task: the *completion* of language; the production of meaningful form. In thwarting the reader's identification of such form—in persisting as *indeterminably* significative reinscription—the inscription is indeed an epitaph for the function of the reader.

Wordsworth's text is a figuration of the nonsemantic, noncognitive conditions of poetic form. The question then arises of whether this involves an identification or *assimilation* of the materiality of the inscription to the substantiality of things, via that figure of remarking or incorporation that conditions the possibility of deixis, perception, or consciousness. That figure—a chiasmus identifying the materiality of the signifier with the phenomenality of the signified—comes into play with strange directness in Inscription 8. This text was entitled, "Inscription intended for a Stone in the Grounds of Rydal Mount," and the title takes on the sense, "inscription *presented to* a stone" as well as "inscription intended to be placed *on* a stone," since the stone is very much the subject and object of the poem. But it is also imagined as a sort of epitaph for the poet ("time will come / When here the tender-hearted / May heave a gentle sigh for him / As one of the departed"). What is startling is that the poem simultaneously performs as a sort of epitaph for the stone. It was rescued by the Bard from the builder's hand, and, "So let it rest," writes Wordsworth; a cancelled version of the line in the manuscript actually reads, "Long may it rest in peace"! The material support *for* the epitaph becomes the subject commemorated *by* the epitaph. And since both the Bard and the stone are the "intended," the signified, of the inscription, there is a transfer of properties and an identification of the Bard with the stone, and of the fictive phenomenality of the signified with the nonfictive materiality of the signifier.

This would mean that the noncognitive element of language, inscription, is being reduced to a cognition, and the intentional, figural dimension of language being assimilated to the status of a natural object. But in this poem, the natural object has been dispelled by the process of inscription. The stone that remains—of which the poem says, "So let it rest"—is the stone singled out by the poet's gesture, the marker of an interruption or intervention in an intentional action of appropriation. It is the marker of an intention that it be the marker of an intention. "So let it rest," means let it rest as a mark, as an unreadable word, like the written word *writing*. "Let it rest": this is also an invitation to let rest a question, an issue, a troubling matter: the matter of language, and whether it determines, or is determined by, thought. "Let it rest" means, Let the matter remain a question. It precisely does not mean, let the stone, the natural object, be. This text inscribes in a succinct injunction the *non*-"intentional structure of the Romantic image": not, "Nun, . . . müssen . . . Worte, wie Blumen, entstehen" (Hölderlin)—"Now, . . . must words . . . originate like flowers"—but, "Nun müssen Steine, wie Worte, bleiben": Now must stones remain, like words.[14]

This is the injunction that "Lines: Written with a Slate Pencil" ends by addressing to the reader. It is care for the materiality of language, and for the specular structure whereby marker and marked are inseparable but irreducible to one another. "Leave / Thy fragments" we now have to read as instructing against the construction of any system that treats as determined the difference between the meaning and its means. For the unfinished task to be inscribed and the unfinished action of inscribing to be inseparable, as they are here, in Wordsworth, means that history remains, and remains because of the figural nature of language, or indeterminable performance. Strangely, that indetermination is the imperative. "Leave / Thy fragments": the line wavers between the body and its dwelling, and between the subject and its signs. These "fragments" are to be "breathing tokens," to quote from another occasional poem of Wordsworth (*Poetical Works* 4:153). Wordsworth's text would link the history, the hope, of men to the conditions of their language. That a *grown* man can freely occupy a space in which he does not inherently belong, can at any hour make himself a not grown, but, rather, *free*man of the spot where building could take place, here rests on the fact that a spot can be marked, a place can be held, by any existing, "full-grown" word, that a word can function as a name for a thing to which it does not inherently belong. For this means that there is no fixed code by which thought determines language or by which a language determines thought; that language remains to be written. Though the inscription checks impatience, it teaches interruption. The rude embryo will never say the last word.

WORKS CITED

Blanchot, Maurice. *L'espace littéraire*. Paris: Gallimard, 1955.

De Man, Paul. *Allegories of Reading: Figural Language in Rousseau, Nietzsche, Rilke, and Proust*. New Haven: Yale University Press, 1979.

———"Hypogram and Inscription: Michael Riffaterre's Poetics of Reading." *Diacritics* 11:4 (Winter 1981), 17–35. Reprinted in *The Resistance to Theory*, pp. 27–53. Minneapolis: University of Minnesota Press, 1983.

———*The Rhetoric of Romanticism*. New York: Columbia University Press, 1984.

Frey, Hans-Jost. "Undecidability." *Yale French Studies* 69 (1985), 124–33.

Fried, Debra. "Repetition, Refrain, and Epitaph." *ELH* 54 (Summer 1986), 615–32.

Hartman, Geoffrey. *The Unremarkable Wordsworth*. Minneapolis: University of Minnesota Press, 1987.

Riffaterre, Michael. Interview. *Diacritics* 11:4 (Winter 1981), 12–16.

———*Semiotics of Poetry*. Bloomington: Indiana University Press, 1978.

———*Text Production*. New York: Columbia University Press, 1983.

Wordsworth, William. *Poetical Works*. Edited by Ernest de Selincourt and Helen Darbishire. Oxford: Clarendon Press, 1958.

———*The Prelude* 1799, 1805, 1850. Edited by Jonathan Wordsworth, M. H. Abrams, and Stephen Gill. New York: Norton, 1979.

———*The Prose Works of William Wordsworth*. Edited by W. J. B. Owen and Jane Worthington Smyser. London: Oxford University Press, 1974.

———*William Wordsworth*. Edited by Stephen Gill. New York: Oxford University Press, 1984.

NOTES

1. Neil Hertz analyzes "the pathos of uncertain agency" in "Lurid Figures," in *Reading de Man Reading*, ed. Wlad Godzich and Lindsay Waters (Minneapolis: University of Minnesota Press, 1989).

2. The distinction between the cognitive and the performative dimensions of language, between meaning and the devices of meaning, is lucidly articulated by Cathy Caruth in "Past Recognition: Narrative Origins in Wordsworth and Freud" (*MLN* 100:5 [December 1984]). In reading Wordsworth's lines on the Blessed Babe "who, when his soul / *Claims* manifest kindred with an earthly soul, / Doth *gather* passion from his mother's eye" (*The Prelude*, 2.241–43), she distinguishes between "the substitutive 'combining in one appearance', which works figuratively to assimilate visual perception to language," and "this 'gathering,'" "a throwing-together (like the poet's 'conjectures'), a bonding which, like a syntax, is *not itself a function of meaning but rather the prop upon which meaning leans, and with which it is immediately confused*" (944–45, my emphasis).

3. Compare Steven Knapp's reading of this passage in "Resolution and Independence" in *Personification and the Sublime: Milton to Coleridge* (Cambridge: Harvard University Press, 1985), pp. 112–14.

4. *Journals of Dorothy Wordsworth*, ed. Ernest de Selincourt (London: Macmillan, 1941), 1:63 (entry for October 3, 1800).

5. In the 1837 text this line is revised to "Is not a Ruin spared or made by time" (*Poetical Works* 4:200). The revised line suggests an idea consistent with our reading of the poem of 1800: that the mound or "rude embryo" is not the product of Time personified as an agent which "spares," creates, or destroys but, rather, of a temporal process characterized by nondialectical discontinuity or "interruption."

6. In *Hegemony and Socialist Strategy: Towards a Radical Democratic Politics* (London: Verso, 1985), pp. 105–114, "Articulation and Discourse," Ernesto Laclau and Chantal Mouffe offer an argument similar to the one advanced here, according to which an adequate conception of history and the possibility of historical change require a performative model of language. Closely congruent with de Man's criticism of Riffaterre's formalist model of the text (see p. 54 above) is Laclau and Mouffe's criticism of Benveniste's interpretation of Saussure on language as a system of "relative" values or differences without positive terms: "to say that the values are 'relative' means that they are relative *to each other*. Now, is that not precisely the proof of their *necessity*?" In a discursive formation constituted in that way, Laclau and Mouffe comment, contingency and the practice of articulation (and historical change) would be impossible (106).

7. De Man, *Allegories of Reading*, p. 269. Compare William Ray, *Literary Meaning: From Phenomenology to Deconstruction* (Oxford: Basil Blackwell, 1984), p. 200, on the link between reference and nonintentional performative.

8. Wordsworth's poem thus defines its own historicity as a function of its undecidable and inescapable relation to the extralinguistic. Closely comparable to the conception of the text proposed here is Laclau and Mouffe's view (see note 6)—linked with the argument that the distinction between discursive and nondiscursive practices is untenable, since every object is constituted as an object of discourse—of "the *material* character of every discursive

structure" (107). In the discursive structure or "language game" of building with building-stones (Wittgenstein), "The linguistic and non-linguistic elements are not merely juxtaposed, but constitute a differential and structured system of positions—that is, a discourse" (108). The point, and the example, are consistent with de Man's ironical image of the literary "monument" (see page 58 above).

This conception of discourse has major consequences for the practice of history. "The first is that the material character of discourse cannot be unified in the experience of a founding subject; on the contrary, diverse *subject positions* appear dispersed within a discursive formation. The second consequence is that the practice of articulation, as fixation/dislocation of a system of differences, cannot consist of purely linguistic phenomena; but must instead pierce the entire material density of the multifarious institutions, rituals and practices through which a discursive formation is structured" (*Hegemony and Socialist Strategy*, 109).

Laclau and Mouffe derive their argument for such a practice of history from a distinction between "articulation" and "mediation" as two different varieties of "'the organization which we are able to give to ourselves'" (94)—a passage drawn from Hölderlin's *Hyperion Fragment*. The present essay derives a similar notion of discourse with consequences for the practice of history from passages of Wordsworth. The nonhistoricist historian "grasps the constellation which his own era has formed with a definite earlier one" (Walter Benjamin, "Theses on the Philosophy of History," *Illuminations* [New York: Schocken, 1969], p. 263). It is that constellation that permits hope. (See below, p. 73, and above, p. 6.)

9. On the stakes and the difficulty of not assimilating the material and performative dimensions of discourse, or its "force," to form, see Jacques Derrida, "Force and Signification," *Writing and Difference* (Chicago: University of Chicago Press, 1978), pp. 3–30.

10. Compare de Man, *Allegories of Reading*, p. 10, and William Ray, *ibid.*, pp. 193–204. Compare also de Man, "Hegel on the Sublime," in *Displacement: Derrida and After*, ed. Mark Krupnick (Bloomington: Indiana University Press, 1983), pp. 149–50, and "Phenomenality and Materiality in Kant" and "Kant and Schiller," in *Aesthetic Ideology*, ed. Andrzej Warminski (Minneapolis: University of Minnesota Press, 1989). Such a conception of "the social" as I evoke here is presented in Ernesto Laclau and Chantal Mouffe, *Hegemony and Socialist Strategy: Towards a Radical Democratic Politics* (London: Verso, 1985), chap. 3. Hans-Jost Frey's discussion of the undecidable referentiality of language, quoted above ("No text can remove itself from a relation to the extralinguistic, and none can determine that relation"), describes the conditions of what Laclau and Mouffe call "the social"; see *Hegemony and Socialist Strategy*, p. 111.

11. On "garments," see Andrzej Warminski, "Missed Crossing: Wordsworth's Apocalypses," *MLN* 99:5 (December 1984), 1000–1002, and "Facing Language: Wordsworth's First Poetic Spirits," in the present volume.

12. Geoffrey Hartman alludes to this inscription in *The Unremarkable Wordsworth*, p. 225, n.14.

13. Paul de Man, reading *Der Wille zur Macht*, in "Rhetoric of Persuasion (Nietzsche)," *Allegories of Reading*, p. 124.

14. These lines from stanza 5 of Hölderlin's "Brot und Wein" are quoted by Paul de Man in the "The Intentional Structure of the Romantic Image" (first published in French in 1960), in *The Rhetoric of Romanticism*. The expression "*non*-intentional structure" to which I resort to characterize Wordsworth's figure is intended to describe my conclusion that, in this Wordsworth text, the figure is not impelled by the "intent of the poetic word to originate in the same manner as . . . 'flowers'" or natural objects (*Rhetoric* 3), but rather by the affirmation of the possibility that natural objects, or substances, have the undetermined, historical, possibly significative status of words or inscriptions. They would not, in that event, be continuous with or masterable by an intention (like a natural growth or like the object of a dialectic). In a similar sense de Man writes of the sheerly "intentional" status of the "natural image" in Romantic poetry: "the word that designates a desire for an epiphany but necessarily fails to be an epiphany, because it is pure origination" (6). The contradiction between the "intention" and the performance of the figure that de Man analyzes in this passage takes place, in Wordsworth's text, between the intentional mode of the poem's rhetoric (the injunction to the reader) and the indeterminable performance that it requires (the performance of reading, of a word that "rest(s)" or remains). The contradiction appears as well as in the conflict between "dwelling" and marking, which is to be found not only in Wordsworth but also, as de Man's critical discussion of Heidegger's interpretation implies, in the poetry of Hölderlin. (See "The Temptation of Permanence," *Southern Humanities Review* 17:3 [Summer 1983], 209–21.)

Secondary Literature
GEOFFREY HARTMAN, WORDSWORTH, AND THE INTERPRETATION OF MODERNITY

DONALD G. MARSHALL

> The greatest advances in interpretation have occurred, moreover, by showing that a false unity has been imposed on an author: in his work there may be another work trying to get out.
>
> —THE FATE OF READING

Geoffrey Hartman's contribution to Wordsworth studies certainly merits reflection. Yet I feel a certain diffidence about my topic, because it may seem indecorously particular. Why should we filter our understanding of Wordsworth or any great poet through the mind of a contemporary critic, even a mind as capacious as Geoffrey Hartman's? But do we in fact have any alternative? Hartman himself has presented "a plea for being aware in the 1970s of the history of scholarship." According to Hartman, "the accumulation of knowledge, like that of capital, makes us deceptively secure. We forget the scarcity that was and the precarious growth of guiding ideas."[1] It is an illusion that we have unmediated access to past works. It is a correlative illusion that the reader or the "community of interpreters" creates the text, so that our task is merely to lay out the method or logic of critical inquiry or simply to describe and resign ourselves to the psychological or institutional compulsions that generate our interpretations. The question, then, is what Hartman makes of Wordsworth and what Wordsworth has made of Hartman. That dialectic is paradigmatic not just for every critic and scholar, but for every reader.

This is, I should add, Hartman's own understanding of interpretation. Elsewhere, I have ventured the formula that Hartman makes himself the self-consciousness of the poet's consciousness.[2] The reciprocity implicit in this relation needs to be stressed: we discover somewhat disconcertingly that—in Blake's biblical phrase—"we become what we behold." Hartman aims to coordinate the tensions between formalist analysis of a poem's internal economy and the historical study of the temporal stream in which it is situated.[3] The two engage each other in the poet's awareness of his own cultural situation—a situation which includes components of social, political, religious, intellectual, and literary history. From this perspective, "reading" Wordsworth in the full sense leads us into an interpretation that not only circles productively between his historical situation and his poetic response to it, but widens to encompass us in our situation as well. Wordsworth's situation is generally formulated as the emergence of modernity, sharpened by the crisis of the French Revolution and all that it implied and entailed. Hartman's way of reading presupposes that we have not yet exited from that historical situation. Reading Wordsworth brings us face to face with what remains problematic for us in modernity and thence, by a kind of retroactive effect (*Nachträglichkeit*), in Wordsworth himself. It is his recognition of and ambivalence toward this insuperable problematic element that I wish to trace in the career of Geoffrey Hartman.

In *The Legitimacy of the Modern Age*, Hans Blumenberg takes "self-assertion" as the "essence of the modern age's understanding of itself."[4] By "self-assertion" he means "an existential program, according to which man posits his existence in a historical situation and indicates to himself how he is going to deal with the reality surrounding him and what use he will make of the possibilities that are open to him" (LMA, 138). The apparent blandness of this definition is deceptive. What it covers is a far-reaching displacement. Comprehensive systems of symbols provided the traditional mediations that integrated the self into society and human existence into nature. In modernism, tradition gives way to the social form of science, which integrates individuals as controlled, rational experimenters in an ongoing project to dominate nature. What science achieves is made possible by our being situated within a world whose rationality cannot be guaranteed, a world which cannot be approached through an exegesis of traditional symbols.

Thomas Paine's *Age of Reason* (1795) draws the consequences with a bluntness that is by no means unintelligent. If a human being's primary question must be, "what is my duty as a moral agent?" then the answer could never come through a historically contingent revelation in a particular language. God's only medium of communication would have to be sensuous observation of a nature available to everybody, and the message would have to lie in reason's discernment in nature of an order akin to itself. In this lingering presumption that nature *is* a message, a medium for our communication with a God, we recognize what Blumenberg calls "re-occupation" (LMA, 65). One era inherits the problems or questions of its predecessor and strives to meet the criterion they set for reflective seriousness, even if doing so "overextends" its own rational resources (LMA, 48). Paine stops just short of the question which will mark the abandonment of the minimum residue he reoccupies, the question, why we should imagine that the order we find in nature is any sort of communication at all? Ultimately for modern science, natural process is not a medium or a message, but merely an object of study.

Kant shows why that doesn't suffice. In answer to the question what is enlightenment, he replies, *sapere aude*: submit everything to reason, to your own judgment.[5] That this could be mere boasting emerges in *Religion within the Limits of Reason Alone*, where Kant tests tradition against this standard.[6] Against any pretension that the human mind can have traffic with transcendance, Kant deploys not only argument, but all the devices of Enlightenment literature as well, devices ultimately based on rage: scorn, irony, sarcasm, satire. He is particularly withering on the slavish temperament to which pietism gives rise. Every traditional religious symbol is hermeneutically stripped down to bare reason: Jesus, whose name is never so much as mentioned, ceases to be God incarnate in historical flesh and blood and deliquesces into the archetype of ideal humanity, given local habitation only in reason and anchored there by nothing stronger than a logical presupposition.

It is not easy to describe Kant's tone: reason is too proud to depend on any historical mediation in its grasp of its own duties, yet it scorns the traditionary comforts that could soften the bitter discovery of its inadequacy to meet its own austere demands. Having demolished endlessly proliferating self-delusions and self-enslavements, Kant pauses at one point to ask whether reason does not suffer an even more destructive illusion in relying solely on the "moral disposition":

> But is there not also perhaps a dizzying *illusion of virtue*, soaring above the bounds of human capacity, which might be reckoned, along with the cringing religious illusion, in the general class of self-deceptions? No! The disposition of virtue occupies itself with something *real* which of itself is well-pleasing to God and which harmonizes with the world's highest good. True, an illusion of self-sufficiency may attach itself thereto, an illusion of regarding oneself as measuring up to the idea of one's holy duty; but this is merely contingent. To ascribe the highest worth to that disposition is not an illusion, like faith in the devotional exercises of the church, but is a direct contribution which promotes the highest good of the world. (RLR, 161)

Clearly he has felt the pinch. Various names from the history of heresy could be attached to this, but it suffices to note the pathos of this rejection of history and mediation, this stoic protest against contingency.

That pathos deepens against the background of Kant's subtly nuanced, dialectic attitude toward reason.[7] Finding reason's limits does not undermine it but establishes it, grounds it on a firm basis. Reason becomes stronger insofar as it is "pure." Moreover, it must purify itself: the critique of reason is the task of reason and also its triumph in every sense, its highest achievement and the achievement which brings it into its strength. And just that purification also demarcates the realm of faith, for what religion is can be seen only when we find what reason is, so that what can be "known" stands distinct from what can only be "thought." Reason is brought to its own tribunal, judged by itself, and hence liberated from any external check, from the censorious controls of dogmatic and instituted forces which would set its borders. This self-operating and self-controlling purification through which reason claims its due of authority and not an iota more gives us at last firm territory. The metaphor is Kant's and it is developed at telling length:

> We have now not merely explored the territory of pure understanding, and carefully surveyed every part of it, but have also measured its extent, and assigned to everything in it its rightful place. This domain is an island, enclosed by nature itself within unalterable limits. It is the land of truth—enchanting name!—surrounded by a wide and stormy ocean, the native home of illusion, where many a fog bank and many a swiftly melting iceberg give the deceptive appearance of farther shores, deluding the adventurous seafarer ever anew with empty hopes, and engaging him in enterprises which he can never abandon and yet is unable to carry to completion. Before we venture on this sea, to explore it in all directions and to obtain assurance whether there be any ground for such hopes, it will be well to begin by casting a glance upon the map of the land which we are about to leave, and to enquire, first, whether we cannot in any case be satisfied with what it contains—are not, indeed, under compulsion to be satisfied, inasmuch as there may be no other territory upon which we can settle; and, secondly, by what title we possess even this domain, and can consider ourselves as secured against all opposing claims. (CPR, A 235–36, B 294–95)

In fact what lies beyond is the realm of transcendental illusions. Though vigilant critique may check their evil consequences, it turns out that we cannot resist their lures, since reason arises out of our status as creatures who know only sensuously and who consequently cannot help seeking intuitions to correspond to our thoughts. These illusions are that the self is a substance we can know; that the world has a design we can discern; and that there is a God, of whose existence we can assure ourselves by sheer argument. When Kant is through, these claims have returned, but only as presuppositions, things we can think but cannot know. Kant thus defines the existential situation of the modern age with an even more searing bluntness than Blumenberg, for he makes it plain both that we cannot stop ourselves from launching on the restless sea of illusion and that any land we think we find there, any traditional symbol, dogma, or doctrine, is merely fogbank or melting iceberg.

The central problem for the modern age, then, is the dilemma of reason. It discovers that it has been definitively thrown back on its own resources, even for the task of surveying those resources and marking its own boundaries. As it takes on this burden, it finds a "beyond," but only in the form of what it must itself presuppose, and to which no mediator gives access. Though Hartman does not explicitly align Wordsworth with Kant in either *The Unmediated Vision* and or *Wordsworth's Poetry*, it seems to me that these are the terms of his reading of Wordsworth. Between the self, whose substantiality can no longer be verified by reflection, and the world, whose design can no longer be demonstrated by the evidence of things seen, the bridge is a God of whose existence reason has no resources for assuring itself and which must be merely presupposed as "the highest condition of the possibility of all that can be thought" (CPR, A334, B391). In Wordsworth, the typical pattern is this: some natural observation forces the mind to recognize its own autonomy as a step to its transformation into "a living soul," to which it is granted to "see into the life of things," to find "a sense sublime / Of something far more deeply interfused ... A motion and a spirit, that impels / All thinking things, all objects of all thought, / And rolls through all things."[8] This principle of generosity or dialectic of love mediates the relation of man to nature but without ever condensing into a fixed or traditional symbol.[9] It is something that hovers beyond any single symbol or series of symbols, located in an unspecifiable interaction or process of exchange often stated in a language of nearly maddening abstraction. Traditional nature description moved through the observed scene to project a transcendent design by means of a diction into which ancient cosmology and modern science flowed equally. As with Kant's Copernican revolution, Wordsworth purges poetry of the dogmatic diction of design and makes the language of poetry continuous with the prose of the world as it appears from the perspective of our own minds—not because of egotism, but because that is all we know. Whether it is all we need to know, whether we still need a symbolic mediation that is not merely personal or occasional, remains unanswered, though Wordsworth is not without hope.

In offering this interpretation, Hartman reopened the dialogue on romanticism by resisting the regnant view that Wordsworth replaced the dogma of design with the dogma of organicism, that is, the doctrine of "the one life within us and abroad" (Coleridge, "The Aeolian Harp"). To many, Hartman seemed to prefer the puzzles of self-consciousness to the achieved faith in the healing and humanitarian power of an imagination nurtured in harmony with nature.[10] As I understand Hartman, he regarded this latter view as an ideology of continuity consolidated into a doctrine by the Victorian poets. In response to their own authentic needs, they picked up the musical analogy to harmony and fused it with the idea of "Bildung."[11] Their doctrine was then transferred to Wordsworthian scholarship—but at the very moment when modern poets began to discern a totally changed spiritual condition, one marked by just that precariousness in the constitution and continuity of a self that Hartman finds in Wordsworth.

Hartman's account of this transposition seems to me convincing.[12] One can see not only in John Stuart Mill,[13] but also in a minor figure like the diarist Francis Kilvert what Wordsworth came to mean to the Victorians.[14] In Kilvert's prose nature descriptions; in his fascination with village graveyards and their decoration on festival days; in his devotion to children, especially little girls; in his pastoral visits to the poor and his careful collection of their stories, songs, and customs; and in his capacity to sustain sympathy and persist in acts of kindness and of love without blurring his realistic vision of rural life—in all these one senses the presence of Wordsworth even before a distant relative visits the neighborhood and Kilvert's impassioned pilgrimage is rewarded with a sight of a lock of the poet's hair. But Kilvert's poetry in fact owes more to Keble than to Wordsworth. The transfer of Wordsworth's spirit to prose is one step in the forging of an Arnoldian critical tradition which Hartman—not unaided, to be sure—began to break open in the fifties.

But what makes Hartman's reading of Wordsworth's poetry convincing is that it is a *reading*. Though it is possible to discern in *Wordsworth's Poetry* a guiding diagnosis of the modern condition, Hartman presents his views through close analysis of key poems and passages. It might thus appear that his dialogue with the tradition of Wordsworth scholarship could be conducted on the common ground of formalist analysis: the question is simply whose reading of Wordsworth's text is correct. That impression might be strengthened when Hartman in the book *Beyond Formalism*, whose title obviously has the flavor of polemic, nevertheless doubts whether the mind can ever free itself of the procedural restraints of formalism "without going through the study of forms. . . . My conclusion is a sceptical one, or else critical in the Kantian sense: to go beyond formalism is as yet too hard for us and may even be . . . against the nature of understanding" (BF, 42). He repeats the point in *The Fate of Reading*, even while associating himself with the then widespread push "to broaden literary study." He accepts that call, but without leaving literature behind for scientific truth, social productivity, or evangelism (FR, viii). One could then conclude that the slogan "beyond formalism" was almost ironic even as Hartman sought—through *Toposforschung, Formgeschichte, Stilgeschichte*, and what he called "psychopoetics"—possibilities for mediating between the self-substantiating form of the artwork and the stream of personal and historical time. This quest was extended under the specific social and political conditions of the sixties—conditions whose afterimage shadows the so-called New Historicism. But this contemporary agenda is also a fresh edition of what we are still thus enabled to see as the central unresolved tension in Wordsworth himself: the task of constituting a moral self is instituted by a false politic's threat to the self's integrity, while the legitimating aim of that task remains the achievement of some form of public address ("a man speaking to men").[15]

Nevertheless, this impression that the issue is one of formalism—both its plain prose medium and the intellectual agenda it inherits from romanticism—is somewhat misleading, for it is not a question of method. The affinity between Hartman and formalism lies in the responsiveness both show the view of the modern spiritual condition evident in modern poetry (since Eliot and Yeats). But Hartman is a phenomenologist from first to last. His insights are anchored to poetic form and style not by analytic procedure, but by his capacity to enter not just the mind of the poet, but also his existential and spiritual situation—to make himself the self-consciousness of the poet's consciousness. That may result in this case from a personal affinity with Wordsworth. His essay "The Interpreter: A Self-Analysis" makes him sound like Wordsworth: he talks of his childhood responsiveness to the senses; of the mass of his later reading and the need to find shelter, a paradise within or a fruitful solitude, where he could yet feel moved by a larger force; and of his sense of superiority vis-à-vis other critics (similar to what Wordsworth felt about his immediate poetic predecessors) and inferiority vis-à-vis art (for Wordsworth, to "nature" and "spirit") (FR, 3–4).

Whatever the personal affinities, Hartman gives what I take to be a decisive hint when he recognizes that in the theme of the refusal and yet quest for mediation, which permeates his thinking from the beginning to the present, he came to realize there was something "more analogous to religious or ritual purification" (FR, 4). I hesitate to introduce the term *religion*, which, as recent polemics have shown, remains something of a red cape in front of the enlightened academic mind. But not the least of Hartman's virtues has been his willingness to pursue his thinking even onto this unhallowed ground. In the modern context, we think of the development of the self as essentially a psychological problem, so that we will read the following in those terms: "Poetry itself is . . . a special realm of self-encounter, enabling the passage from one state of consciousness to another, and with the least damage. For, while to attain selfhood, or rather to accept it, one need simply break with nature by a criminal or ideological position, to achieve manhood more is required. To pass from selfhood to humanity the poet must recover in himself and perhaps for mankind those mediating symbols which destroy false separations or govern the flow of life between true ones. It is an open secret that he is the guardian of those symbols. . . " (WP, 125). In fact, Hartman is here generalizing from "Guilt and Sorrow," which makes clear the religious matrix within which the modern conception of the self emerges. As Hartman puts it with reference to Mircea Eliade, the tension is between the self's experience of the burden of history at all its levels and the ritual abolition of that burden through myth or symbolic action. With the romantics, including Wordsworth, it is precisely the Enlightenment's critique of tradition which frees art to assume the task of converting "self-consciousness into the larger energy of imagination" (BF, 305). Hartman has referred to Wordsworth as an "instinctive phenomenologist." I want to say that "phe-

nomenology" itself emerges out of just this clearing away of traditional dogmas and symbols, which leaves subjectivity as the
starting point of analysis.[16] This is evident in Schleiermacher's
redefinition of "religion" as "feeling," in his discrimination of religion from particular forms or "faiths," and in his consequent attempt to formulate the core "feeling" and dominant tone behind
"a" religion like Christianity.[17]

The problem is that in the wake of critique—and again this
is evident in Kant and Schleiermacher on religion—even when all
the traditional symbols are reinterpreted from the standpoint of
subjectivity, there exists no obvious path, no mediation from the
responsibility and authority of the individual's experience to the
communal, to the stream of history. In Charles Altieri's terms, the
poet is left with the task of constructing a new form of "eloquence," free from traditional rhetoric and grounded in scenic
stagings of the self whose acquired insights can nevertheless be
presented in a language that lays effective claim to public attention.

Thus, Hartman's reading of Wordsworth is not simply a contrary understanding that arises out of and can be reintegrated
within the bounds of a formalist method; rather, it joins itself to
those issues in Wordsworth's poetry which link him to the central
dilemmas of modern thought and culture. One may think of an
analogy to Philo's platonizing reading of the Pentateuch. This is not
to make Moses into Plato or Wordsworth into Kant, for philosophy
does not here "explain" poetry or formulate clearly the poet's confused thinking but itself articulates and responds in different terms
to the same cultural dilemma. Hartman develops a cultural hermeneutics that allows Wordsworth to speak a word to our time. We
are not to suspend our disbelief, to take time out from our concerns to appreciate an alien and incredible doctrine of organic nat-
uralism, but, rather, we are to read Wordsworth according to a different model of history, not subordinated to our agenda but able
to challenge our presuppositions, even our cherished "infidel-
ity."[18]

It is therefore not surprising that Hartman has devoted so
much energy to thinking through the challenge to his own view
of what he describes as "the most effective *countertheological*
movement at present," namely, deconstruction (UW, 111). My

premise is that a countertheology is not an antitheology, but a self-destructive or critical burrowing within. Deconstruction is a kind of alternative diagnosis of the core issue in modern thought, finding it not in the dilemmas of autonomous reason but in reason's occultation of its inevitable secondariness. In his earliest comments on deconstruction, Hartman connects it with the issue of history. He insists on "the historicity of even the most purified kinds of thinking" (of which deconstruction is an extreme example) and contrasts his own "tentative and critical" opposition to conventional history writing with the "transcendentally reductive" mode of undermining that history's "self-idealizing, political humanism" (FR, x). "Some will accuse me, no doubt," he concludes, "of deconstructing without a license" (FR, x).

Increasingly, Hartman comes to see what is at stake as a contrasting understanding of the kind of historicity that relates the interpreter to the artwork. "The decline of hermeneutics," he argues, "is related to a critique of *any* description of life which divides it into 'original' and 'secondary' components—vision and mediation, experience and rationalization, Bible and books" (FR, 17). Voice, the incarnate logos, cannot be an origin—we must live in time unpurged by any voice (UW, 111). "Writing," he adds, "is living in the secondary, knowing it is the secondary" (FR, 18). Hartman accepts the perpetually self-displacing movement of deconstruction that locates value in the secondary. He concedes his early blindness that stressed only nature, body, consciousness, and missed the fact that the chaos he saw was a chaos of forms. He neglected the primacy of writing, the inevitability of a secondariness not naturalized, as Bloom does, in a theorized oedipality drawn from ordinary life (FR, 41–56) but taking a specific linguistic form.[19] Yet he holds to a counter conviction that those who give up the fact of the book drift into a homogenized "philosophy" and lose the tension theology maintains between the Bible as book and as dissolved into proof texts, or, put more generally, "the discrepancy between letter and figurative development [which] was the very space of revisionary shock or 'hermeneutic reversal'" (FR, 13). What is indispensable for Hartman is to provide for the possibility of this reversal, for what he will describe as hesitation or "indeterminacy," the capacity to keep a thing in an "undecided" state before the mind which is thoughtfulness itself (CW, 270).

Hartman ventures that perhaps something has to be forgotten, and as forgotten it becomes the ground (FR, 19).

In quest of this ground, Hartman develops an anaclitic or enclitic interpretation (FR, 14), one that "leans" on the book rather than mirroring or reifying it. In the case of Wordsworth, this comes to mean acknowledging the role of the prior echo, the usurping voice, the pre-text, the intertext in generating imagination in Wordsworth and in complicating the continuity of its expression. Hartman has thus found the path to a remarkable new understanding of the later, "unremarkable" Wordsworth, a path that skirts the *abîme* but does not plunge into it. One could pursue this new understanding in many ways, but I want to follow my colleague Herman Rapaport and listen to the theme of voice and ear.[20] Hartman's defense of a critical style that can range from plain to fancy has called down loud protest.[21] That may have crowded out unfavorable attention to the bold puns that increasingly dot his Wordsworth interpretation. Lucy is seen as a lucy-feric (but not Luciferic) bearer of enlightenment. In the second stanza of "A slumber did my spirit seal," an image of gravitation elides the word *grave*, while echoes of *die* and *urn* are heard in *diurnal* or of *corse* (the older pronunciation of *corpse*) in *course*. The final rhyme, *trees*, anagrammatically elides the word which alternatively rhymes with the *fears* and *years* of the first stanza, namely, *tears* (EP, 145–50). Hartman is certainly aware that noises are distracting and echoes entropic. He is suspicious of echoes heard as harmonies or premature yew-nifications (UW, 144) and tries to respond to the disseminative, disruptive, primary-process feeling of sound. The very title of the key essay, "Words, Wish, Worth" (UW, 90–119) splits the proper name that seals self-continuity, opening a space by and for echo. But at the same time, Hartman follows faithfully Wordsworth's responsiveness in "A Slumber" to the healing power of the barest common speech, "its unconscious obliquity and inbuilt commitment to avoid silence" (EP, 148). The point here is not purity of speech, but commonness. As Wordsworth argued, there is no need to distinguish poetry from prose, an exalted voice from an antithaumaturgical writing, which is inscription's labor of the negative.[22]

The issue can be shown in Hartman's reading (FR, 284–93) of a passage always central to his understanding of Wordsworth:

the "Boy of Winander" episode, written in Germany along with the "Lucy" poems, first published in *Lyrical Ballads* in 1800, heading the section titled "Poems of the Imagination" in the *Poems of 1815*, and finally coming to rest in *The Prelude* (1850: 5.364–397). The Boy stands at twilight beside a lake and by mock whistles rouses the owls to calls that echo through the woods. But when no responsive cry comes, as his mind hangs in suspenseful waiting, the beauty of the scene sinks into his mind with "a gentle shock of mild surprise." Though the Boy died "ere he was ten years old," the poet has often stopped at evening beside his grave and stood "a full half-hour together . . . / Mute." We have here a self split between the Boy and the mature man, the poet.[23] This split self is presented along with a split sound—in the echoes the Boy provokes and in Wordsworth's own syntax and style, as Hartman analyzes them. But for Wordsworth, echo and afterimage are progressively internalized until buried beyond expression. They sink into a muteness, an expressive but unimaginable sound, in contrast to the earsplitting echoing streams and landscapes of conventional pastoral elegy. As with Lucy, we have the sense that the Boy's life has not so much ended as emerged or stepped over into its own indestructibility; the survivor owes his own life or the feeling of life to that exemplary transition.

As Wordsworth suggests in the "Essay on Epitaphs," whether the epitaph is an unanswered cry or crying out by the survivor or the survivor's pain is soothed by the fiction that turns the epitaph into a last word spoken by the departed,[24] elegy seems a voice or writing that arises against the impossibility of response and hence against the futility of saying anything at all. But it seems to me mistaken to set monody as monologue against polyphony as dialogue. Elegy does not just decently cover over silence. It converts silence, trans-mutes it, into voice. We thus find ourselves at the root capacity to hear voices, that is, at the root of that receptivity even to what is most alien, even to what lies just over the border of the human, which is the precondition of dialogue. Hartman frequently touches on the theme of "conversation," which I would see as a transposition in romanticism of the more formal and philosophical conception of dialogue.[25] What elegy makes apparent is the possibility and in fact the necessity of a splitting in self, in voice, in ear as the very precondition of dialogue.

Self-splitting echoing also takes the form of "intertextuality," the relation of this poem to specific texts or literary traditions, but here allusion—like the echo and afterimage of the Boy himself—is so buried that it fades into allusiveness as such, its phenomenology or subjective experience.[26] "This grounding of allusion in experience—in the personal and mortal experience of time," Hartman says, shifts the burden of responsiveness from the mutely meditating poet at the Boy's grave to the reader who ponders this inscription. "Time stretches through this reader into a potentially infinite series of echoes.... This power of recall ... is no simple imitation," Hartman adds, "but a creative response, a venture which extends and renews time" (FR, 291).[27] Hartman emerges with a conception of history as a series of linked ratios: the Boy to Wordsworth, Hartman to Wordsworth, a contemporary reader to Hartman (as mediating a relation to Wordsworth). Such a conception of history does not presuppose continuity and hence evades the deconstructive critique. The Kantian problematic of reason and the self has been relocated in terms of the power of language to curse or bless, wound or heal, where the priority between language and its psychic or ontological force is deliberately not decided (UW, 112). The deconstructive and the hermeneutic are held here in fruitful interchange.

It is important not to underestimate what is at stake here and in Hartman's reflections on the later Wordsworth. Hartman has come to entertain in critical style disseminative echoes and the heightened self-consciousness (not the deepened consciousness), almost the *Verstiegenheit*, they generate.[28] And consequently, he once again finds himself on uneasy or unsettled ground. Between the austerely self-conscious deconstructor and those who forget poetry for the allures of politics, that is, between the extremes of self-consciousness and un-consciousness, Hartman continues to feel, like Wordsworth, dialectically torn.[29] He seeks shadowy middles, genuine mediations, not supplements, and yet[30] he remains scrupulously self-checking and critical. That scrupulosity extends even to a hesitation over Wordsworth, a critical distance that weighs the possible limits of his poetry in an era that hates nothing so much as the middle ground. And yet that scruple is checked by another, a sense that perhaps some of Wordsworth's poems are not weak, but "have the sort of strength we are not yet fit to perceive," a "peculiar textual quality," a "timely utterance" which, again, assigns no priority as between intertextual and intratextual, consciousness and language, wish and word (UW, 112).

Critics used to be frustrated poets. Nowadays, they are more likely to be frustrated commissars (CW, 162). Hartman is not a frustrated, but a published poet, and as always, poetry reveals ambivalence most sharply. His volume *Akiba's Children* includes a series of three blank-verse descriptions of Helvellyn and the landscape near Grasmere. Hartman takes up Wordsworth's characteristic meter, diction, and syntax, but ultimately finds the currents of his own spirit sweeping him in an opposed direction. In the sequence's concluding poem, Hartman addresses Helvellyn. But against "nature and the language of the heart" ("Tintern Abbey"), his mind is drawn to the city and to the visionary style of Blake and Shelley. There the heart is not soothed; its human bonds are forged and tried as in a furnace, where we confront the hell and the heaven whose gates are opened by our ambivalent capacity for dread. Wordsworth's peculiar strength—his faith and resignation—have not resolved our problem. If modernity somehow does not suffice the mind and heart, how must we respond? Shall we seek, laid asleep in body and with an eye made quiet by the power of harmony and joy, to "see into the life of things"? Or must the sleep of reason be filled again with angels climbing the ladder to heaven's gate?[31]

> Glacial striations, the volcanic ridge
> only fancy quakes at; all the heroes
> that humanized this ground with bloody shouts
> or independent words or highland muteness,
> or this your pity that has terror in it,
> they fail to consecrate thy neighborhood
> of so much heaven and so much earth, Helvellyn.
> Had I been born out of thy firmer side
> I might perhaps have cleaved to thee, at last
> showered each season and reviving year
> a ritual cloudburst of memorial song
> over the dedicated brow. But thoughts,
> children of the wind and not of thee,
> or any place on earth, my alien thoughts

bask in thy gentle, steadfast scenery
a moment's moment only, then, outraged
by nothing but the bleating of a sheep,
spurn restless as before thy grassy tenets
and muttonous strength, the panoramic waves
of distant hills and long bluish prospects,
and the too homely church snug at thy base.
Better far the snaky sight of highways
the glare of cities at their head like knots
where people hammer on each other's heart
astonished at the vigor of the chain
that compensates in them earth's titan gods,
possessed—by the real power to possess:
There visions to size up the heart, to make
shudder and say: "How full of dread this place."

NOTES

The following abbreviations, with page numbers, are used in the text for Hartman's books:

AC = *Akiba's Children*. Emory, Va.: Iron Mountain Press, 1978.

BF = *Beyond Formalism: Literary Essays 1958–1970*. New Haven: Yale University Press, 1970.

CW = *Criticism in the Wilderness: The Study of Literature Today*. New Haven: Yale University Press, 1980.

EP = *Easy Pieces*. New York: Columbia University Press, 1985.

FR = *The Fate of Reading and Other Essays*. Chicago: University of Chicago Press, 1975.

ST = *Saving the Text: Literature/Derrida/Philosophy*. Baltimore: Johns Hopkins University Press, 1981.

UV = *The Unmediated Vision: An Interpretation of Wordsworth, Hopkins, Rilke, and Valéry*. New Haven: Yale University Press, 1954. New ed. (slightly revised, with a prefatory note), New York: Harcourt, Brace, 1966.

UW = *The Unremarkable Wordsworth*. Theory and History of Literature, 34. Minneapolis: University of Minnesota Press, 1987.

WP = *Wordsworth's Poetry, 1787–1814*. New Haven: Yale University Press, 1964.

1. My epigraph is from FR, 11. The quotation here is from FR, 282; see also FR, viii, quoted below.

2. See my "Foreword: Wordsworth and Post-Enlightenment Culture," to Hartman, UW, pp. ix–x. The technical philosophical term for this approach is

"hermeneutic phenomenology," which perhaps sounds unduly formidable in English. The fullest account of the approach is Hans-Georg Gadamer, *Truth and Method*, trans. ed. Garret Barden and John Cumming (New York: Seabury, 1975). A revised translation by Joel Weinsheimer and myself is forthcoming from Crossroads/Ungar/Continuum Press.

3. See the manifesto which closes BF, "Toward Literary History."

4. Hans Blumenberg, *The Legitimacy of the Modern Age*, trans. Robert M. Wallace (Cambridge, Mass.: MIT Press, 1983), p. 196. Further references in text abbreviated LMA with page number.

5. Immanuel Kant, "What Is Enlightenment?" in *Critique of Practical Reason and Other Writings in Moral Philosophy*, trans. Lewis White Beck (Chicago: University of Chicago Press, 1949), pp. 286–92.

6. Immanuel Kant, *Religion within the Limits of Reason Alone*, trans. Theodore M. Greene and Hoyt H. Hudson (New York: Harper and Row, 1960). Further references in text abbreviated RLR with page number.

7. Immanuel Kant, *Critique of Pure Reason*, trans. Norman Kemp Smith (New York: St. Martin's, 1965). Further references in text abbreviated CPR with standard page numbers for the first (A) and second (B) edition.

8. "Lines ... Tintern Abbey," lines 48, 95–96, 100–102. Wordsworth, *Poetical Works*, ed. Ernest de Selincourt, 2d ed. (Oxford: Clarendon Press, 1952), 2:259–63.

9. This is particularly Hartman's line of interpretation in UV.

10. An example almost at random is Enid Welsford, "Professor G. H. Hartman's *Theory of the Apocalyptic Imagination*," appendix 3 in her *Salisbury Plain: A Study in the Development of Wordsworth's Mind and Art* (New York: Barnes and Noble, 1966), pp. 157–65, agreeing with the *TLS* reviewer of WP. M. H. Abrams continues to be the most notable exponent of the traditional view.

11. FR, 286. One example of "harmony":

> The Spirit of Nature was upon me there;
> The soul of Beauty and enduring Life
> Vouchsafed her inspiration, and diffused,
> Through meagre lines and colours, and the press
> Of self-destroying, transitory things,
> Composure, and ennobling Harmony.

The Prelude (1850) 7.766–771, ed. Ernest de Selincourt, 2d ed. rev. Helen Darbishire (Oxford: Clarendon Press, 1959).

12. This is the larger theme of Hartman's CW. The emergence of sober, plain prose as a medium of public discourse owes much to Wordsworth's prefaces and critical writings, as interpreted and extended by Matthew Arnold. Hartman, of course, argues for a broader range of styles in criticism.

13. The importance of Wordsworth for Mill is penetratingly analyzed and set in the widest intellectual context by Robert Denoon Cumming, *Human Nature and History: A Study of the Development of Liberal Political Thought*, 2

vols. (Chicago: University of Chicago Press, 1969), a work which those interested in the relation of Wordsworth's poetic achievement to politics neglect at their peril.

14. Robert Francis Kilvert, *Diary*, ed. William Plomer, 3 vols. (London: Cape, 1960).

15. The nature of this tension is seen most clearly, I believe, by Charles Altieri; see his contribution to this volume. Compare also Kenneth R. Johnston, *Wordsworth and "The Recluse"* (New Haven: Yale University Press, 1984), *passim*.

16. *Phenomenology* is obviously a term with a range of meanings. Hartman's frequent attention to Freud may obscure the extreme caution with which he treats psychoanalysis (see "The Interpreter's Freud," EP, 137–54, for a particularly clear critique, which with equal caution entertains the continuing validity of a religious understanding, for example, pp. 150, 152). In *Wordsworth's Poetry*, his developmental model is explicitly Jungian, but my surmise is that Jung is read here in his affinity with the applied phenomenological analyses of religion by Eliade and by Gerardus van der Leeuw. Ludwig Binswanger's phenomenological and existential psychoanalysis seems to me closer in spirit than Freud's to Hartman's project. Our deafness to the specific echoes of Enlightenment religious critique in Wordsworth's labor to constitute a self lead us to a constricted psychological or psychoanalytic understanding, as opposed to a more broadly phenomenological one, which shares common ground with the issue of religion in the wake of critique of (plural) religions. Relevant here is Hans Blumenberg's meditation on the persistence of myth in the era of science; see *Work on Myth*, trans. Robert M. Wallace (Cambridge: MIT Press, 1985), which strategically focuses on the history of the reception of the Prometheus myth, with extensive attention to Goethe. Richard E. Brantley, *Wordsworth's "Natural Methodism"* (New Haven: Yale University Press, 1975), follows a traditional literary-historical approach and assembles evidence of Wordsworth's debt to English evangelical religious currents; he notes that the Wordsworthian constitution of the self is embedded in traditions of Puritan and Methodist spiritual autobiography (esp. chap. 2). This more local context needs, I believe, to be widened to reach back to Augustine and out to German romanticism's wrestling with related issues. Behind Augustine stands Cicero, through whom autobiographical "egotism" links to the stoic social and political ideas which form the consistent core of Wordsworth's thought throughout his career. The historical connections between Wesleyan Methodism and German pietism provide a genealogical link between, for instance, Wordsworth and Schleiermacher.

17. Friedrich Schleiermacher, *On Religion: Speeches to Its Cultured Despisers*, trans. John Oman (New York: Harper and Row, 1958). Religion is defined as "feeling" in the Second Speech, esp. pp. 41–45. In the Fifth Speech, Schleiermacher analyzes the root feeling behind various "faiths," including Christianity. I know no evidence that Wordsworth and Schleiermacher ever so much as heard of each other. But consider this sentence from Schleiermacher: feeling "is the

holy wedlock of the Universe with the incarnated Reason for a creative, productive embrace" (p. 43). Their affinity results from parallel responses to the spiritual condition of their age, not from influence.

18. This is to grant that we read Wordsworth "historically." In a different context, I would deny that claim: Wordsworth belongs to current events, despite the shrinkage in consciousness implicit in the notion that history can be measured in decades. To a journalist who asked what was the significance of the French Revolution, Mao Tse-Tung replied with justified impatience that it was too soon to tell.

19. As in Paul de Man's translation of Bloom's psychological terms into rhetorical figures in his review of *The Anxiety of Influence* in *Comparative Literature* 26 (1974), 269–75.

20. See "Geoffrey Hartman and the Spell of Sounds," in *Rhetoric and Form Deconstruction at Yale*, ed. Robert Con Davis and Ronald Schleifer (Norman: University of Oklahoma Press, 1985), pp. 159–77.

21. These are frequent in reviews of *Criticism in the Wilderness*. A more penetrating and sympathetic, though still critical account is Daniel T. O'Hara, *The Romance of Interpretation: Visionary Criticism from Pater to de Man* (New York: Columbia University Press, 1985), pp. 93–145 (and my review in *Comparative Literature*, forthcoming). O'Hara defines a larger romantic dilemma: the internalized quest for self-identity and immortality leads to an impossible dialectic between influence and originality, that is, the dialectics of "revisionism" or "secondariness." Hartman's style reflects the desire for interpretative authority expressed in "sublime idealizations," coupled with the recognition that these are only fragmentary, arbitrary, and subjective.

22. See Gerald L. Bruns, "Writing Literary Criticism," *Iowa Review*, 12 (1981), 23–43, esp. 36. Bruns describes deconstruction as an "anti-thaumaturgical" theory of language and contrasts it with what Hartman's approach has in common with Heidegger.

23. The early manuscript JJ introduces a first-person singular pronoun into what is otherwise a third-person anecdote, suggesting that the split may be within Wordsworth as well as between Wordsworth and the Boy. See the de Selincourt-Darbishire note to *The Prelude* 5.406.

24. See esp. Wordsworth, *Prose Works*, ed. W. J. B. Owen and Jane Worthington Smyser (Oxford: Clarendon Press, 1974), 2:60.

25. One could trace further the decline from "dialogue" to "conversation" to the modern obsession with "communication." The latter degenerates into the suppression of controversy, either to achieve the totalitarian monotone or in accord with an internalized bureaucratic ideal of minimizing social friction. It thus cooperates paradoxically with aggressive techniques of ideological and deconstructive suspicion to make all talk idle or small. J. Fisher Solomon, "The Concept of the Humanities," *Semiotica*, 64 (1987), 141–56, begins by reviewing Hartman's *Easy Pieces* and opens the broader context of Hartman's theory of the special task of the humanities in a contemporary society governed by a debased

concept of "communication." This is obviously at the center of *Criticism in the Wilderness*.

26. M. H. Abrams and others have noted the allusion to the Twenty-Third Psalm buried in "Tintern Abbey," line 114: "For thou art with me." Because his allusions are so embedded and internalized, Wordsworth's "intertextuality" has been neglected or even denied on behalf of a claim—or charge—of "originality."

27. Hartman distinguishes between "response" as "Rezeption" and as "Empfängnis," a receptivity that is also conception or new creation.

28. This openness to self-consciousness and its heightened style contrasts obviously with the theme of his essay "Romanticism and Anti-Self-Consciousness," *BF*, 298–310.

29. This is doubtless the place to note the now-common accusation that Hartman is an "aestheticist" who neglects "politics." Thus concludes an admirably thorough essay by Michael Sprinker, "Aesthetic Criticism: Geoffrey Hartman," in *The Yale Critics: Deconstruction in America*, ed. Jonathan Arac, Wlad Godzich, and Wallace Martin (Minneapolis: University of Minnesota Press, 1983), pp. 43–65, a conclusion subtly reconsidered by Jonathan Arac, ibid., pp. 189–97. In his essay included in the present volume, Hartman remarks that the privilege which motivates political concerns will not be cancelled by mock polemics against the aesthetic in poetry (see also FR, xi–xiii). But this is not the place to engage the current critical passion for "politics," which in practice is constricted to a narrow slice of partisan politics. It is striking that this accusation so frequently *ends* both essays and further discussion. "The political" can easily function as a "God term," the end, rather than the beginning of thinking (and of thinking about poetry and particular poems). The modern gesture absent-mindedly repeats the accusation against Wordsworth of Hazlitt and other "second-generation" romantics. My own claim is that Wordsworth, particularly in *The Prelude*, is political through and through, though not in a sense of the "political" easily recognized today. The same could be said of Hartman.

30. The phrase is characteristic of Hartman, who could be called the critic of the "and yet": "Every item in the interpreter's ethos should be submitted to a methodical suspicion" (FR, 10). By contrast, for example, Paul de Man's key locution is, "It would be naive to say. . . ."

31. From *Akiba's Children*; the pages are unnumbered.

II

Romanticism
without
Wordsworth

Romanticism without Wordsworth

In "Representative Men" Emerson claims that "[t]he search after the great is the dream of youth and the most serious occupation of manhood." But Emerson also warns us that we had better think hard about the uses we would make of our heroes, our great and representative geniuses. The following essays all offer hard thought not only about Romantic heroes (and heroines), but also about our search for the great and the representative.

In disputing the idea that Wordsworth is the exemplary Romantic poet, James K. Chandler argues not for an alternative candidate, but for a fresh approach to the question of representativeness. Chandler's underlying subject is the nature of literary and cultural history, and if the case against Wordsworth's cultural centrality appears paradoxically at the front and center of his essay, this concentration on Wordsworth must be recognized as a heuristic strategy. Chandler examines and finds mistakenly understood what have to some seemed endorsements by Shelley and Hazlitt of Wordsworth as the writer most representative of the spirit of the age of Romanticism. Shelley's and Hazlitt's positions are more self-consciously self-contradictory than has been credited, Chandler claims, and he sees such unresolvable self-contradictions as working deliberately to block any straightforward assertion of a representative genius of the age.

If some questions of historical and aesthetic representativeness can be perpetually deferred, however, some problems of political representation evidently cannot. Chandler sketches lineaments of Romantic attention to the nature of political representation—in Burke and Shelley, Emerson and Hazlitt—as he urges renewed consideration of the mutual implications of some of the categories of politics and literature.

Marilyn Butler suggests an additional, explicit focus on the politics of literary criticism. Butler seizes the topic of Romanticism without Wordsworth by constructing a fable predicated on a fantasy of a young Wordsworth's execution. The acknowledged shape of a Romanticism truly without Wordsworth might be very different, Butler implies, but not because a singular, potentially transforming genius was prematurely removed from the scene. Wordsworth as the representative Romantic is, Butler claims, essentially a construction of later literary critics and cultures, out of their political aims and disappointments. Butler asks for more recognition of the politics of both the Romantic and the modern cultures, and for increased self-consciousness about contemporary political projections into the literature of the past. Agreeing with Chandler, against M. H. Abrams, Butler asserts that Wordsworth was not in fact, for his contemporaries "the great and exemplary poet of his age." Insisting that this sort of identification of Wordsworth is grounded on an anachronistic modern canon, Butler herself places Byron at the focal point of the Romantics' public vision, and she offers, for contemporary consideration, a detailed recommendation of the historical exemplarity of Southey.

Anachronisms in the modern canon of Romantic literature are also studied by Gary Kelly in his account of the Romantic transformation of the institution of literature. With close attention to the specific historical circumstances of the late eighteenth century, Kelly depicts literature as a "field of struggle" of the professional middle classes, a field on and through which these classes sought to identify and forward their own interests and values. The political dangers of the old hierarchies of genres and discourses were addressed, Kelly claims, by a reconstruction of literature, a reconstruction that appeared to transcend distinctions of class and gender but in fact advanced its own material and sexual politics. The central aim, according to Kelly, was the redemption of prose fiction, and he takes the strategies toward this end to revolve around a reconfiguration of the relation between fact and fiction. Kelly illustrates his thesis with a variety of major and minor novels and quasi-novels of the Romantic period. As he recounts the vicissitudes of their historical reception, he also declares that our current concepts and canons of Romanticism remain subject to errors and opacities, difficulties grounded on our failure to see clearly, even now, that period's political struggle over the institution of literature.

John Murdoch works against a different but related failure to see, in his discussion of the problem of recognizing the political message of visual art. Beginning with a print by Julius Caesar Ibbetson, Murdoch traces the elements of the Picturesque in art at the close of the eighteenth century, but he notes that even as those ideal landscapes were real places, those places, and hence those landscapes, had real politics. The politics on which Murdoch focuses are centered on the role of labor, and he discerns in the visual arts a Georgic tradition: images of work. Murdoch sketches the development and significance of this tradition, its origin as the second of Vergil's three modes of poetry—Pastoral, Georgic, and Epic—and its changing role in the justification of culture—civilization and its hard labors. Particularly significant, Murdoch argues, is the occasional suppression of the Georgic tradition because of its association with political revolution—originally, the mythology of Jupiter's overthrow of Saturn, an insurrection that effects a loss of innocence but makes possible the progress of civilization. Murdoch suggests that eighteenth-century England had absorbed the Georgic and in that way rendered it invisible: settled familiarity with a fixed division of labor makes that division seem itself "natural"; the Georgic is assimilated to the Pastoral and is eventually called Picturesque. But Murdoch shows Ibbetson to have willfully connected his etching to contemporary politics, and he argues that this connection can be used to make visible again a Romantic landscape of labor.

Thus Murdoch's essay, with its consideration of pictorial representation and its detailed account of the way in which history and politics may play a crucial role in what is literally made visible, presents both a new direction and an appropriate conclusion to this set of essays—essays arguing about the nature and criteria of representation, about the methodology of historical criticism and the role of politics in creation and interpretation.

K.H.

Representative Men, Spirits of the Age, and Other Romantic Types

JAMES K. CHANDLER

The 1988 exhibition entitled "William Wordsworth and the Age of English Romanticism" attracted nearly two hundred thousand visitors in New York and Chicago and received widespread coverage in the American press. At Indiana University, the exhibition occasioned the major conference—well attended and reviewed at length in *The Chronicle of Higher Education*—and that conference occasioned the present volume of essays. Since the plans for all this originated with the Wordsworth Trust at Dove Cottage, one can understand the choice of Wordsworth as a focus for the exhibition and the conference. And the heuristic advantages of locating a particular individual at the center of a cultural history surely account in part for the enterprise's popular appeal, an appeal also evident in the sales of *William Wordsworth and the Age of English Romanticism*, the lavishly illustrated volume published as a companion to the exhibit. In view of these circumstances, and this success, it may seem captious to take issue with the chosen marketing strategy. Had it been more evidently and consistently acknowledged as a marketing strategy, or at most a heuristic device, there might indeed have been little to quarrel about. In such a scheme of things, however, the central position provisionally accorded to Wordsworth too often assumes the character of an enduring truth, even among scholars speaking to other

scholars; there is a powerful tendency, conspicuous in the exhibition's own rhetoric, to slip from the cautious suggestion that
Wordsworth is "a center" from which to study Romanticism into
the bold claim that he is "the seminal poet of the age."
Wordsworth's poetry certainly makes a claim for his representativeness of the age, but it cannot be taken at face value, and was
not so taken by his most astute contemporaries.

When, in "The Age of the World Picture," Heidegger formulated a relationship between modernity, epochal consciousness,
and representation, he suggested that the modern age could be
defined precisely by its development of the age-defining world picture.[1] He further speculated that such a picture comes into view
with the emergence of the Cartesian subject—that is, with the surfacing of what, with resonant paranomasia, Wordsworth called
"the picture of the mind." But whenever this picture comes into
view, its age-defining function becomes a major preoccupation in
the decades following the French Revolution. Heidegger seems to
allow as much when he says that the "increasing rootedness of the
world in anthropology, which has set in since the end of the eighteenth century, finds its expression in the fact that the fundamental stance of man in relation to what is, in its entirety, is defined
as a world view."[2] For Heidegger this stance, with its concomitant
forcing back of "what is" into "this relationship to oneself as the
normative realm," is the stance of "representation" in the modern
sense.[3] In contending that Wordsworth's claim to represent his
age cannot be taken at face value, I thus refer to his stance both
as the perceiving subject who pictures his age and as the perceived subject implicitly at the center of that picture. In what follows, however, the cultural claims made for Wordsworth—by
himself and in his behalf by his recent promoters—are less important in themselves than for the more general assumptions they be-
tray about literary and cultural history. My argument here will specifically concern the way in which the likes of Hazlitt and Shelley
figure in the arguments for Wordsworth's representativeness. For
neither Wordsworth's claim to that kind of representation, nor
anyone else's, can be underwritten by appeal to those among
Wordsworth's English contemporaries who most thoughtfully considered these difficult issues.

I

M. H. Abrams's foreword to *William Wordsworth and the Age of Romanticism* makes an appropriate point of departure for this argument since it offers an explicit and familiar defense of the titular configuration and since Abrams himself is largely responsible for popularizing that configuration in our time. "His fellow poets would have understood, and approved, putting Wordsworth at the centre of this exhibition celebrating both the spirit and achievements of English Romanticism," says Abrams, for in spite of reservations they may have had about "some of his opinions and achievements," they "recognized" that he "was the greatest, most inaugurative, and most representative poet of his time."[4] Before considering the question of what Wordsworth might have looked like to his contemporaries, we must notice how Abrams's shift from "greatest" of his time to "most representative . . . of his time" adds a second dimension to his claim for the poet's representativeness. What Wordsworth is supposed to be representing *in* his time, as it turns out, is the time itself, the "Age of Romanticism." To prepare for this shift Abrams needs to establish that it makes sense to talk about such things as "ages" in the first place. Conceding that "[t]he 'Age of Romanticism' is a title imposed by later historians on the four decades after 1790," he goes on to argue for the correspondence of this "title" to a contemporary perception, the self-recognition of a certain "spirit." Writers of 1790–1830

> had recognized that in both its literature and thought it constituted an era that was distinctive, vital, and innovative, and had identified its distinguishing features by the term "the spirit of the age." As Shelley wrote in *A Defence of Poetry* in 1821, "the literature of England has arisen as it were from a new birth." "We live among such philosophers and poets as surpass beyond comparison any who have appeared since the last national struggle for civil and religious liberty, and these writers manifest a common "spirit of the age."[5]

Having introduced the concept of the spirit of the age on the authority of Shelley's comments of 1821, as he did in *Natural Supernaturalism* (1971), Abrams cites Hazlitt, again as before, to support the notion that Wordsworth is the writer "most representative" of that spirit: "'Mr. Wordsworth's genius is a pure emanation of the Spirit of the Age', and it 'partakes of, and is carried along with, the revolutionary movement of our age.'"[6] The authors of the text proper of *William Wordsworth and the Age of English Romanticism* cite the same passage from Hazlitt in their chapter 2, "The Spirit of the Age", and to roughly the same purpose.[7]

The exhibition and its companion publication may thus be seen as giving popular expression to the argument of *Natural Supernaturalism*, where Abrams had stated outright that the "rationale" for his project "was that Wordsworth (as his English contemporaries acknowledged, with whatever qualifications) was *the* great and exemplary poet of the age" (emphasis mine).[8] Disputes over the validity of this claim were carried out in reviews of *Natural Supernaturalism* when it appeared, and they have been summarized in Wayne Booth's generous chapter about that book in his *Critical Understanding*.[9] Some of Abrams's critics have persuasively advocated the candidacy of other writers to stand as "representatives" of "the Age of Romanticism"—Byron, for example.[10] If one wished to accept the framework, one could certainly make a strong case for inserting Scott at its center in lieu of either Wordsworth or Byron. Attempting to pursue this line of thought one step further at the Bloomington conference, the session called "Romanticism without Wordsworth" was organized with the expressed aim of considering the possible "representativeness" of still lesser-known candidates—John Thelwall or the popular novelists or then-celebrated women poets such as Felicia Hemans and Mary Tighe.[11]

But if the objections raised against *Natural Supernaturalism* have failed to check its influence, as the events of last year suggest, the fault may be that the critique has been carried out on the wrong level. It is not enough to present new candidates behind the facehole in the painted cardboard figure of "The Representative Romantic." The picture of the age picture itself, the whole sideshow game, must be called into question. It is a game now played in period studies other than Romantic, but Romanticists may be charged with a special responsibility for it. Whether or not it makes sense to talk about an Age of Romanticism or about

Wordsworth as the best representative of that age, the four decades after the fall of the Bastille do seem to have inaugurated a way of talking about history such that one could begin to speculate about how a cultural period might indeed be representable by the likes of a writer or a philosopher or by any individual other than a head of state. Perhaps the philosophical reorientation toward this view can indeed be traced to Descartes, but it does not much affect the literary representation of history for another century and a half.

In historical writing before 1789, when an "age" is identified in respect to a head of state—the Age of Elizabeth, for example, or of Cromwell—it is normally not the case that the ruler in question is taken to be "representative" of his or her "age" in anything like the modern sense. Hume's *History of England* (1754–62), for example, includes "Appendices" at the end of the various epochs into which it is divided, and these appendices give descriptive, mainly synchronic summaries of the states of society during the long periods which comprise the major sections of the work: for example, "Feudal and Anglo-Norman Government and Manners." The chapters of Hume's actual narrative of events, on the other hand, are normally entitled simply with the names of English monarchs. Whereas the appendices single out no individuals to typify the state of government and manners, the heads of state associated with sections of the narrative tend not to be identified with a particular stage of culture. Eighteenth-century biographical writing corroborates this view from the obverse side. Dr. Johnson's *Lives of the Poets* (1781–83) does not conspicuously offer the subjects of its biographies as representatives or types of the times in which they lived. Thus Leopold Damrosch can argue from the sense that "Johnson's emphasis on the individuality of the imagination is . . . ideally suited to literary biography, rather than to conventional literary history" to the following conclusion: "In the end, therefore, the subjects of Johnson's *Lives* [though dispersed across centuries] appear as contemporaries in the fullness of literary achievement."[12]

The concept of the spirit of the age and the concept of the "representative man" (in roughly Emerson's sense) began to gain currency together, as functions of one another, and they did so in both England and Germany in the decades around the turn of the century.[13] When Emerson himself took up this question in the 1840s, working within the English and German traditions he had learned from the likes of Carlyle, he did not (it must be conceded) consistently offer his representative men as representative of their respective ages. When he says for example that he admires "great men of all classes, those who stand for facts, and for thoughts," he does not seem to have historical categories in mind.[14] His chapters on Plato, Swedenborg, Montaigne, Shakespeare, Napoleon, and Goethe are presented in that (nonchronological) order, and their subtitles employ nonhistorical rubrics: the Philosopher, the Mystic, the Poet, the Man of the World, and the Writer.

In the course of his discussions, however, Emerson does relate the two nineteenth-century figures in the group primarily to the period in which they lived: "I described Bonaparte as a representative of the popular external life and aims of the nineteenth century. Its other half, its poet is Goethe."[15] With Goethe, what is represented is specifically a cultural period, but neither the sense in which it so appears nor the way in which Goethe is said to represent it admits of facile application. Goethe, says Emerson, is

> a man quite domesticated in the century, breathing its air, enjoying its fruits, impossible at any earlier time, and taking away by his colossal parts the reproach of weakness, which, but for him, would lie on the intellectual works of the period. He appears at a time, when a general culture has spread itself, and has smoothed down all sharp individual traits; when, in the absence of heroic characters, a social comfort and cooperation have come in. There is no poet, but scores of poetic writers: no Columbus, but hundreds of post captains with transit-telescope, barometer, and concentrated soup and memmican: no Demosthenes, no Chatham, but any number of clever parliamentary and forensic debaters;— no prophet or saint, but colleges of divinity; no learned men, but learned societies, a cheap press, readingrooms, and bookclubs, without number. There was never such a miscellany of facts. The world extends itself like American trade. We conceive Greek or Roman life, life in the Middle Ages, to be a simple and comprehensible affair; but modern life to respect a multitude of things which is distracting.
>
> Goethe was the philosopher of this multiplicity, hundred-

handed, Argus-eyed, able and happy to cope with this rolling miscellany of facts and sciences, and, by his own versatility, to dispose
of them with ease.[16]

Emerson's handling of Goethe in this, the last of the essays in his
volume, thus opens up some of the paradoxes that abide in his
notion of the culturally representative individual. Although
Emerson's Goethe is the very "type of culture," culture turns out
to be so general and spread out as to *require* heuristic epitomizing
to become intelligible, legible. He is "the soul of his century," but
his was the century of culture's soulless image. It is not that his
stature is a summation of the greatness of his period. The age is
not one of strength, and Goethe does not lend strength to it; he
takes away its weakness. He is the individual capable of standing
for an age that has smoothed down all "sharp individual traits."
    Emerson delivered his lectures in England, after much consul-
tation with his mentor Carlyle, and in respect to such paradoxes
this discussion certainly bears the marks of some of Carlyle's difficult ideas about heroes, hero-worship, characteristics, and signs of
the times. Carlyle saw his own age as defined by the penumbra
of the French Revolution, but nothing characterizes Carlyle's history of that event so conspicuously (in view of its being written
by the man of heroes) as its refusal to represent the Revolution
by means of great representative individuals. That Carlyle developed his theory of heroes in an age without them, and that
Emerson developed his theory of representative great men in an
age without *them*, may not seem so strange on reflection. But it
ought to give us pause about how we construct and depict cultural
periods on the basis of contemporary testimony, and it may cause
us to wonder about the way certain devices of typification have
been used in packaging Romanticism for consumption in a culture
extended, as Emerson said, like American trade.

II

Why the relation of representative writer and represented age
is not tied up so neatly will become clearer, I think, if we return
to Hazlitt's extraordinary collection of essays in *The Spirit of the*

Age, the book that has been used as the rock upon which the modern church of "Wordsworth and the Age of Romanticism" has been built. Leaving aside Hazlitt's specific comments about how Wordsworth's poetry is supposed to have been modeled on the political developments of the French Revolution, we need to take up the more general question of Wordsworth's relation to the announced subject of the collection.[17] Does Hazlitt leave unqualified the force of the pronouncement—always cited straightforwardly and out of context—with which he opens his essay on Wordsworth? "Mr. Wordsworth's genius is a pure emanation of the Spirit of the Age." In what spirit should this declaration be taken?

It sounds straightforward enough. What might initially give us pause, however, is the recollection that Hazlitt makes similar statements, perhaps not quite so definitively couched, about the claims of other writers to represent the spirit of the age and that these claims are quite adverse to the one he advances for Wordsworth. In the essay on Francis Jeffrey, for example, Hazlitt argues that Jeffrey's magazine, *The Edinburgh Review*, is "eminently characteristic of the Spirit of the Age; as it is the express object of the Quarterly Review [earlier discussed by Hazlitt in the essay on Gifford] to oppose that spirit."[18] This seems nearly as forceful an identification of a true representative of the spirit of the age as the assertion made about Wordsworth. The problem is that, as Hazlitt himself as much as says, if one were to single out one antagonist more insistent in his opposition to Wordsworth than any other in the first quarter of the century, it would surely be Jeffrey. Moreover, the spirit of the age is defined in the essay on Jeffrey in terms of intellectual rigor and acumen: the *Edinburgh Review* "asserts the supremacy of intellect." Wordsworth, on the other hand, is said to represent that spirit in spite of "the hebetude of his intellect."[19]

This kind of discrepancy would be easier to ignore if it were the exception in Hazlitt's book, but this is not the case. Consider the opening of Hazlitt's essay "Mr. Coleridge":

> The present is an age of talkers, and not of doers; and the reason is, that the world is growing old. We are so far advanced in the Arts and Sciences, that we live in retrospect, and doat on past achievements. . . . Mr. Coleridge has 'a mind reflecting ages past.'[20]

Mr. Coleridge is the great conversationalist of the age of talkers and the man of retrospection in a time obsessed with past achievements. It is plainly suggested that he is, in these respects, perfectly representative of the age. The opening of the essay on Scott picks out some of the same cultural traits. There Hazlitt calls Scott "undoubtedly the most popular writer of the age" and adds, presumably by way of explanation: "He is just half of what the human intellect is capable of being: . . . he knows all that has been; all that is to be is nothing to him. His is a mind brooding over antiquity."[21] For all this apparent agreement about the retrospectivity of the spirit of the age in the essays on Coleridge and Scott, however, these remarks sort ill with other comments in the volume—for example where Hazlitt speaks of the age's "rash and headlong spirit,"[22] or where, speaking of Gifford's *resistance* to the spirit of the age, Hazlitt says:

> He would go back to the standard of opinions, style, the faded ornaments, and insipid formalities that came into fashion about forty years ago. Flashes of thought, flights of fancy, idiomatic expressions, he sets down among the signs of the times—the extraordinary occurrences of the age we live in. They are marks of a restless and revolutionary spirit: they disturb his composure of mind, and threaten (by implication) the safety of the state.[23]

Saying that the age is essentially retrospective and also that it is essentially prospective involves a contradiction different from the one involved in identifying one representative of the spirit of the age by his faith in "the supremacy of intellect" and another by his own hebetude of intellect. It is nonetheless a forceful contradiction, and Hazlitt's portrait of the moral and poetical character of Wordsworth does not suggest a subsumption of either of these contradictions.

Nor do we find support for the view of Wordsworth's special centrality in the representation of the spirit of the age in the overall organization of Hazlitt's 1825 collection. The essay "Mr. Wordsworth" appears as one among many. It is neither placed first, nor last, nor in the middle of the group. The special claim for Wordsworth, or the specification of the spirit of the age along Wordsworthian lines, might easily have been made in a preface or introductory essay, such as Emerson provided in *Representative Men*. Hazlitt was quite capable of producing such a thing; his *Political Essays* of 1819 were prefaced with several pages of remarks that identified common themes and salient interests among those pieces. The collection of pieces in *The Spirit of the Age*, however, appeared without introduction or preface. From its earliest editions, the book begins straightaway with the essay on Bentham; it is a gallery of "contemporary portraits" without a centerpiece or a docent. In view of the pains Hazlitt has taken to avoid simple solutions to this question of representatives and representations, it would seem most unfortunate to take the first sentence from his Wordsworth essay, no matter how definitive it might sound by itself, as that astute critic's last word on the subject.[24]

The contrast with the 1819 volume of *Political Essays* is relevant in another way in that, although it collects Hazlitt's work from much of the period surveyed in the 1825 volume, it shows no sign of being tempted by the notion of a spirit of the age in the first place. Although the 1819 volume includes several character sketches anticipatory of *The Spirit of the Age*, these earlier essays raise no expectations about how a unified culture might be identified and outlined for, say, 1789–1819. Instead, they tend to make liberal use of specific dates and specific topical references for events of three previous decades; Hazlitt speaks freely of parties, camps, and conflicting constituencies; there are discussions of the characters, not only of individuals but also of Whigs, Tories, Country People, Courtiers, Reformers, and so on. Openly acknowledging this plurality of factions and features in the post-Revolution decades, the 1819 volume is inclined to dwell neither on the period's singularized "spirit" nor (consequently) its contradictions. When Hazlitt does speak of the "spirit of contradiction" in 1819, he does so in reference to one of several traits he finds in the character of the reformer.[25]

In *The Spirit of the Age*, however, in the very act of positing the notion of a unified spirit, Hazlitt has constructed a scheme of contradictions. Not only are the contradictions discernible, they are even emphasized by Hazlitt's arrangement of things. Writers are contrasted with other writers both within essays (Mr. Campbell and Mr. Crabbe) and between essays (Lord Byron and Sir Walter Scott), and where two paired figures are both accorded representative status, they nonetheless may be said to agree on virtually nothing:

> Lord Byron and Sir Walter Scott are of writers now living the two, who would carry away the majority of suffrages as the greatest geniuses of the age.... We shall treat of them in the same connection, partly on account of their distinguished pre-eminence, and partly because they afford a complete contrast to one another. In their poetry, in their prose, in their politics, and in their tempers, no two men can be more unlike. (p. 69)

In addition to contradicting one another, writers also contradict themselves. Robert Southey is first described by Hazlitt as having "a look at once aspiring and dejected." Wordsworth's muse is "distinguished by a proud humility." For most of these figures it is alleged that their strength lies in their weakness: Coleridge's procrastinating talkativeness, for example, is just the underside of his ability to see all sides of a question. There is no single set of coordinates, however, on which such multiple contradictions can be plotted.[26] Nor, again, is there a single figure—either in the sense of a particular contradictory trope (such as Abrams's governing oxymoron "natural supernaturalism") or in the sense of a particular person (Wordsworth as Waverley)—in which the entire scheme can be subsumed.[27]

If Hazlitt's positing of the spirit of the age brings the contradictions to notice, the contradictions have implications for what "the spirit of the age" itself can be imagined to mean. It may help here to recall that Althusser initially deployed the now-familiar notion of overdetermination in order to distinguish between the functions of contradiction in the Hegelian and Marxian conceptions of history and periodicity. If, says Althusser,

> a vast accumulation of "contradictions" comes into play *in the same court*, some of which are radically heterogeneous—of different origins, different sense, different *levels* and *points* of application—but which nevertheless "merge" into a structural unity, we can no longer talk of the sole, unique power of the general "contradiction." Of course, the basic contradiction [between the forces and relations of production] dominating the period (when the revolution is "the task of the day") is active in all these

"contradictions: and even in their "fusion." But, strictly speaking, it cannot be claimed that these contradictions and their fusion are merely the pure phenomena of the general contradiction. The "circumstances" and "currents" which achieve it are more than its phenomena pure and simple.... This means that if the "differences" that constitute each of the instances in play ... "*merge*" into a real unity, they are not "*dissipated*" as pure phenomena in the internal unity of a *simple* contradiction.[28]

The period model in which the differences among the instances in play at a given moment are "dissipated as pure phenomena in the internal unity of a simple contradiction" is, for Althusser, Hegel's, and it is the one that I have argued most closely suits the world picture of Romanticism-as-Wordsworth-as-"Natural Supernaturalism"—or for that matter, Romanticism-as-Byron-as-"Faithful Skepticism," or Romanticism-as-Scott-as-"Progressive Conservatism." The simplicity of this kind of contradiction, as Althusser explains, "is made possible only by the simplicity of the internal principle that constitutes the essence of any historical period."[29] Although Hazlitt's *Spirit of the Age* brings the reformer's "spirit of contradiction" conspicuously into play, he makes every effort to block the identification of a simple contradiction to which his representation of his age could be said to reduce (in the way that phenomena reduce to an essence). Just this resistance to simplification, it seems to me, is wherein the greatness of the book's achievement lies. Such resistance is indeed built into Hazlitt's critical style, which was regarded by some of his first readers as a public menace. In a relatively well-disposed review, nonetheless thoroughly preoccupied by Hazlitt's "figurative and epigrammatic style," a writer for *The Monthly Review* wrote of the prose in *The Spirit of the Age*: "Every thing shines as through a prismatic medium. The result is, that we retain nothing distinctly of what he says. It is a sort of confused memory of sounds, like the clashing of musical instruments."[30]

But why, if all this is true of the book, does Hazlitt call Wordsworth "the pure emanation of the spirit of the age"? Any good answer to this question requires notice of one of Hazlitt's favorite (because anarchic) figures: catachresis. Since we normally speak of spirits as being "embodied" in persons, the word we ought to have seen where "emanation" appears is "incarnation." "Emanation" was used then, and is still used now, to suggest a relatively immaterial effluence from a relatively material source. Since the spirit of the age is already, for Hazlitt, immaterial, the notion of an emanation from it, indeed a "pure emanation," is strongly redundant. This might be carelessness or a casual joke, but it would be more in keeping with what a contemporary reviewer called Hazlitt's "paradoxical and caustic genius" to see in it a certain mockery of Wordsworth's pretensions.[31] The essay on Wordsworth attempts to capture what it is that Wordsworth aspires to, and it would not be difficult to argue, even on the basis of the poetry Hazlitt would have seen, that Wordsworth's writings aspire to the condition, exactly, of being read as a "pure emanation" of the spirit of the age.

Hazlitt would not, of course, have seen the completed *Prelude*, but the parts he would have seen (such as the "Bliss was it in that dawn to be alive ..." passage published in *The Friend*) would have corroborated such a view of Wordsworth. Furthermore, the Prospectus to *The Recluse* (the same text which Abrams makes his recurring point of departure and return in *Natural Supernaturalism*) is a text that Hazlitt knew well. In that ambitious document, Wordsworth represents the "age"—post-Milton, post-Enlightenment—precisely by an act of subsuming it into the patterns of his own mind and character. He makes its hopes his hopes and its disappointments his disappointments. And, by way of sublimation ("pure emanation"?), he also seeks to make *his* recompenses *its* recompenses. In his writings about Wordsworth all through his life, certainly from the largely sympathetic review of *The Excursion* onward, Hazlitt resisted Wordsworth's "internalization of quest romance"—his way of offering his own experience as an epitome of his historical culture and his narrative of that experience as the resolution of its contradictions. It is of considerable relevance in this connection that in the last of his 1818 *Lectures on the English Poets*, his contemporary commentary "On the Living Poets," Hazlitt does not make any reference to Wordsworth's "representativeness" of the contemporary developments he surveys. He calls him "the most original poet now living," but this claim, needless to say, stands in no clear relation to a straightforward claim for his representativeness. Moreover, Hazlitt employs neither the concept of the spirit of the age nor that of representative man in "On the Living Poets." For him, this discourse is a development of the writings of the mid-1820s, and, as I have argued, it is deeply ironized and decentered there.

In what amounted to a trial run for *The Spirit of the Age*, Hazlitt published five of his "contemporary portraits" in numbers of *The New Monthly Magazine* for 1824—all under the pluralized rubric, tellingly, of "Spirits of the Age."[32] Wordsworth is not included in this group of five—Bentham, Irving, Scott, Tooke, and Eldon—and can hardly be said to epitomize them. Hazlitt makes his rubric singular for the great 1825 collection, but, again, the irreducible multiplicity of representatives and representations of the spirit of the age aims precisely to refuse both epitome and reduction—and yet Abrams and his followers appeal to Hazlitt's authority for accepting and indeed celebrating the representative status that Wordsworth claimed for himself.[33]

III

To examine the discussion of such matters in Shelley, the other authority cited by Abrams in support of his cultural configuration, is to find even less corroboration for present assumptions about Wordsworth and the Age of Romanticism. Shelley is actually credited in the OED with the first English use of the phrase "the spirit of the age," in a letter to Charles Ollier in early 1820.[34] Abrams cites Shelley's more celebrated use of the term in "A Defence of Poetry," where it appears in the final paragraph of the existing text and leads to the famous culminating claim that "poets are the unacknowledged legislators of the world." That final paragraph of the "Defence," however, is a virtual transcription of the conclusion of chapter 1 of a work that Shelley had begun more than a year earlier (in November 1819), *A Philosophical View of Reform*:

> The persons in whom this power [of communicating intense and impassioned impressions respecting man and nature] takes its abode may often, as far as regards many portions of their nature, have little tendency to [MS: *correspondence with*] the spirit of good of which it is the minister. But although they may deny and

abjure, they are yet compelled to serve, that which is seated on the throne of their own soul. And whatever systems the[y] may [have] professed by support, they actually advance the interests of Liberty. It is impossible to read the productions of our most celebrated writers whatever may be their system relating to thought or expression without being struck by the electric life which there is in their words. They measure the circumference or sound the depths of human nature with a comprehensive and all penetrating spirit, at which they are themselves perhaps the most sincerely astonished for it [is] less their own spirit than the spirit of their age. They are the priests of an unapprehended inspiration, the mirrors of gigantic forms which futurity casts upon the present; the words which express what they conceive not, the trumpet which sings to battle and feels not what it inspires; the influence which is moved not but moves. Poets and philosophers are the unacknowledged legislators of the world.[35]

If Shelley is interested in the question of how and by whom the spirit of the age shall be represented, however, his way of addressing it is no simpler nor more direct than Hazlitt's. Wordsworth clearly seems to be one of the writers alluded to in this passage, especially in the remarks about "their system relating to thought and expression," but he is certainly not singled out. From the beginning Shelley's comments pluralize their referent: "we live among such philosophers and poets as surpass beyond comparison any who have appeared in our nation since its last struggle for liberty."[36] For Shelley, furthermore, it is not so much that the "spirit" of a privileged writer "corresponds" to the putative spirit of the age but, rather, that in manifesting itself through a given writer, the spirit of the age displaces the work of the personal spirit. This spirit is not only "unapprehended" by the person it makes its instrument, it also can stand powerfully at odds with his or her personal-authorial opinions and intentions. For example, if we suppose that, in addition to Wordsworth, Shelley is also thinking here of Byron, the contemporary poet whom there is reason to think he held in at least equal esteem with Wordsworth, then he is well aware of being faced with two "representative" writers whose authorial views and intentions (as he was well aware) were deeply at odds. As with Hazlitt, therefore, but for slightly different reasons, Shelley's ideas about representing the spirit of the age lead him to posit a plurality of "representatives" and to incorporate unsimplified contradiction in their representational function.

What lends special distinction and complexity to Shelley's account is his attention to an aspect of the question of representation which is only glimpsed in Emerson and Hazlitt: representation of peoples in such legislative institutions as the English Parliament and the still-young American Congress. Setting up a knotty conceit during his introductory remarks in *Representative Men*, Emerson says that "each material thing has its celestial side; has its translation through humanity into the spiritual and necessary sphere, where it plays a part as indestructible as any other." The conceit runs this way:

> The gases gather to the solid firmament: the chemic lump arrives at the plant, and grows; arrives at the quadruped, and walks; arrives at the man, and thinks. But also the constituency determines the vote of the representative. He is not only representative but participant.[37]

If Emerson's style "calls for philosophy," as Stanley Cavell has suggested, it here seems to call not only for philosophy of science but for political philosophy as well. For if "the man" in this passage represents the entire diachronic process of philogeny, the (great) man (also? equally? analogously?) represents the mass of population that ascends toward him in human society. The political metaphor of representation by suffrage—which here incorporates the notion of the political representative as the synecdoche of the represented—itself seems to strive, against some resistance, metaphorically to govern the entire discussion of human representativeness.[38] For his part, Hazlitt, in establishing the representativeness of Byron and Scott, had said that they would "carry away the majority of suffrages as the greatest geniuses of the age." In this age of developing mass readership, Hazlitt's couching of his comments about literary popularity in the terms of political suffrage is, again, more than a casual metaphor, even if it remains an underdeveloped one.[39]

As Catherine Gallagher's work has recently brought into sharp focus, discussions of literary representation or representativeness in the Victorian period often intersect with the dominant political topic of the day: the issue of reform in political representation.[40] No one, as far as I know, certainly not the Victorians whom Gallagher persuasively analyzes in these terms, makes the relation between these two aspects of representation so explicit a subject for reflection as early as does Shelley in *A Philosophical View of Reform*. But, remarkable as it is, the *View* has not been a widely read essay, partly on account of its presumed eclipse by "A Defence of Poetry," which, although composed later and also left unfinished, was published eighty years earlier than the *View*, in 1840.[41] It has been too little recognized, certainly among those who cite Shelley's remarks casually, that his discussion of spirits of the age and poet-legislators (that is, representative men) appears in a discussion of the stages of reform in political representation, or that this is a discussion composed at the moment of the most severe crisis for the reform movement: the months after the Peterloo Massacre.

The scope of the *View* is vast, even before Shelley comes to his economic history of England since 1641 in chapter 2 or his prophetic sketch of the theory of passive resistance in chapter 3. His first chapter attempts nothing less than a history of the relation of poetic vitality and political progress since the end of the Roman Republic. This ambitious project was motivated by Shelley's sense of a dilemma in confronting at once a political system he found intolerably oppressive and a reform movement he found intolerably obsessive about changing the mechanisms of parliamentary representation. At the end of May 1820, Shelley told Leigh Hunt that the *View* was "intended as a kind of standard book for the philosophical reformers politically considered, like Jeremy Bentham's something, but different & perhaps more systematic."[42] Shelley had been more explicitly critical of Bentham's (and Beccaria's) plans for reform in a letter to Hunt just weeks earlier, on April 5.[43] It is perhaps not surprising, therefore, that the doctrine of utility should have special prominence in Shelley's history, or that the outcome of this history is to suggest how circumscribed is the doctrine of utilitarianism both in its horizon of vision and in its theory of representation.

Shelley dates the effective genesis of utility to what he sees as the beginning of the modern period, the enlightened "new epoch" that arrives with the seventeenth century. The heroes of Shelley's seventeenth century are Bacon, Spinoza, Hobbes, Bayle, and Montaigne, writers who "regulated the reasoning powers, criticized the past history, exposed the errors by illustrating their causes and their connection, and anatomized the inmost nature of social man" (p. 8). When Shelley distinguishes a second generation of important metaphysicians in the new epoch–Locke, Berkeley, Hume, and Hartley—he defines their achievement in respect to how they illustrated the consequences of their predecessors' new thought. Their views were "correct, popular, simple, and energetic, but not profound." A third generation of metaphysicians, the French philosophes, were even more popularizing and pragmatic than their English contemporaries, but with a better excuse. Considered as philosophers, the error of this "crowd of writers in France" consisted in their limitedness of view; "they told the truth but not the whole truth" (p. 9). Shelley's excuse for them is that "[t]his might have arisen from the terrible sufferings of their countrymen" which led them "rather to apply a portion of what had already been discovered to their immediate relief, than to pursue one interest, the abstractions of thought, as the great philosophers who preceded them had done, for the sake of a future and a more universal advantage" (p. 9). The writing of the *View* itself is demonstrably caught between these two conflicting impulses, the pragmatic drag on his philosophical aspirations finally achieving strength enough to lead him to abandon the work altogether in favor of embarking on "A Defence of Poetry."

The doctrine of utility that will come to figure so importantly in 1819 is simply the eighteenth century's application of the principles of the new, yet incomplete metaphysics to the field of politics. Shelley describes the labors and limitations of the political philosophers at some length, but summarizes their achievement as "the establishment of the principle of Utility as the substance, and liberty and equality as the forms according to which the concerns of human life ought to be administered" (p. 10). This is the principle, of course, that stands prominent in the Benthamite program for reform that is at once Shelley's topic and point of departure.

How representation and thus "representative men" figure in the argument becomes apparent when Shelley illustrates the powers and limitations of the concept of utility by reference to the revolutions of America and France. The importance of the former, for Shelley, is that it issued in a system of government that he calls "the first practical illustration of the new philosophy" (p. 10). Happy that this system marks an enormous gain over "the insolent and contaminating tyrannies under which, with some limitation of these terms as regards England, Europe groaned" at the time of the Revolution, Shelley also confesses that it is "sufficiently remote . . . from the accuracy of ideal excellence" (pp. 9–10). As compared with the old governments of Europe and Asia, the United States holds forth the example "of a free, happy, and strong people" and of "an immensely populous, and as far as the external arts of life are concerned, a highly civilized, community administered according to republican forms":

> It has no king, that is it has no officer to whom wealth and from whom corruption flows. It has no hereditary oligarchy, that is it acknowledges no order of men privileged to cheat and insult the rest of the members of the state, and who inherit a right of legislating and judging which the principles of human nature compel them to exercise to their peculiar class. It has no established Church, that is it has no system of opinions respecting the abstrusest questions which can be topics of human thought, founded in an age of error and by prosecutions, and sanctioned by enormous bounties given to idle priests and forced thro' the unwilling hands of those who have an interest in the cultivation and improvement of the soil. *It has no false representation, whose consequences are captivity, confiscation, infamy and ruin, but a true representation. The will of the many is represented by the few in the assemblies of legislation and by the officers of the executive entrusted with the administration of the executive power almost as directly as the will of one person can be represented by the will of another.* (p. 11; emphasis mine)

Although it seems as if Shelley's America has it all, the incompleteness of the American revolution, and therefore of the utilitarianism that it embodies, and *therefore* of its system of representation, becomes clearer when Shelley turns to his second major case in point: "The just and successful Revolt of America corresponded with a state of public opinion in Europe of which it was the first result. The French Revolution was the second" (p. 13). Shelley regards this revolution, like the American one, as only a partial success. But in this case, as not in the American example, the evidence of its flaw is palpable and spectacular in the record of the Reign of Terror.[44] For Shelley, the explanation for the Reign of Terror, and thus for the failure of the Revolution to achieve what its proponents had hoped of it, lies less in the history of French politics, in the narrow sense, than in French poetics: "The French were what their literature is [excluding Montaigne and Rousseau, and some few leaders of the . . .] weak, superficial, vain, with little imagination, and with passions as well as judgements cleaving to the external form of things" (p. 13–14).

The counterpart of this suggestion in Shelley's analysis of the American example can be found in the way he qualifies his claim that America is a community administered according to republican forms and is "highly civilized" only "as far as the external arts of life are concerned." The external arts are the technological or mechanical arts, what we sometimes call the "useful" arts, and they are identified here as engaging only with "the external form of things." The implied internal forms, which they cannot reach, should probably be identified with those "forms of human nature" into which Bacon and his colleagues inquired. For such purposes, only the internal arts are fit, the arts Shelley summarizes under the name of "literature" or, more typically, "poetry."

This recognition sheds light on the question of how Shelley can suggest that, in spite of all the indications to the contrary, England now stands in a more advantageous political position than America and France. Donald Reiman's transcriptions of the *View*'s manuscripts in *Shelley and his Circle* include an important and hitherto unpublished note scribbled under Shelley's discussion of the strengths and limitations of the American experiment:

> Its error consists not in the representing the will of the People as it is, but in not providing for the full development the most salutary condition of that will. For two conditions are necessary to a theoretically perfect government, & one of these alone is adequately fulfilled by the most perfect of practical government the Republic of the United States. To represent the will of the People as it is. To provide that that will should be as wise and just as possible. To a certain extent the mere representation of the public will produces in itself a wholesome condition of it, and in this extent

America fulfills imperfectly & indirectly the last & most important condition of perfect government.[45]

Although there are two necessary conditions here, to some extent the existence of the first is sufficient for the production of the second, and to that extent there is only one condition. But that extent is evidently limited. The truest representation of the national will is also the best and most beautiful. It is that representation that improves as it reflects. This notion is the basis for the famous claim about poetic legislators which concludes the argument of chapter 1, gives way to the quasi-utilitarian analysis of chapters 2 and 3 of the *View*, and which eventually issues in the full-scale critique of utilitarianism, as personified in Peacock, that one finds in "A Defence of Poetry."

Although its social miseries may be less severe than England's, America lacks the poetic genius to represent its contemporary state—the spirit of its age—to itself. It lacks a public medium in which sympathetic identification and acknowledgment can take place. No one in America in 1819, for example, could have represented the age so effectively as what we find even in a minor sonnet such as Shelley's "England in 1819"—composed contemporaneously with chapter 1 of the *View*—let alone the more celebrated English works of that year. America, Shelley said, has "no false representation . . . but a true representation." In its elected President and Congress, "the will of the many is represented by the few . . . almost as directly as the will of one person can be represented by the will of another." But in the writings of great poets the national will represents itself fully, despite even the intentions of the poets themselves to the contrary. Poetic mimesis is the representation, not of the will of one person by the will of another, but of the national will to itself. This is the kind of representation that improves on its subject in a powerful way. And, on the Rousseauist principle that it is in the nature of the human will to improve itself, only that kind of will which improves what it represents can be said to represent that will truly.

Shelley's *View*, then, surveys how eighteenth-century forms of legislative representation, having challenged divine-right monarchy, themselves begin to give way to emergent institutions of cultural representation: poet-legislators. But Shelley plainly saw this work of a nation's cultural self-representation as a collective enterprise, one that involved a company of poets singing, like the nightingales in *Prometheus Unbound*, both in and of an ever-expanding horizon of inclusion. Many of his works, *Prometheus Unbound* prominent among them, contest the representation, such as he finds it in the writings of his contemporaries, of this work of representation itself. Charles Robinson has suggested that Byron is that "great contemporary" to whom Shelley alludes in his Preface to *Prometheus Unbound*. If "the 'forms' which 'modified' *Prometheus Unbound* were Byron's *Prometheus* and *Manfred*," Robinson argues, "Shelley borrowed from Byron's Promethean poems only to subvert their metaphysics."[46] I believe this is exactly right, as long as the subverted "metaphysics" can be understood to include Byron's attempt to offer his representation of the Napoleonic or Promethean will as itself representative of an idealized national will. If the representative claims of Byronism are critiqued in *Prometheus Unbound*, the representative claims of Wordsworthianism are critiqued in another great work of Shelley's great year, *Peter Bell the Third*, and likewise those of Rousseauism two years later in *The Triumph of Life*. In representing the work of national representation, indeed, Shelley refused pride of place not only to Byron and Wordsworth and Rousseau, but also to Coleridge, Southey, Moore, Hunt, Godwin, Keats, and Scott.

In this respect, then, Shelley arrives at a position that may look and be something like Hazlitt's. In perhaps one respect Shelley may surpass Hazlitt in his approach to a position such as the one from which Althusser offers his critique of Hegelianism. In speaking of Hegelian contradiction as "made possible *only* by the simplicity of the internal principle that constitutes the essence of any historical period," Althusser goes on to explain that "the reduction of *all* the elements that make up the concrete life of a historical epoch (. . . institutions, customs, ethics, art, religion, philosophy, and even historical *events*. . . .) to *one* principle of internal unity, is itself only possible on the absolute condition of taking the whole concrete life of a people for the externalization-alienation of an internal spiritual principle, which can never definitely be anything but the most abstract form of that epoch's consciousness of itself."[47] The natural supernaturalism of Wordsworth's Prospectus to *The Recluse* and the faithful skepticism of Byron's *Manfred*—or again, the progressive conservatism of *Waverley*—are each of them offered as oxymoronic representations of the age's consciousness of itself. From this confident fiction of epochal self-consciousness derives what Shelley called the "didacticism" of such programs; it is what Keats, working out of Hazlitt, called the sense of "palpable design." Shelley persistently fostered a generous suspicion of this claim of an individual will to represent the general will, even (indeed especially) for those among his contemporaries whom he regarded as possessed of greatest genius.

How does Shelley's representation of the spirit of the age escape its own critique? Perhaps it just does not and cannot. But if one reads his most famous passage on the subject closely, one might begin to see a way. It is the rousing ending of "A Defence of Poetry," the sentences reprised from the conclusion of chapter 1 in *A Philosophical View of Reform*:

> It is impossible to read the compositions of the most celebrated writers of the present day without being startled with the electric life which burns within their words. They measure the circumference and sound the depths of human nature with a comprehensive and all-penetrating spirit, and they are themselves perhaps the most sincerely astonished at its manifestations, for it is less their spirit than the spirit of the age. Poets are the hierophants of an unapprehended inspiration, the mirrors of the gigantic shadows which futurity casts upon the present, the words which express what they understand not; the trumpets which sing to battle, and feel not what they inspire: the influence which is moved not, but moves. Poets are the unacknowledged legislators of the world.[48]

Shelley's paragraph is a study in unresolved and unresolvable contradictions. Poets are said to measure and plumb a human nature, spatially conceived, and apparently itself unchanging, with a spirit of time and change. In this the spirit of the age seems to be their instrument, what they measure and plumb with. But the metaphor is quickly turned around to suggest that the poets indeed are the instruments wielded by the spirit—trumpets, for example, the insensate means by which a trumpeter inspires a hearer. Two other metaphors seem vaguely to line up this way: the hierophants of the unapprehended inspiration and the words that expressed what they understand not. But the famous last sentence, so often quoted out of context, contradicts the new formation at yet another angle. Following the metaphors of the trumpet and the hierophant, and the words metaphors, poets ought to be called the "unacknowledging" legislators. This would also be consistent with their being called the influence which moves without being moved. It would seem to have been the spirit that was unacknowledged, not the poets. Indeed, it is by no means clear by whom poets are to be acknowledged.

Shelley's representation of the spirit of the age disallows reduction to a single formula, oxymoronic or otherwise, about the epoch's consciousness of itself. In this respect, though Hazlitt could not have seen it, Shelley's passage would have made an appropriate epigraph for Hazlitt's *Spirit of the Age* four years later. Its style is indeed equally answerable to the description of Hazlitt's in *The Monthly Review*: "Every thing shines as through a prismatic medium. The result is, that we retain nothing distinctly of what he says. It is a sort of confused memory of sounds, like the clashing of musical instruments." It courts expectations that it will not meet, and it refuses to allow the spirit of the age to become an affair of consciousness or self-comprehension.

IV

The forms of historical representation in what we call the Romantic period are far subtler than either the "old historicists" or their newer revisionists normally allow. A thorough study of the issues I have broached here would take up the type-of-the-age heroes that Scott developed in the *Waverley* novels, which have descended to us in a far more simplified form than I think Scott ever imagined. It would also look carefully at historical representatives and representations in such *Waverley*-inspired works as Shelley's *The Cenci* and Byron's *Don Juan*. Eventually, one would also go back to the text in which the issues of representation in politics and aesthetics find their most powerful mutual articulation, Burke's *Reflections on the Revolution in France*. Burke saw himself as responding to a charge brought by English sympathizers with the revolution—a charge he correctly saw as aimed precisely at the constitution's provision for popular representation: "The Revolution Society has discovered that the English nation is not free," he says, and then paraphrases the critique he had found in Richard Price's radical pamphlet on the subject:

> They are convinced that the inequality in our representation is a "defect in our constitution *so gross and palpable*, as to make it excellent chiefly in *form and theory*." That a representation in the legislature of a kingdom is not only the basis of all constitutional liberty in it, but of "*all legitimate government*; that without it a *government* is nothing but an *usurpation*;"—that "when the representation is *partial*, the kingdom possesses liberty only *partially*; and if extremely partial it gives only a *semblance*; and if not only extremely partial, but corruptly chosen, it becomes a *nuisance*." Dr. Price considers this inadequacy of representation as our *fundamental grievance*; and though, as to the corruption of this semblance of representation, he hopes it is not yet arrived to its full perfection of depravity; he fears that "nothing will be done towards gaining for us this *essential blessing*, until some great abuse of power again provokes our resentment, or some great calamity again alarms our fears, or perhaps till the acquisition of a *pure and equal representation by other countries*, whilst we are *mocked* with the *shadow*, kindles our shame.[49]

Burke carries out his counter-critique by attacking the concept of "pure and equal representation," and he does so by reference to what he sees as the metaphysical warrant that is offered for it, a platonizing metaphysic that sees representation as mere reflection or "shadow." In spelling out what he calls the "adequate representation" provided by the English system, he argues that political representation is in a deep sense constitutive and that it is constitutive in the way that poetic representation is constitutive. When Burke insisted that political representation must be grounded primarily on property, he also insisted that property must be unequal by its nature. But then he proceeds to give an account in which this "unequal representation" can result in a higher-order equality when it is represented unequally by means of the "pleasing illusions" that inheres in the code of chivalry, that system of manners whose characteristic form of representation is poetic romance.

The question of who shall represent the English looms large

in the *Reflections* from the start. Burke tells his ostensible correspondent, Victor de Pont, that he undertook the letter to him in
order to correct the latter's impression that the new correspondence societies in London were the proper representatives of the
English nation or that their representations of that nation were in
any sense authoritative. Burke is most sensitive about his own vul-
nerability to a charge of presumption on this score: "I have no
man's proxy. I speak only for myself," he disclaims.[50] But of course
Burke does speak for and represent the English in 1790, not because he has membership in the English parliament, which he
scarcely mentions, but because he remains chivalric in sentiment
and, just as important, romantic in his utterance. That this was just
the point of the paean to Marie-Antoinette and the narrative of the
October Days was only partly recognized by Thomas Paine when
he spoke of the "poetical liberties" Burke had taken with his narrative and when he called Burke's entire argument a "dramatic
performance."[51] Hazlitt called attention to this aspect of Burke's
political writing when, in one of his earliest "contemporary portraits," he depicted him as the most poetical of England's politi-
cians.

As the sense of a 1789–1815 period took shape in the years
after Waterloo, Burke's romantic answer to the question of who
should represent the English in the revolutionary crisis led to the
question of who should represent the English in the romantic-
revolutionary age. That latter question, as we have considered it
here, involves some difficult issues about historical typology in
early nineteenth-century literature. I have obviously not offered
a definitive answer to this question but have preferred instead to
urge that it be recognized as a question with at least modest cultural and political stakes and that we do not permit discussion of
it to be prematurely foreclosed in the interest of a campaign to
"clothe in priestly robe / A ... single spirit singled out
... / ... for holy services." At the very least, we must refuse to
credit oversimplified historical appeals to the remarkable contemporary analysts—Emerson, Hazlitt, Shelley, Burke—who first engaged the complex diffusion of post-French Revolution literary
and political culture.

NOTES

1. "The world picture does not change from an earlier medieval one into a modern one, but rather the fact that the world becomes a picture at all is what distinguishes the essence of the modern age"; Martin Heidegger, *The Question concerning Technology and Other Essays* (New York, 1977), p. 130.

2. Ibid., p. 133.

3. "To represent means to bring what is present at hand, before oneself as something standing over against, to relate it to oneself, to the one representing it, and to force it back into this relationship to oneself as the normative realm", ibid., p. 131.

4. Jonathan Wordsworth, Michael C. Jaye, and Robert Woof, *William Wordsworth and the Age of English Romanticism* (New Brunswick, N. J., 1987), p. vii.

5. Ibid., p. vii.

6. Ibid., p. viii.

7. Ibid., p. 27.

8. M. H. Abrams, *Natural Supernaturalism* (New York, 1971), p. 14.

9. Wayne C. Booth, *Critical Understanding: The Powers and Limits of Pluralism* (Chicago, 1979), pp. 139–75.

10. See Jerome McGann, "Romanticism and the Embarrassments of Critical Tradition," *Modern Philology* 70 (1973), 252–53.

11. On this last point, see especially Marlon Ross's study of how the women poets of the period were erased in the subsequent representations of literary history; *The Contours of Masculine Desire* (New York, forthcoming).

12. Leopold Damrosch, *The Uses of Johnson's Criticism* (Charlottesville, Va., 1976), p. 162.

13. See Dwight Culler's recent survey of emergent English cultural history in the early nineteenth century in *The Victorian Mirror of History* (New Haven, 1985), pp. 20–73; for more on the eighteenth-century context see J. G. A. Pocock, *Virtue, Commerce, and History* (Cambridge, 1985). The two classic intellectual histories of the larger subject are, of course, Friedrich Meinecke, *Historism*, trans. J. E. Anderson (New York, 1972), and R. G. Collingwood, *The Idea of History* (Oxford, 1946).

14. Ralph Waldo Emerson, *Collected Works* (Cambridge, Mass., 1971–   ) 4:13.

15. Ibid., 4:156.

16. Ibid.

17. I have addressed the problems with Hazlitt's more specific claims in *Wordsworth's Second Nature* (Chicago, 1984), pp. 4–6.

18. William Hazlitt, *Collected Works*, ed. P. P. Howe, 21 vols. (London, 1932), 11:127.

19. Ibid., pp. 127, 86.

20. Ibid., pp. 28–29.

21. Ibid., p. 57.

22. Ibid., p. 130.

23. Ibid., p. 116.

24. Every lover of Hazlitt, that great hater, must feel the force of David Bromwich's comment that "We live at a time of immense sophistication in criticism, yet the state of our dealings with Hazlitt might suggest other thoughts than the consoling one that we have advanced beyond him"; in *Hazlitt: The Mind of a Critic* (New York, 1983), p. 13.

25. Hazlitt, *Works*, 7:14.

26. It seems to me that Roy Park's rich chapter on *The Spirit of the Age*, and indeed his excellent book as a whole, is diminished rather than enhanced by his drive to reduce Hazlitt's thinking to a polarity of abstraction and particularity; *Hazlitt and the Spirit of the Age* (Oxford, 1971), pp. 206–36. The contradictions summarized above, for example, do not so reduce.

27. John Kinnard has gone as far as anyone in his insistence on the discrepancies in *The Spirit of the Age*; *William Hazlitt: Critic of Power* (New York, 1978): "What emerges is a composite portrait of the age, whose unity of character is now seen to inhere precisely in its inconsistencies, in the dramatic logic of its discords—a polarity of conflict often very different in its motives from the tensions and contentions of the age as the combatants themselves were defining them" (p. 304). But, perhaps weakened by an underdeveloped sense of contradiction in Hazlitt, Kinnard's discussion goes on to accept at face value the notion that Wordsworth's genius is given the privileged position in the value "as being thoroughly expressive of its time" (319). See also Herschel Baker's brief but useful comments on the unresolved "antinomy" in Hazlitt's contradictions in *William Hazlitt* (Cambridge, Mass., 1962), p. 440.

28. Louis Althusser, "Contradiction and Overdetermination" in *For Marx* (New York, 1977), p. 102.

29. Ibid., p. 103.

30. *The Monthly Review* (May 1825), 107:1. A year earlier, the same periodical's review of Hazlitt's *Characteristics* noted that "many of these 'Characteristics' are evidently the result of temporary feeling, and are contradicted in different parts of the volume"; (February 1824), 103:221.

31. Ibid., p. 221.

32. *New Monthly Magazine* (1824) 10:68, 187, 246, 297 and 11:17.

33. To their credit, the authors of the text proper of *William Wordsworth and the Age of English Romanticism* attempt to qualify their apparent initial endorsement of Abrams's view when they come to Byron: "It is no longer possible, however, to decide with Hazlitt that Wordsworth was 'a pure emanation of the Spirit of the Age', and Byron some form of alien. In many ways they seem to be at opposite poles. . . . Yet it is between these two poles that the age must be defined" (p. 45). This sense of what it is no longer possible to decide seems a step in the right direction. But where the authors go wrong, from the perspective of the present argument, is in the simplified view they think Hazlitt holds and in the failure of their own simple "polarity" to measure up to the rich texture of cultural contradiction that I have tried to describe in Hazlitt's book.

34. "But it is the spirit of the age & we are all infected with it"; *The Letters of Percy Bysshe Shelley*, ed. F. L. Jones, 2 vols. (Oxford, 1964), 2:189.

35. Shelley, *Complete Works*, eds. Roger Ingpen and Walter E. Peck, 10 vols. (London, 1928), 7:19–20. All subsequent references cited by page number in the text.

36. Ibid., pp. 991–92.

37. Emerson, *Works*, 4:7.

38. For a philosophical survey of various models of political representation see Hannah Pitkin, *The Concept of Representation* (Berkeley, 1967).

39. See Jon Klancher's discussion "Radical Representations" in *The Making of English Reading Audiences, 1790–1832* (Madison, Wisc.: 1987), pp. 98–134.

40. See especially part 3 of Gallagher's *The Industrial Reformation of English Fiction* (Chicago, 1985), pp. 188–267.

41. Exceptions to the rule of neglect can be found in K. N. Cameron, *Shelley: The Golden Years* (Cambridge, Mass., 1974), pp. 127–49; P. M. S. Dawson. *The Unacknowledged Legislator* (Oxford, 1980), *passim*; and Donald Reiman's introduction to the transcription of the text of the *View* in *Shelley and his Circle*, 6:945–61.

42. Shelley, *Letters*, 2:201.

43. Ibid., 2:181.

44. Of the unhappy response of the "oppressed" against the "tyrants" in the later stage of the Revolution, Shelley writes:

> Their desire to wreak revenge, to this extent, in itself a mistake, a crime, a calamity, arose from the same source as their other miseries and errors, and affords an additional proof of the necessity of that long-delayed change which it accompanied and disgraced. If a just and necessary revolution could have been accomplished with as little expense of happiness and order in a country governed by despotic as [in] one governed by free laws, equal liberty and justice would lose their chief recommendations and tyranny be divested of its most revolting attributes. (p. 13)

45. *Shelley and His Circle 1773–1822*, ed. Donald H. Reiman (Cambridge, Mass.: 1973), 6:977.

46. Charles Robinson, *Shelley and Byron* (Baltimore, Md.: 1976), p. 114.

47. Althusser, *For Marx*, p. 103.

48. *Shelley's Poetry and Prose*, eds. Donald H. Reiman and Sharon B. Powers (New York, 1977), p. 508.

49. Edmund Burke, *Reflections on the Revolution in France* and Thomas Paine, *The Rights of Man* (Garden City, N.Y.: 1973), p. 68.

50. Ibid., p. 98.

51. Ibid., p. 296.

Plotting the Revolution

THE POLITICAL NARRATIVES OF ROMANTIC POETRY AND CRITICISM

MARILYN BUTLER

In September 1793, William Wordsworth was in London looking for literary work so that he could support his French mistress and their baby. At Joseph Johnson's bookshop in St Paul's Churchyard one frosty autumn morning William found waiting for him a fateful letter franked in France. Annette wrote to say that the baby Caroline had a fever; she might die without learning to say the word *Papa*. William impetuously took the noon mail to Folkestone, and three days later was in a Paris more dangerous even than the year before. It was October 7, 1793, the day when the first of the Girondins, the journalist Gorsas, was to be guillotined. William knew Gorsas slightly, and that reckless, selfless courage which seems to have been characteristic drew him to the fatal scene. As he stood in the crowd, a distinctive figure in his English greatcoat, an informer recognized and denounced him. The rest is history (and of course sentiment: who can forget the wartime movie, and the heartrending delivery of the last speech by the young Ronald Colman?). The name of William Wordsworth will always be remembered for its pathos, the very essence of what we mean by "romantic": the (alas) minor English poet who went to his death rather than abandon his French girl and their child.

Rehearsing yet again the well-known story, with all its mythicized accretions, almost tempts me to a flight of fancy about the poems Wordsworth could have written if he hadn't met that cruel end. He might have been the Milton of his age; he might have cast himself as an epic hero, the Adam of a new *Paradise Lost*; his native Lake District might by now have been turned into a gigantic traffic jam every summer. Who can estimate what a difference his survival might have made to the English ecology and to English literature?

But it's hard to imagine that a poet of Wordsworth's cast—we do after all have *Descriptive Sketches* and *An Evening Walk*—could have turned the course of poetry singlehandedly in the exceptional period that followed his death. Wordsworth came out of the eighteenth-century country tradition of Thomson, Gray, and Cowper. The high road of English poetry during the French revolutionary wars was, we know, of quite another kind: it had to do not with retirement in pursuit of what—the self? God?—but with nationhood and power and with the impossibility, so traumatizing for alienated middle-class poets, of standing aside in wartime from a communal, national engagement. What we now call English Romanticism (borrowing the loose-fitting German term) had to do with the characterization of the central state—that way of coming to terms with the "platoon" to which we belong, in Burke's word, when the degree to which we *do* belong is in real doubt. For the existing British constitutional arrangements debarred most members of the literary community, whether readers or writers, from a role in the state, yet the unprecedented size and coherence of the market for books gave writers a voice in the national community, in its public sphere, that they had never enjoyed on their own account before. At once endowed with influence and denied power, English writers around 1800 are preoccupied with the topic of external authority and its corruptions.

One theme after all binds Blake (whom contemporaries barely knew) to Scott and Byron (by whom they were dazzled): that theme is empire and its imagined overthrow, which is both longed for and dreaded. The nature of the British state was transformed in fact though not yet in law in the decade following 1795 by the effective annexation of the Indian subcontinent from Ceylon to the Himalayas: liberals followed Ferguson, Gibbon, and Burke in thinking it transformed for the worse. First Cornwallis, then Marquis Wellesley, Wellington's brother, completed the subjection of 562 petty Indian states, a program of expansion matching that of the rival empire in Europe headed by Napoleon. The scale of these events ensured that the period's dominant modes were not in the end personal, meditative, and lyric, as might have been predicted in more ordinary times from what went before. The attractive Cowper became quickly superseded, and no wonder. He had to compete with allegorical narratives enacting revolution—Blake's *America*, Landor's *Gebir*, Campbell's *Pleasures of Memory*, Southey's *Thalaba the Destroyer*, Byron's *Bride of Abydos* and *Corsair*. And then, since accounts of war didn't end with war, Moore's *Lalla Rookh*, Shelley's *Revolt of Islam*, Keats's *Hyperion*.

The poets of the turn of the century displace and generalize the revolutions they re-create. It is inadequate to suppose they merely obsessively repeat literal recent events in France, however horrifically these are perceived. Whether they envisage the monstrous fall of the state, or the fall of the monstrous state, the topic is most dreadful because it implies the rejection and the imagined dismemberment of their own community. Abstracted, the revolution-in-the-head assumes all kinds of forms. These include the free enjoyment of sexual love, and its withering away; the coming of the empire of poetry, and the exposé of the bad faith of all great poems yet written.

Most of the better English poets of the period take from French ideologues a tendency to look askance at old regime literature, the arts, scriptures, and mythologies. They read them as from primitive times, the products both of the state and of "the state of things," fictions that encourage repetition and invariance and so may be used by rulers. Thus Blake's *First Book of Urizen* challenges (by parodying) the biblical First Book of Moses. Shelley's *Prometheus Unbound* takes on the lost Aeschylean drama and *Paradise Lost*. Byron in *Cain* mocks Genesis once more, and he writes a sequel, *Heaven and Earth*, which exploits a noncanonical sacred text, the long-lost Ethiopic Book of Enoch brought back from Abyssinia by James Bruce. These representative poems of the period are sometimes classed as biblical or Miltonic, unhelpful terms unless it is acknowledged that the poems deconstruct their host-text, in an interest that seemed at the time ideological even if modern critics prefer to treat it as stylistic. The impulse is disaffected and hardly ever utopian: these half-enfranchised republicans of letters insert themselves into the public sphere without apparent confidence in that process of remaking of which their own poems are the prototype. "Reality" isn't usually the cosmic republic envisaged in act 4 of *Prometheus Unbound*, but a dying landscape, the stricken worlds shown in Crabbe's *Eustace Gray* and *Peter Grimes*, Byron's *Darkness* and *Cain*, act 2, Mary Shelley's *Last Man*.

If, then, Wordsworth the solitary walker had lived, what could he have done with his consoling cloud-capped mountains but provide a sideshow, a poetry of feeling and privacy which would have made him as marginal in posterity's eyes as the five hundred–odd women poets of the period between Charlotte Smith and L.E.L. (Letitia Landon)?

Happily, we have the latest findings from the Dove Cottage scholars' workshop: he did live. Annette was too busy with Caroline to catch the post with that letter; by the time she could get out, weeks later, Caroline was better; in any case, the missive was impounded by an Anglophobe official at Montreuil, on the road to Calais. So William was able to write away with a marginally clearer conscience for the next quarter of a century, and, even while Byron, the period's poetic celebrity, was still alive, some shrewd observers were guessing that Wordsworth would play tortoise to Byron's hare. Or, as the historicist would prefer to put it, that more Anglophone literary intellectuals of succeeding generations would prefer to model themselves on Wordsworth than on Byron—for reasons they will freely give, and for reasons they will not.

In 1825, William Hazlitt, an aging radical of not quite fifty, impishly tried in *The Spirit of the Age* to embarrass the new right of his day by promoting controversial early Wordsworth, the author of the *Lyrical Ballads*, as *the* Wordsworth; it was impudent because by 1820 it was Anglican Wordsworth, the bard of the River Duddon, whom responsible critics adopted as the poet to topple Byron from his bad eminence.[1] Hazlitt's was the last throw of the generation of the 1790s, for by the late 1820s German transcendentalism and Anglican high culturism were the new rage, notably at the Cambridge where the young Tennyson was studying. The intellectuals of the second quarter of the nineteenth century—the era of Keble, Carlyle, and Newman in England and of Emerson in America—worked, among other things, to prepare the way for *The Prelude*, that great Victorian poem. This was the generation which coopted, selected, interpreted, and effectively constructed the "high" Wordsworth the profession as we know it has also on the whole preferred to celebrate.

A century later, from about 1950, another conservative generation in America has again found itself in flight from European revolutions. So it's Wordsworth-time again, and he is being assiduously revised and, after a fashion, rewritten by a critical technique resembling the novelist's free indirect speech. Editing of Wordsworth sometimes seems to err on the creative side, but this is nothing compared with that free translation of his thought processes into a modernist vocabulary which has appropriated him as a man of the later twentieth century. The task of inventing a new language for him has been facilitated by disposing of the old one, by stripping him of almost all his own contemporaries and associates and thus ensuring we do not learn his natural vocabulary of thought and feeling. He has been provided instead with an arbitrary and factitious peer group, including (the contents vary a little, according to whether you're reading Hartman or Poirier, Bloom or Bromwich) Kant, Hegel, Carlyle, and Emerson—who has found himself, surely not by accident, at the central point in my line. It proceeds with Nietzsche (always), Freud (sometimes), and Wallace Stevens (always again). The problem here is that a person is known by the company he keeps. By wishing these colleagues on Wordsworth we perform an act of interpretation as surely as when we subject his text to a refined close reading. And the operation of reading Wordsworth "through" Emerson generally turns out to be at most half a close reading. As on the whole prose writers, the line of modern prophets isn't commonly subjected to an exacting linguistic analysis. Their words tend to be received as more or less scriptural injunctions to the world to adopt certain life choices. It is through the commentaries of Carlyle, Emerson, and Nietzsche that we begin to feel the significance of the musings of Wordsworth in *The Prelude*, "Tintern Abbey," *The Excursion, The White Doe of Rylstone*. Those poems are moralized, spiritualized, and unmistakably politicized, and they come to signify European intellectuals' will to reject the material revolution made in France.

Historicists are, or should be, analysts of the growth of stories and mythologies, including their own. That is why this essay is about fabling, by the Romantics and by modern critics when we represent the Romantics. Narratives are among the strongest and most transmissible of interpretative mechanisms. Though the Emersonian Wordsworth is everywhere to be found, we are not paying enough attention to when and where he came from and what he is doing in our midst.

One gloomy hypothesis is that we are witnessing an example of collective professional narcissism. What better models for (male) literary academics than a line of THINKING MEN who are plainly idealized versions of themselves? But the cult of philosophical Wordsworth plainly has other implications, so that the enthusiastic empathizing with William of so many otherwise sophisticated Wordsworthians need not, thank heaven, be taken too much at face value. Once Wordsworth's poems are filled out with commentaries from Emerson, Nietzsche, and the rest, they inevitably begin to assume more general values, they become models for a culture. Incidentally—is it incidental?—this postwar Atlantic pantheon of sages plainly serves the ends of cultural nationalism. The nineteenth-century line of thinkers now so earnestly pressed into service as mentors for the young were themselves leading cultural nationalists in that era of affirmative leadership: Carlyle in Britain, Emerson in America, above all the line from Hegel to Nietzsche in Germany.

In Cambridge, England, in January 1988 I heard a talk by the Harvard social historian Daniel Bell on the shifting political alignment of the New York or eastern Jewish literary intelligentsia between the thirties and the present day. He spoke with strong approval of the affirmative, socially constructive role of this intelligentsia, and of the central part played in its work by the teaching of literature. He praised the pioneering role in the 1950s of his own university, Columbia, and of his own group, which included Lionel Trilling. He did not suggest that the motive driving their seminars and their journalism was a disinterested zeal to teach or to get to know writers of the last two centuries better.

He saw a shift in social philosophy and in political allegiance prompted by intellectuals' need, at the outset of the Cold War, to distance themselves from Stalin's Russia. This has led by a smooth progression to the repositioning of American Jewish intellectuals right of center and to their political acceptability in Reagan's America.

The date Bell was looking at, around 1950, happens to coincide with the most notable ideological shift in twentieth-century northeast American perceptions of Romanticism. (The term sometimes used, Anglo-American, obscures the relative localism of the phenomenon and makes accurate analysis more difficult.) The present impressive wave of American neo-Romanticism emerged after the war, for example, with Northrop Frye's book on Blake, *Fearful Symmetry* (1947), and Morse Peckham's article, "Toward a Theory of Romanticism" (1951), later amplified as *Beyond the Tragic Vision* (1962). Over time, one of Frye's most underrated successes has been the general acceptance of his simplistic, schematic notion of Enlightenment literary history: the eighteenth century is a period he deems scarcely worthy of serious critical attention on account of its paucity of vision or (religious) enthusiasm. Though nowadays Peckham's is less of a name to conjure with than Frye's or René Wellek's, he too has bequeathed to late twentieth-century culture part of a paradigmatic plot of its own origins.

Peckham's book places the birth of the modern consciousness at the tragic close of the eighteenth century. According to his compelling if simplified account, the intellectuals of 1800, the Goethes, Beethovens, and Wordsworths, saw past the eighteenth-century demolition of God and saw through its project of democratization and material progress. They proposed a new project, one open admittedly only to the intellectual minority—a search for the self and for the God within. Peckham is interesting for my purposes because his language makes it plain that he is writing not so much literary history but an essay about his own intellectual times. The key pages in his book come at the end of part 1, "The End of Ancient Thinking," before he can enter the new space, literary modernism, the world made by "The Alienated Vision" of ex-radicals. For the generation of 1800, Peckham says,

... thinking for the most part in isolation, ... the French Revolution was the ultimate test. Here was a vast political endeavor in which an enormous effort was made to put the Enlightenment faith into practice ... What was its lesson? It released social, emotional and moral forces of which the Enlightenment tradition had been totally ignorant, which the vaunted nature, and reason, and enthusiasm, and empiricism had never discovered. And it showed that those forces could be controlled only by a brutal and repressive tyranny which—and here was the real horror—was in itself perfectly justifiable on Enlightenment principles.[2]

After a decade of Cold War it's not the French Revolution Peckham has in mind but the Russian; not Napoleon's evil empire but Stalin's.

Of the talented critics known as the Yale-Cornell group, only M. H. Abrams has a reputation primarily as a literary historian. Yet in spite of their importance as theorists or at least as striking critical innovators, in spite of their brilliance as close readers in the older new critical or newer deconstructive mode, Hillis Miller, Geoffrey Hartman, Harold Bloom, and Paul de Man tend to acknowledge the need for literary history. They become de facto historians, if simple and untheoretical ones, by treating Romanticism as a specific cultural event in place and especially time (the moment of the disappearance of God, the recovery of religion, the emergence of modern consciousness).[3] This is unmistakably the same narrative Peckham did much to popularize, though the linguistic methodology of Peckham's successors filters out overt allusions to politics. A shyness about limiting ideological origins is, to be sure, a common feature in the evolution of stories, myths, and traditions. As ever with such stories, the task set the modern analytical reader is to identify and isolate the Other. For Us, the sensitive, individualistic, self-cultivating good guys modeled by Emerson, the Other is the undifferentiated mindless mass of consumers—the quaffers of, along with other cans, canned entertainment; the crass materialists, that is, of our own Western world. But these people are not opposed, they are tragically duplicated by their apparent antagonists—the materialist ideologues, the thought-police, the goose-stepping uniformed hordes of the East.

In fact, though Peckham had features of today's plot in place by 1962, he didn't yet have our hero, William, who perhaps was

not securely installed at the center of the new counterrevolutionary Romanticism until M. H. Abrams elevated *The Recluse* into a
symbolically central role in *Natural Supernaturalism* (1971).
Abrams there explains his decision wholly to omit Byron, probably
the age's own candidate as leading poet, by observing that Byron
ironically opposes the "vatic stance" allegedly to be found in the
other leading English Romantics. Wordsworth, by contrast, "(as his
English contemporaries acknowledged, with whatever qualification) was the great and exemplary poet of his age."[4] But as what
purports to be a statement of fact this is misleading. From 1797,
for example, in what we have chosen to call Wordsworth's Great
Decade, he mostly figured in the public mind as a follower of Southey. It was Southey, with two collections of ballads in 1797 and
1799, who was already celebrated for this form of literary slum-
ming; Wordsworth's lyrical ballads could never in his lifetime be
sufficiently dissociated from Southey's ballads, which were polemical broadsides. Francis Jeffrey could not even review Southey's
epic *Thalaba the Destroyer* for the first number of the *Edinburgh
Review* without in fact concentrating on Southey's ballads instead
and attacking them for their manifest political unsoundness. It was
in this article of 1802 that Jeffrey described for the first time a
whole sect of "literary dissenters," headed by Southey, in which
Wordsworth merely figured, unnamed, as the author of its manifesto, the Preface to the *Lyrical Ballads*.[5] The smear of religious
sectarianism places the group accurately enough among the politicized unitarians of Bristol and the Midlands. The later term *Lake
poets* evokes a more private, gentlemanly literary circle and plays
its part in isolating poetry and poets from civic and religious divisions and from commercial contamination—a crucial stage in the
modern definition of literariness.

Wordsworth was a poet constructed for his contemporaries
on a body of deliberately iconoclastic and popular verse by Southey. It may be alleged that, by what de Man calls our "refinement
of linguistic perception," we have simply corrected that first ignorant view of where Wordsworth stood and of what matters about
his poetry. But work along these lines cannot retrospectively undo
what Southey's presence must have done to Wordsworth. Our no-
tions of ourselves, even a great poet's, are largely formed by what
contemporaries say about us and write about us. Wordsworth, and

Coleridge too, sat for a group portrait around Southey. I have dwelt elsewhere on the literal sense in which the word *exemplary* may be better applied to Southey than to Wordsworth.[6] That article has something to say about the role of Southey's narrative poem in the evolution of Wordsworth's most significant narrative poem, *The Prelude*, and it also investigates the reappearances of Southey's structures and images in the nineteenth-century literature of colonialism, high and low, beginning with Shelley and Byron. It would be fatuous to introduce Southey with the aim of adding one more writer to the canon, thus perpetuating a current methodology marked by its restricted range of intellectual interests and by its in-professional preoccupation with verbal and aesthetic categories. Southey is merely a convenience in the case I want to argue in favor of a concern with the external relations of a poem or a poet, for it happens that all six of the Romantic poets we now think major demonstrably had literary relations with Southey. These are at their weakest in the texts of Blake and Keats and at their strongest in the best poems of Coleridge—which is why I take one of the latter as my principal example.

Coleridge followed Southey into both medieval ballad and oriental fable: in Coleridge's productive poetic years, 1797 and 1798, he wrote more poems of these distinctively Southeyan kinds than poems associated with the more personal and "natural" manner of his new partner, Wordsworth. Just what the popular manner signified to Southey doesn't emerge until 1801, in the highly ambitious syncretic narrative poem *Thalaba the Destroyer*. Victorian editions often print Southey's romance epics without the notes, which has the effect at once of making them more reverent and respectable (for the notes are often scurrilous) and less intellectually sophisticated. The notes rehearse analogues for different episodes in the text from many cultures, characteristically leading to the conclusion that the particular story is fictitious and that moreover its currency exposes human credulity. In drawing this moral, Southey was, I believe, refuting Coleridge's attempt in *The Ancient Mariner* to defend Christianity by incorporating its apparent crudities and "superstitions" into a record of faith, the "panharmonicum" of the universal church.[7] No less than *The Ancient Mariner, Thalaba the Destroyer* is a cunning cultural palimpsest. First readers must have thought Southey's poem the more palimpsestic, before Coleridge added the glosses to *The Ancient Mariner* in 1817. But in *Thalaba* the ballads, fairy tales, and superstitions—survivals, corruptions, of primitive oral literature—are molded into a single narrative, which both speaks for the unacceptable court cultures of the later Middle Ages and Renaissance and radically challenges them. Here in *Thalaba* we have a pioneering example of a genre dear to Abrams and to Frye, a quest-romance in twelve books. But the quest already has a goal alien to the transhistorical idealizations of those critics, and the romance has a different value if the folktales on which it is built also retain their distinctive form and manner and so introduce the impermanences and divided interests of life in place and time.

Readers who move in and out of the footnotes of *Thalaba*, which entails entering and leaving the discourses of many centuries, can't avoid adopting a historical perspective. More specifically, their vantage point is characterized as "enlightened"; the reader is typecast as a progressive. The plot suggests maturation, not so much the perfectibility of the individual as the evolution of the human race. Thalaba is a Bedouin herdsman, a nomad, a man without landed property who descends as an iconoclast on Baghdad and other corrupt cities of the plain, imposing by force their return to an ideal republican simplicity. Models for this hero could include Mohammed (famously described by Gibbon), Luther, and Blake's Orc, whom I don't propose to prove Southey knew. Models for the author as a primitive moralist range from Isaiah and Jeremiah to the Rousseau who wrote *On the Origins and Foundations of Inequality among Men*. Models for a text which is the symbolic history of the life of a nation through its cultural stages to its fall include the Bible, in Robert Lowth's strikingly secularized reading of that text as both a poem and a history;[8] Homer, who in Thomas Blackwell's socio-historical reading becomes the historian of ancient Greece's transition from pastoralism to commerce;[9] and Gibbon again, as a reader of the rise and fall of the greatest of Western empires, the Roman.

Only limited claims to poetic originality can be made for Southey and his generation. The dictum that a new art was born either in response to or in reaction against the French Revolution is just more baggage from the nineteenth-century German cultural nationalists. James Macpherson drew on many of the same sources in the 1760s to frame his symbolic history of the Gaels. Blake's prophetic books share the same understanding of primitive literature as national and impersonal. Landor's strange, impressive poem *Gebir* (1798) turns Bonaparte's adventure of that year into a primitive epic, profoundly concerned with the clash of cultures, Eastern and Western, courtly and primal, and as such it is Southey's immediate, acknowledged model.

The interest of Southey is not in the texture of his poetry, line by line, word by word, for he lacks that density, so characteristic of advanced written culture, which invites close reading. We don't close-read much of Blake either. But Southey in *Thalaba* and in *The Curse of Kehama* can claim our attention as a sophisticated narratologist who challenges the subjective, empathetic plot of spiritual autobiography that his ex-partner Coleridge was developing. While the beginning and end of *Thalaba* rewrite *The Ancient Mariner*, the central episode of Southey's poem (books 6 and 7) has equally strong links with a Coleridge poem most of Southey's readers could not have read, the fragment *Kubla Khan*.

According to Southey's narrative, Thalaba, who has a mission to root out some false religionists, a powerful group of magicians, comes on a wonderful walled garden among the mountains, a place at first described as resembling Eden. But, as readers of Spenser would well know, book 6 is never going to be journey's end: it's a false destination, a deceitful Paradise, constructed by a magician called Aloadin to beguile and entrap innocent questers. This is an appropriate center in an orientalist poem. Though the topos of the paradisal garden belongs to the sacred literature of the West no less than the East, the notion of the garden as dangerously seductive is peculiarly potent in the early literary history of orientalism: it classically represents that medieval Western view of the East as soft, degenerate, amoral, corrupt, despotic. Southey quotes three such Western travelers in his notes, Purchas, Odoricus, and Mandeville. He suspects that the source of all three accounts is the same, possibly Odoricus, but to include all three is nevertheless rhetorically essential. It enables him to hint at the universality of myth and to illustrate this by extending his coverage to Persia, Cathay, and Abyssinia. The single story told in books 6 and 7 is seen to stand for rich oriental civilizations as a whole; its wicked deceiving Eastern despot models represent corrupt court cultures anywhere. Southey's note, which glosses a line in book 7 on "The Paradise of Sin," is given here with only minor omissions from Odoricus and Mandeville:

The Paradise of Sin

In the N.E. parts of Persia there was an old man named Aloadin, a Mahumetan, which had inclosed a goodly vally, situate between two hilles, and furnished it with all variety which nature and art could yield; as fruits, pictures, rilles of milk, wine, honey, water, pallaces, and beautifull damosells, richly attired, and called it Paradise. To this was no passage but by an impregnable castle; and daily preaching the pleasures of this Paradise to the youth which he kept in his court, sometimes would minister a sleepy drinke to some of them, and then conveigh them thither, where being entertained with these pleasures four or five days, they supposed themselves rapt into Paradise, and then being again cast into a trance by the said drink, he caused them to be carried forth, and then would examine them of what they had seene, and by this delusion would make them resolute for any enterprize which he should appoint them; as to murther any prince his enemy, for they feared no death in hope of their Mahumetical Paradise. But Haslor or Ulan, after three years siege, destroyed him, and this his fool's Paradise.—*Purchas.*

In another place, Purchas tells the same tale, but calls the Impostor Aladeules, and says that Selim the Ottoman Emperor, destroyed his Paradise.

The story is told by many writers, but with such difference of time and place, as wholly to invalidate its truth, even were the circumstances more probable.

Travelling on further towards the south, I arrived at a certaine countrey called Melistorte, which is a very pleasant and fertile place. And in this countrey there was a certeine aged man called Senex de Monte, who round about two mountaines, had built a wall to inclose the sayd mountaines. Within this wall there were the fairest and most chrystall fountaines in the whole world: and about the sayd fountaines there were most beautiful virgins in great number, and goodly horses also; and, in a word, every thing that could be devised for bodily solace and delight, and therefore the inhabitants of the countrey call the same place by the name of Paradise.

The sayd olde Senex, when he saw any proper and valiant young man, he would admit him into his paradise. Moreover, by certaine conducts, he makes wine and milk to flow abundantly. This Senex, when he hath a minde to revenge himselfe, or to slay any king or baron, commandeth him that is governor of the sayd Paradise, to bring thereunto some of the acquaintance of the sayd king or baron, permitting him a while to take his pleasure therein, and then to give him a certeine potion, being of force to cast him into such a slumber as should make him quite voide of all sense, and so being in a profounde sleepe, to convey him out of his paradise: who being awaked, and seeing himselfe thrust out of the paradise, would become so sorrowfull, that he could not in the world devise what to do, or whither to turne him. Then would he go unto the foresaide old man, beseeching him that be might be admitted againe into his paradise: who saith unto him, you cannot be admitted thither, unlesse you will slay such or such a man for my sake, and if you will give the attempt onely whether you kill him or no, I will place you againe in paradise, that there you may remaine alwayes. . . .

And when the Tartars had subdued a great part of the world, they came unto the sayd olde man, and tooke from him the custody of his paradise; who being incencensed thereat, sent abroad divers desperate and resolute persons out of his forenamed paradise, and caused many of the Tartarian nobles to be slain. The Tartars, seeing this, went and besieged the city wherein the sayd olde man was, tooke him, and put him to a most cruell and ignominious death.—*Odoricus.*

The most particular account is given by that undaunted liar, Sir John Mandevile.

"Beside the Yle of Pentexoire, that is, the Land of Prestre John, is a gret Yle, long and brode, that men clepen Milsterak; and it is in the Lordschipe of Prestre John. In that Yle is gret plentee of godes. There was dwellinge somtyme a ryche man; and it is not long sithen, and men clept him Gatholonabes; . . . . And he had let muren all the mountayne aboute with a strong walle and a fair. And withinne the walles he had the fairest gardyn that any man might behold; and therein were trees beryinge all maner of frutes that ony man cowde devyse, and therein were also alle maner vertuous herbes of gode smelle, and alle other herbes also that beren faire floures, and he had also in that gardyn many faire welles, and beside the welles he had lete make faire halles and faire chambres, depeynted alle with gold and azure. And there weren in that place ... many dyverse stories; and of bestes and of bryddes that songen fulle delectabely, and moveden be craft that it semede that thei weren quyke. ... And he had also in that place the faireste damyeles that myghte ben founde under the age of 15 zere, and the fairest zonge striplynges that men myghte gete of that same age; and all thei weren clothed in clothes of gold fully rychely, and he seyde that tho weren angeles. And he had also let make three welles faire and noble, and all envyround with ston of jaspre, of cristalle, dyapred with gold, and sett with precious stones, and grete orient perles. And he had made a conduyt under erthe, so that the three welles, at his list, on scholde renne milk, another wyn, and another hony, and that place he clept paradys. And whan that ony gode knyght, that was hardy and noble, came to see this Rialtee, he would lede him into his paradys. ... And he woulde let make dyverse instruments of musick to sownen in an high tour, so merily, that it was joye for to here, and no man scholde see the craft thereof; and tho, he sayde, weren Aungeles of God, and that place was paradys. ... And thanue worde he maken hem to drynken of certeyn drynk. ... And than wolde he schewe hem his entent and seye hem, that zif thei wolde go sle such a lord, or such a man, that was his enemye, or contrarious to his list, that thei scholde not drede to don it, and for to be sleyn therefore hemselfe; for aftir hire dethe he wolde putten hem into another paradys, that was an hundred fold fairere than ony of the tothere: and there schole thei dwellen with the most fairest damyseles that myghte be, and pley with hem ever more. And thus wenten many dyvense lusty bacheleres for to sle grete lords, in dyverse countrees, that weren his enemyes, and maden hemself to ben slayn in hope to have that paradys. And thus often tyme he was revenged of his enemyes by his sotylle disceytes and false cauteles. And whan the worthe men of the contree hadden perceyved this sotylle falshod of this Gatholonabes, thei assem-bled hem with force, and assayleden his castelle, and slowen him, and destroyden all the faire places, and alle the nobletees of that paradys."————Sir John Mandeville.[10]

The story Southey takes from the travel writers to put so cen-trally in his text *is* a story, which responds to a narratological and typographical reading more richly than to a close reading of its words. Above all, it is a narrative which in much poetry and drama of around 1800 sees service as a fable of revolution. It echoes the version of world history spelled out by Constantin Volney, that

Foucault of the day, in his influential polemic of 1791, *The Ruins*. According to Volney's fictional Legislator, populations are kept quiet by being told religious tales; they are enchanted, like the inmates of Southey's garden. When the gullible masses cease to be gulled, they will overthrow their rulers. The task of the revolutionary artist, says Volney, is to retell the fables of enchantment as actions which resolve themselves in millenarian denouements. Godwin and Shelley were among Volney's English followers; the poets Blake, Landor, and Southey established his impressive place in English poetry. It is the Volneyan vision of historical change that provides the dynamic for the onward-thrusting plots of Southey's magical oriental adventure yarns. Southey's adolescent type of fantasy-fiction first repeats, then hearteningly dissolves, darker popular fantasies, myths about vengeful punitive gods and sacralized monarchs called Jupiter, Jehovah, Kehama, Aloadin.

Southey's notes must have existed before he went off to Portugal in the summer of 1800 to write the text of his poem, since he sent *Thalaba* directly to the publisher from Portugal the following year. His ambition to write an epic illustrating each of the world's great religions dates from his schooldays, and much of the research for the first two, the Welsh or Bardic *Madoc* (1805) and the Mohammedan *Thalaba* (1801), seems to have been done in the mid-1790s, when he had access to the Bristol lending library. Southey may well have drawn Coleridge's attention to Purchas. He may have done much more and shown him his little anthology of travelers' oriental gardens, for Coleridge's poem after all makes unexplained the transition from Cathay to Abyssinia that occurs naturally in Southey's note. Moreover, Coleridge surely *had* been reading Mandeville, even though Purchas is the only traveler he gives as his source. For some features of the tale are present in all three travelers and in Coleridge's and Southey's poetic versions of the tale: the mountain(s), the fortified wall, damsels, the fountain, the river, a pleasure-palace, the repetition of the word *Paradise*. Mandeville and Coleridge alone have the music, the perfume, the underground chamber, and a glimpse of lovemaking by supernatural lovers.

In the travelers' tales the story has a clear structure, to which Southey's poeticized version remains essentially faithful. (1) The garden is well populated by victims of the enchanter's spell. (2)

The enchanter cruelly expels his victims from the garden. (3) The victims long to reenter, they try to re-create the place imaginatively, they would commit crimes to get back in. (4) Because his many dupes endanger them, the enchanter's neighbors attack the fortress and kill the old man.

In the travel tales, as in Southey's poetic version, the enchanter's creation is less importantly his solid artifacts (the garden, pleasure-palace, and so on), for these would remain in a sense his possessions, as a poem can be considered to belong to a poet. But where the garden is represented as a populated place, it becomes an image of society, and the falseness its magician fabricates is the delusory mind-set of its inhabitants. The overthrow of *this* garden by an undeluded outsider becomes therefore a version of the revolutionist's plot. Though potentially an allegory also for the conquest of a neighboring territory, or even for a mass religious conversion, it seems to be used by Southey, following Volney, as a metaphor for the exposure of false religious consciousness or of false ideology.

But if that is a familiar contemporary reading of the story of the Eastern enchanter's garden, it is not, famously, the story Coleridge gave to the first readers of *Kubla Khan* in 1816. *Kubla Khan* appeared surrounded with its own notes on its sources and its own myth of origins. This celebrated piece of editorializing has tended to accompany the poem ever since, often preceding it as in E. H. Coleridge's Oxford edition of 1912:

KUBLA KHAN
Or, A Vision In A Dream. A Fragment.

The following fragment is here published at the request of a poet of great and deserved celebrity [Lord Byron], and, as far as the Author's own opinions are concerned, rather as a psychological curiosity, than on the ground of any supposed *poetic* merits.

In the summer of the year 1797 [1798], the Author, then in ill health, had retired to a lonely farm-house between Porlock and Linton, on the Exmoor confines of Somerset and Devonshire. In consequence of a slight indisposition, an anodyne had been prescribed, from the effects of which he fell asleep in his chair at the moment that he was reading the following sentence, or words of the same substance, in "Purchas's Pilgrimage": "Here the Khan

Kubla commanded a palace to be built, and a stately garden thereunto. And thus ten miles of fertile ground were inclosed with a
wall."* The Author continued for about three hours in a profound
sleep, at least of the external senses, during which time he has
the most vivid confidence, that he could not have composed less
than from two to three hundred lines; if that indeed can be called
composition in which all the images rose up before him as *things*,
with a parallel production of the correspondent expressions,
without any sensation or consciousness of effort. On awaking he
appeared to himself to have a distinct recollection of the whole,
and taking his pen, ink, and paper, instantly and eagerly wrote
down the lines that are here preserved. At this moment he was
unfortunately called out by a person on business from Porlock,
and detained by him above an hour, and on his return to his room,
found, to his no small surprise and mortification, that though he
still retained some vague and dim recollection of the general pur-
port of the vision, yet, with the exception of some eight or ten
scattered lines and images, all the rest had passed away like the
images on the surface of a stream into which a stone has been
cast, but, alas! without the after restoration of the latter!

KUBLA KHAN

In Xanadu did Kubla Khan
A stately pleasure-dome decree:
Where Alph, the sacred river, ran
Through caverns measureless to man
   Down to a sunless sea.
So twice five miles of fertile ground
With walls and towers were girdled round:
And there were gardens bright with sinuous rills,
Where blossomed many an incense-bearing tree;
And here were forests ancient as the hills,
Enfolding sunny spots of greenery.

But oh! that deep romantic chasm which slanted
Down the green hill athwart a cedarn cover!
A savage place! as holy and enchanted

*In Xanadu did Cublai Can build a stately Palace, encompassing sixteene miles of plaine
ground with a wall, wherein are fertile Meddowes, pleasant Springs, delightfull Streames,
and all sorts of beasts of chase and game, and in the middest thereof a sumptuous house
of pleasure.'—*Purchas his Pilgrimage*: Lond. fol. 1626, bk. 4, chap. xiii, p. 418.

As e'er beneath a waning moon was haunted
By woman wailing for her demon-lover!
And from this chasm, with ceaseless turmoil seething,
As if this earth in fast thick pants were breathing,
A mighty fountain momently was forced:
Amid whose swift half-intermitted burst
Huge fragments vaulted like rebounding hail,
Or chaffy grain beneath the thresher's flail:
And 'mid these dancing rocks at once and ever
It flung up momently the sacred river.
Five miles meandering with a mazy motion
Through wood and dale the sacred river ran,
Then reached the caverns measureless to man,
And sank in tumult to a lifeless ocean:
And 'mid this tumult Kubla heard from far
Ancestral voices prophesying war!
   The shadow of the dome of pleasure
     Floated midway on the waves;
   Where was heard the mingled measure
     From the fountain and the caves.
It was a miracle of rare device,
A sunny pleasure-dome with caves of ice!

   A damsel with a dulcimer
   In a vision once I saw:
   It was an Abyssinian maid,
   And on her dulcimer she played,
   Singing of Mount Abora.
   Could I revive within me
   Her symphony and song,
   To such a deep delight 'twould win me,
That with music loud and long,
I would build that dome in air,
That sunny dome! those caves of ice!
And all who heard should see them there,
And all should cry, Beware! Beware!
His flashing eyes, his floating hair!
Weave a circle round him thrice,
And close your eyes with holy dread,
For he on honey-dew hath fed,
And drunk the milk of Paradise.
   1798.

Among Coleridge's transformations of the story in *Kubla Khan*, none is more significant and fundamental than the emptiness of the garden in the first thirty-six lines; without its dazzled, drugged inhabitants, the beautiful spot has no function except to give pleasure to its solitary maker. Coleridge's editorializing in 1816 ensures that his reader will follow a subject-centered lead, first to Kubla himself, then to his empathizing maker. His claim that the fragment is a "psychological curiosity" coupled with his yarns about its dream origins and the cannily circumstantial man from Porlock all reinforce his theories of poems as consciously or unconsciously their individual writer's creations. But the facts of the poem's provenance do not support these claims to authorial autonomy, which are implicitly claims to the autonomy of literature as a sphere. We have relevant information, literary and textual in nature though extrinsic to *this* poem, which shows that work of its type—the popular ballad and oriental pastiche of the period—is implicated in matters of state and of ideology.

I hope I do not give the impression of imposing on this poem a political reading which belongs to the consciousness of our period rather than of Coleridge's. For, on the contrary, I take Coleridge here to be fully in command of his meaning, and doing what Marjorie Levinson in her chapter on "Tintern Abbey" suggests that Wordsworth is doing:[11] rewriting a narrative previously in the public sphere so that it becomes a private fable, political no longer. Coleridge's commentary of 1816 further impedes a politicized reading by providing alternative "sources" for the poem that lead away from Southey and *Thalaba*. By 1816, *Thalaba the Destroyer* was one of the best-known poems of the poet laureate of the day, and since it supplied its own source materials, the travel tales too were coopted into literature's public domain. Readers could see that the drugged outcast with whom Coleridge's fragment ends comes from the passages Southey gathered, not from Purchas's account of Kubla. Coleridge's "explanation" must have looked particularly shifty to a close reader of Southey such as Shelley, who in 1814 began a prose version, never finished, of the story of the Assassins. It is yet another variant of the story of the earthly paradise, quite probably inspired by *Thalaba* and ironically adjusted by Shelley to reinforce its traditional function as anti-

Christian propaganda. This is one of many examples—*Alastor*, 1816, is another—of Shelley's politicized retellings of Southey's political narratives. In 1816 as much as in 1798, for Coleridge to *empty* the paradisal garden of people and of politics must also read as a political move.

An issue that bears as centrally on the career of Paul de Man as of Wordsworth and Coleridge is that of the close relations throughout the modern period between sophisticated literature and hostility to politics, or quietism. T. S. Eliot, who in his day established the prestige of refined linguistic criticism and the dogma of the autonomous poem, was notable for his discovery that almost all the poets who rose thereby in critical esteem were religious and political conservatives. Since Eliot's day New Criticism and its successor, the Yale-Cornell variant of depoliticized deconstruction, has repeated that discovery for the Romantics. From the late 1940s "Romanticism" has steadily risen in academic esteem, but a cluster of quietist poems has risen fastest of all. Yale and Yale-influenced critics in the 1980s attend to a shortlist of poems by Wordsworth, Keats, and Shelley and neglect the rest of Wordsworth and Shelley, Byron with the partial exception of *Don Juan*, the poems of Coleridge, and (most significant of all) the intransigently political Blake. Even Shelley and Keats are presented by Yale-Cornell critics in versions engorged by (a version of) Wordsworth. The quietist poet and the quietist critic have this above all in common, a rejection of politics so comprehensive and doctrinaire that they appear to have left themselves no vocabulary in which to write analytically about their own sociopolitical positions.

Jacques Derrida has ably marshaled textual and contextual evidence to support the view that de Man was never a fullhearted or outright Nazi.[12] In deconstruction of the de Man type, Yale and Cornell may indeed have acquired an analytical methodology which Derrida seems justified in representing as historically more French (and thus cautious, skeptical, "enlightened," leftist) than German (mystical, visionary, counterrevolutionary, rightist). From this performance it is clear that an able historian of ideas and historical materialist was lost in Derrida. But it is odd that Derrida accompanies a meticulous examination of de Man's early Belgian journalism as the products of specific events in wartime, occupied

Belgium, which appeared in a singular format (a collaborationist newspaper), with an impression of de Man's mature work, done in America, as entirely and privately his own. In a rich, important, and importantly flawed passage, Derrida describes "the effective and fruitful history," that is, de Man's later criticism, as "the 'real' history." "The 'real' events" [externality in 1940–42] add up to much less than "what was *his history*, the only one."[13] Derrida omits the contingent circumstances and the politics of contemporary America—apart from a single footnote about antisemitism in Ivy League universities, a suggestive clue which is never followed up.[14] Instead he appears to endorse unskeptically de Man's leading *critical* principle in the pieces in the collaborationist newspaper—that art and politics are separate spheres. Yet Derrida's methodology as he writes about German hegemony in 1940 subverts that proposition. "Literature is an independent domain having a life, laws and obligations belonging only to it," and "The world war has brought about a profound upheaval in the political and economic world. But artistic life has been swayed relatively little."[15] It is this professedly neutral but commonly rightwing posture of abstraction and abstentionism—and *not* deconstruction—that runs through de Man's career, giving him the space to work in the collaborationist newspaper (even if often ambivalently) and facilitating his absorption into Emersonian Yale and Cornell.

Coleridge's omission of the garden's inhabitants is a quietist maneuver, representing in the apparent smallness of its scale the largeness of its implications. Without his subjects the ruler loses his malignity. A story, like a sentence, provides its own formal arrangement of elements—characters, objects and events—which are to be understood by their fixed relations to one another. As with all transformations within a genre or to a received text, changes are particularly significant and emphatic to those in the know—as at least one other person and potential reader, Southey, was. Southey becomes more significant as both a projected reader of *Kubla Khan*, one capable of noting its innovations, and as the author of comparable texts by which other potential readers would have been conditioned. Southey's prior existence as a published, celebrated writer guarantees that Coleridge's authorial maneuvers, alterations, suppressions will not go unnoticed. Which is why the modern analytical reader must seek to know such circumstances and contingencies as manifestly condition the poem which responds to them. It is not marginal but central to observe that Coleridge refrains from telling *Kubla Khan* as a story about superstition or false consciousness imposed on numbers of people from above, or from describing the paradisal garden as though it could serve as a metaphor for a wicked court.

By the standards of refined linguistic criticism Southey's narrative poems are less accomplished than those of Wordsworth and Coleridge. This does not mean that his medium, the externalized or symbolic narrative, is unfit for serious critical attention. We do, after all, attend to the poets Blake and Shelley, and to novelists such as Godwin, Lewis, Mary Shelley and Maturin when they explore a dreadful court (or household) and the role and actions of a terrific patriarch. These works employ a language, in part visual and dramatic, of image, setting, relationship, symbolic event, which has its own poetry and its given social significance. Fragments of this language, and still more often suppressions of it, show like scars in the poetry of Wordsworth and Coleridge. Because of the currency of that other poetic discourse, the repeated claim that the paradigmatic Romantic narrative is the Song of Myself must surely fail.

Even Wordsworth, slipping in his youth off the barricades, gains something of will, of purposefulness, of artistic autonomy, if we can show that he did not just fall insensibly into an elegiac mood allegedly constitutional to Romantic poets. His loneliness cannot be generalized away as the intellectual malaise (or crowning insight) of 1800. Comparison with the texts of their contemporaries establishes precisely this, for Wordsworth as for Coleridge. The modes of their poetry, including the self-reflexivity, the literariness, and the dense linguistic texture, are themselves signs which operate outside the poem and signify the political preferences they were actively adopting even as they composed—so too, of course, do the shifts of mode and of priority characteristic of those modern admirers of Wordsworth (especially), who have made an icon of his poetry and sought to repeat even its significant silences in their criticism.

NOTES

1. See, for example, *London Magazine* 2 (1820), 4–5, where the journal's diarist, perhaps the editor John Scott, concedes that Byron's *Beppo* and *Don Juan* "trespass on the fences of society, and are therefore dangerous to its security." Wordsworth, on the other hand, though his earlier, familiar compositions still "startle," proved himself in his latest poems (on the River Duddon) "the loftiest and most effulgent mind of the age."

2. Morse Peckham, *Beyond the Tragic Vision* (New York: Braziller, 1962), p. 84.

3. Hillis Miller's *The Disappearance of God* (Cambridge, Mass.: Harvard University Press, 1963) is paradigmatic literary history for Yale-Cornell purposes. Hartman calls for "a genuinely reflective history writing" in *The Fate of Reading* (Chicago: University of Chicago Press, 1975), p. xiii. Bloom's *The Visionary Company* (1962) is essentially a literary history, and further developed as one in the revised edition (Ithaca: Cornell University Press, 1971), which has a new historical essay as introduction; the modernist historical literary genealogy underlies his later essays dealing with Romantic authors, including the psychoanalytic work of the mid-1970s. Northrop Frye's essay "The Drunken Boat," in his *The Stubborn Structure* (1970) repeats the formula implicit in his book on Blake, *Fearful Symmetry* (Princeton: Princeton University Press, 1947), of an apocalyptic moment: "What I see first of all in Romanticism is the effect of a profound change," dated now, significantly, after rather than before the French Revolution, "around the 1790–1830 period" (pp. 203, 200). Jacques Derrida attributes to Paul de Man a strong (and he seems to think saving) belief throughout his career in literary history and its autonomy. "It does not merge with sociopolitical history either in its rhythms or in its causal determinations. Historicism, and especially 'vulgar' historicism, would consist in mapping one history onto the other, in ignoring . . . the temporality proper to literary history, the duration of the waves within its depths that one must know how to listen for over and above the swirls and agitation of the immediate'; "Paul de Man's War," *Critical Inquiry* 14 (Spring 1988), 627.

4. M. H. Abrams, *Natural Supernaturalism* (New York: Norton, 1971), p. 14.

5. [F. Jeffrey,] *Edinburgh Review* 1 (1802), 63; rptd. *Southey: the Critical Heritage*, ed. L. Madden (London: Routledge and Kegan Paul, 1972), p. 68.

6. This lecture has appeared in somewhat different forms in *TLS*, December 4, 1987, pp. 1349–60; as *Literature as a Heritage* (Cambridge: Cambridge University Press, 1988); and as "Repossessing the Past," in *Rethinking Historicism* (Oxford: Blackwell, forthcoming), jointly with Marjorie Levinson, J. J. McGann and Paul Hamilton.

7. See *Literature as a Heritage*, pp. 14–16.

8. R. Lowth, *Lectures on Hebrew Poetry*, Latin ed., 1753, trans. G. Gregory (London, 1787).

9. Thomas Blackwell, *An Enquiry into the Life and Writings of Homer* (London, 1735).

10. R. Southey, *Thalaba the Destroyer* (1802) 2:65–70. Southey's travel writers are the British Samuel Purchas or Purches (1575–1626), whose *Pilgrimage* first appeared in 1613; the Frenchman Odoricus or Odoric (?1286–1331), whose first-hand experiences of Cathay and India were widely influential; and Sir John Mandeville, died 1372, whose *Travels* may have been essentially through other peoples' books.

11. M. Levinson, *Wordsworth's Great Period Poems* (Oxford: Blackwell, 1986), pp. 14–57.

12. "Paul de Man's War," *Critical Inquiry* 14 (Spring 1988), 590–652.

13. Ibid, p. 650.

14. Ibid, p. 592n.

15. Ibid, p. 613 and 628, quoting articles by de Man in *Le Soir*, December 2, 1941, and March 4, 1941. Compare Derrida's gloss on de Man's view of the autonomy of literary history, quoted note 3 above.

The Limits of Genre and the Institution of Literature

ROMANTICISM BETWEEN
FACT AND FICTION

GARY KELLY

Literature was implicated in the Romantic revolutions in two ways. It was a field of struggle for self-definition of the classes who produced and consumed literature, principally the professional middle classes. It was also the major institution available for representing the interests, culture, and values of those classes as the "national" interest, culture, and values while concealing the fact that it did so. For literature to accomplish this, however, its older, class- and gender-based distinctions of genre, fact and fiction, literary and subliterary had to be reconstructed. This was accomplished by changing literature from a humanist institution of "polite learning" designed to serve court culture, *and* from an Enlightenment institution of demystification and social criticism designed to oppose court culture and serve a coalition of gentry and professional classes, into a written verbal art, centering and ordering all other discourses of language, written or spoken, to represent and serve the interests of the professional middle classes, who were led by the Romantic revolutionaries.[1]

By the late eighteenth century many in the professional middle classes were moving away from subordination to or even coalition with the upper classes and pushing for social, cultural, and political hegemony. In doing so they were assisted by major social changes: urbanization, the professionalization of state and society, and the commercialization of culture (which removed it from the patronage of the upper classes, though not from their leadership and domination).[2] At the same time, many in the professional classes still wanted to cling to familiar emulation of their "betters," while others tried to establish new coalitions with politically conscious artisans and lower middle classes. An important manifestation of these changes and conflicts was referred to at the time as "the rise of the reading public." This development was sometimes celebrated as a sign of progress and improvement, sometimes deplored as a degeneration of taste and culture (especially when it was pointed out that most people were reading fiction), and sometimes condemned as a cause of social insubordination. The eclipse of a writing culture of patronage based on shared humanist values and education by a commercialized, emulative culture of fashionable literary consumption created new uncertainties, confusions, and anxieties about social and institutional control of writing and print and, indeed, about who constituted the "reading public" and what they wanted. The ending of perpetual copyright in 1774 had opened the way for the new kinds of entrepreneurship in publishing and bookselling that dominated the Romantic period, led by such famous or infamous figures as Colburn and Constable.[3] There was a rapid increase in reprint series of "classic" English literature, in handbooks for aspirants to polite literature, in critical reviews and literary periodicals, and in other products to feed the appetite of upwardly mobile middle classes for the literary culture and practices of their "betters." At the same time, "modern novels" (so called to distinguish them from earlier, courtly novels, romances, and novellas) seemed to disseminate values and practices of the upper classes, especially in "fashionable novels," or novels of manners.[4] On the other hand, leaders in the provincial and Nonconformist Enlightenments, in rising urban centers such as Birmingham, Manchester, Norwich, and Sheffield, were using print, reading clubs, and public libraries to spread their own values and culture, while radicals such as William Godwin saw the rise of the reading public as a historic opportunity to do away with all governments, court as well as republican.[5] Finally, the huge sales of

Tom Paine's *Rights of Man* to artisans and petty bourgeois reformers gave alarming insight into the potential social distribution and uses of print—alarming even to professional middle-class reformers. Thus in the late eighteenth century, literature in the broad sense, like the pushing classes themselves, remained deeply divided between emulation of older, genteel values and practices and cultivation of more self-consciously professional and bourgeois ones; accompanying these changes was an underlying anxiety about the further spread of print culture to classes which had not hitherto been considered as participating in it.

Ambivalence is seen in the hierarchy of genres and discourses both within and outside literature. Within the domain of literature, broadly speaking, were the *belles-lettres* (poetry, familiar essays, prose fiction, and dramatic writing); more or less factual discourses such as history, travels, biography, and memoirs; theology, sermons, and religious tracts; controversial prose (and verse); scientific and philosophical (though not technical) writing; and, doubtfully, educational writing and writing for children. The review periodicals, miscellany magazines, and rhetoric handbooks of the late eighteenth century all use these categories to some extent; they also accord the highest status to those discourses and genres usually practiced by professional men (though not necessarily professional writers), especially factual and controversial kinds, and allowing belletristic treatment. The lowest literary status was accorded those kinds merely entertaining, practical, or practiced mainly by women. The *belles-lettres* had a double nature: literature of the highest kind on "serious" subjects (that is, in the domain of men), artistically well wrought, and written by men and mere elegant diversion from more "solid" and "useful" reading (that is, reading for professional life). The miscellany magazines served the market for *belles-lettres* of the latter kind.[6] Outside of literature were the nonliterary or subliterary kinds of print, especially newspapers and the cheap reading matter of the common people, "street literature," as it was called. Beyond the print forms, but exercising a powerful force on them as British society continued to shift from a largely oral culture to one dominated by print, was the large universe of spoken discourse, with its own genres. The discourses and genres of widest social diffusion—speech, the newspaper, and prose fiction—had no literary status.

Orality and fiction were, furthermore, associated with subordinate groups in British society—women, the lower classes, and children—and with subordinate, colonialized peoples in the empire (especially orientals).

These divisions and hierarchies were too dangerous to be allowed to persist, as the French Revolution and increasing social conflict in Britain seemed to demonstrate. One response was the Romantic revolution in literature and in other discourses of language; other responses were censorship and schemes of national education. The literary revolution was designed to reconstruct literature as written verbal art transcending the other discourses and genres of writing and speech while leaving literature firmly in control of the professional middle classes or their self-appointed leaders (among whom were the Romantic revolutionaries). Because literature of this kind appeared to transcend the class-based and gender-based distinctions of genre and discourse (it did not in fact do so), it could claim to represent (in both senses) the whole of British society (and the empire). Because it seemed to transcend mere professional, practical writing while itself remaining a kind of writing, it could validate or legitimate the entire culture of writing while concealing the fact that that culture was the property of only one part of society. Furthermore, literature as written verbal art could retain the character of the older, genteel, nonprofessional *belles-lettres* but avoid their tendency to emulate gentry and even courtly literary culture. At the same time, it could relegate commercial literature, however widely disseminated, to marginal cultural and social status, thus disarming it and its purveyors in the struggle for cultural and social hegemony, and thus also helping conceal the actual commercial basis of the new literature. By raising non- or subliterary discourses and genres, especially speech and prose fiction, to literary status, the new literature could subordinate popular discourses while exploiting them. Finally, by foregrounding its artistic character, the new literature could disguise its own politics, thus disseminating them more effectively.

Whatever politics they served, Romantic revolutionaries tried to carry out this program in various ways and with varying degrees of success; the rest of this essay assesses their efforts to mediate prose fiction, fact, and literariness. Fiction in verse form can be passed over here, since poetic form had for centuries legitimized fictional narratives, and much Romantic narrative poetry continued to fictionalize the factual, historical, and mythic, as well as the autobiographical, from Coleridge's conversation poems and Wordsworth's *Prelude* to Scott's and Southey's long poems, Shelley's, Keats's, and Blake's mythic poems, and Moore's and Byron's novels in verse. But prose fiction posed large obstacles to appropriation by literature during the Romantic period, because of its wide social distribution and its association with fashion and commercialized culture and with subordinate social groups. Yet because of these very drawbacks, prose fiction of all kinds had to be "redeemed"—saved for literature by the Romantic revolutionaries if they were to use it to effect the social, cultural, and political reconstruction of Britain in their own interests. Their program for redemption of prose fiction was correspondingly comprehensive, if only partly successful.

The fiction of oral culture, to begin with, was expropriated by antiquarians, forgers, and novelists in order to invent a historically and socially particular "national" literature and culture. Popular fiction in print presented a different problem and evoked different responses. Middle-class social reformers deplored popular chapbook fiction as the repository of the popular moral economy, and thus as the seedbed of social rebellion—a "sans-culotte library."[7] Only with great reluctance did such reformers themselves adopt fiction as a way of supplanting traditional popular fiction, in projects such as Hannah More's Cheap Repository in the 1790s and the Religious Tract Society's massive publication program after 1799. On the other hand, artisan political radicals sometimes viewed chapbook fiction as opiates of the people, spreading a debased version of upper-class values and practices, rather than as a "sans-culotte library."[8] Yet there is ample testimony, in the autobiographies of John Clare, Hugh Miller, and even such political radicals as Samuel Bamford, to the power of cheap popular fiction to transform the self-consciousness and social awareness of many lower-class readers.[9] The power of fiction in print to detach some lower-class young people from the traditional, customary moral economy may have been a necessary first step to acquiring political consciousness. Meanwhile, popular cheap fiction, of the traditional or the newer sort, became an object of interest to serious novelists such as Walter Scott and Bulwer Lytton; Godwin made a chapbook instrumental in the plot of *Caleb Williams*; and Pierce Egan (who earned a bit of money writing chapbooks) even wrote a popular thriller into his enormously successful carnivalesque novel, *Life in London*.

At the same time, there was increasing concern about the fiction reading of middle-class children. Formerly, such children had been allowed to read popular chapbook fiction—the supposedly childish literature of the common people was considered appropriate for middle-class children. But, increasingly, middle-class parents were warned against leaving their children too long in the care of servants, from whose folktales they would absorb too much of the oral "premodern" culture, superstitions, irrationality, and false consciousness of the common people. Maternal supervision and then the supervision of impoverished but educated female gentlefolk—governesses—would ensure against that contamination by the lower classes. Books written specifically for middle-class children would exclude both the traditional chapbooks and the oral folk-narrative. The new middle-class children's literature, as historians of the genre have demonstrated, was relentlessly didactic, devoted to "domestic realism," and eager to subdue fiction and narrative to fact.[10] Mere fictionality, narrativity, and the fabulous were to be excised, or at most used only to sugar the pill of instruction and decorate the straight path to acquisition of the intellectual capital and self-discipline necessary to the middle class, and especially to the professional middle-class child. Furthermore, this Romantic children's literature differentiated little between girls and boys; the same inward qualities, if not accomplishments, were expected from both, though as the middle-class child approached adulthood increasing differentiation between the character and the roles of males and females was reflected in the literature for "youth."

For the "modern novel" the acts of literary redemption were more diverse, and difficult, with tendencies and emphases shifting throughout the Romantic period. The shifts themselves attest to the continuing status of the "modern novel" as an article of fashionable consumption within a commercialized culture which prized novelty (called "originality" in "serious" literature). In general, though, four different strategies were used to convert the novel from an effeminate, commercialized, subliterary discourse widely seen as inimical to professional middle-class aims and ideology, from "the trash of the circulating libraries" into literature. This redemption was to be accomplished while retaining the novel's wide distribution among the power-holding or power-desiring classes and its acknowledged effectiveness as a vehicle of ideological communication among those classes.

The first strategy was to incorporate elements of factual and primarily argumentative discourse, of familiar Enlightenment kinds of social criticism, as in the novels of Dr. John Moore—highly respected in the early Romantic period—and in the novels of the English Jacobins such as Thomas Holcroft, William Godwin, and Mary Wollstonecraft.[11] Most who used this strategy were men, for Enlightenment literature was a predominantly male practice. A second, more feminine strategy was to incorporate elements of acknowledged literary kinds, especially the *belles-lettres*, as in the novels of Fanny Burney, Charlotte Smith, and Ann Radcliffe. This kind of novelist aimed to be serious and moral while remaining acceptably feminine, ladylike, and apparently oriented to the aesthetic rather than to the political (though no less political for that). A third strategy, related to the second, then, was concentration on elements of domestic realism—another acceptably feminine strategy, pursued by the three women novelists already mentioned, but including others, such as Jane West, Elizabeth LeNoir, Elizabeth Hamilton, Maria Edgeworth, Mary Brunton, Amelia Opie, Jane Austen, and Mary Mitford.[12] These women, most from good professional middle-class families and some on the fringes of the gentry, practiced the fiction of the local, domestic, and "realistic," precisely at the expense of aristocratic, courtly, public, officially political, and "romantic" (as a pejorative term) values and practices, thus fulfilling their destiny within the anticourtly but still patriarchal middle-class ideology of woman, even if in the literary domain. This gender-based differentiation of theme and form persisted throughout the Romantic period; indeed, one could argue that it was one aspect of the Romantic revolution and of Romantic feminism, reinforced rather than refuted by a feminist such as Mary Wollstonecraft and her unfinished novel *Maria: or, the Wrongs of Woman*. For Wollstonecraft's novel, too, though firmly based on particular historical, legal, and sociological research, was devoted to the local and domestic. In fact, many of these women writers included in their novels prefaces, footnotes, or other apparatuses affirming the factual basis of their fictions; many also included condemnations of "mere novels" or "the trash of the circulating libraries." But the important point is that study of the local, the domestic, and the "real" could enable those relegated there to participate in national and political issues, especially since national politics and planning seemed unable to cope with the crises in British society. As Elizabeth Hamilton showed in *The Cottagers of Glenburnie*, national social reform would begin in those domains supervised by women, the domestic and the local. In this sense there was little difference between a "Jacobin" such as Wollstonecraft and an "Anti-Jacobin" such as Hamilton.

A fourth strategy for redemption of the mere novel, related to the third but practiced more often by men, was appropriation of factual discourses, especially history, antiquarianism, travels, historical memoirs, and what we now call folklore (then called popular antiquities). The great figure here, of course, was Walter Scott, though he was preceded by such antiquarians as Joseph Strutt (whose *Queen-Hoo Hall* Scott completed after Strutt's death) and, more important, by certain women writers of "national tales" and "historical" or "biographical romances," such as Maria Edgeworth, Lady Morgan, and the Porter sisters. The social-historical novel represented "national" origins, culture, history, and destiny in a period of severe international crisis and domestic economic and social dislocation; after the Napoleonic wars such novels in the 1820s turned to the problem of "national" purpose and leadership. It is doubly significant, then, that Scott was considered, even in his own time, as the one novelist who had demonstrated the full literary potential and status of the novel—"literary" in a sense beyond the mere belletrism of earlier and contemporary women novelists (whose work, nevertheless, Scott himself admired and recognized as, in certain respects, superior to his own).

Yet for all their success in redeeming the "modern novel" for literature, all four of these strategies left the novel differentiated according to gender and genre and still mired in associations with subliterary fashionable pursuits and commercialized consumption.

Another strategy was to subordinate the fictional elements, in an overt way, to some other factual or accepted literary discourse, resulting in a kind of quasi-novel, recognizable as such. Women authors often did this in writing for children, but surveying history, botany, or domestic economy in fictional form remained a literary labor of low esteem, if considered literary at all. Religious writers also wrote quasi-fictions to make theology and morality more attractive (the Lord taught in parables), but although such tracts as the Reverend Legh Richmond's *Annals of the Poor* sold in the millions and exhibited the Romantic literary sensibility of their authors, they could not be considered mainly literary. The quasi-novel seems, rather, to have appealed to men (rarely to women) interested in questioning, challenging, or transgressing generic and discursive boundaries for political, philosophical, intellectual, satirical, or other reasons. In this respect, most quasi-novels represented a rejection of commercialized and fashionable culture. Thus the quasi-novel remained marginal in the Romantic period, but a kind of literature worth examining more closely because it is still little known and because of the light it sheds on the problematic relationship of fact, fiction, and literariness in Romantic literary culture. Of course, there were quasi-novels before the Romantic period, such as the Socratic or Lucianic dialogue, Varronian satire, and didactic writing such as Rousseau's *Emile* or Barthélemy's prerevolutionary *Voyage du jeune Anacharsis*. Enlightenment quasi-novels such as Barthélemy's were usually ways of disseminating learned culture combined with social criticism. In the Romantic period, these kinds of quasi-novel continued to be written, but other kinds were added as the struggle for ideological self-definition and leadership within the book-writing, novel-reading classes intensified. Some Romantic quasi-novels seem designed less to gain a wider readership for social criticism than to define or decenter the authority of writing in a literary culture obsessed with authorial authority and deeply disturbed by the increasing numbers of obscure readers obviously outside the historic institutions of literary culture and therefore beyond the power of those institutions to enforce a community of readers. Such Romantic quasi-novels deliberately pose problems of reading and problems of generic recognition. Thus the challenges they posed became more acute as Romantic literary culture developed from the 1790s to the 1820s.

An example of the late Enlightenment quasi-novel with emergent Romantic elements is the English Jacobin John Thelwall's *The Peripatetic; or, Sketches of the Heart, of Nature and Society; in a Series of Politico-Sentimental Journals, in Verse and Prose, of the Eccentric Excursions of Sylvanus Theophrastus; Supposed to be Written by Himself* (1793). Here *eccentric* means wandering, off-center, marginalized, therefore individual, truthful, authentic, central. The eccentric is perforce original, a genius in the late eighteenth-century use of the word; the uniquely individual is supposed to have unique authority, authority written in the transgressive form and style of the work, authority perhaps only knowable through writing. *The Peripatetic* combines verse and prose, meditation and dialogue, tale and essay, political oratory and literary criticism, fable and history, sensibility and enlightenment, lyricism and social criticism, the personal and the public. It attempts to reorder the distinction and hierarchy of genres and discourses inherited from a culture of patronage and its subservient learned culture to give a new meaning, shape, and (hence) power to "philosophical" discourse, in the special, radical sense of "philosophy" prevalent in the revolutionary decade.

The turn away from the overtly political quasi-novel after the 1790s is seen clearly in the gentleman clergyman Thomas Frognall Dibdin's *Bibliomania; or, Book Madness: A Bibliographical Romance*, published in 1809, greatly expanded in 1811, and expanded again in 1842. The text is a frame narrative with a series of dialogues dealing with the history, symptoms, and cure of bibliomania; it argues for "the right use of literature"—literature here meaning written or printed knowledge. Paradoxically, the book itself is concerned with and manifests an obsession for the book as object. Every typographical device is exploited, the "main" text is embarrassed with footnotes that spill over to page after page, there are numerous supplements, illustrations, and indexes, and the book is choked with absurdly learned, detailed, recondite information. It is an extravaganza, clearly not meant to be read through, a monument to its subject, the classic of Romantic bibliophily, and a challenge to commercial, professional, and utilitarian ideas of the book. At the same time, it insists on almost every page on the inescapable, even glorious materiality of the book.

The rapid professionalization of criticism in the age of the new professional literary journals led to the great quasi-novel of Romantic criticism, the "Noctes Ambrosianæ," which appeared in *Blackwood's Magazine* from 1822 to 1835, written by Wordsworth's disciple, John Wilson ("Christopher North"), and others. "Noctes Ambrosianæ" is ambitious and extravagant, the most richly literary and topical of any Romantic quasi-novel, or perhaps any text of the Romantic period. In the dialogues and debates of the "Noctes" we have the same topics—almost anything of interest to a professional man—treated seriously in the other parts of *Blackwood's*, but turned into play as "North" and his confreres relax at Ambrose's. (Among other things, "Noctes Ambrosianæ" is a send-up of Aulus Gellius' scholarly miscellany, *Noctes Atticæ.*) Here the intellectual chiefs of *Blackwood's* are presented in quasi-genteel, off-duty mode. This is a pretense, of course. Nothing in *Blackwood's* is more serious, professional, and political than the "Noctes," with its construction of literary, cultural, and social authority through pseudo-debate and pseudo-dialogue, centering, after all, the elegant, nervous, personal, yet standard English of "North" in the face of deviant sociolects and dialects of other characters, such as "the Ettrick Shepherd," James Hogg. A sign of the representativeness of the "Noctes's" factuo-fictional literariness is that Hogg's revenge, the great novel *Confessions of a Justified Sinner*, which plays fact, fiction, literariness, and speech against one another in a more radical way, sank without a trace on its publication in 1824. In short, the "Noctes" was an important and highly influential attempt to gentrify literary and critical discourse without relinquishing its professional character, and power.

Rivaling the "Noctes" as a carnival of genres and discourse is Robert Southey's most interesting work, *The Doctor, &c.*, written from 1813 and published from 1834 to 1847. Supposedly the life and opinions of Doctor Daniel Dove of Doncaster, it encompasses an encyclopedic range of topics, essays, stories (including the classic children's story, "The Three Bears"), quotations, languages, poems, sociolects and dialects, and styles in a maze of chapters, "interchapters," "arch-chapters," and "extraordinary chapters." Appropriately, the frontispiece shows the author from the back as he faces a wall lined with books. The Shandean device is carried through into a complex reflexiveness on the act of writing, as the reader is forced at many points to reflect on text-making as process, and on reading as a process governed by the same idiosyncracies of subjectivity that are supposed to govern writing. Doctor Dove himself, though lost sight of for much of the time in this normally digressive text, represents the rural, gentrified professional man central to the embourgeoisement of rural England and to the cultural ideals described by Martin Wiener in *English Culture and the Decline of the Industrial Spirit.* The reader is not, however, asked to come into the text on the level of Dove but on the level of the narrator, the carnival master implicitly superior to both gentry and professional bourgeoisie, on the transcendental plane of the literary.

As relentlessly literary, but eluding all generic and discursive categories, including that of quasi-novel, is William Hazlitt's *Liber Amoris: or, The New Pygmalion* (1823). Constructed from documents of Hazlitt's life during his infatuation with his landlord's daughter, *Liber Amoris* is obviously literary in its lyricism, its allusiveness, its celebration of imaginative gusto in the face of sordid social convention, oppressive marriage laws, political disappointment, and the unknowability of the desired other. So, too, it is a work of Romantic irony, but turned inside out as the reader is not only forced to share the protagonist's uncertainty about the beloved, but is also left in uncertainty as to the generic status of the text itself. This text refuses to divulge its identity as fact or fiction, and thus remains "mere" writing, therefore above fact or fiction, therefore qualifying as literature. *Liber Amoris* exposes the limitations of genre and discourse as these limitations were being used to construct literature during the Romantic period, literature as we still know it and teach it. Not surprisingly, critical opinion at the time was divided as to what *Liber Amoris* was, and it too sank with little trace on publication; later in the century Richard Le Gallienne published an edition with original documents, purporting to reveal thereby the truth at last. *Liber Amoris* is still regarded as a failure and an embarrassment; in fact, I would argue, its "failure" exposes the inadequacies of our concepts and canons of Romanticism.

In summary, then, the quasi-novel deals with generic and discursive limits of fact and fiction in a variety of ways, from politics to play to indeterminacy. To this extent, quasi-novels share the project of novels that simply incorporate elements of factual, belletristic, learned, religious, or poetic discourse. Only occasionally, as with Hazlitt, does a quasi-novel undermine even this revolutionary project.

The "major" novelists of the period, Austen and Scott, handled the problem of the subliterary status of prose fiction and the bounds of fact and fiction in different ways. It is true that Austen has been taken by Scott, Wordsworth, and others in her time and after to be a domestic realist of a certain kind.[13] Yet, I think, Austen's achievement was to transform "the trash of the circulating libraries" into literature by a certain play with fictional conventions, in particular the conventions of the novel of manners, sentiment, and emulation as revised by Fanny Burney and Maria Edgeworth. Austen's novels play with fictional conventions so as to engage the reader in a particular exercise of reading, an exercise of moral, intellectual, *and* aesthetic judgement. At the same time, Austen's protagonists have imposed on *them* a task of reading self and others within the fictional world. Austen's use of reported interior speech and thought, together with narrative irony, enables her to mesh these two different kinds of reading, two different kinds of worlds. Thus fiction-as-literary-discourse assumes a special prominence in the moral and intellectual subject who, as Austen's protagonist or as Austen's reader, is forced to bring together gentry and professional ideology and practice. Austen's "realism" is, then, a by-product of enforced critical reading through fictional conventions of the day; the reader well read in "the trash of the circulating libraries," a socially and historically particular kind of writing, will be the reader most qualified to read Austen's novels, but at the same time most susceptible to reading them as merely a superior kind of "novels of the day," that is, ephemeral and subliterary. Thus, unlike the ephemeral "novels of the day," to be rented, read, and returned, Austen's novels are textured so that rereading discloses more of their literariness to the reader now schooled in how to read them. They disclose the surplus beyond story, what Scott may have meant when he referred to their "finishing-off," their "exquisite touch." By engaging in and with the

subliterary "modern novel" in just this way, Austen could also retain the particular gender inflection assigned to such usually despised reading, as merely feminine, but she did so without relinquishing the class basis of her argument, for male readers. And
because her novels make silk purses out of sows' ears, Austen can
relinquish the belletristic decorations often found in novels that
would be literature in her day; she can also drop the "factual" elements, such as "an essay on writing, a critique on Walter Scott, or
the history of Buonaparté"[14] to be found in novels that would be
"solid" or "useful" reading. Each of *her* novels bears the proudly
provocative subtitle, "A Novel," though her contemporaries had
to wait till after her death to read the defense "only a novel" in
Northanger Abbey—probably the best-known statement in English about the novel.

Scott's response to the limits of genre and discourse looks
quite different from Austen's. As we have seen, in his own time
Scott was widely supposed to have established the literary potential of the "modern novel," mainly by combining realism of character and history with the hitherto despised and dangerous discourse of fiction.[15] His sense of the difference between these
discourses and his ambivalence about his work in the novel "line"
(he often used trade metaphors to refer to his writing) were both
strong. In March 1826 he wrote in his journal, "I am begun *Nap*[o-
leon] *Bon*[apart] again which is always a change because it gives
me a good deal of reading and research whereas *Woodstock*
[which he had just finished] and such like being extempore from
my mother wit is a sort of spinning of the brains of which a man
tires"—or should that be "of which a *man* tires" (but a woman
doesn't)?[16] Somewhat earlier, in the preface to the first series of
Tales of the Crusaders, Scott has "the Author" propose forming
with his various narratorial personae a joint stock company "for
the purpose of writing and publishing the class of works called the
Waverley Novels." When the personae refuse to cooperate, "the
Author" threatens them:

> "—I will discard you ... I will leave you and your whole hacked
> stock in trade—your caverns and castles—your modern antiques
> and your antiquated moderns.... I will vindicate my fame with
> my own right hand.... I will lay foundations better than on quick-

sands. I will rear my structure of better materials than painted cards; in a word, I will write HISTORY!"

"The Author's" creatures are incredulous; one remarks, "'The old gentleman forgets that he is the greatest liar since Sir John Mandeville,'" to which another replies, "'Not the worse historian for that ... since history, you know, is half fiction.'"

Scott was also an excellent historian and critic of the novel and deeply interested in and concerned about the canon and the social function of literature. It is *Woodstock* (1826), a novel of the aftermath of civil war, that contains Scott's most extended figural reflection on the socially unifying function of "national" literature, in the debate between Sir Henry Lee, young Charles II, and Markham Everard on the relative merits, moral and aesthetic, of Shakespeare, Davenant, and Milton (chap. 25; vol. 3, chap. 1). As readers of *Woodstock* knew, history had resolved the debate, dropping the king's favorite (in both senses), Davenant, and canonizing *both* Shakespeare and Milton, just as they knew that the author of the book in their hands was also in the process of being canonized. A couple of years earlier, Scott had been the prime mover in the opening of a new Edinburgh academy for sons of the burghers and the nearby gentry, and one of the school's innovations was to be to have "a class for the study of English Literature."[17] But Scott himself could not resolve whether or not his novels were literature, properly speaking.

Most critical discussion of Scott in his day (including his published and private discussions of himself), focused on, first, the ease, rapidity, and apparent carelessness of the composition of the Waverley novels; second, the copiousness of the author's knowledge of the discourses of literature and of history; third, the move from poetic to prose narrative; fourth, the politics of the novels; and, fifth, the fusion or confusion in them of history and romance, fact and fiction.[18] The combining of fiction and fact delighted most readers and critics—some even thought the Waverley novels could be used as quasi-fiction for the young was already being used, to teach "useful" information to the intellectually immature or inferior (including women). Some critics, however, saw the combination as a trivializing of the noble discourse of historiography, as making Scott's politically tendentious views of history seem based in fact; they considered them too poetical and "romantic" and simply inaccurate. What most could admire was the Great Unknown's evident command, through allusion, of "literature" in the full sense—both factual and belletristic discourses, as well as what was just emerging as canonical "national" literature. Furthermore, this literariness could be seen as a gentleman's culture. Scott's literariness was also put to the purpose of reinforcing the historiographical authoritativeness, and thus the political authority, of his narratives. This literariness differs from both the ladylike literariness of a writer such as Ann Radcliffe and the masculine Enlightenment literariness of a Dr. John Moore. Further authority was gained by Scott's development of the figural mode of narrative he had realized so successfully in his enormously popular verse narratives. As for the rapidity and carelessness of composition of the Waverleys, Scott was of course responding to the demands of a commercialized fiction product he himself had done a lot to create, yet the carelessness, too, has a rhetorical purpose: it registers for the professional literary intellectual the distance between "the Author of Waverley" and the Waverley novels, between the Great Unknown and his world-famous works. The fact is that Scott's readers wanted a kind of literary factual fictions, not the exposé of their compositional politics mounted by James Hogg in his *Confessions of a Justified Sinner*.

Perhaps it is appropriate that Hogg's novel began to come to the notice of critical literature in the early twentieth century, just as Scott's work was ceasing to be considered as serious literature, or even a popular classic. Scott remained a popular classic as long as the coalition of gentry and professionals he called for held sway in Britain—this in spite of increasing condescension toward him on the part of leading professional intellectuals in Britain. Yet outside of Britain, Scott was—*and is*—a major author in a way no other writer of the Romantic period, and no other writer of English apart from Shakespeare, has been. Scott provided professional middle-class writers in many countries with what he had already provided for Britain—a major form for representing or inventing what Benedict Anderson calls the "imagined community" of the nation—a community which Anderson argues could only be made possible by two forms of "print capitalism," the newspaper and the novel of the type mastered by Scott—the literary factual fiction.[19] In his partial resolution of the relations of fact, fiction, and literariness within the social limitations of genre and discourse in his time, Scott contributed enormously, more than any other writer of his age, to the Romantic literary revolution, a revolution whose issues and ramifications are still critically present to us today.

NOTES

1. Raymond Williams, *Keywords: A Vocabulary of Culture and Society* (Glasgow: Fontana/Croom Helm, 1976), p. 153.

2. See Geoffrey Holmes, *Augustan England: Professions, State and Society 1680–1730* (Boston: G. Allen and Unwin, 1982); Lawrence Stone and Jeanne C. Fawtier Stone, *An Open Elite? England 1540–1880*, abridged ed. (New York: Oxford University Press, 1986); Neil McKendrick, John Brewer, and J. H. Plumb, *The Birth of a Consumer Society: The Commercialization of Eighteenth-Century England* (London: Europa, 1982); and P. J. Corfield, *The Impact of English Towns 1700–1800* (New York: Oxford University Press, 1982).

3. A. S. Collins, *The Profession of Letters: A Study of the Relation of Author to Patron, Publisher and Public, 1780–1832* (1928; Clifton, N.J.: Augustus M. Kelley, 1973); and John Sutherland, "Henry Colburn, Publisher," *Publishing History* 19 (1986), 59–84.

4. Joseph Bunn Heidler, *The History, from 1700 to 1800, of English Criticism of Prose Fiction* (Urbana: University of Illinois Press, 1928); W. F. Gallaway, Jr., "The Conservative Attitude toward Fiction, 1770–1830," *PMLA* 55 (1940), 1041–59; Gary Kelly, "'This Pestiferous Reading': The Social Basis of Reaction against the Novel in Late Eighteenth- and Early Nineteenth-Century Britain," *Man and Nature/L'homme et la nature* 4 (1985), 183–94; and Terry Lovell, *Consuming Fiction* (New York: Verso, 1987).

5. Devendra P. Varma, *The Evergreen Tree of Diabolical Knowledge* (Washington, D.C.: Consortium, 1972); Paul Kaufman, "English Book Clubs and Their Social Import," in *Libraries and Their Users* (London: Library Association, 1969), 36–64; Gary Kelly, *English Fiction of the Romantic Period 1789–1830* (New York: Longman, 1988), chap. 1.

6. R. D. Mayo, *The English Novel in the Magazines 1740–1815* (Evanston, Ill. and London: Northwestern University Press and Oxford University Press, 1962), chaps. 1 and 5.

7. Gary Kelly, "Revolution, Reaction, and the Expropriation of Popular Culture: Hannah More's *Cheap Repository*," *Man and Nature/L'homme et la nature* 6 (1987), 147–59.

8. For example, Thomas Frost, *Forty Years' Recollections: Literary and Po-*

litical (London: Sampson Low, 1880), 7–9; for a working-class radical's view of the effect of novels, see Richard Carlile, *The Gauntlet: A Sound Republican Weekly Newspaper*, February 10, 1833, pp. 2–3.

9. David Vincent, *Bread, Knowledge and Freedom: A Study of Nineteenth-Century Working-Class Autobiography* (London: Europa, 1981), chap. 5.

10. Geoffrey Summerfield, *Fantasy and Reason: Children's Literature in the Eighteenth Century* (London: Methuen, 1984); and, earlier, F. J. Harvey Darton, *Children's Books in England: Five Centuries of Social Life*, 3rd ed. rev. (Cambridge: Cambridge University Press, 1982), chaps. 5–11.

11. Gary Kelly, *The English Jacobin Novel 1780–1805* (Oxford: Clarendon, 1976); and Marilyn Butler, *Jane Austen and the War of Ideas* (Oxford: Clarendon, 1975), chaps. 2 and 3.

12. Mary Poovey, *The Proper Lady and the Woman Writer: Ideology as Style in the Works of Mary Wollstonecraft, Mary Shelley, and Jane Austen* (Chicago: University of Chicago Press, 1984). On the gendering of literary genres within Romantic culture see Irene Tayler and Gina Luria, "Gender and Genre: Women in British Romantic Literature," in *What Manner of Woman: Essays on English and American Life and Literature*, ed. Marlene Springer (New York: New York University Press, 1977), pp. 98–123; and *Romanticism and Feminism*, ed. Anne K. Mellor (Bloomington: Indiana University Press, 1988). On the women novelists mentioned here, see Ann H. Jones, *Ideas and Innovations: Best Sellers of Jane Austen's Age* (New York: AMS, 1986), and Kelly, *English Fiction of the Romantic Period*, chap. 3.

13. See B. C. Southam, ed., *Jane Austen: The Critical Heritage* (London: Routledge and Kegan Paul, 1968).

14. *Jane Austen's Letters to Her Sister Cassandra and Others*, ed. R. W. Chapman, 2d ed., corr. (Oxford: Oxford University Press, 1959), p. 300.

15. See John O. Hayden, ed., *Scott: The Critical Heritage* (New York: Barnes and Noble, 1970).

16. *The Journal of Sir Walter Scott*, ed. W. E. K. Anderson (Oxford: Clarendon, 1972), p. 122 (March 31, 1826).

17. J. G. Lockhart, *The Life of Sir Walter Scott, Bart.* (London: Adam and Charles Black, 1893), p. 526.

18. Hayden, ed., *Scott*.

19. Benedict Anderson, *Imagined Communities: Reflections on the Origin and Spread of Nationalism* (London: Verso, 1985).

The Landscape of Labor
TRANSFORMATIONS OF THE GEORGIC

JOHN MURDOCH

The print of an ass pulling a cart appears in the middle of a small volume published by Julius Caesar Ibbetson in 1817.[1] The other prints show groups of animals, cows and sheep, and people similarly engaged in characteristic rural occupations, leading asses, guiding carts, gathering firewood. Publications like this appeared frequently in the first quarter of the nineteenth century, and their currency undoubtedly arose from the demand in the market for instruction books on drawing—books that taught both what to draw and how to draw it. Although etching is not the most appropriate technique for demonstrating graphic effects—soft ground etching with aquatint was used by David Cox to simulate the effect of pencil and watercolor in his *Series of Progressive Lessons* (1811 and numerous later editions), and lithography was already available as a facsimile medium for an even greater range of effects—Ibbetson successfully communicates through the etched line a sense of variegated broken lights and interesting texture in his subject.

These are key words, for Ibbetson was a painter and draughtsman profoundly affected by the aesthetic movement known as the Picturesque, within which these simple, commonly accessible stimulants to the human senses were understood as producing a pleasurable and appreciative response—especially suitable, in-

Print by Julius Ibbetson, inscribed "To the Manes of Gilbert Wakefield,"
1817. Copyright Trustees of the Victoria & Albert Museum

deed peculiar, to the experience of looking at pictures. Groups of
animals and human figures could be incorporated into landscapes
to impart this pleasurable ocular stimulus of the Picturesque, and
simultaneously to evoke associations of Arcadian imagery from the
Claudian landscape tradition. Ibbetson, like many artists, poets and
lay tourists went north in the years around 1800 to find their own
Arcadia in the English Lake District. His finished landscapes in
which Windermere and Grasmere are instantly recognizable thus
record with topical precision the moment at which the educated
class decided that the ideal landscape had a present reality. As a
real place, it has a social structure, a culture, and a politics.

That figure of the peasant in the print, with his load of faggots,
refers to the ancient rights of gathering firewood from the com-
mons and enclosures by "hook or by crook"—that is, by pulling

dead wood from trees and thickets without cutting it. The fat man in clerical dress is known to be Richard Watson (1737–1816), absentee bishop of Llandaff, proprietor of Calgarth New Hall on the eastern shore of Windermere, just across from John Christian Curwen at Belle Isle. Curwen and Watson were both intensely interested in agrarian reform. In 1798, Curwen planted on Claife Heights "by the desire of my respected friend Dr. Watson . . . thirty thousand larches" and a good number of oaks to render sylvan and fruitful the view across Windermere from Calgarth.[2] In such new plantations, trimmings produced a valuable early return on investment: common rights to firewood are never, I think, mentioned in the literature of planting wastelands.

The inscription on the print reads: "To the Manes of Gilbert Wakefield." In 1801 everyone knew who Gilbert Wakefield was.

He was born in 1756, the son of a clergyman; he was a scholar and fellow of Jesus College Cambridge; ordained deacon in 1778, appointed to a curacy in Stockport, then in Liverpool, where he worked to arouse public opinion against the slave trade. Without proceeding in his holy orders, he resigned his curacy on a matter of theological principle (his Unitarian beliefs were incompatible with the Thirty-Nine Articles) and became a schoolmaster to support himself, his wife, and an increasing family while he prepared for the press his first major work, an edition of the *Georgics*, which appeared in 1788. Politically his opinions were humanitarian, liberal, and pacific.

> He had long upon principle been an enemy to war, thinking it absolutely incompatible, unless as a measure of direct defence, with Christian morality, and especially detesting it when employed to usurp upon the rights of mankind and overthrow the plans of liberty. He thought it bore this character when it was waged against the principles of the French revolution, an event which in its commencements he, in common with many other philanthropists, hailed as the promise of a much improved state of human affairs (John Aiken, a colleague's son from Warrington, quoted from *DNB*).[3]

DNB goes on:

In 1798 the bishop of Llandaff, wrote an "Address to the People of Great Britain," an ordinary party tract in defence of Pitt and the war and the new "tax upon income." Wakefield instantly published a "Reply" which, as he says, "was never written over twice, and was finished for the press in the compass of a single day." The "Reply" was a remarkable *tour de force* of mingled eloquence and enthusiasm. Wakefield contended that the poor and the labouring classes would lose nothing by a French invasion, and declared that if the French came they would "find him at his post among the illustrious dead." It also contained charges of corruption against the civil and ecclesiastical system of the day, and detailed numerous accusations against the bishop of Llandaff as an absentee and pluralist. A prosecution followed of Wakefield, his publisher (Cuthell), and his printer, and all three were convicted. After the conviction of the printer and publisher Wakefield was tried separately in February 1799. Erskine offered to defend him for nothing, Wakefield having exhausted his means in paying the expenses of his publisher; but the offer was declined, and he defended himself in an able and outspoken address. On conviction he was released on bail, and ... was committed to the king's bench prison, where Fox, Lord Holland, and the Duke of Bedford, and others ... visited him. In May he was sentenced to two years' imprisonment in Dorchester goal, and to give security for good behaviour for five years. On his conviction Fox wrote to him as follows: "The liberty of the press I consider as virtually destroyed by the proceedings against Johnson and Jordan; and what has happened to you I cannot but lament therefore the more, as the sufferings of a man whom I esteem in a cause that is no more." In May 1799 Wakefield was taken to Dorchester goal where his family ... were allowed to visit him frequently; and his confinement, thanks to influential friends, was rendered fairly supportable. A long correspondence, since published, passed between him and Fox, chiefly on matters of scholarship. The large sum of money (£5,000) that was raised for him by his friends and sympathisers—for Wakefield was never rich—relieved him and his family of pecuniary anxiety. He devoted part of his time to the poorer prisoners and part to literature ... he wrote constantly to Fox, and ... translated select essays of Dio Chrysostom and prepared a work on Greek metres, which was published, under the title of "Noctes Carcerariae" (London, 1801), shortly after his release. On this happy event, 29 May 1801, he returned to Hackney, and projected a series of lectures on Virgil. He died at Hackney of typhus fever on 9 Sept. 1801, and was buried near the east end of St Mary Magdalene's Church, Richmond.

In making his point that the British laborer had nothing to gain from supporting Pitt and the war party, Wakefield had quoted Aesop's Ass, who, on being exhorted to flee on the approach of its master's enemy, stopped to inquire whether the enemy would not also load it with burdens. Many intellectuals, not only those of the immediate Holland House group, agreed with this subversive view of events in France. Wakefield was obviously far from friendless, and as we probe more deeply into the names and places in the *DNB* account, the sense of a circle of like-minded people becomes increasingly strong.

Thus, Wakefield was involved in antislavery campaigns in Liverpool. Also involved in the Liverpool antislavery movement was William Roscoe, patron of a recent arrival in the city, J. C. Ibbetson; Roscoe put Ibbetson in touch with his brother-in-law Daniel Daulby, a man of similar opinions and activity in the slavery question who settled in Rydal in 1796. Daulby took up farming. He wrote to Roscoe in August 1796, "Margaret [his wife] enters into the true spirit of farming . . . she makes her fifth cheese tonight from the two cows which have given seven pounds of Butter fat."[4] Daulby was an active patron of Ibbetson, who settled in Rydal in 1798/99, just when Wakefield was hitting the headlines with his attack on their neighbor down the road at Calgarth, Bishop Watson. Ibbetson's etching commemorating this attack, and dedicated "To the Manes of Gilbert Wakefield," completes the circle.

What does this suggest? Certainly not that we are at the center of an active Fifth Column of dangerous proletarian radicals. This is, on the contrary, high Whiggery—displaced from Holland House to the north of England but wearing nonetheless its characteristic face. The clue perhaps is contained in the Aesopian fable—turned so elegantly by Wakefield to dissociate the Foxite policies from Pitt's war on Liberty. For the fable projects a far from revolutionary attitude to the question of Labor.

The paradox for us, but not for Wakefield, is that a political statement of such instantly subversive import could at the same time disclose such a profound acceptance of the political status quo. In terms of class politics the real message of the fable is that Labor is inevitable. Come the French invasion, come Napoleon himself, the lot of the laborer is to *work*. Work is hard and unremit-

ting, but because it is not slavery it is not and should not be without reward in a just society. In a just society, by means of rebellion
if necessary, the lot of the laboring classes can be prosperous and
happy. But work is still undeniably necessary, the condition on
which all prosperity depends. It is not coincidental that Gilbert
Wakefield was the editor of the *Georgics*, for the *Georgics* provide
the defining myth of the prosperity that can be achieved through
hard work in the aftermath of rebellion and civil war, when the
strong just ruler comes, bringing Justice for all. For English Whigs
contemplating French politics of the 1790s in the light of British
history after the Glorious Revolution the Georgic was of special
relevance.

What are the *Georgics*? The term refers to the long poem in
four books by Virgil, on agriculture and the keeping of bees. Together with the *Eclogues* or *Bucolics* and the *Aeneid*, it constitutes
the middle term of the Virgilian triad: Pastoral, Georgic, and
Epic.

As three kinds of poetry, these modes correspond with basic
masculine activities. The Pastoral provides an image of leisure, the
Georgic provides an image of work, and the Epic provides an
image of conflict, war and heroism. In terms of individual human
development, Virgil's own progress from the *Eclogues* to the *Georgics* to the *Aeneid* could be represented as a progress from the
"low style" of Pastoral to the "middle style" of Georgic and finally
to the "high style" of Epic. In some instances, Pastoral equates with
childhood, and the Georgic and the Epic with alternative forms
of the human lot of the adult; the Georgic is necessarily encountered first and leads, as occasion demands, to the Epic. But these
modes are not simply chronological or necessarily exclusive of
one another. Elements of the Pastoral are contained in the Georgic, and elements of the Georgic are certainly contained in the
Epic.[5] The vital element of overlap between Georgic and Epic
seems to be signaled by Virgil in the similarity between the opening of the *Aeneid*: "Arma virumque cano ..." (I sing of the arms
and the man) and the lines of the first georgic: "Dicendum et
quae / sint duris agrestibus arma"—In Dryden's translation:
"Nor must we pass untold what arms they wield, / Who labour
Tillage and the furrow'd field."[6] So the *Georgics* also celebrate her-

oism and struggle, not with sword and spear but with rake and reap-hook, harrow and plough:

> Without whose aid the Ground her Corn denies
> And nothing can be sown and nothing rise.
> The crooked plough, the share, the towring height
> Of waggons, and the cart's unwieldy weight;
> The sled, the tumbril, hurdles and the flail,
> The fan of Bacchus, with the flying sail:
> These all must be prepared, if ploughmen hope
> The promised blessing of a bounteous crop. (ll. 241–48)

And in this way is civilization built. As Anthony Low points out, "Various etymological puns on [the Latin word] *cultus*, meaning both tilled and civilised, permeate the *Georgics* and belong to the texture of Western language."[7] So, in this *culture*, farming is the model of all the other human activities that follow from it in practice, all those necessary activities which together build the state. And this building operation is necessary because the Virgilian world view, like the Christian, postulates a sort of Fall, a loss of the landscape of Eden, in which there was plenty without toil, in which the fruits of the earth grew without need of plough or tillage.

In the first book of the *Georgics* this loss of ease is attributed to Jupiter in his guise of the Greek Zeus who overthrew the primal god Cronus (the Roman Saturn) and thus brought the Saturnian or Golden Age to an end. Jupiter, father of agriculture, makes possible the progress of man from the childlike state of innocence to that of civilization. Jupiter makes possible the very concept of progress. This is Dryden again, from *Georgics*, book 1:

> The Sire of Gods and Men, with hard decrees,
> Forbids our Plenty to be bought with Ease:
> And wills that Mortal Men, inur'd to toil,
> Shou'd exercise, with pains, the grudging Soil.
> Himself invented first the shining Share,
> And whetted Humane Industry by Care:
> Himself did Handy-Crafts and Arts ordain;
> Nor suffer'd Sloath to rust his active Reign.
> E're this, no Peasant vex'd the peaceful Ground;

Which only Turfs and Greens for Altars found:
No Fences parted Fields, nor Marks nor Bounds
Distinguish'd Acres of litigious Grounds:
But all was common, and the fruitful Earth
Was free to give her exacted Birth.
Jove added Venom to the Viper's Brood,
And swell'd, with raging Storms, the peaceful Flood:
Commission'd hungry Wolves t'infest the Fold,
And shook from Oaken Leaves the liquid Gold:
Remov'd from Humane reach the chearful Fire,
And from the Rivers bade the Wine retire:
That studious Need might useful Arts explore;
From furrow'd Fields to reap the foodful Store:
And force the Veins of clashing Flints t'expire
The lurking Seeds of their Coelestial Fire.
Then first on Seas the hollow'd Alder swam;
Then Sailers quarter'd Heav'n, and found a Name
For ev'ry fix'd and ev'ry wandring Star:
The *Pleiads, Hyads*, and the Northern Car.
Then Toils for Beasts, and Lime for Birds were found,
And deep-mouth Dogs did Forrest Walks surround:
And casting Nets were spread in shallow Brooks,
Drags in the Deep, and Baits were hung on Hooks.
Then Saws were tooth'd, and sounding Axes made;
(For Wedges first did yielding Wood invade.)
And various Arts in order did succeed,
(What cannot endless Labour urg'd by Need?) (ll. 183–218)

Because they are so important, it is worth emphasizing some key phrases in the passage, the so-called *Jupiter Theodicy*, which justifies the ways of God to Man in the Virgilian ante-type of Christianity:

    —*hard Decrees*: the idea that it is God's will that men should work hard;

    —the *pains* of work: by extension, poverty and fear of want to enforce production;

    —the Georgic or agrarian state is contrasted with the primal state in which there were no boundaries, fences, or enclosures— no property, for all was common and the riches of the earth were free;

—Jupiter even introduces evil—poison, ravening wolves, and so on—as threats to enforce constant anxiety and vigilance;

—raging storms at sea and the birth of technology: navigation, fishing, forestry, and even the arts, crafts and culture.

These things, which are civilization, which are the state, follow from the loss of primal leisure or bliss. They partly, or even largely, compensate human beings for that loss. In the sense that the *Georgics* follow from the *Eclogues*, so does the state of labor follow from the state of play, and it is therefore the Pastoral that resembles most closely primal otium. But unlike primal otium, the Pastoral may not be irrecoverable. It is merely an alternative to the Georgic state, and in Virgil's first *Eclogue* the suggestion seems to be that its blissfulness can only be realized, at least in the dialogue form of the verse, by contrasting it with the miseries of exile. The blissful state of Tityrus is contrasted with that of Meliboeus, who has been ejected from his estate in the aftermath of war. Meliboeus complains:

> Beneath the Shade which Beechen Boughs diffuse,
> You *Tity'rus* entertain your Silvan Muse:
> Round the wide World in Banishment we rome,
> Forc'd from our pleasing Fields and Native Home:
> While stretch'd at Ease you sing your happy loves;
> And *Amarillis* fills the shady Groves.
> (John Dryden, *Virgil's Pastorals*, I, ll. 1–5; *ibid*, p. 873.)

Tityrus on the other hand has been restored to his patrimony—for him the loss of bliss has not been a final and irretrievable event like the loss of Eden. He answers Meliboeus:

> These blessings, friend, a deity bestowed
> For never can I deed him less than god
>
> He gave my kine to graze the flowery plain
> And to my pipe renewed the rural strain.

The identity of this god is clear—in Dryden anyway it is clear from the printed argument to the first Pastoral, for it is none other than Augustus ("never can I deem him less than God") who has restored Tityrus to bliss. One needs to remember that in Virgil—

especially in Virgil, one might say—the idea of the Pastoral as well as the Georgic is thus constructed politically. Already in Virgil the Pastoral is a privilege held on the condition of a strong and well-disposed sovereign power; it is not a condition separate from or above the idea of government. Nor is it a state without work as such but one in which work is, as Milton describes it in book 5 of *Paradise Lost*, both easy and fruitful:

> On to their morning's rural work they haste
> Among sweet dews and flowers; where every row
> Of fruit trees over-woody reached too far
> Their pampered boughs, and needed hands to check
> Fruitless embraces; or they led the vine
> To wed her elm; she, spoused about him, twines
> Her marrigeable arms, and with her brings
> Her dower the adopted clusters to adorn
> His barren leaves; (ll. 211–19)

Pastoral ease has this in common with the Garden of Eden: both are the happy, privileged lot of the innocent who acknowledges and is grateful for godly benificence. And it is through that positive association of willing grateful acquiescence under absolute authority with innocence that the Pastoral develops its negative association with the sophistry and wickedness of "politics." The Pastoral becomes that Other Place and Other Time in which the struggles for power and position, for wealth and prestige at court can be left behind. For the political class the Pastoral is the reward for and recreation after the business of city and court.

But what of the location of the Pastoral state? Where does the dialogue between Tityrus and Meliboeus take place? The answer is surprising, at least for those of us who think of Pastoral sheep-rearing country as typically upland. Dryden tells us that "when Augustus had settled himself in the Roman Empire, that he might reward his veteran troops for their past service, he distributed among 'em all the lands that lay about Cremona and Mantua: turning out the right owners for having sided with his enemies" ("Argument," *Pastoral* I). These are flat lands, the fat plains of Lombardy, an agricultural landscape if ever there was one, not at all the pastoral hills and valleys celebrated by the postclassical Greek poets, Theocritus, Bion, and Moschus.

In fact, the scene shifts in the *Eclogues* from Lombardy to Dalmatia, and it is likely that for Virgil the landscape of the Pastoral, this Arcady, was primarily an imaginative resource rather than a single or particular place. Arcadia was thus reformulated as a type of landscape—mountainous, wooded and well watered, the domain of Pan, the tutelary deity of the shepherds who were its inhabitants.[8] The later Latin poets, contemplating the landscape of Virgil and Horace as it were from afar, tended to locate it wherever, outside the city, the mind could wander: in the Roman Campagna, on the supposed site of Horace's villa, or even, as in Petrarch, in the hills of Transalpine Gaul about Avignon.

On to this landscape, with its inescapable Meliboean association of lament for lost blessings, the seventeenth century grafted the poignant phrase, "et in Arcadia ego,"[9] and extended its strict sense to mean "I too once lived in Arcadia," thus opening the way for Arcadian, upland landscape to become a potential symbol of the lost state of childhood in Romantic imagery. The seventeenth-century landscape painters working in Rome confirmed this developing imagery of the Pastoral as located in a mountainous, sheep- and goat-rearing country, a dreamland in which recognizable scenes of the Roman Campagna and the Appenines were populated by gods and goddesses, shepherds and maidens.

For already in the seventeenth century it was becoming difficult even to imagine a Pastoral mode of life taking place anywhere but in a hilly country. What we might call *cultural* conditioning made it unlikely: not only the Virgilian tradition but agrarian economics meant that flat land was Georgic and hilly land was Pastoral. So the characteristic figure in the Pastoral landscape was that of the shepherd, lying in the shade, dallying with pretty shepherdesses, almost always making music, dancing, and feasting.

These characteristics of the Pastoral were undoubtedly attractive but there was, clearly, also a down side. Viewed from Britain—a definitively Georgic country of enclosures, agrarian reform, of corn, and of barley to feed horses for heavy transport, a country of scientific, technical, and industrial progress—the Pastoral way of life seemed backward. The negative face of leisure is idleness, and the positive face of industry is wealth. The cultural construction of the Pastoral as the Other Place, was thus reinforced by the Englishman's observation of Rome and its environs as he encountered them as a traveler from rich northern Europe: a ruined civilization, an object of melancholy reflection confirming the Englishman's sense of himself as having grown beyond this state, taking on the burdens of a fallen world and reaping the corresponding benefits of freedom and prosperity.

After 1648 and the end of the wars of religion, Italy had begun to lose its image, familiar to us from Shakespeare and from the Jacobean tragedians, as the site of Macchiavellian politics and sinister soutaned priests communicating by the back stairs. No longer powerful politically, Catholic Italy was seen as the past, increasingly as the site of lost innocence, pre-Reformation, before the revolt against the state of sheeplike innocence, against the priest-pastor, which had taken place in England in the mid-sixteenth century. That revolution against the Catholic church created the hard state of individual conscience and responsibility, in which the duties of self-improvement, hard work, and the division of labor were the necessary conditions of progress.

And yet the dominant literary mode throughout the period of the English Reformation was the Pastoral. It prevailed in conjunction with the Epic, at the expense of the Georgic, through the period of the founding of the British nation-state. The reason, which perhaps should concern us only in passing, was surely the need to present the Tudor monarchy in the guise, not of Jupiter, the usurper and inventor of adversity, but of Saturn, the "legitimate." Elizabeth's characteristic self-presentation was therefore as Astraea, the goddess whose return to earth signified the return of the Saturnian Golden Age of Justice and Plenty—the mode, in other words of the Pastoral. Georgic, the mode associated with the postlapsarian state, after the Golden Age, which provided access to its prosperity only on the condition of hard and incessant labor, was profoundly uncongenial to a court culture that was promoting the Reformation Church as a return to primal rectitude. It would have been a gift to Counter-Reformation propaganda to characterize the British polity as, in any sense, fallen, even though seeking to rise by hard effort. Within this political culture, therefore, the cult of Astraea and of Saturn, the cult of Saturnian *Melancholy*, constitute a metaphor for the political legitimacy necessary for a state so recently separated from the traditional structure of European authority. The absence of the Georgic from a culture that otherwise regarded itself as descended from Aeneas, the founder of Rome (because Brutus, the founder of the British state, according to Geoffrey of Monmouth, was the great-grandson of Aeneas), was a simple necessity of state propaganda and politics until, roughly, the end of the wars of religion in 1648.

By this time, British political self-consciousness was being transformed by the experience of civil war and the imminent execution of the "legitimate" king by the "usurper" Cromwell, celebrated by Marvell as a Georgic hero rising as a matter of personal destiny to the Epic occasion:

> [He] Who from his private Garden, where
> He lived reserved and austere,
> As if his highest plot
> To plant the bergamot
> Could by industrious valour climb
> To ruine the great work of time
> And cast the kingdom old
> Into another Mold. ("An Horatian Ode," ll. 29–36)[10]

The "great work of time" may be a punning allusion again to Cronus (or Saturn), the whole passage thus equating Cromwell with Jupiter, and with the incarnation of Jupiter, Augustus Caesar. For, as Aeneas is informed in book 6 of the *Aeneid*, out of a period of civil war will come a Child, who shall be a strong man ruling with Justice and Peace, "who shall establish in Latium a second time the Golden Age throughout the fields where Saturn once was king." Edmund Waller, the royal panegyrist, had once indiscreetly identified Cromwell as Augustus in his "Panegyrick on my Lord Protector" of 1654, but like Cowley and Dryden he was clearer by 1660 that it was the Restoration and the figure of Charles II that were correctly Augustan. And it is the arrival of this Augustan self-image which signals the admittance of the Georgic into the culture of the ruling class. Thomas May translated the *Georgics* in 1628; John Ogilvy did so in 1649, with further editions in 1650, 1654, 1665, 1668, 1684. But the most influential translation, decisively, was Dryden's of 1697. With Dryden one is at the verge of that age which is still ordinarily referred to as Augustan—the age of Dryden and Pope, of Queen Anne and George I, of agricultural revolution, of enclosures, and of the quintessentially Georgic poem, James Thomson's *Seasons*, published in parts successively beginning with *Winter* from 1726.[11]

The Georgic is the characteristic mode of eighteenth-century writing about landscape. Indeed one might say that it is *the* characteristic eighteenth-century cultural mode, essentially related to other such characteristic phenomena as the country house and the landed estate—the whole system of gentry values which explicitly contrasted the virtues of agricultural self-sufficiency—"eating one's own mutton"—in the country with the extravagance and parasitism of urban life. The country estate, on which the owner pressed ahead with agricultural reforms, provided a site on which the ruling class as well as the laboring class could each be identified as engaged in work to build up the prosperity of the country.[12] This is Arthur Young:

> It is the business of the nobility and gentry who practise agriculture, and of authors who practise and write on it, to help forward the age; to try experiments on newly introduced vegetables, and if they are found good, to spread the knowledge of them as much as possible; to endeavour to quicken the motions of the vast but unwieldy body, the common farmers. Common farmers love to grope in the dark: it is the business of superior minds, in every branch of philosophy, to start beyond the age, and shine forth to dissipate the night that involves them.[13]

Unsurprisingly, the gentry opt for the part of the task that does not involve manual labor, that part which, in the new theoretical dichotomy proposed by the Georgic economist Adam Smith, was "head-work," the labor of thought and invention, directing the toil of others. So when you see in landscapes by George Lambert the figures of the gentry in the landscape, apparently watching the reapers at work, you may take it that the gentry too are working. And the meaning of the landscape thus constructed is that prosperity, the wealth of nations, and happiness are the result, dearly bought, of gentry and laborers working together on the land for the common good. We may say that this is a convenient ideology for the ruling class to promote—one in which they direct and others are directed—but it is not quite true to say that the ideology is not intended to promote gentry *leisure*.

It does not necessitate the maintenance, as it were, of an Arcadian space, the possibility of the Pastoral, as a special privilege for the gentry. For within the terms of their Georgic ideology, within the terms of their self-identification as members of an Augustan ruling elite, work was part of the common lot of mankind. Gentry privilege was the Georgic privilege of directorship.

Lambert's *Hilly Landscape* (Tate Gallery, London) is thus, it seems to me, the full, proper, and simple expression of the eighteenth-century Georgic, a landscape in which the process of thinking about *how* landscape is constructed, a process in which the Georgic Committee of the Royal Society had since the early 1660s given the lead, reaches some sort of temporary rest. Landscape has become the face of Augustan political hegemony. At this point, the absorption of the Georgic into the collective cultural consciousness, into a region almost *beyond* consciousness and therefore beyond question, requires that it should become practically invisible. The landscape which represents the blessedness acquired through Jupiterian revolt, through hard, unremitting work—through *culture* in the fullest sense—has to change in some way its "nature." Its origins in political revolt require concealment; its dependence on hard, unremitting labor requires it as well. So various things happen: the Georgic is assimilated to the Pastoral, so that in literature and painting they are often almost indistinguishable. Think of *The Fleece*; think of *The Seasons*; think of Robert Bloomfield's *The Farmer's Boy* and imagine a painting illustrating it by Ibbetson which is as perfect a reformulation of Georgic elements—laborers, ploughs, the accoutrements of labor—into an image of Golden Age Plenty as Samuel Palmer later achieved at Shoreham.

By the mid-eighteenth century, the "aestheticization" of the Virgilian triad, its reformulation in terms of purely aesthetic categories, had taken place so that the Georgic was Beautiful and the Epic was Sublime. Burke's contribution to the process, to some extent isolated in its originality and extreme sensationism, can be taken as typical in one respect. In his thesis, the experience of the Beautiful was caused by certain objective qualities, such as smoothness or greenness, impinging on the senses: no need to ask who *made* the smoothness or the greenness; no need to ask what these qualities told of their own causation: the labor of ploughing, harrowing, seeding, and mowing was entirely transposed into its material effects, and the material effects themselves have been subsumed into what we would call abstractions. It was Burke's most intelligent reader, Uvedale Price, who completed the reformulation of the Virgilian triad by separating out the special qualities of wooded valleys, hills and streams, cows and sheep, the characteristics of the Pastoral landscape, and calling them Picturesque.

We started with the image of Ibbetson's 1801 etching, a print published in a series apparently intended to offer exemplary lessons in drawing technique. Everything about the print—its scratchy textural qualities as an etching, the broken lights of the foreground, the portly cleric whose vicarage might doubtless be up the lane, the broken-down donkey with its staring coat, the ragged peasant, the piled-up faggots, the distant group of rough children—is formulaic Pricean Picturesque. Like the other prints in the series, it is apparently part of the enclosed, abstracted discourse of art and aesthetics. And yet, as we have seen, this is not all that it is. Undeniably and explicitly, it is something else as well—located by its inscription in contemporary politics and itself a perfectly conscious statement on the issues. We have seen also how the peremptory, immediate political realities of the situation—the threats of French invasion and the war against liberty as well as the local issues of enclosure, land improvement, woodland management, landlordism, absenteeism, clerical pluralism—must have loomed hugely in the aftermath of Wakefield's death. So much so that they served also to occlude the issue which is suddenly and startlingly brought up in the Aesopian fable, that the lot of the laborer is nonnegotiable; it is not even on the agenda of those who go to prison for opposing Pitt's war policy. So out of the Picturesque, formulated by Price (like Wakefield in correspondence with Charles James Fox) against the background of events in France and outbreaks of millenialist labor revolt at home, we thus begin to see shadows and highlighted figures that previously had been rendered invisible. Through the Picturesque, Labor returns to the landscape: the Picturesque landscape is peopled, it is as in Ibbetson's print actually made up of people, their habitations and the marks that they make over the landscape—the rutted tracks, the broken trees, the evidences of life led—in uncorrupt simplicity and without the corrupting influences of Taste or Self-Consciousness—at the level of subsistence. At this point the landscape of Labor is being transformed into the landscape of Nature: Labor, provided it is Mindless, is equated with Nature. And Nature has the capacity to assimilate all Labor, even Mindful Labor—even the Labor of False Taste—into itself and redeem it. But then Nature herself in this avatar is more than half transformed into Time and like Time—Old Chronos, to reverse the pun—she seems more and more at home in the Golden Age, a figure sitting on the granary floor in Autumn, as Palmer has her, the reaper's scythe balanced against the doorpost.

The critical literature of the Picturesque has left this moment of the subject ill-served. It is difficult to see even in Ann Bermingham's brilliant account of the Picturesque a sense of it as an intersection of interests that we otherwise recognize in Augustanism, in Tory neo-feudalism, in Ruskinian and Morrisite laborism.[14] The Picturesque was constituted at the point of the ruling class's response to an apparently genuine popular insurrection. It represented the adaptation of that class's view of its physical landed environment to what were seen as new pressures. It produced new icons for the common edification, but almost at once, within the first decade of the nineteenth century, the terminology of the Picturesque was seen as feebly inadequate. So the hunt was on for an authentically grand manner of address, something that would mediate the insights of the Picturesque without its preciosity, that would be patriotically of the nation and would connect it unmistakably to the classical tradition. This, I think, was the brief that Turner and Constable took on as they passed through their early manhood in the Picturesque years of the 1790s.

NOTES

1. *Etchings, by the late Julius Caesar Ibbetson, consisting of groups of cattle, in six plates, and groups of rustic figures, in eight plates* (London: Harvey and Darton, 1817).

2. I am indebted to Dr. Robert Woof for the quotation.

3. *Dictionary of National Biography*, ed. Leslie Stephen and Sidney Lee (London, 1908), 20:452–5.

4. To William Roscoe, August 4, 1796; quoted again from Robert Woof.

5. Anthony Low, *The Georgic Revolution* (Princeton, 1985). This brilliant book has influenced heavily what I have written here.

6. John Dryden, *The Works of Virgil: Containing his Pastorals, Georgics and Aeneis. Translated into English Verse* (London, 1697), ll. 239–40, quoted from *The Poems of John Dryden*, ed. James Kinsley (Oxford, 1958), II, 924, 239–240. All references to both the *Georgics* and *Eclogues* are from this edition.

7. Low, *Georgic Revolution*, pp. 8–9.

8. Arcadia: "A country in the centre of the Peloponnesus, bounded on the north by Achaia, on the west by Elis, on the east by Argolis, and on the south by Laconia and Messinia. It was very mountainous, though at the same time diversified with fruitful valleys and well-watered by an abundance of streams. The Arcadians were for the most part Shepherds . . ." (J. Lemprière, *Bibliotheca Classica* . . . , [Reading, 1788]).

9. "Ego" in this famous phrase is death: death in the afternoon, death in the midst of happiness, death which comes and justifies the anxious certainty that happiness presages death. This anxiety and fear of mutability is present in the pastoral tradition at least from the Theocritan laments over the death of Daphnis and is shockingly realized in the image of the skull—"Et in Arcadia Ego"—in Guercino's pastoral of c. 1621–23 (Rome, Galleria Corsini). The tomb in Poussin's more famous image c. 1630–35 (Paris, Louvre) is similarly a *memento mori*, and the motto, traced out by the innocent finger of the shepherd, refers also primarily to death. But the image opens the way to the profounder interpretation, that of self-alienation from innocence and bliss, and it is this which has become, romantically, the predominant understanding of the subject. See Erwin Panofsky, "Et in Arcadia Ego," in *Philosophy and History: Essays Presented to Ernst Cassirer* (Oxford, 1936).

10. Quoted from Low, *Georgic Revolution*, p. 12.

11. J. W. Johnson, "The Meaning of 'Augustan,'" *Journal of the History of Ideas* 19 (1958), 507–22.

12. This is intended to make a small point of difference from John Barrell in *The Dark Side of Landscape* (Cambridge, 1980), a book which made it possible to discuss the presence—or the absence—of human figures in landscape painting. Before Barrell, figures were discussed by art historians as staffage, well or ill drawn. It has always seemed to me that art historians reacted initially against the labor-history of landscape because they had never been taught about the Georgic tradition, and it was their habit to use the term Pastoral with little consciousness of its stricter application. These terms are, of course, familiar to literary historians.

13. Quoted from Low, *Georgic Revolution*, p. 120.

14. Ann Bermingham, *Landscape and Ideology* (London, 1987).

III

American Counterpoints

American Counterpoints

Romantic literature is famous, or infamous, for its historically unprecedented emphasis on nationality, and this third group of essays, though focused on a single tradition, raises the troubling question of cultural boundaries. What is distinctive about *American* Romanticism? And since the question itself is a Romantic legacy, why should such a radically subjective movement, with its myth of the autonomous self, have been drawn toward the contingent, if not constrictive idea of a national literature?

From our present perspective, the attractions of nationalism as a poetic vehicle are apt to seem less evident than its dangers, but with the exhaustion of sectarianism and religious passion as symbols of group identity in the eighteenth century, emergent nationalities provided a ready theater for the casting of dominant and submissive (or rebellious) roles, and so for the dramatization of such perennial oppositions as old and new, strong and weak, static and mobile. No doubt, specific postures were further influenced by the traditional images of a *representative* heroism and of a *body* politic: Virgilian in France, Virgilian and biblical in England, more singularly biblical in the covenantal and prophetic ideologies of America.

The question of distinctive differences is a matter less for historical than for literary reflection. In American Romanticism, collective identity becomes what Blake would have called an emanation, the embodiment of an imaginative vision, which in its repudiation of all actual forms acquires a limitless potential virtue. The notion of an American literature is thus as resistant to definition as the notion of a sacred literature. One can at best define what it is not, and this negative logic extends to those attributes or expressions of the American genius treated here: Nature and its immanent counterpart or "younger brother" Democracy, whose "history," as Whitman writes, "[always] remains unwritten." The idea is resumed in the "terrible query" that stands as the title to one of Whitman's last essays: "American National Literature: Is there any such thing—or can there ever be?" The issue for Whitman is no longer the slavish dependence on English models, nor the lack of public interest in the arts. He is not suggesting that great literature will never be written by Americans (he considered *Leaves of Grass* a modern supplement to the Bible), nor that national differences are necessarily fatuous (he delighted in elaborating lists of American characteristics), but rather that the idea of America itself is essentially mythic and elusive.

The stories devised to explain the particularity of the "American" by recent critics (from Matthiessen and Winters, through Bloom, Poirier, and Bercovitch, to Weisbuch and Pease, among others) share a common repertoire of mythic figures. They tend to play on James's trope of "privation," or on Emerson's trope of "transition" and its pragmatist variants, or on the old Puritan trope of corporate teleology. None of the following essays offers a global replacement, but all assume the burden of alterity or *ex*centricity inherited from the nineteenth century. As a result, their concerns stand subtly apart from the issues and categories proposed in the general introduction, making them representative of those "American Counterpoints" that are their subject. The best writing on American literature, like the best of American literature in general, has been unusually chary of critical ideologies, of movements and schools. Its claim (one might say its enabling fiction) is rather its radical independence, its freedom from social determinations— though certainly not from ethical dilemmas or social responsibilities.

This is evident immediately in David Bromwich's essay, which addresses the comparative issue directly, transcending the isolationism still common in American Studies while recalling the classic title of its leading exponent, Perry Miller's "From Edwards to Emerson." Bromwich evaluates the cost of self-trust in Wordsworth's "Intimations Ode" by reading it twice, once on its own and again as reflected in Emerson's essay "Self-Reliance." Locating the debate in the ode between imaginative power and social obligation, between autonomous intuition and the claims of common sympathy, he shows how similar constraints are repudiated by

Emerson, whose enlarged notion of character includes social identity as one of its aspects, an expression of that alienation by which the self recognizes its own genius. Emerson's relative insulation from social guilt coincides with an antipathy toward memory and repetition, shared by most of the writers of the misnamed American Renaissance. Bromwich suggests that it is the retrospective ethos of Wordsworth, for whom imaginative power is associated with recollection, that prepares the way for the opposing movements of natural piety and social consciousness against which imagination must continually struggle. By contrast, Emerson's notion of the self as unrecuperable because never yet realized obviates the need for expiation and allows a greater independence from usage, voluntary thoughts, and consistency itself—as from the regret that gives to Wordsworth's poetry its superior pathos.

Although the prestige of Emerson as an imaginative writer has kept pace with the revaluation of Romanticism in general and is now no longer contested, his insistence on genius and the "all-sufficiency of private Character" carries socially aversive or elitist overtones—more salient when one hears their echo in the writings of Nietzsche—which are apt to seem unpalatable from the perspective of ethical or political philosophy. This is the main focus of the essay by Stanley Cavell, who, in dialogue with John Rawls's influential critique of the doctrine of moral perfectionism, attempts to preserve a place for Emersonian self-reliance within the ethical tradition of American democracy. The problem faced by Emerson is in a sense his own invention, strikingly at odds, for example, with Franklin's "bold and arduous project of arriving at moral perfection." Where democracy and genius to Franklin were still natural allies, in league against the constraints of caste, Emerson, more troubled by the feints of equality, had urgently to proclaim his view of the American scholar as a kind of gospel, opposed both to experience and to his own darker intuition that the grounds of commonality are in weakness, moral debility, and subjection to fate. Approaching self-reliance as a compensation for guilt rather than a denial or evasion of responsibility, Cavell advances a paradoxical claim for perfectionism as a "training for democracy," which he understands now to mean a training against the trials of disillusionment. Like John Jay Chapman, who ambiguously identified Emerson's work with the cry of a man "crushed by democracy," Cavell reads the call to self-reliance as a projection of our own predicament, thus making of Emerson one of our own rejected thoughts and illustrating the definition of thinking as vocation with which his essay opens.

The arrogance and obduracy latent in moral perfectionism are counterbalanced in Emerson by a paradoxical emphasis on poverty, the "iron band" that both provides the basis for genuine community and, as a figure for imaginative need, "makes in morals the capital virtue of self-trust." But Emerson's "bleak rocks" are a place as well as a state of mind, as Barbara Packer shows in the third essay. Packer's subject is the representation of the American landscape, and in particular the celebration of absence or wildness as a sign of originality. The burden of self-definition faced by American writers and artists in the early part of the nineteenth century set a premium on originality and helped generate the characteristic confusion, so productive for subsequent generations, between the authentic and the primordial. For American writers like Emerson, deprived of the old-world genii loci, "the Eden of God is bare and grand." Their attraction for the "bare common" begins already with Anne Bradstreet and extends forward to the winter meditations of Stevens, the primal landscapes of London, Jeffers, and Faulkner, and the strength-in-desolation annals of Mary Austin and Rachel Carson, for whom nature is the site of a radical ascesis. Packer concentrates on the generation of poets and painters immediately preceding Emerson, giving us in particular a new appreciation of William Cullen Bryant, whose early vision of an American Adam confronting the unnamed vastness is followed to its fulfillment in the deserted Eden poems of Robert Frost.

Frost's example, whether one takes him as developing or deflecting Romantic conventions, suggests that American Romanticism extends beyond the usual chronological divisions. John Irwin's essay on Hart Crane and the figuration of origins in *The Bridge* advances this claim explicitly. In Crane's fragmented epic, the internalized quest characteristic of Romantic poetry is re-externalized, projected out onto the physical body of America, and the nation, remade in the poet's own image, assumes the place of the inaccessible object. The austerity of a landscape purged of the human—the tradition described in Packer's essay—thus becomes the grounds for an extravagant animation and eroticization of the very map of America. In important ways, Crane's basic strategy is analogous to that of Whitman, whose song of the self was already a song of the nation, but the overwhelmingly primitive animations of Crane, for whom the virgin continent takes the archetypal form of the three-fold goddess—mother, lover, and destroyer—are more graphic. Irwin charts the deep history of these identifications, analyzing the corpse which lies buried in "Indiana," the heart of the map and one of the hitherto undervalued centers of the epic. Focusing on the changes Crane made in the original conception of the poem, he traces the psychological pressures that transformed a potentially nostalgic elegy for a lost past into a more paradoxical prophecy of rupture and effacement, of migrations that "void memory" rather than bind it to a time or a place.

"There is no history; only biography" was Emerson's maxim, and Irwin's essay, which appeals to psychoanalytical insights to illumine the "juxtaposition of personal and national history in *The Bridge*," might thus be seen as an Emersonian response to the inquisitorial perspicuities of the New Historicists in the preceding section. Indeed, all four of the present essays share with the tradition they interpret a certain defiance not of history but of historical deductions, a preference for possibility at the expense of definition. This emerges in their treatment of the "American," and also in their approach to the literary in general, their tendency to locate meaning in the unassimilable juncture between author and text, or in the spaces between one text and another. Thus, all contribute substantially to what a generation ago would have passed as source criticism—elucidating with new precision the influence of Wordsworth on Emerson, of Emerson on Nietzsche, of Bryant on Frost, and of Crane's family life on his poetry—yet they wear their critical discoveries casually, relegating them to the margins of more speculative engagements. To approach criticism as itself a kind of romance or quest, in which all knowledge is by definition provisional and tentative, is to achieve yet another transformation of Emerson's optative mode. Perhaps this explains why appreciation rather than subversion or demystification is so prominent in these essays, which, as "aversive" conversations, turn away from the specious battles for truth.

H.M.

From Wordsworth to Emerson

DAVID BROMWICH

My title says a little more than it means. I will not really
be telling how to get from Wordsworth to Emerson, or describing
the forces that intervened to create some sort of continuity between them. Instead, I want to point to something in Wordsworth
and something in Emerson, and to show by description why they
belong together. I have in mind a thought which impresses both
writers with its difficulty—a thought which resists the intelligence
but which both choose to treat as a communicable truth. It has
to do with the soul and the complex ideas by which the soul may
be defended. Words like *hope* and *trust* sometimes give a name
to such ideas, and I will be alluding to other names presently. Let
me now suggest only the general grounds of argument. Emerson
was as happy to declare, as Wordsworth was reluctant to admit,
the thought they shared about self-trust, or our ability to "keep
/Heights which the soul is competent to gain." In elaborating this
contrast between them, I mean to offer an illustrative anecdote
concerning the growth, in the nineteenth century, of an individualism which was noncontractual and nonpossessive.

There has been a debate about the Immortality Ode among
modern critics of Wordsworth in which most readers feel they
have to take a side. In the terms given by that debate, the poem
is about growing old, or about growing up. Either way, it has a
motive related to the poet's sense that he stands at a transition between two kinds of activity. These belong, first, to the imagination,

which alone suffices for the creation of poems; and, second, to the "philosophic mind" by which a poet may be accommodated to the proper sympathies of human life. Wordsworth's position on the good of such sympathies is ambiguous. Because they come from unchosen attachments, they can seem to compel us like the force of custom, "Heavy as frost, and deep almost as life." On the other hand, the acts (including acts of love) that we perform from sympathy are just such as we might have performed freely had our minds been unconstrained by an habitual self-regard. In this way the philosophic mind appears to be allied with the poet's imagination after all.

The puzzle remains why Wordsworth should have been so equivocal—compared to other writers of his time—about the sympathies he might expect to share with his readers. He says in the Preface to *Lyrical Ballads* that the poet must give pleasure and that, "Except this one restriction, there is no object standing between the Poet and the image of things."[1] It is odd to think of pleasure, in a sense that allies it with communication, as *limiting* the poet's own sight of the image of things. Maybe the suggestion that the reader's pleasure can hold back the poet's seeing goes some way to explain Wordsworth's uncertainty about how far common sympathies may hinder imagination.

Of course in the debate I mentioned, questions like these are referred to the antithesis between childhood (which is linked with poetic powers) and the philosophic mind (which is linked with "the soothing thoughts that spring / Out of human suffering"). But I do not want to guess at Wordsworth's supposed feelings about his own fate as a poet because I do not think the motive of the poem can be found anywhere in this area. The motive is not Wordsworth's failure or success in cheering himself up but rather a feeling close to guilt. It is a guilt, however, respecting what might as well have been a source of pride: namely, the poet's knowledge that there are certain thoughts all his own, which he, having lived his life and felt the sentiments associated with it, can understand and cherish as no one else can do. What Wordsworth would like to say in this poem is something Emerson does say in "Self-Reliance": "Absolve you to yourself, and you shall have the suffrage of the world."[2] But the ideas of obligation in which Wordsworth believed made him reject that as an impossible gesture. What the ode ends up saying is something more like, "Absolve you to the world, and you shall have the suffrage of yourself." The world, however, believes in the suffrage of no power but itself, and it cannot ever wholly absolve him.

From Burke and other moralists, Wordsworth inherited an idea of morality as formed by common interests and tending to subordinate the individual to the community. On this view personal liberty and social order stand in an uneasy tension with each other. The choices of conscience are not beyond challenge, and they are hard to generalize from, being themselves only the internalization of worldly reason and prejudice. It is by coming to know the passions, affections, and sentiments we share with others that we recognize our relationship of mutual attachment to others in a society; by such attachment, in turn, that we are able to see the good of the duties we impose on ourselves as obligations; and by this whole picturing of our selves within the scene of other people's thoughts, feelings, and condition of life that we start to be moral beings and so are humanized. From the beginning of his career, Wordsworth talked in this way about morality; and against this background in another ode, he defined a personal imperative of duty. But in one respect the morality I have described—antirationalist, and noncontractual, though it was—spoke in a language that was not his. It seemed to allow no reckoning with the thoughts that made his imagination unlike anyone else's.

For the thoughts that define one's personal character always have to come, says Wordsworth, from an aspect of oneself (a faculty, perhaps) that relates to another aspect of oneself (an instinct, perhaps). These thoughts come to light through the imagination's action upon a deposit so elusive that to catch the sense of it Wordsworth mixes metaphors and calls it a *spot* of *time*. The thoughts in question, that is to say, are discovered by a thinking and writing later self, in a search across moments from an earlier life that can now be looked on as a scene of indefinite striving or possibility. It is for this reason that throughout *The Prelude* Wordsworth describes childhood, in the personal sphere, with the same figures of speech he reserves for the French Revolution in the political sphere. I think Hazlitt was right therefore when he assumed that the phrase, "What though the radiance which was once so bright / Be now for ever taken from my sight," referred at once to youth itself and to the youth of the revolution. But, if that is so, one may conclude that the observance of homecoming in this poem has likewise a double reference. Wordsworth is turning back from the French Enlightenment morality of nature to the still-abiding English morality of sentiments and affections; and, at the same time, from the liberty of an unchartered life to the necessary constraints of a community. Certainly the poem has a good deal of the pathos one associates with an ambivalent return: "We will grieve not, rather find / Strength in what remains behind."

But that only alters the question a little. To whom, or what, does Wordsworth feel answerable for the rightness of his return? Or again (though it is much the same question), to what causes does he lay the unhappiness of his departure? These difficulties the ode does not solve; nor can it, given the nature of the man who wrote it. For Wordsworth's former self-betrayal, like his present self-expiation, is twofold. By wandering to a site of radical enlightenment and reformation, he had turned against England, the place that nursed him, the home (in the largest sense) of all the childhood rovings that first gave him an idea of freedom. And yet by giving up France and its radiance now, and taking on himself the bonds of a native life, he surrenders the very freedom that has been for him a condition of self-knowledge, and that has made him conscious of his separable membership in a community. The last lines of the ode emerge in so unbroken a cadence that one can fail to notice how strangely they recur to the note of ambivalence.

> Thanks to the human heart by which we live,
> Thanks to its tenderness, its joys, and fears,
> To me the meanest flower that blows can give
> Thoughts that do often lie too deep for tears.

We live by the human heart; but the thoughts come to *me*. The shared joys and fears of this conclusion recall the wedding, the funeral, and other ceremonial occasions that have appeared rather grimly in the more conventional part of the poem. Amid all this grand evocation of public observances is one who stands alone aware of thoughts the meanest flower can give; just as, earlier in the poem, with children culling flowers on every side, only the child Wordsworth could feel "The Pansy at my feet / Doth the same tale repeat."

Plainly something in the poem, including one part of Wordsworth, wants us to be able to say that these solitary thoughts are the same as those "soothing thoughts that spring / Out of human suffering." In that case they would truly belong to Wordsworth's new and comparatively selfless existence. But the poem only half conceals an allusion to the fact that his thoughts are of a different kind. They can often be, it says, "too deep for tears," which means that they come with no affections of the usual sort. So a principle of self, and even of self-reliance, has tacitly been declared at the end of a poem that aimed from the first at an other-regarding dedication of the poet's imaginings. The result must appear difficult, almost opaque, if placed beside the poem's moral directives elsewhere. A person gazing earnestly at the meanest flower will look anomalous compared to someone contemplating a picturesque landscape of fountains, meadows, hills, and groves. But for Wordsworth it is enough to know that his choice is intelligible to him. I take the end of the ode to suggest that any venture of Wordsworth's life, however it affects the community he lives in, will be justified only in the light of a personal principle from which finally there is no appeal—not even to responses like tears, which others can be imagined to share. Leigh Hunt thought that tears were "the tributes, more or less worthy, of self-pity to self-love. Whenever we shed tears, we take pity on ourselves; and we feel . . . that we deserve to have the pity taken."[3] I think this helps in reading the last line of the ode. Wordsworth's conviction about his own thoughts has deepened beyond the want even of an appeal to *self*-sympathy. He no longer expects others to pass in sad review the events of his life (as if those events added up to a tale worthy of their pity). And he tells us that he himself is unable to see his life in this way.

I have concentrated thus far on the end of the ode both because it is decisive and because it is memorable. But, in looking back on the poem, one may come to feel that its frequent turnings, the very traits that make it an ode, were the result of an effort to control and render outstanding what is always inward in the poet's thoughts. I can give two examples of this, the first structural and general, the second figural and particular. The poem, we know, was written in two parts, the first four sections at one time and then the last seven; and it does feel as if it had been written that way. The whole first part is imagined by Wordsworth with a persistent intensity of grief for himself: it is "I," writing about me and the things that are mine. "Two years at least," according to the Fenwick Note, elapsed between the last line of the fourth section ("Where is it now, the glory and the dream?") and the first line of the fifth ("Our birth is but a sleep and a forgetting"), and if we ask what has come into the poem in that time, the answer is the "we" that steals upon us quietly and that dominates the rest of the ode.

This is, if I may put it so, the first Arnoldian consolation in English poetry. It works its way by various ruses in the next several sections: first Wordsworth tries out the myth of preexistence, then he supposes the child a foster-child nursed by mother earth (so he has already lost something; there never was a time when he had not lost it); then, in a curious and unassimilable satirical bit, he dandles and pokes the child some more, and pushes him back among his proper companions, regarding him now as a conscious, imitative being ("A six years' Darling of pigmy size!"). In this perspective the address to the child as "Mighty Prophet! Seer blest!" which strikes many readers as hyperbolic, may have seemed to Wordsworth a compensation for the liberty he took with the child in the preceding sections.

So much for the structural effort of control—the movement from I to We, from an inward and incommunicable subject to an outward and common one—and Wordsworth's feeling that this is both a necessary passage and a focus of new anxieties. For the figural representation of that effort, I turn to the ninth section, in which, as I read it, nothing at last is controlled. The hope that nature, being the source of a shared sentiment, will therefore be translatable to other people, seems here as precarious as ever. Wordsworth has spoken of "Delight and liberty, the simple creed / Of Childhood," but now he adds:

> Not for these I raise
> The song of thanks and praise;
> But for those obstinate questionings

Of sense and outward things,
Fallings from us, vanishings;
Blank misgivings of a Creature
Moving about in worlds not realised,
High instincts before which our mortal Nature
Did tremble like a guilty Thing surprised:
But for those first affections,
Those shadowy recollections,
Which, be they what they may,
Are yet the fountain light of all our day,
Are yet a master light of all our seeing;
Uphold us, cherish, and have power to make
Our noisy years seem moments in the being
Of the eternal Silence....

Note that, in this analysis of thought, Wordsworth gives three distinct moments, with corresponding kinds of moral agency, which seem to stand for three different phases of consciousness. In the creed of childhood liberty, the child possesses himself without knowing that he does. Grown up and joined to our mortal nature, he will be unable to imagine such freedom except in grown-up terms, as a prompter of fear and guilt. But Wordsworth is interested in neither of these moments, neither of the extremes. He chooses rather to celebrate the child-consciousness at the moment of farewell, when the boy is just starting to know the "blank misgivings" (blank, because why should he feel them?) that signify his passage into the moral life of society. His instincts even at this moment are high, for he is sure, without having to be conscious, of his difference from other people and the rightness of that difference.

Yet the common moral life deals not so much with high instincts as with middling hopes and fears and prudential arrangements, and, once committed to these, the child will participate in our mortal nature. He is, however, thereby diminished only with respect to his own instincts, which he has disappointed. What is cryptic about the whole passage is that it speaks as if the loss related mostly to perception; the "fallings from us, vanishings" are fallings and vanishings from sight; and we know (among other sources, again, from the Fenwick Note) that perception formed a large part of Wordsworth's thinking about the idealisms of childhood. However, on the interpretation I have sketched, the great lines of the ninth section were not written by a man reflecting on the character of his perceptions. In all of these metaphors, the tenor belongs to morality and not metaphysics—but morality in the reverse of Wordsworth's usual self-distrustful sense. The child himself was a principle all his own before he could ever reflect on the fact; but his individual character, his soul, becomes definite to him only as he begins to see it passing; and he sees that happen vividly whenever he is imposed on by other people's claims.

Such, then, is the moment Wordsworth selects for thanks and praise: the moment when, having fallen part way from our selves, we discover that we exist, and look for certain traces of past seeing to uphold and cherish. But that is not quite right either. By resorting to normal ideas of cause, effect, and agency to explain Wordsworth's conception, I have distorted it. According to the grammar of the lines, we do not uphold and cherish anything; rather, it is those recollections, instincts, misgivings, in their very falling from us, that uphold and cherish *us*: they compose whatever we are; and we are nothing else, even if the consequent sense of ourselves has come from nothing but impressions caught in flight. Wordsworth's practice of self-recovery does not reach beyond this fact which resists all further discussion. The knowledge we have of our own identity is the representation, by a conscious self, of something fugitive in the life of a creature not yet individuated, with whom we share some memories and a name.

Emerson read the ode early and pondered it often, and was, in fact, among the first to have called it an Ode on Immortality. I want to begin this inquiry into his relationship to the poem by asking what he meant by a difficult sentence in the first paragraph of "Self-Reliance": "In every work of genius we recognize our own rejected thoughts; they come back to us with a certain alienated majesty." What kind of thoughts did Emerson mean? One feels that he was trying to describe, and trying not to illustrate, a scene of the uncanny return of something repressed in ourselves—just the kind of scene Wordsworth did commonly illustrate, as in the boat-stealing episode of *The Prelude*. I do not tell myself (Emerson would thus be saying), till I discover it unbidden in some external thing, how thoroughly a principle of self-trust governed even the things I could care for. That principle has made the world over, in keeping with my character and moods; so that I suppose for me to respond to them, they must always have been mine.

In the light of this clue I think it is worth recalling the history of the composition of "Self-Reliance." Emerson occasionally mentions Wordsworth in his lectures of the 1830s, though some of his praise is rather equivocal.[4] Then in January 1839 at the Masonic Temple in Boston, he delivers a lecture on genius, with a draft of some remarks he will work in to "Self-Reliance":

> To believe your own thought,—that is genius. . . . In every work of genius, you recognize your own rejected thoughts. Here as in science the true chemist collects what every body else throws away. Our own thoughts come back to us in unexpected majesty. We are admonished to hold fast our trust in instincts another time. What self-reliance is shown in every poetic description! Trifles so simple and fugitive that no man remembers the poet seizes and by force of them hurls you instantly into the presence of his joys.[5]

Fugitive and *instincts* have come back to him from the ode. And a little further on, he generalizes: "The reason of this trust is indeed very deep for the soul is sight, and all facts are hers; facts are her words with which she speaketh her sense and well she knoweth what facts speak to the imagination and the soul."[6] However, between the two passages above Emerson needed to quote some poetry; he chose the lines about skating that later went into *The Prelude*, beginning "So through the darkness and the cold we flew," and ending "Till all was tranquil as a summer sea." It is one of the earliest quotations I know by any critic of materials from Wordsworth's autobiographical poem; though the passage was available to others where Emerson found it, in the four-volume edition published in Boston in 1824.

He quoted well from a new source, but he was thinking about the ode, of which "Self-Reliance" gives an original reading. If for us now, his individualism is generally accounted more radical than Wordsworth's, that is because he made himself be the sort of reader Wordsworth could not afford to be. Across the divide of those vanishings, and writing wholly from the side of our mortal nature, Wordsworth had come to have too many misgivings. The particular use of Emerson therefore, for someone interested in English Romanticism, is that he recovers a revolutionary idea of Wordsworth's aims. But, as in Wordsworth after 1797 or so, it is a revolution without a social medium in which to operate. The beautiful sublimation that Wordsworth had performed, by speaking of the French Revolution in a parable about childhood, Emerson continues by speaking of American democracy in a parable about the self. And on a single point of terminology, the two authors do converge. The individual power which they aim to preserve they call neither the child nor the self but the soul.

Yet in the sentence of "Self-Reliance" that I began with, much of Emerson's thought turns on his use of a rarer word, "alienated." It can have a religious sense of course, and maybe that is the primary one here: having alienated myself from the god who is my self, I find that my face is turned toward him again in every meaningful look I give or receive. But there is also a social sense of the word (the alienation of property) which stays near the surface with almost the force of a pun. I have alienated myself from my own estate; but wherever I cast my eye I find it still before me. That would be sufficiently Wordsworthian; and it fits in with the following sentence from "Self-Reliance," about the power we can call upon if we have once been strong in the past: "That is it which throws thunder into Chatham's voice, and dignity into Washington's port, and America into Adam's eye." So the two metaphors that alienation can imply—the religious one about sight and the social one about property—are suggested together in Adam's gaze at his lands. It is important that the lands be inherited as naturally as an instinct, and not earned as the reward of labor or service. For Emerson will also want to say: "Prayer that craves a particular commodity, anything less than all good, is vicious."

I shall return later to Wordsworth's and Emerson's ideas of property. Besides, there is a connection between the Immortality Ode and "Self-Reliance" which ought to concern us more. I mean the path by which Wordsworth moves from his intimations to the glimpse of the "immortal sea which brought us hither"; by which Emerson is able to pass from the accusing philanthropists who muddle his thoughts to the conception of an aboriginal Self. Both proceed by means of an inverted genealogy. Wordsworth says, "The Child is Father of the Man." Emerson says, "Is the acorn better than the oak which is its fulness and completion? Is the parent better than the child into whom he has cast his ripened being? Whence this worship of the past?" Which is very strange, until one realizes it is playing against the Wordsworth, and even then it is not much less strange. Wordsworth's little allegory itself is grotesque if one tries to picture it rather than reason about it. But once we scale it down from allegory to mere exaggeration, it seems to say that the child is both wiser, in his closeness to the source of things, and at the same time more capable than the father, in having not yet had to acquiesce in the ways of custom and habit. Because he establishes the character the man will have to obey, the child is father to him. On the other hand—what *could* Emerson have meant? One expects the acorn will be compared to the oak as the child to the parent, but he works it the other way around, and says the oak is the child "into whom [the parent] has cast his ripened being." So the child there stands above the parent by being the realized thing that is livelier to the imagination than the potential thing. The child, in his characteristic independence, outranks the parent in his thoughtless conformity, as the fully developed entity does the inchoate or elementary.

One cannot help being struck as well by a difference in the function of the metaphors. The child, as Wordsworth sees him, can actually come before, precede, influence the man *in the continuity of a single life*, and in that sense be his own father. But there is no sense in which the child Emerson imagines (with the integral strength Emerson imputes to such a creature) will admit that the parent came before, preceded, or influenced him in any but the trivial manner in which an acorn comes before an oak. The reason Emerson can do without this admission is that he is not in fact talking about the continuity of a single life. Why look to virtuous actions, he asks, when you have before you the man who is himself the embodied virtue? Start thinking about acts and you scatter your forces. On this view the composition of a life by particular choices of conduct toward others looks like a chimerical aspiration. Even the possibility of knowing days "bound each to each by natural piety" may come to seem an invention of institutional morality which one could very well do without. I am alluding here to Wordsworth's use of the phrase *natural piety* in the epigraph to the ode: as far as I know, *The Prelude* is the first work of moral reflection in which virtue is made to depend on a conscious attempt to compose a life of such naturally linked actions.

Emerson would have found this way of thinking antipathetic, for to judge particular acts somehow implies judging them from outside; which is done by rules, or at least by conventions of judgment; which, in turn, bring to mind the kind of scrutiny that can make society "a conspiracy against the manhood" of each of its members. But there may be another clue to his reaction in the word *piety*. It shares a root with *expiation*, about which Emerson has this to say: "I do not wish to expiate, but to live. My life is for itself and not for a spectacle." To the extent that Wordsworth does regard his life as a spectacle, his thinking seems to be in line with ordinary republican sentiments about how one has to live with respect to others. One acts, that is, under a consciousness of fortune and men's eyes. By contrast, Emerson has already so far sacrificed consistency, and with it even the aim of being the hero of his own life, that he is hardly susceptible to much anxiety about the story others may make of it. Indeed the very idea of story is non-Emersonian. He says, still in "Self-Reliance," that "all history resolves itself very easily into the biography of a few stout and earnest persons," and he might as fairly have added that biography itself is only the insight of believing persons into "a great responsible Thinker and Actor working wherever a man works." We sympathize with such a man and want to imagine his life in just the degree that we find our own thoughts come back in his with a certain alienated majesty.[7]

I said earlier that Emerson, like Wordsworth, appeals from an idea of the self to an idea of the soul. Here is the passage from "Self-Reliance" in which he declares his faith:

> The magnetism which all original action exerts is explained when we inquire the reason of self-trust. Who is the Trustee? What is the aboriginal Self, on which a universal reliance may be grounded? What is the nature and power of that science-baffling star, without parallax, without calculable elements, which shoots a ray of beauty even into trivial and impure actions, if the least mark of independence appear? The inquiry leads us to that source, at once the essence of genius, of virtue, and of life, which we call Spontaneity or Instinct. We denote this primary wisdom as Intui-

tion, whilst all later teachings are tuitions. In that deep force, the last fact behind which analysis cannot go, all things find their common origin. For the sense of being which in calm hours rises, we know not how, in the soul, is not diverse from things, from space, from light, from time, from man, but one with them and proceeds obviously from the same source whence their life and being also proceed. We first share the life by which things exist and afterwards see them as appearances in nature and forget that we have shared their cause. Here is the fountain of action and of thought. Here are the lungs of that inspiration which giveth man wisdom and which cannot be denied without impiety and atheism. We lie in the lap of immense intelligence, which makes us receivers of its truth and organs of its activity. When we discern justice, when we discern truth, we do nothing of ourselves, but allow a passage to its beams. If we ask whence this comes, if we seek to pry into the soul that causes, all philosophy is at fault. Its presence or its absence is all we can affirm. Every man discriminates between the voluntary acts of his mind and his involuntary perceptions, and knows that to his involuntary perceptions a perfect faith is due. He may err in the expression of them, but he knows that these things are so, like day and night, not to be disputed. My wilful actions and acquisitions are but roving; the idlest reverie, the faintest native emotion, command my curiosity and respect. Thoughtless people contradict as readily the statement of perceptions as of opinions, or rather much more readily; for they do not distinguish between perception and notion. They fancy that I choose to see this or that thing. But perception is not whimsical, but fatal. If I see a trait, my children will see it after me, and in course of time all mankind,—although it may chance that no one has seen it before me. For my perception is as much a fact as the sun.

When Emerson writes "We lie in the lap of immense intelligence," I think he means that our nurse or foster-mother (the same one who "fills her lap with pleasures all her own") is *not* the earth. We do not belong to someone who can speak for nature and human nature, and by doing so wean us from ourselves, and make us forget the glory from which we came. Rather that intelligence is simply ourselves. So that the receding of its power from us is a tendency of life to which we need not submit. Emerson, of course, can make his claim the more plausibly because he conceives of the soul as somehow beyond the reach of our experiential self: it is "that science-baffling star, without parallax, without calculable elements . . . the last fact behind which analysis cannot go."

Seeking a clue to his intentions here, let us recall that in the paragraph quoted above, as in some other celebrated passages, Emerson speaks of the soul's force in a metaphor borrowed from electromagnetism. The soul makes a current of being, and can do so merely by having brought two things into relation, like a coil of wire with a magnet. This explains his confidence about the fatality of perception once a given character and the physical universe have been brought into contact with each other. For the power that is generated as a result may appear to be both timeless and oddly undifferentiated. True, one of Emerson's aims is to concentrate all energy in the present: it seems to be part of his larger project of disencumbering the self, and America, of a grave and incapacitating reverence for the past. But though the entire figure concerning magnetism has this form, it is intended above all as a metaphor about process, and the power in question can hardly be constant or static. We come to know it, indeed, only in moments of passage from one state to another—that is to say, in fallings from us which are also fallings toward something deeper in ourselves. As Emerson remarks a little further on, in a striking revision of the ninth section of the ode: "Life only avails, not the having lived. Power ceases in the instant of repose; it resides in the moment of transition from a past to a new state, in the shooting of the gulf, in the darting to an aim. This one fact the world hates; that the soul *becomes*. . . ."

Wordsworth had placed the moment of repose in the past, though it is a question whether he really thought it belonged there: he seems to have wanted to defend himself from the knowledge that it might still lie in the future. When, in the "Ode to Duty," he writes "I long for a repose that ever is the same," it is a longing against both imagination and freedom.

Emerson for his part believed that individual power tends to harden soon enough into just such a repose; but he wants us to believe that the opposite is always possible; and his departure from Wordsworth is connected with his own violent hatred of memory. To the conspicuous faith of the ode, that our memories leave the deposit from which our profoundest thoughts derive,

Emerson replies in "Self-Reliance": "Why should you keep your head over your shoulder? Why drag about this corpse of your memory, lest you contradict somewhat you have stated in this or that public place? Suppose you should contradict yourself; what then?" We are once again at the point where natural piety, consistency of opinion, and a respect for duties laid upon oneself as actor in the spectacle of social morality, come to seem names for the same thing. Wordsworth, however reluctantly, is responsive to their call, and Emerson is not.

Every other divergence I have noticed between Wordsworth's and Emerson's reading of the self plainly follows from their opposite prejudices about memory. But I want to close by remarking a slightly different, almost physical, correlative of the self which both writers treat allusively and which may bring out a permanent difference in the social backgrounds from which English and American Romanticism took shape. The self-trust of an individual in the writing of both Wordsworth and Emerson has something to do with the secure possession of property. Wordsworth uses a complex word for the motive by which property and the self are linked: the word is *hope*. Thus we are told of the hero of "Michael" that the news of his forfeit of lands

> for a moment took
> More hope out of his life than he supposed
> That any old man ever could have lost.

Hope, in this Wordsworthian grammar, has to be represented as a partitive substance, like land or earnings. But hope for Michael is the imaginative measure of that practical thing, property. To put it another way, a strong self like Michael finds in property the sanction of his individual way of life. The model both for the poet, who dwells in effort and expectation and desire, and the citizen who lives an exemplary life of natural piety, is the return to a given spot of earth by a Cumbrian freeholder. It was of such people that Wordsworth observed in his letter of 1801 to Charles James Fox: "Their little tract of land serves as a kind of permanent rallying point for their domestic feelings.[8]

On the face of things Emerson, notwithstanding his popular

reputation, has a much more disdainful view of property, and in "Self-Reliance" preeminently. He says near the end of the essay that "the reliance on Property, including the reliance on governments which protect it, is the want of self-reliance." (It is pertinent that he also says, "Fear and hope are beneath [the soul]. There is somewhat low even in hope.") And yet, Emerson is always close to a figurative language that keeps in view associations of property; as, for example, in the long passage above, with its rhetorical question, "Who is the Trustee?" He seems, in short, to have been interested in property as a material instance of a principle which the soul prefers to keep ideal. Though not, therefore, connected as cause and effect, secure property and self-reliance know each other as versions of autonomy, and are perhaps justly suspicious of each other's claims. But Emerson writes of a society in which this kind of sanction could be taken more for granted than in England. Little of the available land in America had yet been either claimed or enclosed. It is in fact the apparent detachment of the self from property that makes Emerson so elusive a guide to readers who expect a writer like him to be involved in the work of social criticism, whereas Wordsworth, though his politics at any time of his life are difficult to characterize, has been steadily serviceable to radical as well as reactionary communitarians.

Maybe Emerson's unsatisfactoriness here, his intention not to satisfy interests like these, marks a more general refusal of the spectacle of expiation. It may also seem to mark the point at which we have to start reading him against no writer earlier than himself. I have been arguing only that the peculiar quality of his detachment was a possible development from Wordsworth. He said of Wordsworth in *English Traits* that "alone in his time, he treated the human mind well, and with an absolute trust. The Ode on Immortality is the high-water mark which the human intellect has reached in this age. New means were employed, and new realms added to the empire of the muse, by his courage." This is conventional language but for Emerson its meaning was not conventional. The high-water mark had to be very high indeed to reach us, as far inland as we were in conformity and habitual practices. And, for Wordsworth, whose deference to the bonds of custom was great in exact proportion to his self-doubt, to show the thoughts of the soul must have seemed an even stranger undertaking than it has been for his successors, who have had his own example to invigorate them. All I have tried to explain in this essay is what Emerson rightly called Wordsworth's *courage*.

NOTES

1. "Preface to *Lyrical Ballads*," in *Selected Poems and Prefaces*, ed. Jack Stillinger (Boston, 1965), p. 454. All quotations of Wordsworth's poems are from this edition.

2. "Self-Reliance," in *Selections from Ralph Waldo Emerson*, ed. Stephen E. Whicher (Boston, 1957), p. 149. All quotations of "Self-Reliance" are from this edition.

3. Leigh Hunt, *Imagination and Fancy* (London, 1883), p. 302.

4. He more than once refers to Wordsworth's poetic talents as "feeble." I take it he meant by this to deny Wordsworth the power of a rich inventiveness while granting him a power much stranger and less parochially literary.

5. *The Early Lectures of Ralph Waldo Emerson*, ed. Robert E. Spiller and Wallace E. Williams (Cambridge, Mass., 1972), 3:77. The overt echoes of the ode in "Self-Reliance," of which I have little to say here, may be useful to list for the reader who hoped for a different kind of commentary. They seem to me these: "[A boy] cumbers himself never about consequences, about interests.... But the man is as it were clapped into jail by his consciousness." "[Man] dares not say 'I think', 'I am', but quotes some saint or sage. He is ashamed before the blade of grass or the blowing rose."

6. Ibid., 3:78.

7. Carlyle wanted the majesty to return, unalienated, in the life of a hero, who would make a great figure for a race, and not merely for individual readers. The choice has broad consequences for his thinking about history. It cannot be for him (what Emerson says it is) "an impertinence and an injury if it be any thing more than a cheerful apologue or parable of my being and becoming." The Carlyle parable is gloomy because it always belongs to a whole people, over the heads of the individuals who recall it.

8. *Early Letters of William and Dorothy Wordsworth* (1787–1805), ed. Ernest De Selincourt (Oxford, 1935), p. 262.

Emerson's Aversive Thinking

STANLEY CAVELL

In recommending Emerson, despite all, to the closer attention of the American philosophical community, I hope I may be
trusted to recognize how impertinent his teachings, in style and
in material, may sound to philosophical ears—including, from
time to time, my own. But what else should one expect? My recommendation is bound to be based—unless it is to multiply
impertinence—on something as yet unfamiliar in Emerson, as if
I am claiming him to remain a stranger. In that case to soften his
strangeness would be pointless—which is no excuse, I do realize,
for hardening it. About my own sound it may help to say that while
I may often leave ideas in what seems a more literary state, sometimes in a more psychoanalytic state, than a philosopher might
wish—that is, a philosopher might prefer a further philosophical
derivation of the ideas—I mean to leave everything as in a sense
provisional, the sense that it is to be gone on from. If to a further
derivation in philosophical form, so much the better, but, I would
not lose the intuitions in the meantime—among them the intuition that philosophy should sometimes distrust its defenses of philosophical form.

It is common knowledge that Emerson's "The American
Scholar" is a call for Man Thinking, something Emerson contrasts
with thinking in "the divided or social state," thinking, let us say,
as a specialty. I do not know of any commentary on this text that
finds Emerson to be thinking about the idea of thinking. Uniformly,

rather, it seems that he and his readers understand well enough what he is calling for, that it is something like thinking with the whole man. I suppose this can be taken so because there has been, since Emerson's time, or the time he speaks for, a widespread dissatisfaction with thinking as represented in Western philosophy since the Enlightenment, a dissatisfaction vaguely and often impatiently associated, I believe, with an idea of Romanticism. Emerson is, in his way, locating himself within this struggle when he calls on American thinkers to rely on and to cheer themselves: "For this self-trust, the reason is deeper than can be fathomed—darker than can be enlightened" (75).[1] As if he anticipates that a reader might suppose him accordingly to be opposed to the Enlightenment, he also says, "I ask not for the great, the remote, the romantic; . . . I embrace the common, I sit at the feet of the familiar, the low," a claim I have taken as underwriting ordinary language philosophy's devotion to the ordinary, surely one inheritance of the Enlightenment.

Existentialism—in the years in which it seemed that every mode of thinking antagonistic to analytical philosophy was called Existentialism—was famous for some such dissatisfaction with philosophical reason, expressed for example by Karl Jaspers in his book on Nietzsche originally published in 1935:

> That the source of philosophical knowledge is not to be found in thinking about mere objects or in investigating mere facts but rather in *the unity* of *thought and life*, so that thinking grows out of the provocation and agitation of the whole man—all this constitutes for Nietzsche's self-consciousness the real character of his truth: "I have always composed my writings with my whole body and life"; "All truths are bloody truths to me."[2]

"Cut these sentences and they bleed." Philosophy, as institutionalized in the English-speaking world, has not much felt attacked by or not vulnerable to such criticism—partly because the style and animus of the criticism is so foreign as to suggest simply other subjects and partly, and sufficiently, because since Frege and the early Russell, analytical philosophy can see what thinking is or should be, namely, reasoning.

In taking on Emerson's view of thinking I am not advocating his view over or characterizing it against a view more familiar to us (such as a view of reason as rationality), but, rather, I am calling attention to an attitude toward or investment in words that Emerson's view seems to depend on, an attitude allegorical of an attitude or investment in our lives that I believe those trained in professional philosophy are trained to disapprove of. The disapproval of the attitude interests me as much as the attitude itself. If we were asked whether our philosophizing demands of us anything we would think of as a style of writing, our answer would waver, perhaps because our motivation in writing is less to defend a style than to repress style, or allow it in ornamental doses. In speaking of disapproval, accordingly, I am not raising a question of taste, of something merely not for us, but a question of intellectual seriousness and illicitness. However glad we may be to think of ourselves as intellectually fastidious, I do not suppose we relish the idea of ourselves as intellectual police.

I should perhaps confess that an ulterior stake of mine in speaking of Emerson's attitude to words is that—to begin specifying a suggestion already made—I find J. L. Austin and the later Wittgenstein to participate in an aspect of the attitude, that which places an investment in the words of a natural language that can seem antithetical to sensible philosophizing. Half a lifetime ago I began writing philosophy by defending J. L. Austin's practice with ordinary language against criticisms of it articulated by Benson Mates.[3] I did not answer Mates's criticisms because I could not account for that investment in the ordinary. I still cannot. This failure pairs with my inability to answer Barry Stroud's question twenty years later about whether my *Claim of Reason* amounted to a claim to find a general solution to skepticism.[4] I wanted to answer by saying that by the end of the first two parts of that book I had convinced myself not only that there is no such solution, that to think otherwise is skepticism's own self-interpretation, but also that it was work for an ambitious philosophy to attempt to keep philosophy open to the threat or temptation to skepticism. This left me what I named as Nowhere, and it led me, in the fourth part of my book, to particular regions usually associated with literature—especially to aspects of Shakespearean and certain Romantic texts—in which I seemed to find comic and tragic and lyric obsessions with the ordinary that were the equivalent of something (not everything) philosophy knows as skepticism. Emerson became increasingly prominent an inhabitant of these regions. His investment in the ordinary is so constant and so explicit that, perhaps because of the very strangeness and extravagance of his manner, it may indicate afresh why a philosopher might spend a reasonable lifetime looking for an account of it.

The first half of this essay takes its bearing from pertinences Emerson's "American Scholar" address bears to Heidegger's sequence of lectures translated as *What Is Called Thinking?* (all citations of Heidegger are from this text); the second half sketches an implied moral outlook in Emerson that helps account for a philosophical disapproval of his work. The outlook is a kind of Moral Perfectionism for which Emerson's writing is definitive and with respect to which it is a dominating influence on, among others, Nietzsche. Moral Perfectionism has for various reasons found no home in modern moral philosophizing, and this is tied up with the fact that Emerson has found no home in modern philosophizing.

The guiding thought directing me to Emerson's way of thinking is his outcry in the sixth paragraph of "Self-Reliance": "Self-reliance is [the] aversion [of conformity]," by which I take him to mean both that he is averse to society's demand for conformity, specifically that his writing expresses his self-reliance (his self-consciousness, his thinking) as aversive to society's incessant demands for his consent—his conforming himself—to its doings and that his writing must accordingly be the object of aversion to society's consciousness, to what it might read in him. When in a comparable outcry a few paragraphs later Emerson writes, "Every word they say chagrins us," he is not, as the context might imply, expressing merely his general disappointment at some failure in the capacity of language to represent the world, but expressing at the same time his response to a general attitude toward words that is causing his all but complete sense of intellectual isolation.

The isolation is enacted in "The American Scholar," whose occasion is enviably if not frighteningly distinctive. Whomever Emerson invokes as the class of scholars that Commencement Day at Harvard the summer of 1837—his audience, himself (whether as poets, preachers, or philosophers)—the principal fact about the class is that it is empty, the American Scholar does not exist. Then who is Emerson? Suppose we say that what motivates Emerson's thinking, or what causes this call for the American scholar, is Emerson's vision of our not yet thinking. Is this fact of American history—that we are, still find ourselves, looking for the commencement of our own culture—worth setting beside the intricate formulation whose recurrences generate Heidegger's *What Is Called Thinking?*: "Most thought-provoking in our thought-provoking time is that we are still not thinking." It probably does not matter that the translation cannot capture the direct force in the relation of *bedenklich* to *denken* and the senses of *bedenklich* as doubtful, serious, risky, scrupulous—it would mean capturing the idea of the thing most critically provoking in our riskily provocative time, that we are still not really provoked, that nothing serious matters to us, that our thoughts are unscrupulous, together with the surrealistic inversion of the Cartesian thought that if I am thinking then I cannot be thinking that perhaps I do not think. In Heidegger, if I am thinking then precisely I must be thinking that I am (still) not thinking. I say the translation does not matter because one who is not inclined as I am, at least intermittently, to take Heidegger's text as a masterpiece of philosophy will not be encouraged to place confidence in a mode of argumentation which invests itself in what is apt to seem at best the child's play of language and at worst the wild variation and excesses of linguistic form that have always interfered with rationality. For someone who has not experienced this play in Heidegger, or in Emerson, the extent of it is indescribable; even to the sympathetic it can from time to time appear as a kind of philosophical folly.

I pick two instances from the essay "Experience" in which Emerson's thought is, on a certain way of turning it, a direct anticipation of Heidegger's. Emerson writes: "I take this evanescence and lubricity of all objects, which lets them slip through our fingers then when we clutch hardest, to be the most unhandsome part of our condition." You may either dismiss, or savor, the relation between the clutching fingers and the hand in handsome as a developed taste for linguistic oddity, or you might further relate it to Emerson's recurring interest in the hand (as in speaking of what is at hand, by which, whatever else he means, he means the writing taking shape under his hand and now in ours) and thence to Heidegger's sudden remark, "Thinking is a handicraft," by which he means both that thinking requires learning and makes something happen, but equally that it makes something happen in a particular way since the hand is a uniquely human possession: "The hand is infinitely different from all grasping organs—paws, claws, fangs . . . (16)." (It matters to me in various ways to recall a seminar of C. I. Lewis's on the Nature of the Right, given at Harvard in the academic year 1951–52—the year Heidegger delivered the lectures constituting *What Is Called Thinking*—in which Lewis emphasized the hand as a trait of the human, the tool-using trait, hence one establishing a human relation to the world, a realm of practice that expands the reaches of the self. The idea seemed to me in my greenness not to get very far, but it evidently left me with various impressions, among others one of intellectual isolation.) Emerson's image of clutching and Heidegger's of grasping, emblematize their interpretation of Western conceptualizing as a kind of sublimized violence. (Heidegger's word is *greifen*; it is readily translatable as "clutching.") Heidegger is famous here for his thematization of this violence as expressed in the world dominion of technology, but Emerson is no less explicit about it as a mode of thinking. Overcoming this conceptualizing will require the achievement of a form of knowledge both Emerson and Heidegger call reception, alluding to the Kantian idea that knowledge is active, and sensuous intuition alone passive or receptive. (Overcoming Kant's idea of thinking as conceptualizing—analyzing and synthesizing concepts—is coded into Emerson's idea that our most unhandsome part belongs to our condition. I have argued elsewhere that Emerson is transfiguring Kant's key term *condition* so that it speaks not alone of deducing twelve categories of the understanding but of deriving (schematizing) every word in which we speak together (speaking together is what the word condition says), so that the conditions or terms of every term in our language stand to be derived philosophically, deduced.[5]

Now reception, or something received, if it is welcome, implies thanks, and Heidegger, in passages as if designed to divide readers into those thrilled and those offended by them, harps on the derivation of the word *thinking* from a root for *thanking*, and interprets this particularly as giving thanks for the gift of thinking, which is what should become of philosophy. Does it take this thematization to direct attention to one of Emerson's throwaway sentences which, as essentially every Emersonian sentence, can be taken as the topic of the essay it finds itself in, in this case of "Experience": "I am thankful for small mercies." To see that this describes the thinking that goes on in an Emersonian sentence you would have first to see the joking tautology in linking his thankfulness with a *mercy*, that is to say a *merci*; and recognize "small mercy" as designating the small son whose death is announced at the beginning of "Experience," an announcement every critic of the essay comments on, a child never named in the essay but whose death and birth constitute the lines of the father's investigation of experience—and it is the philosopher's term experience Emerson is (also) exploring, as in Kant and in Hume—an effort to counteract the role of experience as removing us from instead of securing us to the world. The idea, again argued elsewhere, is that Emerson's essay "Experience" enacts the father's giving birth to Waldo—the son that bears Emerson's name for himself, hence declares this birth (as of himself) as his work of writing generally, or generously.[6] The clearer the intricacies become of the identification of the child Waldo with the world as such, the deeper one's wonder that Emerson could bring himself to voice it socially, to subject himself either to not being understood or to being understood—yet another wonder about intellectual isolation. I myself am convinced that Emerson knew that such devices as the pun on *thankful* and *mercy* were offensive to philosophical reason. So the question is why he felt bound to give offense. (An opening and recurrent target of Dewey's *Experience and Nature* is thinkers who take experience to "veil and screen" us from nature. Its dissonance with Emerson is interesting in view of Dewey's being the major American philosopher who declared Emerson without reservation to be a philosopher—without evidently finding any use for him. For Dewey the philosophical interpretation of experience was cause for taking up scientific measures against old dualisms, refusing separation. For Emerson the philosophical interpretation of experience makes it a cause for mourning, assigning to philosophy the work of accepting the separation of the world, as of a child.)

Further connections between Emerson's "American Scholar" and Heidegger's text on thinking will continue to come up, especially when Nietzsche makes a steadier appearance, since it is in Nietzsche, wherever else, that some explanation must be sought for the inner connection between a writer (such as Heidegger) who calls for thinking *knowing* the completed presence of European philosophy, or facing its aftermath, as if needing to disinherit it and a writer (such as Emerson) who calls for thinking *not* knowing whether the absence of the philosophical edifice for America means that it is too late for a certain form of thinking here, or whether his errand just is to inherit remains of the edifice. Nietzsche is the pivot because of his early and late devotion to Emerson's writing together with his decisive presence in Heidegger's *What Is Called Thinking?* Accordingly I end the first half of this essay by listing a few further thoughts on "The American Scholar" anyone will have to notice who wishes to follow Emerson's sense of thinking.

It is a sense of thinking as, generally, a double process, or a single process with two names, transfiguration and conversion. For instance: "A strange process, . . . this by which experience is converted into thought, as a mulberry leaf is converted into satin. The manufacture goes forward at all hours" (70). And again:

> The actions and events of our childhood and youth are now matters of calmest observation. . . . Not so with our recent actions,— with the business which we now have in hand. Our affections as yet circulate through it. . . . The new deed . . . remains for a time immersed in our unconscious life. In some contemplative hour it detaches itself . . . to become a thought of the mind. Instantly it is raised, transfigured; the corruptible has put on incorruption. (70–71)

Transfiguration is to be taken as a rhetorical operation, Emerson's figure for a figure of speech—not necessarily for what rhetoricians name a known figure of speech, but for whatever it is that he will name the conversion of words. In "Self-Reliance" he calls the process that of passing from Intuition to Tuition, so it is fitting that those who find Emerson incapable of thought style him a philosopher of Intuition, omitting the teacher of Tuition. Tuition is what Emerson's writing presents itself to be throughout: hence, of course, to be articulating Intuition. It is when Emerson thinks of thinking, or conversion, as oppositional, or critical, that he calls it aversion. This bears relation not only to Emerson's continuous critique of religion but also to Kant's speaking of Reason, in his always astonishing "Conjectural Beginning of Human History," as requiring and enabling "violence" (to the voice of nature) and "refusal" (to desire), refusal being a "feat which brought about the passage from merely sensual to spiritual attractions" and uncovers "the first hint at the development of man as a moral being" (56–57). And Emerson's aversion bears relation to Heidegger's discussion of why thinking in his investigation of it "is from the start tuned in a negative key" (29).

The reverse of the unhandsome in our condition, Emerson's clutching, Heidegger's grasping—call the reverse the handsome part—is what Emerson calls being drawn and what Heidegger calls getting in the draw, or the draft, of thinking. Emerson speaks of this in saying that thinking is partial, Heidegger in speaking of thinking as something the human is inclined to. Heidegger's opening paragraphs work inclination into a set of inflections of *mögen,* *vermögen,* and *Möglichkeit*—inclination, capability, and possibility. Emerson's "partiality" of thinking is, or accounts for, the inflections of partial as "not whole" and as "favoring or biassed toward" something or someone. Here is Emerson weaving some of this together:

> Character is higher than intellect. Thinking is the function. Living is the functionary. . . . A great soul will be strong to live, as well as strong to think. Does he lack organ or medium to impart his truths? He can still fall back on this elemental force of living them. This is a total act. Thinking is a partial act. Let the grandeur of justice shine in his affairs. Let the beauty of affection cheer his lowly roof. Those "far from fame," who dwell and act with him, will feel the force of his constitution. (72)

"Affairs," "lowly roof," and "constitution," are each names Emerson is giving to functions of his writings. A number of clichés, or moments of myth, are synthesized here, opening with a kind of denial that virtue is knowledge, continuing with the Existentialist tag that living is not thinking, picking up a Romantic sound ("lowly roof") to note that strong thoughts are imparted otherwise than in educated or expert forms, and hitting on the term *partial* to epitomize what he calls at the beginning of his address "the old fable" "that the gods, in the beginning, divided Man into men, as the hand was divided into fingers, the better to answer its end" (thus implying that Man has an end, but that to say so requires a myth).

When Emerson goes on to claim to have "shown the ground of his hope in adverting to the doctrine that man is one" (75), the apparent slightness of this, even piousness, in turning toward a doctrine, as if his hopes are well known, and well worn, may help disguise the enormity of the essay's immediate claim for its practice, that is, for its manner of writing. The passage (citing thinking as partial) proposes nothing *more*—something total—for thinking to be; *living* is total, and if it is strong it shows its ground, which is not to say that it is *more* than thinking, as if thinking might leave it out. Thinking *is* a partial act; if it lacks something, leaves something out, it is its own partiality, what Kant calls (and Freud more or less calls) its incentive and interest (*Triebfeder*).

Since the lives of this people, Emerson's people, do not yet contain thinking, he cannot, or will not, sharing this life, quite claim to be thinking. But he makes a prior claim, the enormous one I alluded to, namely, to be providing this incentive of thinking, laying the conditions for thinking, becoming its "source," calling for it, by what he calls living his thoughts, which is pertinent to us as far as his writing is this life, which means: as far as "the grandeur of justice shine(s)" in the writing and "affection cheer(s)" it. This is the importance of his having said, or implied, that since in the business we now have in hand, through which our affections as yet circulate, we do not know it, it is not yet transfigured, but remains in "our unconscious life," the corruptible has not yet put on incorruption. But what is this corruptible life, this pretransfigurative existence of his prose, unconscious of itself, unconscious to us? It is, on the line I am taking, one in which Tuition is to find its Intuition, or in which Emerson's thinking finds its "material" (as psychoanalysis puts it), as in the opening two paragraphs of "The American Scholar" it "accepts" its topics in hope and understands hope as a sign, in particular of "an indestructible instinct," yet an instinct that thinking must realize as "something else," as if thinking is replacing, by transfiguring, instinct (as Nietzsche and as Freud again will say).

I focus on the reluctance and the indefiniteness of Emerson's definition of his topic, and his notation of this anniversary event as the "sign of the survival of the love of letters among a people too busy to give to letters any more" (to letters any more than love, and hope, and instinct), and I take Emerson to mean that his topics are our everyday letters and words, as signs of our instincts; they are to become thought. So that thinking is a kind of reading. But thought about what? Reading for what?

Sign suggests representation. How can "The American Scholar" represent the incentive of thinking without at the same time presenting it, showing it? If thinking were solving problems the incentive would be the problems, or could be attached to the solutions. But Emerson's crack about our being "too busy to give to letters any more" exactly suggests that we are busy solving things. When he opens by defining the anniversary on which he is speaking as one of hope and perhaps not enough of labor, he means of course that our labors are largely devoted otherwise than to letters—which is what everyone who cared was saying in explanation of the failure of America to found its own letters, its own writing, and its own art. But Emerson also means that letters demands its own labor and that we do not know what this other labor (the one that produces letters) is, that it is also a mode of thinking. Labor—as a characterization of thinking—suggests brooding. An interplay between laboring as reproductive and as productive (as the feminine and the masculine in human thought) suggests Emerson's relentlessness concerning the interplay of the active and the receptive or passive in our relating to the world. (Thinking as melancholy reproduction characterizes Hamlet.) The other labor of thinking—devoted to letters—is accordingly one that requires a break with what we know as thinking. (Wittgenstein says our investigation has to be turned around, Heidegger says we have to take a step back from our thinking.) The incentive to this other mode will presumably consist in recognizing that we are not engaged in it, not doing something we nevertheless recognize a love for, an instinct for. Then Emerson's task is to show to that desire its satisfaction. Which is to say: This writing must illustrate thinking. This means at the least that it must contain thought about what illustration is, what an example is.

In "The American Scholar" Emerson's transfiguration of illustration is his use of the word "illustrious." For example: "[The scholar] is one who raises himself from private considerations ["innermost" he sometimes says] and breathes and lives on public ["outermost"] and illustrious thoughts" (73). In Emerson's way of talking, this is a kind of tautology. It is a favorite idea of Emerson's that the passage from private to public ideas is something open to each individual (as if there is in the intellectual life the equivalent of the Moral Law in the moral life, an imperative to objectivity). In "Self-Reliance" he speaks of a man who is able to reachieve a certain perspective that society talks us (almost all of us) out of, as one whose opinions would be "seen to be not private but necessary" (149), and in "The American Scholar" he phrases what he will call the ground of his hope that man is one, by saying "the deeper [the scholar] dives into his privatest, secretest presentiment, to his wonder he finds this is the most acceptable, most public and universally true" (74). The contrast to the private, which the *most* private can reach, is characterized in the former passage as necessary, in the latter as universal, thus exactly according to the characteristics Kant assigns to the a priori, something I suppose Emerson to know. But why would Emerson speak of illustrating the a priori conditions of thinking as illustrious? Surely for no reason separate from the fact that the illustration of thinking as attaining to the necessary and universal illustrates the conditions shared by humanity as such; such thoughts are illustrious exactly because they are completely unexceptional, in this way representative.

This thought produces some of Emerson's most urgent rhetoric, some of the most famous: At the opening of "Self-Reliance": "To believe your own thought, to believe that what is true for you in your private heart is true for all men,—that is genius." "In every work of genius we recognize our own rejected thoughts; they come back to us with a certain alienated majesty." Self-evidently no one is in a position to know more about this than any other, hence in no position to *tell* anyone of it, to offer information concerning it (this is the Ancient Mariner's mistake, and his curse). So clearly Emerson is not talking about science and mathematics. Then what is he talking about? Whatever it is, he properly— conveniently, you might think—describes himself as *showing* his ground. But if his ground, or anyone's, will prove to be unexceptional (except for the endlessly specifiable fact that it is one's own life on that ground), why the tone of moral urgency in showing it, declaring it? Is thinking—something to be called thinking—something whose partiality or incentive is essentially moral, and perhaps political?

Before responding to this let us confirm Emerson's transfiguration of the illustrative in its other occurrence in "The American Scholar": "The private life of one man shall be a more illustrious monarchy, more formidable to its enemy, more sweet and serene in its influence to its friend, than any kingdom in history" (76). The idea is that the illustrious is not, or shall not be, merely a particular result of monarchy but monarchy's universal cause, and the paradox alerts us to consider that while of course monarchy is derived as the rule of one (for whoever is still interested in that possibility) it may also come to be seen to speak of the *beginning or origin* of one, of what Emerson calls "one man," the thing two sentences earlier he had called "the upbuilding of a man," that is, of his famous "individual." (Hence the paradox of a private life as an illustrious monarchy is to be paired with the idea, in the generation of Jefferson and Adams, of the natural aristocrat. They knew that *that* was a paradoxical idea—as if democracy has its own paradox to match that of the Philosopher King.) When this process of upbuilding, or origination, is achieved, then, as the final sentence of "The American Scholar" puts it, "A nation of men will for the first time exist"—or as Marx put the thought half a dozen years after Emerson's address, human history will begin. For Emerson you could say both that this requires a constitution of the public and at the same time an institution of the private, a new obligation to think for ourselves, to make ourselves intelligible. (What goes on inside us now is merely obedience to the law and voices of others—the business Emerson calls conformity. That no thought is our own is what he signals by interpreting the opening fable of his essay, concerning the Gods' original division of Man into men, to mean that "Man is thus metamorphosed into a thing" (64). That we are already (always already) metamorphosed sets the possibility and necessity of our transfiguration. Then what were we before we were metamorphosed? Emerson speaks not only of our conversion; which is to say, rebirth; he also says that we are unborn.)

If we are things, we do not belong to Kant's Realm of Ends, we do not regard ourselves as human, with human others, which seems to mean for Emerson that we are not, that our existence is not, human. For Kant the Realm of Ends might be seen as the realization of the eventual human city. For Emerson this is not the culmination of the moral life but its inception. Is this a sensible difference?

Here we cross to the second part of my essay, to follow out a little the questionable tone of moral urgency in Emerson's descriptions of thinking. My thought is that a certain relation to words (as an allegory of my relation to my life) is inseparable from a certain morallike relation to thinking, and that the morality and the thinking that are inseparable are of specific strains—the morality is neither teleological (basing itself on a conception of the good to be maximized in society) nor deontological (basing itself on an independent conception of the right) and the thinking is some as yet unknown distance from what we think of as reasoning. An obvious moral interpretation of the image of figuring from the innermost to the outermost is that of Moral Perfectionism (as currently understood) at its most objectionable, the desire to impose the maximization of one's most private conception of good on all others, regardless of their talents or tastes or visions of the good.

I remarked that Moral Perfectionism has not found a secure home in modern philosophy. There are various reasons for this homelessness, and the title Perfectionism may cover a number of views. I am taking Emerson and Nietzsche as my focal examples here, and thinking of them, I surmise that the causes for disapproval will orbit around two features or themes of their outlook: (1) A hatred of moralism—of what Emerson calls "conformity"—so passionate and ceaseless as to seem sometimes to amount to a hatred of morality altogether (Nietzsche calls himself the first antimoralist; Emerson knows that he will seem antinomian, a refuser of any law, including the moral law). (2) A second reason for Perfectionism's homelessness is its expression of disgust with or a disdain for the present state of things so complete as to require not merely reform, but a call for a transformation of things, and before all a transformation of the self—a call that seems so self-absorbed and obscure as to make morality impossible: what is the moral life apart from acting beyond the self and making oneself intelligible to those beyond it?

A thought to hold on to is that what Emerson means by conformity is to be heard against Kant's idea that moral worth is a function of acting not merely in conformity with the moral law but for the sake of the law. Kant famously, scandalously, says that a mother who cares for her child out of affection rather than for the sake of the moral law exhibits no moral worth. Kant does not however say that this woman exhibits no excellence of any kind— just not of the highest kind, the kind that makes the public life of mutual freedom possible, that attests to the realm of ends. Emerson's perception can be said to be that we exhibit neither the value of affection nor the worth of morality (neither as it were feminine nor masculine virtues), but that our conformity exhibits merely the fear of others' opinion, which Emerson puts as a fear of others' eyes, which claps us in a prison of shame.

This in turn is to be heard against John Rawls's impressive interpretation of Kant's moral philosophy in which he presents Kant's "main aim as deepening and justifying Rousseau's idea that liberty is acting in accordance with a law that we give to ourselves" and emphasizes that "Kant speaks of the failure to act on the moral law as giving rise to shame and not to feelings of guilt."[7] A text such as Emerson's "Self-Reliance" is virtually a study of shame, and perceives what we now call human society as one in which the moral law is nowhere (or almost nowhere) in existence. His perception presents itself to him as a vision of us as "bugs, spawn," as a "mob"; Nietzsche will say (something Emerson also says) "herd." It is a violent perception of a circumstance of violence. How do we, as Emerson puts it, "come out" of that? How do we become self-reliant? The worst thing we could do is rely on ourselves as we stand—this is simply to be the slaves of our slavishness: it is what makes us spawn. We must become averse to this conformity, which means convert from it, which means transform our conformity, as if we are to be born again. How does our self-consciousness—which now expresses itself as shame, or let us say embarrassment—make us something other than human? I have elsewhere tried to show that Emerson is taking on philosophy's interpretation of self-consciousness in its versions in both Descartes and Kant.[8]

In Descartes, self-consciousness, in the form of thinking that I think, must prove my existence, human existence. In "Self-Reliance" Emerson says explicitly that we are ashamed to say "'I think'," "'I am'," from which it follows that we do not exist (as human). And I find this pattern in Emerson (of discovering our failing of philosophy as a failure of our humanity) also to be interpreting Kant's idea of freedom as imposing the moral law on oneself. It is for Emerson not so much that we are ashamed because we do not give ourselves the moral law—which is true enough— but that we do not give ourselves the moral law because we are already ashamed, a state in need of definition. Again: it is not that we are ashamed of our immorality; we are exactly incapable of being ashamed of *that*; in that sense we are shameless. Our moralized shame is debarring us from the conditions of the moral life. That debarment or embarrassment is for Emerson, as for Kant, a state other than the human since it lacks the humanly defining fact of freedom. That we are perceived as "bugs" says this, and more. Bugs are not human, but they are not monsters either; bugs in human guise are inhuman, monstrous.

How does Emerson understand a way out, out of wronging ourselves, which is to ask: how does Emerson find the "almost lost ... light that can lead [us] back to [our] prerogatives" (p. 75)? Here is where Emerson's writing, with its enactment of transfigurations, comes in. Its mechanism may be seen in Moral Perfectionism.

What Moral Perfectionism means is taken in *A Theory of Justice* to have two versions, moderate and extreme. In the moderate version its principle is one among others and "[directs] society to arrange institutions and to define the duties and obligations of individuals so as to maximize the achievement of human excellence, in art, in science, and culture." Then how shall we understand Emerson's and Nietzsche's disdain for the cultural institutions, or institutionalized culture, of their day (including universities and religions and whatever would be supported by what Rawls describes as "public funds for the arts and sciences"), a disdain sometimes passionate to the point of disgust? The distribution of nothing of high culture as it is now institutionalized is to be maximized in Emersonian Perfectionism, which is in that sense not a teleological theory at all. What Nietzsche calls "the pomp of culture" and "misemployed and appropriated culture" is, on the contrary, to be scorned. Nor is anything to be maximized in what this Perfectionism craves as the realm of culture, the realm to which, as Nietzsche puts it, we are to consecrate ourselves, the path on which, as Emerson puts it, we are to find "the conversion of the world." There is, before finding this, nothing specific to ask the maximization of, and one can also say that the value of the culture in question is already universally distributed or else it is nothing—which is to say it is part of a conception of what it is to be a moral person, call this the capacity for self-criticism.

What I mean is explicit in what Rawls calls the extreme version of Perfectionism, in which the maximizing of excellence is the sole principle of institutions and obligations. *A Theory of Justice* epitomizes this in the following selection of sentences from Nietzsche's second Untimely Meditation, *Schopenhauer as Educator*:

> Mankind must work continually to produce individual great human beings—this and nothing else is the task. . . . for the question is this: how can your life, the individual life, retain the highest value, the deepest significance? . . . Only by your living for the good of the rarest and most valuable specimens.

This sounds bad. Rawls is certainly right to reject anything of the kind as a principle of justice (compare page 328). And if Nietzsche is to be dismissed as a thinker pertinent to the foundation of the democratic life then, so it may seem, is Emerson, since Nietzsche's Meditation on Schopenhauer is, to an as yet undisclosed extent, a transcription and elaboration of Emersonian passages. Emerson's dismissal here would pain me more than I can say, and if that is indeed the implication of *A Theory of Justice*, I want the book, because of my admiration for it, to be wrong in drawing this implication from itself. In Nietzsche's Meditation on Schopenhauer the sentence, "Only by your living for the good of the rarest and most valuable specimens," continues with the words, "and not for the good of the majority." The majority is then, however, characterized still further in that sentence: it is not part of constitutional democracy that one is to live for the good of the majority— something Rawls's book is the demonstration of, for those committed to democracy. If not for the good of the majority, then is one to live for the good of each (for each societal "position")? No doubt this is not just making rational choices that have justifiably unequal benefits for all (the Difference Principle), but it may yet be a life taken within the commitment to democracy. There will doubtless be perfectionisms that place themselves above democracy or that are taken in the absence of the conditions of democracy. The former might describe a timarchy, an oligarchy, or a dictatorship. These are not my business, which is rather to see whether Perfectionism is necessarily undemocratic. I might put my thought this way: The particular disdain for official culture taken in Emerson and in Nietzsche (and surely in half the writers and artists in the one hundred fifty years since "The American Scholar," or since Romanticism) is itself an expression of democracy and commitment to it. Timocrats do not produce, oligarchs do not commission, dictators do not enforce arts and culture that disgust them. Only within the possibility of democracy is one committed to *living* with, or against, such culture. This may well produce personal tastes and private choices that are, let us say, exclusive, even esoteric. Then my question is why this exclusiveness should be not just tolerated but treasured by the friends of democracy.

There are two further problems with the final sentence among those Rawls quotes from Nietzsche concerning living for rare specimens and not for the majority. First, Nietzsche's word translated as "specimens" is *Exemplare*, faithfully translated as "exemplars" later (in *Friedrich Nietzsche: Untimely Meditations*, Cambridge University Press, 1983), by the same translator from whom Rawls takes his Nietzsche sentences (R. J. Hollingdale, in his earlier *Nietzsche: The Man and His Philosophy*, Louisiana State University Press, 1965). The biological association of "specimens" suggests that the grounds for identifying them (hence for assessing their value) are specifiable independently of the instance in view, of its effect on you; its value depends on this independence; specimens are samples, as of a class, genus, or whole; one either is or is not a specimen. Yet the acceptance of an exemplar, as access to another realm (call it the realm of culture; Nietzsche says, echoing a favorite image of Emerson's, that it generates "a new circle of duties"), is not grounded in the relation between the instance and a class of instances it stands for but in the relation between the instance and the other for whom it does the standing for, the delegating. ("Archetype," translatable as "exemplar," is the word Kant, for example, uses to refer to Christ.) Second, Nietzsche goes on to begin characterizing the life of culture, and it seems not to be one accessible to a *particular* class of exemplars. It can perhaps be understood as a life lived for the good of each. It doubtless demands exclusiveness, so its good is inherently not maximizable. But neither is it inherently unjust, requiring favored shares in the distribution of good. Its characteristic vice would not be envy but perhaps shirking participation in democracy. (Then the question becomes: If it is not shirking then *what* is its participation?)

> The young person should be taught to regard himself as a failed work of nature but at the same time as a witness to the grandiose and marvelous intention of this artist. . . . By coming to this resolve he places himself within the circle of *culture*; for culture is the child of each individual's self-knowledge and dissatisfaction with himself. Anyone who believes in culture is thereby saying: "I see above me something higher and more human than I am; let everyone *help* me to attain it, as I will help everyone who knows and suffers as I do."[9]

In the next sentence the "something higher," desire for which is created in self-dissatisfaction, is marked as "a higher self as yet still concealed from it."

Could it be clearer that this higher self is not—not necessarily and in a sense not ever—that of someone *else*, but is a further or eventual state of the self now dissatisfied? Nietzsche continues: "Thus only he who has attached his heart to some great man is by that act *consecrated to culture*; the sign of that consecration is that one is ashamed of oneself without any accompanying feeling of distress, that one comes to hate one's own narrowness and shrivelled nature" (163). "Attaching one's heart," here to some great man, is, let us say, acting toward him in love, as illustrated by Nietzsche's writing of his text on Schopenhauer. But the author of that text is not consecrating himself to Schopenhauer—Schopenhauer, as everyone notes, is scarcely present in the text. If what you consecrate yourself to is what you live for, then Nietzsche is not living for Schopenhauer. It is not Schopenhauer's self that is still concealed from the writer of this text. The love of the great is, or is the cause of, the hate of one's meanness, the hate that constitutes the sign of consecration. ("The fundamental idea of culture, insofar as it sets for each one of us but one task [is]:

to promote the production of the philosopher, the artist and the saint within us and without us and thereby to work at the perfecting of nature" [*ibid.*]. This is said to set one in the midst of "a mighty community." Obviously it is not a present but an eventual human community, so everything depends on how it is to be reached.)

Many, with Rawls, have taken Nietzsche otherwise than as calling for the further or higher self of each, each consecrating himself/herself to self-transformation, accepting his or her own genius, which is precisely not, indeed it is the negation of, accepting one's present state and its present consecrations to someone fixed, as such, "beyond" one. Perhaps it was necessary for Nietzsche to have left himself unguarded on this desperate point. Emerson provides an explanation and name for this necessary ambiguity in the passage of "The American Scholar" of which Nietzsche's on the relation to greatness is a reasonably overt transcription (with sensible differences):

> The main enterprise of the world for splendor, for extent, is the up-building of a man (76). . . . In a century, in a millennium, one or two men; that is to say, one or two approximations to the right state of every man. All the rest behold in the hero or the poet their own green and crude being,—ripened; yes, and are content to be less, so *that* may attain to its full stature. (75)

But Emerson does not say that this contentment is the best or necessary state of things. For him, rather, it shows "What a testimony, full of grandeur [in view of what we might become], full of pity, [in view of what we are], is borne to the demands of his own nature [by the poor and the low], to be brushed like flies from the path of a great person, so that justice shall be done by him to that common nature which it is the dearest desire of all to see enlarged. . . . He lives for us, and we live in him" (76). But as we stand we are apt to overrate or misconstrue this identification. Emerson continues:

> Men, such as they are, very naturally seek money or power. . . . and why not? for they aspire to the highest, and this in their sleepwalking they dream is highest. Wake them and they shall quit the false good and leap to the true, and leave governments to clerks and desks. This revolution is to be wrought by the gradual domes-

tication of the idea of Culture.... Each philosopher, each bard, each actor has only done for me, as by a delegate, what one day I can do for myself. (76)

Here there simply seems no room for doubt that the intuition of a higher or further self is one to be arrived at in person, in the person of the one who gives his heart to it, this one who just said that the great have been his delegates and who declares that "I" can one day, so to speak, be that delegate. I forerun myself.

In the so-called Divinity School Address, delivered the year after "The American Scholar," Emerson will in effect provide the originating case of our repressing our delegation and attributing our potentialities to the actualities of others, the case of "Historical Christianity['s] dwell[ing], with noxious exaggeration about the *person* of Jesus," whereas "The soul knows no persons." Evidently Emerson is treating this form of worship or consecration, even if in the name of the highest spirituality, as idolatry. (Here is a site for investigating the sense that Perfectionism is an attempt to take over, or mask, or secularize, a religious responsibility, something Matthew Arnold is explicit in claiming for his Perfectionism in *Culture and Anarchy*, something Henry Sidgwick criticizes Arnold for in "The Prophet of Culture."[10])

In Emerson's way of speaking, "one day" ("Each philosopher ... has only done, as by a delegate, what one day I can do for myself ...") always also means today; the life he urgently speaks for is one he forever says is not to be postponed. It is today that you are to take the self on; today that you are to awaken and to consecrate yourself to culture, specifically, to domesticate it gradually, which means bring it home, as part now of your everyday life. The urgency about today is the cause of Emerson's characteristic allusions to the gospels. In "The American Scholar" it is more than an allusion: "For the ease and pleasure of treading the old road ... [the scholar] takes the cross of making his own"—a road Emerson characterizes in that passage as one of poverty, solitude, stammering, self-accusation, and "the state of virtual hostility in which he seems to stand to society, and especially to educated society" (73). In "Self-Reliance" the parody is as plain as the allusion: "I shun father and mother and wife and brother when my genius calls me. I would write Whim on the lintels of the door-post." The shunning reference is to the call to enter the kingdom of heaven at once, today, the call to follow me, and Emerson's parody mocks his preachiness (which he evidently finds necessary) while it acknowledges that the domestication of culture is not going to be entered on today yet insists that there is no reason it is postponed; that is, no one has the reason for this revolution if each of us has not. It is why he perceives us as "[bearing] testimony, full of grandeur, full of pity, . . . to the demands of [our] own nature," a remark transcribed in Nietzsche as "[regarding oneself] as a failed work of nature but at the same time as a witness to the grandiose and marvelous intentions of their artist." Bearing testimony and witnessing are functions of martyrdom. In Moral Perfectionism, as represented in Emerson and in Nietzsche, we are invited to a position that is structurally one of martyrdom—not, however, in view of an idea of the divine but in aspiration to an idea of the human.

What can this mean?[11] And how does thinking as transfiguration bear on it? Which is to ask: How does Emerson's way of writing, his relation to his reader, bear on it? Which in turn means: How does his writing represent, by presenting, the aspiration to the human?

Before going on to sketch an answer to this pack of questions, it may be well to pause to say another word about my sense that the view Emerson and Nietzsche share is not simply to show that it is tolerable to the life of justice in a constitutional democracy but to show how it is essential to that life, a treasure for it. The question I ask myself is for the point of Perfectionism's emphasis, common from Plato and Aristotle to Emerson and Thoreau and Nietzsche, on education and character and friendship, where that is pertinent for a democratic existence. That emphasis of Perfectionism, as I have said, may be taken to serve an effort to escape the mediocrity or leveling, the vulgarity, of equal existence, for oneself and perhaps for a select circle of like-minded others. There are undeniably aristocratic or aesthetic Perfectionisms. But in Emerson it should be taken as part of the training for democracy. Not the part that must internalize the principles of justice and practice the role of the democratic citizen—that is clearly required, so obviously that the Perfectionist may take offense at the idea that this aspect of things is even difficult, evince a disdain for ordinary temptations to cut corners over the law. The training and character Emerson requires for democracy I understand as preparation to withstand not its rigors but its failures, character to keep the democratic hope alive in the face of disappointment with it. (Emerson is forever turning aside to say especially to the young not to despair of the world, and as if he is speaking not to a subject but to a monarch.) That we will be disappointed in democracy, in its failure by the light of its own principles of justice, is implied in the original position in which its principles are accepted, a perspective from which we know that justice will in actual societies be departed from and that the distance of any actual society from justice is a matter for each of us to assess for ourselves. I will speak of this as our being compromised by the democratic demand for consent, so that the human individual meant to be created and preserved in democracy is apt to be undone by it.

Now I go on to sketch in answer to the question how Emerson's writing (re)presents the aspiration to the human, beginning from a famous early sentence of "Self-Reliance" I have already had occasion to cite: "In every work of genius we recognize our own rejected thoughts. They come back to us with a certain alienated majesty." The idea of a majesty alienated from me is a transcription of the idea of the *sublime* as Kant characterizes it. Then the sublime, as has been discussed in recent literary theory, bears the structure of Freudian transference.[12] The direction of transference—of mine to the text, or the text's to me in a prior counter-transference (or defense against being read)—seems to me an open question. In either case reading as such is taken by Emerson as of the sublime.

This comes out in Emerson's (and Thoreau's) hilarious denunciation of books, in the spectacle of their writing books that dare us to read them, and dare us not to, that ask us to conceive that they do not want us to read them, even that they are teaching us how—how *not* to, that they are creating the taste not to be read, the capacity to leave them. Think of it this way: if the thoughts of a text such as Emerson's (say that on rejected thoughts) are yours, then you do not need them. If its thoughts are *not* yours, they will not do you good. The problem is that the text's thoughts are neither exactly mine nor not mine. In their sublimity as my rejected—repressed—thoughts, they represent my further self. (To think otherwise, to attribute the origin of my thoughts simply to the other, thoughts which are then, as it were, implanted in me—some would say caused—by let us say some Emerson, is idolatry.)[13]

In becoming conscious of what in the text is (in Emerson's word) unconscious, the familiar is invaded by another familiar—the structure Freud calls the uncanny, and the reason he calls the psychoanalytic process itself uncanny. Emerson's process of transfiguring is such a structure, a necessity of his placing his work in the position of our rejected and further self, our "beyond." One of his ways of saying this is to say "I will stand here for humanity" as if he is waiting for us to catch up, or catch on. When this is unpacked it turns out to be the transfiguration of a Kantian task. To say how I track for a moment Emerson's play, pivotally and repeatedly, on inflections of standing up (and upright) in relation to standing for and in relation to standards.

"Standing for humanity," radiating in various directions as *representing* humanity and as *bearing* it (as bearing the pain of it) links across the essay with its recurrent notation of postures and of gaits (leaning and skulking among them—postures of shame) of which *standing* or uprightness, is the correction Emerson seeks, his representative prose. This opens into Emerson's description of our being drawn by the true man, as being "constrained to his standard." (Emerson says he will make "this" true—I assume he is speaking of his prose—and describes the true man as "measuring" us.) Now *constraint*, especially in conjunction with conformity, is a Kantian term, specifically noting the operation of the moral law on us—of the fact that it applies only to (is the mark of) the human, that is, only to a being subject to temptation, a being not unmixed in nature, as beasts and angels are unmixed. If you entertain this thought, then the idea of *standard* links further with the Kantian idea that man lives in two worlds, that is, is capable of viewing himself from two *standpoints* (in Kant's term). It is this possibility that gives us access to the intelligible world—the realm of ends, the realm of reason, of the human—"beyond" the world of sense. If Emerson assigns his pages as standards (flags and measures) and if this is an allusion to, an acceptance of, the Kantian task of disclosing the realm of ends, then what is its point?

The point of contesting the Kantian task is presumably to be taken in the face of its failure, or parody, its reduction to conformity. In picking up its standard—and transfiguring it—Emerson finds the intelligible world, the realm of ends, closed to us as a standpoint from which to view ourselves individually (our relation to the law no longer has *this* power for us). But at the same time he shows the intelligible world to be entered into whenever another represents for us our rejected self, our beyond, causes that aversion to ourselves in our conformity that will constitute our becoming, as it were, ashamed of our shame. Some solution. Well, some problem.

Kant describes the "constraint" of the law as an imperative expressed by an ought. For Emerson, we either *are* drawn beyond ourselves, as we stand, or we are *not*; we recognize our reversals or we do not; there is no ought about it. It remains true that being drawn by the standard of another, like being impelled by the imperative of a law, is the prerogative of the mixed or split being we call the human. But for Emerson we are divided not alone between intellect and sense, for we can say that each of these halves is itself split. We are halved not only horizontally but vertically—as that other myth of the original dividing of the human pictures it—as in the *Symposium*, the form of it picked up in Freud, each of us seeking that of which we were originally half, with which we were partial.

Here, in this constraint by recognition and negation, is the place of the high role assigned in Moral Perfectionism to friendship. Aristotle speaks of a friend as "another myself." Emerson enacts the position as a *further* myself. If one does not recognize Emerson in that position, his writing will seem, to its admirers misty or foggy, to its detractors ridiculous. (*Almost* everyone gets around to condescending to Emerson.)

How can philosophy have got itself into the position of having to be accepted on intimate terms *before* it has proven itself? It seems the negation of philosophy.

If Emerson is wrong in his treatment of the state of conformity and of despair in what has become of the democratic aspiration, he seems harmless enough—he asks for no relief he cannot provide for himself—whatever other claims other Perfectionisms might exert. But if Emerson is right, his aversion provides for the democratic aspiration the only internal measure of its truth to itself—a voice only this aspiration could have inspired, and, if it is lucky, must inspire. Since his aversion is a *continual turning away* from society, it is thereby a continual turning *toward* it. Toward and away; it is a motion of seduction—such as philosophy will contain.

The idea of the self as always to be furthered is not expressed by familiar phantasies of a noumenal self, nor of the self as entelechy, either final or initial. May one imagine Emerson to have known that the word "scholar" is related in derivation to "entelechy"—so that by the American Scholar he means the American self? Then since by Cartesian and by Kantian measures the self in America does not exist, America does not exist—or to speak in proper predicates, is still not discovered as a new, another, world.

And the question might well arise: Why does Emerson take on the Cartesian and Kantian measures? Why does he put English on the terms of philosophy? Instead of transfiguring these terms, why not take the opportunity of America as one of side-stepping philosophy, as one more European edifice well lost? Why does Emerson care, why ought we to care, whether he is a philosopher? Why care when we come to his page, his standard, whether the encounter with our further self, the encounter of reading, the access to an intelligible world, is a *philosophical* one? Evidently because the gradual domestication of culture he calls for—what he names his revolution—is a philosophical one. How?

How is this domestication—call it finding a home for humanity; Emerson and Thoreau picture it as building a house, another edification—how is this a task for philosophy? We may take for granted Plato's description of his task in the *Republic* as creating a "city of words," hence accept it that philosophy in the Western world unfolds its prose in a depicted conversation concerning the just city. Emerson's house of words is essentially less than a city, and although its word is not that of hope, its majesty is not to despair, but to let the "grandeur of justice shine" in it, and "affection cheer" it. Kant had asked: what can I hope for? Emerson answers: for nothing. You do not know what there is hope for. "Patience—patience [suffering, reception] ... abide on your instincts"—presumably because that is the way of thinking. For him who abides this way, "the huge world will come round to him"—presumably in the form in which it comes to Emerson, one person at a time, whose turning constitutes the world's coming around—the form in which you come to your (further) self.

In coming to Emerson's text from a state of alienated majesty, we (each of us as Emerson's reader) form an illustrious monarchy with a population of two. It illustrates the possibility of recognizing my finitude, or separateness, as the question of realizing my partiality. Is the displacement of the idea of the whole man by an idea of the partial man worth philosophy?

I see it this way. Emerson's perception of the dispossession of our humanity, the loss of ground, of nature as our security, or property, is thought in modern philosophy as the problem of skepticism. The overcoming or overtaking of skepticism must constitute a revolution that is a domestication for philosophy (or redomestication) because, let us say, neither science nor religion nor morality has overcome it. On the contrary they as much as anything cause skepticism. Is philosophy left to us, even transformed? Well, that is my question; I think it is philosophy's question, which accordingly now comes into its own—as if purified of religion and of science.

I can formulate my interest in Emerson's situation in the following way. Domestication in Emerson is an issue, or urgency, of the *day*, today, one among others, an achievement of the everyday, the ordinary, now, here, again. In Wittgenstein's *Philosophical Investigations* the issue of the ordinary is the issue of the siting of skepticism, not as something to be overcome, as if to be refuted, as if it is a *conclusion* about human knowledge (which is skepticism's self-interpretation), but to be placed as a mark of what Emerson calls "human condition," a further interpretation of finitude, a mode, as said, of inhabiting our investment in words, in the world. This argument of the ordinary—as what skepticism attacks, hence creates, and as what counters, or recounts, skepticism—is engaged oppositely in a work such as Heidegger's *What Is Called Thinking?*—hence engaged between these visions of Wittgenstein and of Heidegger. (It may present itself as an argument between skepticism and sublimity, between transfiguration down and transfiguration up.) It is why I am pleased to find Emerson and his transfigurations of the ordinary to stand back of both Wittgenstein and Heidegger. They are the two major philosophers of this century for whom skepticism remains alive for philosophy, whose burden is philosophy's, and it is, to my mind, utterly significant that in them—as in Emerson—what strikes their readers as a tone of continual moral urgency or religious or artistic pathos is not expressed as a *separate* study to be called moral philosophy or religious philosophy or aesthetics. The moral of which—or the aesthetics of which—I draw as follows: What they write is nothing *else* than these topics or places of philosophy, but is always nothing but philosophy itself. Nothing less, nothing separate, can lead us from, or break us of, our shameful condition. It is what perfectionists always find a way to say.

Needless to say—is it?—in calling for philosophy Emerson is not comprehensible as asking for guardianship by a particular profession within what we call universities. I assume what will become "philosophy itself" may not be distinguishable from literature—that is to say, from what literature will become. Then that assumption, or presumption, is, I guess, my romanticism.

I come back to earth, concluding by locating what I have been saying in relation to a passage from John Stuart Mill's *On Liberty* which should be common ground. I adduce it with the thought that what I have been saying suggests to me that Perfectionism, as I perceive the thing that interests me, is not a competing moral theory but a dimension of any moral thinking. Kant found an essential place for perfection in his view of it at the end, as it were, of his theory, as an unreachable ideal relation to be striven for to the moral law; in Emerson this place of the ideal occurs at the beginning of moral thinking, as a condition, let us say, of moral imagination, as preparation or sign of the moral life. And if the precondition of morality is to be established in personal encounter, we exist otherwise in a premoral state, morally voiceless. Mill's passage, while no doubt not as eager to court the derangement of intellect as Emerson's prose has to be, is no less urgent and eloquent in the face of human dispossession and voicelessness:

> In our times, from the highest class of society down to the lowest, every one lives as under the eye of a hostile and dreaded censorship. Not only in what concerns others, but in what concerns

themselves, the individual, or the family, do not ask themselves—
what do I prefer? . . . or, what would allow the best and highest
in me to have fair play, and enable it to grow and thrive? They
ask themselves, . . . what is usually done? I do not mean that they
choose what is customary, in preference to what suits their inclination, except for what is customary. Thus the mind itself is
bowed to the yoke: even in what people do for pleasure, conformity is the first thing thought of; they like in crowds; they exercise
choice only among things commonly done; peculiarity of taste,
eccentricity of conduct, are shunned equally with crimes: until by
dint of not following their own nature, they have no nature to follow: their human capacities are withered and starved; they become incapable of any strong wishes or native pleasures, and are
generally without either opinions or feelings of home growth, or
properly their own. Now is this, or is it not, the desirable condition of human nature?[14]

I call attention to the toll of that Millian word "desirable." In a passage in *Utilitarianism*, Mill famously conceives the claim that anything is desirable—on analogy with the claim that anything is visible or audible—to rest finally on the fact that people do, or
presumably under specifiable circumstances will, actually desire
it. Philosophers never used to tire of making fun of that passage
from *Utilitarianism*. Yet the drift of it still strikes me as sound.
According to it, the question at the conclusion of the quotation
from *On Liberty* becomes: Do you, his reader, or would you under
any circumstances, desire this censored condition of mankind?
The eloquence of the passage is to awaken the reader to the question, to show that it is a question. The implication seems to be
that until we each give our answers to the question, one by one,
one on one, we will not know what it is to which we are giving
our consent.

NOTES

Though first delivered as part of the Indiana Romanticism conference, this
essay was written knowing that a version of it would also constitute the first of
my three Carus Lectures delivered later the same month, March 1988, at the

meetings of the Pacific Division of the American Philosophical Association. So this text bears the marks of that knowledge of an eventual professional audience of philosophers, which I would not wish to disguise.

1. Ralph Waldo Emerson, *Selections from Ralph Waldo Emerson*, ed. Stephen E. Whicher (Boston: Houghton Mifflin, 1957). All further references will be to this edition.

2. Karl Jaspers, *Nietzsche: An Introduction to the Understanding of His Philosophical Activity*, trans. Charles F. Walraff and Frederick J. Schmitz (Chicago: Henry Regnery Co., 1965), p. 386.

3. Stanley Cavell, *Must We Mean What We Say?*, (rpt., Cambridge: Cambridge University Press, 1976).

4. This was part of Stroud's contribution to a panel held on my recently published *Claim of Reason* at the 1980 meetings of the Eastern Division of the American Philosophical Association. His contribution was published under the title "Reasonable Claims: Cavell and the Tradition," in *The Journal of Philosophy* 77 (November 1980): 731–44.

5. "Emerson, Coleridge, Kant," reprinted in *In Quest of the Ordinary* (Chicago: University of Chicago Press, 1989), pp. 105–130.

6. "Finding as Founding," in *This New Yet Unapproachable America* (Chicago: University of Chicago Press, 1989).

7. John Rawls, *A Theory of Justice* (Cambridge, Mass.: Harvard University Press, 1973), p. 256.

8. "Being Odd, Getting Even," in *In Quest of the Ordinary*, pp. 105–130.

9. Nietzsche's word *Exemplare* is faithfully translated as "exemplars" by R. J. Hollingdale in his translation of "Schopenhauer as Educator" (included in his edition of Nietzsche's *Untimely Meditations* [Cambridge: Cambridge University Press, 1983]), p. 162. Hollingdale is the same translator from whom Rawls takes his Nietzsche sentences. They are drawn from Hollingdale's much earlier *Nietzsche: The Man and His Philosophy* (Baton Rouge: Louisiana State University Press, 1965). The translation of *Exemplare* as "specimens" can be found on p. 127 of that book and is invoked on p. 325 of *The Theory of Justice*. The revised version of the Hollingdale book that is currently available, under the title of *Nietzsche* (Boston: ARK Paperbacks, 1985), now omits this passage. Further confusion is introduced by the fact that Hollingdale has a second, completely different book available with exactly the same title (*Nietzsche*, London: RKP, 1973). It is perhaps worth remarking that the earlier, inadequate English translation of "Schopenhauer as Educator" by James Hillesheim and Malcolm Simpson, which Hollingdale's recent translation has finally replaced, also translates *Exemplare* as "specimens" (*Schopenhauer as Educator*, South Bend, Ind.: Regnery/Gateway, 1965).

10. *Miscellaneous Essays and Addresses*, ed. E. M. Sidgwick and A. Sidgwick (London: Macmillan, 1904).

11. Whatever it means it suggests why I cannot accede to the recent proposal, interesting as it is in its own terms, of taking Perfectionism to be exemplified

by the well-rounded life. See Thomas Hurka, "The Well-Rounded Life," *Journal of Philosophy* (December 1987), 727–46.

12. See Thomas Weiskel, *The Romantic Sublime* (Baltimore: Johns Hopkins, 1986); Neil Hertz, *The End of the Line* (New York: Columbia, 1985), chaps. 1 and 3. I go into these matters in the penultimate footnote to my essay "Psychoanalysis," in *The Trial(s) of Psychoanalysis*, ed. François Meltzer (Chicago: University of Chicago Press, 1988), pp. 257–58. This note was added when the essay was reprinted from its original appearance in *Images in Our Souls: Cavell, Psychoanalysis, and Cinema*, ed. Joseph H. Smith and William Kerrigan (Baltimore: Johns Hopkins, 1987).

13. "The Politics of Interpretation," in *Themes Out of School* (San Francisco: North Point Press, 1984), pp. 27–59.

14. J. S. Mill, "On Individualism," in *On Liberty*, ed. Elizabeth Rapaport (Indianapolis: Hackett, 1985), pp. 58–59.

"Man Hath No Part in All This Glorious Work"
AMERICAN ROMANTIC LANDSCAPES

BARBARA L. PACKER

The Duke of Dorset, doomed hero of Max Beerbohm's *Zuleika Dobson*, at one point spends an evening at his Oxford club attempting to be civil to an American guest, a Rhodes scholar. The Duke regrets that he finds the American "rather oppressive," since he has always fancied himself one of America's defenders.

> The Duke was not one of those Englishmen who fling, or care to hear flung, cheap sneers at America. Whenever any one in his presence said that America was not large in area, he would firmly maintain that it was. He held, too, in his enlightened way, that Americans have a perfect right to exist.[1]

The Duke merely wishes they would not exercise this right at Oxford. All foreigners are an intrusion there, of course, but Americans are "the most troublesome—as being the most troubled—of the whole lot."

> They were so awfully afraid of having their strenuous native characters undermined by their delight in the place. They held that the future was theirs, a glorious asset, far more glorious than the past. But a theory, as the Duke saw, is one thing, an emotion another. It is so much easier to covet what one hasn't than to revel in what one has.[2]

The terms in which the Duke expresses his ambivalence should sound familiar, for they are the ones in which the "problem" of American poetry has been discussed since the beginning of the nineteenth century. Henry James's famous list of the items of high civilization missing in America, from the preface to his book on Hawthorne, is probably the best known, but the habit of numbering America's "disastrous lacks" has remained such a staple of American cultural self-criticism that when Randall Jarrell came up with his own list in the course of an essay on Wallace Stevens he concluded it with a kind of shrug. *Of course* America lacks "delicacy, awe, order, natural magnificence and piety, 'the exquisite errors of time' and the rest";[3] isn't that something we have always taken for granted?

From the beginning American poets have had to make a Muse of deprivation. In 1801 the Scottish-born writer Hugh Henry Brackenridge was inspired by the dialect poems of a fellow immigrant to try his hand at tetrameter couplets in the style of Burns. Brackenridge's poem recounts his experiences as a young immigrant to the Western Pennsylvania frontier. Many of the memories are comic—as when Brackenridge recalls the day he met a skunk on his father's new farm and disastrously mistook it for some sort of indigenous American cat. But once, at least, their wistfulness rises beyond the personal. In the Latin poetry he reads at school Brackenridge encounters a landscape with creatures even stranger than skunks:

> Soon after this I gaed to Latin:
> And read a buke, I kenna what in,
> That talk'd o' things that whir in bushes
> Dryads, Hamadryads, Muses,
> On tops o' hills wad sing leke Mavies,
> And in the shady woods, and cavies . . .[4]

He is sure he has never seen any of these creatures. At length he decides that the clearing of the forest at the frontier's edge is responsible for their flight:

> Thought I it maun be this vile clearing
> And grubbing up the trees, and bleering,
> And burning brush and making fences,

> That scares these things out o' their senses;
> And drives them frae our fields and patches;
> For who sees any, now, or catches
> A moor-land deity or Nymphy,
> That roosts in trees, or wades in lymphy?
> Or hears a musy in the thicket,
> Just as you wad hear a cricket?

The young poet remains hopeful that the gods, though banished, still survive somewhere beyond the edge of advancing civilization.

> May be in places farther back
> The vestige may na be sae slack;
> Where woods are green and country new,
> The breed may yet remain, a few ...

Brackenridge may seem an unlikely choice for Representative American Poet. His public poems had been dutifully written in blank verse or couplets. He had hailed the rising glory of America or celebrated the inauguration of Thomas Jefferson in verses equally uninspired. Suddenly, at the end of his career, Brackenridge found himself liberated into fluency by the task of describing in a dialect he had forsaken his hopes of finding in a land barely civilized some trace of the myths left by a culture long since vanished. Brackenridge may have been the first American poet to draw energy from such a convergence of negative forces, but he was hardly the last.

In 1948, W. H. Auden, surveying the century and a half of American poetry since Brackenridge and trying to define what distinguished it from English poetry of the same period, found himself making his own list of lacks:

All European literature so far has presupposed two things: a nature which is humanized, mythologized, usually friendly, and a human society in which most men stay where they were born ... Neither of these presuppositions was valid for America, where nature was virgin, devoid of history, usually hostile; and society was fluid ... [5]

Taking a night journey across the country by plane, measuring the distance between the widely spaced lights below, the visiting Englishman is startled into realizing how thinly settled the country still is, how empty. And this circumstance gives the American poet at least one curious imaginative advantage:

> Many poets in the Old World have become disgusted with human civilization but what the earth would be like if the race became extinct they cannot imagine; an American like Robinson Jeffers can quite easily, for he has seen with his own eyes country as yet untouched by history.[6]

One way of characterizing what the Romantic revolution meant to American literature is to say that it changed people's attitudes toward the emptiness Auden notes: from considering it a calamity, American poets began to see it as a challenge and, finally, as a resource. Albert von Frank has argued in a recent book that nineteenth-century American culture is best understood as a contest between two kinds of provincialism—the provincialism of the conservative whose "intense regard" for a "transplanted culture" leads him to wage a battle to preserve and transmit that culture in an environment always conceived as threatening, and the provincialism of the liberal who sees in the inevitable attenuation of the parent culture an opportunity for the new land's art.[7] What makes the contest agonizing is that the conservative and liberal attitudes frequently coexist within the same person, and even within the same poem.

Consider an early fragment of Bryant's. Like many poems of the period, "The Burial-Place" is about graveyards and, like many American poems, about graveyards that have something wrong with them. In the Old World, graveyards link the present to the past, suggest a path from the sensible to the transcendent. If the death they mark is a severing of individual ties, they nevertheless stand for the continuities of custom and society. The absence of graveyards in the American wilderness—at any rate, of familiar sorts of graveyards—is one measure of its cultural emptiness. English poets may indeed make us aware of the social differences that exist between them and the simple country people whose graves inspire their meditations, but American poets muse on graves whose difference from their own is far greater and more disturbing. Freneau's envy at the innocent trust in immortality reflected by Indian burial customs, the pity and fear Longfellow feels at the sight of tombstones marking the graves of the Sephardic Jews of

Newport, whose faith throughout centuries of Christian persecution stands in reproach to his own culture's cruelty and civilized scepticism—what American poets find when they pause by the graves of the dead is not fellowship but the consciousness of disjunction.

Bryant's poetic fragment hardly deserves mention with Freneau's or Longfellow's, and it measures a much smaller dislocation. "The Burial-Place" is little more than a longing account of the superiority of the landscaping in English graveyards. Still, in its confusions and ambivalences it sketches out a plot that American poetry would find itself reenacting many times in the century that followed.

The obtrusive archaizing of the first lines announces Bryant's poem as "conservative" from the outset.

> Erewhile, on England's pleasant shores, our sires
> Left not their churchyards unadorned with shade
> Or blossoms . . .[8]

The English dead are surrounded with the forms of "vegetable beauty":

> There the yew,
> Green even amid the snows of winter, told
> Of immortality, and gracefully
> The willow, a perpetual mourner, drooped;
> And there the gadding woodbine crept about,
> And there the ancient ivy.

But the Puritans left these "simple customs of the heart" behind them; possibly, as Bryant thinks, because the absence of familiar and beloved English flowers made them reluctant to try native substitutes. After a time these "gentle rites / Passed out of use." But when Bryant turns to describe what the graveyards of New England now look like, he suddenly gives us a vision of ugliness that startles his meditation into energy.

> Naked rows of graves
> And melancholy ranks of monuments
> Are seen instead, where the coarse grass, between,

Shoots up his dull green spikes, and in the wind
Hisses . . .

Spondees are always a sign of pleasure in Bryant; "Thanatopsis" might almost have been written to demonstrate how many spondees a blank verse line can sustain. Here, the way the two stressed syllables of "coarse grass" expand to three in "dull green spikes," then tumble over into that splendidly Miltonic trochee, with its suggestions of the Satanic—"in the wind / Hisses"—show Bryant the poet secretly enjoying the very bleakness Bryant the melancholy provincial deplores. In his description of the English graveyard he so admires, Bryant is smooth, graceful, and wearisomely conventional; the native graveyard makes him rough, angry, and momentarily interesting.

Bryant's early poetic education had taken him through the whole history of eighteenth-century English poetry; at ten or eleven he had devoured Pope's *Homer*, and afterward passed on to Thomson, to Cowper, to Blair. The best lines of "Thanatopsis" move with an authority that explains the excited response of Bryant's countrymen; here at last was a poet who spoke with authority, and not as the scribes:

> The hills
> Rock-ribbed and ancient as the sun,—the vales
> Stretching in pensive quietness between;
> The venerable woods—rivers that move
> In majesty, and the complaining brooks
> That make the meadows green; and, poured round all,
> Old Ocean's gray and melancholy waste,—
> Are but the solemn decorations all
> Of the great tomb of man.[9]

It is easier to smile at the melancholy sentiments of the poem than to notice the flashes of originality that enliven it. The hills are "rock-ribbed and ancient as the sun," as if Bryant shared Blake's perception of an ancestral human form beneath the contours of the visible world. The syntax is of the kind Donald Davie would call "objective," meant to suggest in its exfoliation a process in the natural world. Each named element of the landscape flows into the one beyond it, balked here and there by the ever-varying placement of the caesuras, until everything is surrounded by the great gray melancholy waste of Ocean. Then that, too, is revealed to be yet another decoration for the "great tomb of man." By transforming nature into funerary art Bryant neatly evades the problem of cultural inferiority that was later to trouble him in "The Burial-Place." If our graveyards are bleak, our landscapes are sublime.

As an unwilling law student in the office of Wendell Phillips, Bryant solaced himself by devouring the *Lyrical Ballads*. What effects that encounter had on him can be seen in a poem he wrote the next year. Entitled "Inscription for the Entrance to a Wood," it exhorts a nameless "Stranger" to turn to Nature as balm for the guilt and misery of the human world:

> Even the green trees
> Partake the soft contentment; as they bend
> To the soft winds, the sun from the blue sky
> Looks in and sheds a blessing on the scene.
> Scarce less the cleft-born wild-flower seems to enjoy
> Existence, than the winged plunderer
> That sucks its sweets.[10]

The Bryant poem blends the metrical pattern of "Tintern Abbey" with the sentiments of "Expostulation and Reply." Just this sort of weak solution of Wordsworth or Byron *was* American poetry in the 1820s and 1830s. We know that Bryant's verse was one of the things Emerson had in mind when he launched his famous attack on the imitativeness of American art in "The American Scholar" and complained in his journal: "Our poetry reminds me of the cat-bird who sings so affectedly & vaingloriously to me near Walden. Very sweet & musical! very various! fine execution! but so conscious! and such a *performer! not a note is his own*, except at last, *miow, miow*."[11] But not every poem of Bryant's is what Harold Bloom would call a disaster of influence. The justly famous "To A Waterfowl" shows a more fruitful assimilation of the themes and techniques of English Romantic poetry than the unconscious parody of "Inscription for a Wood." Bryant's anxiety as he watches a lone waterfowl migrating northward against a sunset sky, his identification with the bird, and the consolation he draws from his recollection that a higher power guides both seem at first to have nothing about them that mark them as particularly "Romantic"; any meditative poet of the Age of Johnson might have said something similar.

What is new about the poem, what made it seem so fresh and original to its first readers, lies, rather, in its imagery, which reflects Bryant's new freedom to glory in the exhilarations of the infinite, and in its form, which manages to break free of the addictive cadences of the blank-verse line or the elegiac quatrain. Those sweet poisons have always been maddening to American poets. To write in traditional meter is a quick way of borrowing the resonance and authority of six centuries of English verse. Unfortunately, unless you wage constant war against the meter you have chosen, your highest success will be a kind of ventriloquism. Against this undertow American poets of the nineteenth century fought back with increasingly violent metrical strategies: the Finnish meter of *Hiawatha* or the hexameters of *Evangeline*, the crude hymn-meters of Dickinson, Whitman's expanding and contracting lines.

Bryant's modest experiment in "To A Waterfowl" is hardly so radical, yet it gives him a flexibility missing from his blank verse. By shortening the first and last lines of the stanza to trimeters while preserving the alternating rhyme scheme (a trick he seems to have picked up from some of Southey's lyrics), Bryant manages to achieve effects of considerable complexity within a relatively simple scheme. The stanzas seem to billow out and contract again with the thoughts that move from the tiny figure of the waterfowl to the immensities of sky and earth that lie beneath its flight. A phrase like "the abyss of heaven" is a catachresis Wordsworth might have admired, and indeed the poem, beneath its unexceptionable piety, manages to convey a powerful appetite for the infinite. Bryant professes fear, but what he expresses is something closer to desire:

> Whither, midst falling dew,
> While glow the heavens with the last steps of day
> Far, through the rosy depths, dost thou pursue
> Thy solitary way?[12]

In the stanza that asserts the faith—

> There is a Power whose care
> Teaches thy way along a pathless coast—
> The desert and illimitable air—
> Lone wandering, but not lost

—what we remember is not the consolation but the line "the desert and illimitable air." *Desert* is a grammatical pun of a kind later much favored by Dickinson; as one hears the stanza the word at first seems to be a substantive, like *coast*, as if deserts were part of the waterfowl's route. Only at the end of the line is it clear that the word *desert* is an adjective modifying *air*, sensory ballast for the formidably abstract *illimitable*. Yet the ambiguity remains just long enough to convert the air into a real wasteland, an airy Sinai for the waterfowl to cross before it reaches the promised land of its nesting ground. Like the thoughts of Belial as Wordsworth described them in his fragmentary essay "The Sublime and the Beautiful," the waterfowl "tolerate[s] neither limit nor circumscription," and what Bryant seems to envy is not so much the assurance of its safe arrival as the wildness of its flight.[13]

In succeeding decades Bryant, Cole, and Allston, the first generation of American Romantics, began to see just what aspects of European Romanticism might be appropriated for American development. Not every subject was promising. William Blake might be able to use the idea of the American Revolution to fuel apocalyptic poetry, but on this side of the Atlantic it served as the occasion for ceremonial oratory, stodgy public self-congratulation. The French Revolution was another matter, and it had some sympathizers here, but poets who were radical politically were often artistic reactionaries. When Joel Barlow wrote his famous poem "The Hasty-Pudding" in 1793 he was an émigré standing for election as a deputy to the French Convention from the province of the Savoy (a Savoyard dish of polenta triggered his New England memories), but he wrote his poem in the polished couplets of *The Rape of the Lock*.

As for another favorite subject of European Romantic poetry—ruins, the Gothic, all those places where landscape is interpenetrated by history—America obviously fared badly here too. In "The Prairies" Bryant tries to do what he can with the mys-

terious mound-builders of the Great Plains, even pointing out desperately that the mounds were being built, or, rather, heaped, at
the same time as the Parthenon. For the most part American poets
faced a landscape devoid of history, empty of castles, villages, wayside crosses, Roman roads, anything that might lead the meditative
mind from the present back into the mysterious past. Like Bryant
in his ugly, weedy graveyard, the American poet can only murmur
sadly, "They do it better in Grasmere."

But when it came to the landscape itself—the vast, the threatening, the unexpected, the sublime—we clearly had the Europeans beaten. If you want to confront terror, be shrunken into insig-
nificance, then rebound into triumphant self-assertion, you are
better off in the Rockies than in the Alps, where the nearness of
other human beings dissipates the terror that belongs to the true
sublime. The European categories—sublime, beautiful, picturesque, and so on—seem poor ways of describing American scenery anyway. When Emerson made his second journey to Britain
in 1847–48, he found himself being quizzed by Englishmen curious about the American landscape. He was not sure what to tell
them:

> There, I thought, in America, lies nature sleeping, evergrowing,
> almost conscious, too much by half for man in the picture, and
> so giving a certain *tristesse*, like the rank vegetation of swamps
> and forests seen at night . . . ; and on it man seems not able to make
> much impression. There, in that great sloven continent, in high
> Alleghany pastures, in the sea-wide sky-skirted prairie, still sleeps
> and murmurs and hides the great mother, long since driven away
> from the trim hedge rows and over-cultivated garden of En-
> gland.[14]

The thought of American nature is oppressive, like swamp air, and
sad, and the continent itself is a sloven—yet it preserves a sense
of the numinous and occult that Europeans with their humanized
landscape have lost. Like Brackenridge, Emerson locates the
mythic beyond the frontier, though his goddess is not a Greek
muse but the mighty mother of the earliest Indo-European religion.

It began to occur to American writers that the difference between our landscape and the landscape of Europe might be made

a source of power, not a cause for envy and regret. The change in Bryant's attitude can be seen in a sonnet he wrote in 1829 to his friend Thomas Cole, the poet and painter. The sense of provincial impoverishment felt by any American artist in the early nineteenth century was naturally felt more acutely by plastic artists, who had to travel to Europe to encounter for the first time the masterpieces of their art. Cole is about to depart on such a tour, and Bryant encourages him to become a kind of representational ambassador to Europeans, showing them in pictures the sort of things Emerson despaired of conveying in words:

> Lone lakes—savannas where the bison roves—
> Rocks rich with summer garlands—solemn streams—
> Skies, where the desert eagle wheels and screams—
> Spring bloom and autumn blaze of boundless groves.[15]

But he also issues a warning. Europe is beautiful, yes, but different, and that difference can tame or destroy the one thing an American artist possesses:

> Fair scenes shall greet thee where thou goest—fair,
> But different—everywhere the trace of men,
> Paths, homes, graves, ruins, from the lowest glen,
> To where life shrinks from the fierce Alpine air.
> > Gaze on them till the tears shall dim thy sight,
> > But keep that earlier, wilder image bright.

The prosiness of the second line in this passage should not obscure its metrical genius: the way it forces us to come down hard on the final phrase—"everywhere the trace of *men*" with a shudder of Gothic horror. Men are conceived here as a form of pollution, and we root for the fierce Alpine air that makes life shrink from it. Bryant's greatest fear for Cole is that he will lose the "wildness" his experience of inhuman nature conveys, and so lose the one thing that makes him original.

Expulsion from the Garden of Eden, Thomas Cole
American, 1801–1848
Oil on canvas, 39 x 54 in. (99 x 137.2 cm.)
Gift of Mrs. Maxim Karolik for the Karolik
Collection of American Paintings, 1815–1865
Courtesy Museum of Fine Arts, Boston

He found in Cole a sympathetic audience, a kindred spirit—as Asher Durand's famous painting labels him. Already by 1826, Cole had grown restive under the conventions of European landscape painting as they were then understood by his patrons. He had wanted to paint his "Falls of Kaaterskill"—an autumn landscape of forests, thunderstorms, and waterfalls—without including human figures. But his patron had objected, suggesting instead that Cole include an Indian and a few deer. The tiny Indian visible at the center of the finished painting may represent Cole's concession to his patron's wishes.[16]

Not so the equally diminutive figures in another sublime landscape Cole painted a year or so later. It is hard to imagine a painting of "The Expulsion of Adam and Eve from the Garden" that does not include Adam and Eve, but Cole comes close to achieving it. What is remarkable about this theatrical canvas (see illustration) is how completely the scale of Cole's human figures alters the emphasis of the traditional story. The fear, grief, and guilt of the human figures are dwarfed by the self-sufficient majesty of nature; our first parents look less like recently deposed rulers of the world than like misbehaving tourists evicted from Yellowstone National Park. If we are expected to feel sympathy with anything in the painting, it is hardly the tiny pair of scurrying figures; we identify instead with the garden, which rejoices in being innocent again, free of the corrupting human presence that had disturbed its ecology of joy.

Ten years after "The Expulsion of Adam and Eve from the Garden" Cole painted a landscape entitled "Schroon Mountain." Like "Falls of Kaaterskill," "Schroon Mountain" is a wild autumn scene, but this time there is not even a hint of human presence. What moved Cole about the Adirondacks was the sense they gave of "the sublimity of untamed wildness and the majesty of the eternal mountains." They symbolized to him "quietness—solitude—the untamed—the unchanged aspect of nature." He even wrote a poem in which the spirit of Schroon Mountain is allowed to speak in his own voice, and what the spirit chiefly rejoices in is his isolation: he sings his "hymn of gladness all alone."[17]

But why should the American poet or painter rejoice in a sublimity that makes him unnecessary?[18] Bryant gives a hint of one answer when he begins "The Prairies," a blank-verse meditation commemorating his first journey to the frontier in 1832, by noting that these "gardens of the Desert," these "unshorn fields, boundless and beautiful" are things "for which the speech of England has no name."[19] The terrible monopoly the mother country has on the mother tongue is broken, at least for an instant: *prairies* is an American word for a wholly American kind of landscape. (That this moment of liberation does not last, that the poetic diction of England is harder to shed than its referential vocabulary, becomes painfully apparent a few dozen lines farther on when Bryant speaks of guiding his "steed" "o'er the verdant waste.")

Bryant praises the prairies' "encircling vastness," but the sublimity of natural objects is no guarantee that the poetry describing them will be equally sublime. What fascinates him, besides the sheer vastness of the space, is its uncanny mixture of motion and rest. The hillocks of the prairie

> stretch
> In airy undulations, far away,
> As if the Ocean, in his gentlest swell,
> Stood still, his rounded billows fixed
> And motionless forever. Motionless?—
> No—they are all unchained again. The clouds
> Sweep over with their shadows, and, beneath,
> The surface rolls and fluctuates to the eye.

The passage may owe something in technique to the many sublime cloud scenes that occur in Thomson's *Seasons*:

> Rent is the fleecy mantle of the sky;
> The clouds fly different; and the sudden sun
> By fits effulgent gilds th'illumined field
> And black by fits the shadows sweep along.
> A gaily-checkered heart-expanding view
> Far as the circling eye can shoot around.[20]

Or it may be indebted to the ice-skating scene in Wordsworth's *Prelude*, when the cliffs, appearing to continue spinning by the boy when he stops skating, gradually become "feebler and feebler" until they subside into a rest as "tranquil as dreamless sleep."[21] But neither Thomson nor Wordsworth would likely have exclaimed, as Bryant did looking at his prairies, "Man hath no part

in all this glorious work." The prairies are empty of men and virtually untouched by them; even the mysterious mound-builders
were transient, and the Red Men who succeeded them ephemeral.
Toward the close of the poem Bryant tries to work up enthusiasm
for the progress of civilization—the approaching white men
whose imported bees already buzz on an alien landscape. But his
heart is not in it. We can feel his relief when the poem ends by
shattering this vision of civilization:

> All at once,
> A fresher wind sweeps by, and breaks my dream,
> And I am in the wilderness alone.

Bryant loves the wilderness because it is original, but there
are other reasons for valuing it as well. In an essay on Robert Frost,
Auden comments on the bleakness of Frost's landscape and sees
in it an accurate reflection of Nature's hostility to man on the
American continent. This bleakness engenders qualities—
toughness, honesty, stoicism—that Auden admires in poets as
much as in citizens. But originality and stoicism are not the end
of Nature's gifts to man in America.[22]

"The Oven-Bird" is a brilliant and funny American version of
"To a Skylark" or Keats's Nightingale Ode. It is ostensibly a com-
plaint in the manner of Bryant's "The Burial-Place" about the ugliness of American bird-song and, by implication, about the sorry
plight of the American poet who can find no other symbol for his
art. But Frost's ear for dialect and his technical mastery make his
poem a bitter comedy of diction, not a collapse into bathos. Consider two of the poem's opening lines:

> There is a singer everyone has heard,
> He makes the solid tree-trunks sound again.[23]

That makes a credible distich, the sort of thing one might find in
the better blank-verse poems of Bryant or Emerson. But of course
Frost's poem doesn't really go that way; in the poem itself those
lines are woven together with lines of a different provenance.

> There is a singer everyone has heard,
> Loud, a midsummer and a mid-wood bird.

> He makes the solid tree-trunks sound again.
> He says that leaves are old and that for flowers
> Mid-summer is to spring as one to ten.

The clumsy caesura after the first syllable of the second line is brilliant, like a similar metrical joke in Chaucer's portrait of Absolon—"But sooth to seyn, he was somdeel squaymous / Of fartyng, and of speche daungerous"[24]—it functions as the prosodic equivalent of onomatopoeia. More subtle is the kind of double rhythm certain lines establish as they shuttle between formal pentameter rhythm and the colloquial rhythms of American speech. Frost was fascinated by this problem, which his move to England in 1912 had made more immediate. In a letter to Robert Bridges, Frost wrote:

> The living part of a poem is the intonation entangled in the syntax idiom and meaning of a sentence. It is only there for those who have heard it publicly in conversation. It is not for us in any Greek or Latin poem because our ears have not been filled with the tones of Greek or Roman talk. It is the most volatile and at the same time the most important part of poetry.[25]

So little has contemporary criticism concerned itself with this intonational punning that I am not aware of a term for it, though it is the source of the humor in that little Frost poem Randall Jarrell once called a Stanford-Binet test of the imagination:

> But Islands of the Blessed, bless you, son,
> I never came upon a blessed one.[26]

In "The Oven-Bird" Frost creates lines which invite two kinds of performance: one decorous, elegiac, serious; one Yankee, funny, and mean.

> He says that leaves are old and that for flowers
> Mid-summer is to spring as one to ten.
>
> .   .
>
> And comes that other fall we name the fall
> He says the highway dust is over all.

The undersong of the colloquial is, after all, the oven-bird's only music, his margin of originality—and it may be Frost's as well.

> The bird would cease and be as other birds

> But that he knows in singing not to sing.
> The question that he frames in all but words
> Is what to make of a diminished thing.

The "diminished thing" the oven-bird asks about may be variously interpreted: summer as compared to spring, middle age as compared to youth, the oven-bird as compared to the nightingale, the American poetic tradition as compared to the English. But the last line is only elegiac if you stress the word *diminished*. If you stress the word *make*, then Frost, like Milton's Mammon (the most American of all the devils) is merely telling us to seek our own good from ourselves.

The title "The Most of It" might, in fact, be considered Frost's answer to the oven-bird's question: what do you make of a diminished thing? Yet the title is also curiously self-abnegating, since the "great buck" so powerfully represented in the poem is hardly a diminished thing; it is, in fact, the link between representation and myth.

Brackenridge had hoped to find a muse in a thicket. The solitary figure in Frost's poem, too, hopes to wake an answer from the universe, but only hears "the mocking echo" of his own voice "from some tree-hidden cliff across the lake." Several critics have noted the resemblance to Wordsworth's Boy of Winander, but it seems to me that Frost also wished to suggest more ancient parallels. An epithet like "boulder-broken" sounds like something out of Homer, just as the plight of Frost's solitary man recalls the frustration of Odysseus or Telemakhos at tantalizing visits from gods who always appear in disguise.

> He would cry out on life, that what it wants
> Is not its own love back in copy speech,
> But counter-love, original response,
> And nothing ever came of what he cried
> Unless it was the embodiment that crashed
> In the cliff's talus on the other side.[27]

Embodiment sound like one of Wordsworth's curiously concrete abstractions; the meter even requires us to elide the preceding article with it. But the hope this sublime abstraction expresses is proved false, for as the embodiment swims nearer, the speaker can see that it is not embodied love, not embodied anything.

As a great buck it powerfully appeared
Pushing the crumpled water up ahead,
And landed pouring like a waterfall
And stumbled through the bush with horny tread,
And forced the underbrush—and that was all.

Hope changed to awe, awe to disappointment—if Frost were Wordsworth we might expect here a sudden recovery in which the mind recognizes sublimity in its own capacity for making deifying mistakes. Instead the poem ends anticlimactically, and we are left meditating not on the mind but on the great buck at the moment of its epiphany, when its size and power make the perceiver for a moment uncertain whether he sees a great buck or some god—say, Zeus—in the shape of a great buck, forcing the underbrush on some errand of desire or fury. What Frost seems to suggest is that American longing and American nostalgia are both mistaken. Myth lies neither behind us, in Europe, nor beyond us, on the frontier, but in those moments when perception becomes uncanny, and suddenly finds in the deserted landscape a more than human power.

NOTES

1. Max Beerbohm, *The Illustrated Zuleika Dobson, or, An Oxford Love Story*, intro. by John Hall (Milan: The Folio Society), pp. 120–21.

2. Beerbohm, *Zuleika Dobson*, p. 121.

3. Randall Jarrell, "Reflections on Wallace Stevens," in *Poetry and the Age* (New York: Farrar, Straus, and Giroux, 1953), p. 134.

4. From "A Dogrel Said to be by Auld Brackie on the Scots-Irishman," *Tree of Liberty*, June 20, 1801; quoted in Claude M. Newlin, *The Life and Writings of Hugh Henry Brackenridge* (Princeton: Princeton University Press, 1932), p. 5. I am indebted to Albert J. von Frank's discussion of Brackenridge's dialect poems in his excellent recent study, *The Sacred Game: Provincialism and Frontier Consciousness in American Literature, 1630–1860* (New York: Cambridge University Press, 1985), pp. 42–45.

5. W. H. Auden, "American Poetry," in *The Dyer's Hand and Other Essays* (New York: Faber and Faber, 1963), pp. 357, 363–64.

6. Auden, "American Poetry," p. 359.

7. Von Frank, *Sacred Game*, pp. 6–9.

8. William Cullen Bryant, "The Burial-Place: A Poetic Fragment," in *The Poetical Works of William Cullen Bryant*, ed. Parke Godwin, 2 vols. (New York: D. Appleton, 1883), 1:28.

9. Bryant, "Burial-Place," 1:18–19.

10. Ibid., 1:24.

11. Ralph Waldo Emerson, *The Journals and Miscellaneous Notebooks of Ralph Waldo Emerson*, ed. William Gillman, et. al., 16 vols. (Cambridge: Harvard University Press, 1960–81), 8:173.

12. Bryant, "Burial-Place," 1:26.

13. William Wordsworth, *The Prose Works of William Wordsworth*, ed. W. J. B. Owen and Jane Worthington Smyser, 3 vols. (Oxford: Clarendon Press, 1974), 2:354; quoted in Frances Ferguson, *Wordsworth: Language as Counter-Spirit* (New Haven: Yale University Press, 1977), p. 115.

14. *The Complete Works of Ralph Waldo Emerson*, ed. Edward Waldo Emerson, 12 vols. (Boston: Houghton Mifflin, 1903–1904), 5:288.

15. Bryant, "Burial-Place," 1:219.

16. See *American Paradise: The World of the Hudson River School* (New York: Metropolitan Museum of Art, 1987), pp. 120–22. "Falls of Kaaterskill" is reproduced on page 121.

17. *American Paradise*, pp. 134–35.

18. For a provocative discussion of this question, see Richard Poirier, "Writing Off the Self," in *The Renewal of Literature: Emersonian Reflections* (New York: Random House, 1987), pp. 182–223. Poirier's remark that "we are not required to think of loss or reduction or self-dissolutions as if it were synonymous with deprivation" was my starting point for this essay, and my debt to him should be apparent throughout.

19. Bryant, "Burial-Place," 1:228–32.

20. James Thomson, "Autumn," from *The Seasons* (London: C. Whittingham, 1802), ll. 36–41.

21. William Wordsworth, *The Prelude, or the Growth of a Poet's Mind*, ed. Ernest de Selincourt and Helen Darbishire, 2nd ed. (Oxford: Clarendon Press, 1959), Book 1, ll. 462–63.

22. Auden, "Robert Frost," in *The Dyer's Hand*, pp. 337–53.

23. Robert Frost, *The Complete Poetry of Robert Frost*, ed. Edward Connery Latham (New York: Holt, Rinehart and Winston, 1967), p. 119.

24. Geoffrey Chaucer, "The Miller's Tale," *The Works of Geoffrey Chaucer*, ed. F. N. Robinson, 2nd ed. (Boston: Houghton Mifflin, 1957), p. 50.

25. Quoted in Lawrence Thompson and R. H. Winnick, *Robert Frost: A Biography* (New York: Holt, Rinehart and Winston, 1981), p. 176.

26. Frost, *Complete Poetry*, p. 363.

27. Frost, *Complete Poetry*, p. 338.

Back Home Again in Indiana
HART CRANE'S *THE BRIDGE*

JOHN T. IRWIN

Several years ago I published a book called *American Hiero-glyphics*, that dealt with the influence of the decipherment of the Egyptian hieroglyphics on the literature of the American Renaissance and used this rather specialized area of inquiry as a means of raising larger questions about the figuration of the self and the search for origins in that form of late romanticism that is nineteenth-century American symbolism. It is this question of origins and their figuration, as posed in the writings of the American Renaissance, that I would like to pursue here into twentieth-century American poetry. One of the most common poetic figures in the English romantic tradition for the quest for origins (whether the origin of the self, of language, or of the human) is, of course, the search for the source of a river. In the wake of the publication of Sir James Bruce's *Travels to Discover the Source of the Nile* (1790), this figure for the pursuit of origins appears in works as various as Shelley's *Alastor*, Coleridge's "Kubla Khan," Book 6 of Wordsworth's *The Prelude*, and George Darley's *Nepenthe*, to name a few. In the American Renaissance the most striking examples of the figure are found in the works of Poe, whether in the unfinished *The Journal of Julius Rodman* (about a man who explores the Louisiana Territory ten years before Lewis and Clark, looking for, among other things, the source of the Mississippi) or in *The Narrative of A. Gordon Pym* (about a journey to the polar abyss). One might wonder for a moment what a journey to the polar abyss has to do with the search for the source of a river. The trope linking the two derives from the classical notion of the ultimate circularity of the waters of the earth: the notion that the waters of the oceans flow into the earth through openings at the poles, travel through subterranean passages to the equator, where they issue forth in springs and fountains that are the sources of great rivers that in turn flow back to the seas and thence to the polar abysses. As in any circular system, origin and end coincide, so that the search for the source of a great river can be approached from the opposite direction through a voyage to the polar abyss. (We might recall in this regard that in Book 6 of *The Prelude* Wordsworth correctly locates the source of the Nile in Abyssinia, and that in *Pym* the languages which the hero encounters in the vicinity of the polar abyss—Arabic, Coptic, and Ethiopic—are the languages of the Nile valley.)

Perhaps the most notable use of this romantic trope in twentieth-century American poetry occurs in Hart Crane's *The Bridge*, an epic representation of the search for American origins. Part of the poem's action involves a phantasized journey by its speaker back in time to the pre-Columbian world of the Indians to observe a primal scene of origin in which a people and a land are joined in the sacred marriage of the Indian chief Maquokeeta (whose name means "Big River") and the maiden Pocahontas, symbol of the virgin continent. And the metaphoric vehicle for this return to origin is the speaker's journey down the Mississippi River to the abyss of the Gulf. In his role as native son imaginatively present at, imaginatively participating in, the generation of the American self, Crane found that the work of depicting a primal scene of national origin inevitably involved for him a reassessment of the emotions associated with his personal origin, an examination of the way in which his stormy relationship with his parents affected his imagining of that central scene in which the seminal river pours into the abyss. That Crane understood this quest as a romantic project is clear from his 1930 response to Allen Tate's review of the poem: "The fact that you posit *The Bridge* at the end of a tradition of romanticism may prove to have been an accurate prophecy, but I don't yet feel that such a statement can be taken as a foregone conclusion. A great deal of romanticism may persist—of the sort to deserve serious consideration."[1]

In pursuing this inquiry into the figuration of origins in *The Bridge*, I want to focus in particular on the "Indiana" section of the poem. In his 1927 letter to his benefactor Otto Kahn, which outlines the plan and progress of *The Bridge*, Crane, noting that the "Indiana" section "is not complete as yet," describes it as "the monologue of an Indiana farmer; time, about 1860. He has failed in the gold-rush and is returned to till the soil. His monologue is a farewell to his son, who is leaving for a life on the sea. It is a lyrical summary of the period of conquest, and his wife, the mother who died on the way back from the gold-rush, is alluded to in a way which implies her succession to the nature-symbolism of Pocahontas" (*L*, 307). What interests us in this description of "Indiana" is that the roles assigned to the father and mother in this section as it was conceived in 1927 are reversed in the published version of 1930. In its completed form "Indiana" is the monologue not of a father but of a mother: it is the wife of the Indiana farmer who bids farewell to her son as he leaves for a life on the sea. And, conversely, the parent who dies on the way back from the gold rush is the father rather than the mother. The question, then, is what occurred during the two-year period between Crane's description of "Indiana" in the letter to Kahn and the completion of the poem, to cause this reversal in the roles that had originally been projected for the father and mother.

We know that the single most important event in Crane's personal life during this period was the definitive break he made with his mother in the spring of 1928 and the subsequent reversal in his long-standing opposing attitudes toward his parents. Since at least late adolescence Crane had been close to his mother, who, seeing her own "artistic" temperament reborn in her son, encouraged his poetic career, and either at odds with or estranged from his father, for whom success in business was an ideal inherited from his own father that he had tried to pass on to his son, an ideal in relation to which Hart could never be anything but a failure. When Grace and Clarence Crane's marriage began to fall apart, their son became both a prize to be won and a weapon to be wielded in the battle between them. Crane's alliance with his mother lasted from the time of his parents' divorce in 1917 until

the early months of 1928, even though his precarious finances required that he remain on civil terms with Clarence Crane (or C.
A. as he was called), to whom he periodically applied for loans.
At this period Crane and his mother were both living in Los Angeles. Hart was acting as secretary and companion to Herbert Wise,
and Grace was staying with her ailing mother in a bungalow in
Hollywood. In February 1928, Hart, perhaps in response to
Grace's requests that he introduce her to his Hollywood friends
or fearing that she might hear of his escapades, told his mother
that he was a homosexual. There are conflicting reports about
Grace's immediate reaction to the news, but Crane told a friend
that she was "visibly upset" and that "for days afterward she
seemed to him cold and contemptuous."[2] Whatever the truth was,
the disclosure of his homosexuality placed an enormous strain on
his relationship with his mother, a strain that was soon com-
pounded when, after quitting his job with Wise at the end of February, Crane moved in with his mother and grandmother in mid-
March. His grandmother was dying, and Hart spent part of each
day serving as her nurse and companion while at the same time
coping with his mother's own "nervous collapse." For the next two
months the relationship between Hart and Grace steadily wors-
ened. Unterecker describes Crane's

> growing conviction that his mother's love for him had degener-
> ated into a brutal possessiveness. . . . Not only did he discover that
> Grace was jealous of his love for his grandmother; he also
> discovered—recalling his past—a lifelong pattern of jealousy:
> Grace "guarding" him from any deep affection for his father, for
> his other relatives, for the girls whom, in a more conventional
> boyhood, he might have come to love. . . . She would never volun-
> tarily, he felt, allow him to love anyone other than her; nor, he
> was sure, would she ever allow him a life substantially indepen-
> dent of her. (p. 540)

By the end of May 1928, Crane was desperate to leave, and
after packing surreptitiously for a week, he stole away from the
bungalow in the dead of night heading for New York, never to see
his mother again. If, as Emerson says, poets write with actions as
well as with words, then the route that Crane chose in leaving his
mother to return to the east was a symbolic statement whose gloss

is to be found in *The Bridge*. After traveling by train from Los Angeles to New Orleans, he continued by ship through the Gulf of Mexico and up the East Coast to New York. In a letter dated June 14, 1928, written to his father after his return, he gave some indication of the significance of this journey in his description of a day he spent in New Orleans: "The boat ride down the delta of the Mississippi (we were from 10 till 5 p.m. completing it) was one of the great days of my life. It was a place I had so often imagined and, as you know, written about in my River section of *The Bridge*. There is something tragically beautiful about the scene, the great, magnificent Father of Waters pouring itself at last into the oblivion of the Gulf!"[3] In recounting his boat ride on "the great, magnificent Father of Waters" to his own father, Crane evokes this transitional place he "had so often imagined," this threshold where the seminal river pours itself into the oblivion of the gulf, as a "tragically beautiful . . . scene"—a primal scene in a Oedipal tragedy, I would suggest. Pausing in New Orleans at mid-continent, midway in his flight from his mother, Crane recalled the "River section of *The Bridge*" and the quester's imaginative identification with the hobo Dan Midland, whose body was cast into the Mississippi to descend to the submarine, amniotic world of the Gulf. He may have sensed even then that his eastward flight from his mother would turn out to be a circular journey like all of those in *The Bridge*, a journey whose turnings would finally bring him back to the oblivion of the Gulf four years later.

In spite of periodic setbacks, Hart's relationship with his father improved steadily after his break with Grace. Hart's new sense of the way in which his mother had turned him against his father was matched by a new willingness on Clarence Crane's part to admit that his own life was no model for his son's. In July 1928, the elder Crane wrote Hart:

> You and I agree now as never before that your father has made a failure of his life because he has paid too much attention to hard work and not enough to play. I have been too ambitious for things that really did not amount to anything at all. . . . It was born in my father to be saving and energetic. All of my younger life he kept me at it until I got the same impression of things . . . so I kept at it and kept at it. . . . Now, I don't want you to do this way, for I have lived to see the folly of it all. . . . I think you write well, and

unquestionably have better than an average ability for it, but no business is any good unless it pays a dividend and if writing does not pay a dividend then you have to do something else.... I cannot tell you what to do. On that subject my advice has been all wrong for many years. (*L*, 627–29).

But while Crane grew closer to his father, he became increasingly hostile toward his mother, until the one he had always loved best came to seem his nemesis. Unterecker describes the elaborate precautions that Crane took during the rest of his life to keep his mother from learning of his whereabouts: "Each flight—prompted always by terror that she might persuade him to return—led to an orgy of drunken escape and complex moves from place to place as, swearing friends to secrecy, he attempted to cover his trail.... So long as she lived, he felt, she would continue to hunt him down" (p. 542). It is significant that while Crane was working on *The Bridge* and its vision of a return to national origin, a return whose anthropomorphic representation was the son's return to the womb of the triple goddess (the virgin-mother-whore Pocahontas), he was fleeing desperately from his own mother. In February 1929, Crane wrote to his friends the Rychtariks from Paris, "My mother has made it impossible for me to live in my own country" (*L*, 338).

That Crane understood what was involved psychologically in his mother's obsessive attachment is clear from a letter he wrote to Grace's sister-in-law Zell in the late fall of 1928: Grace "is profoundly attached to me, really loves me, I know. But there are mixtures of elements in this attachment that are neither good for her nor for me. Psychoanalysis reveals many things that it would be well for Grace to know" (Unterecker, p. 565). Crane's mention of psychoanalysis no doubt reflects the knowledge of psychoanalytic theory that he had acquired during the fall of 1928 from his friend Solomon Grunberg, who was part owner of a bookstore Crane frequented and who practiced as a lay analyst at the time Crane knew him. Unterecker reports that though Hart "declined Grunberg's offer to explore his mind ('If I let myself be psychoanalyzed, I'll *never* finish *The Bridge*!'), he did, on long walks, take advantage of Grunberg's listening silences, his offhand leading questions, his summaries of pertinent 'classical' cases" (p. 566). During October and November of 1928, "Hart worried incessantly about his relationship to his mother and father, Grunberg said; and, once, on one of their meanderings, Hart talked about the nightmares he had been having, nightmares that made insomnia preferable to sleep" (Unterecker, p. 566). Unterecker records two of the dreams that Crane recounted to Grunberg, dreams that not only shed light on Crane's relationship with his parents at this period but also suggest the way in which his differing attitudes toward his father and mother affected his imagining of the primal scene of origin in *The Bridge.*

Before examining these two dreams in some detail, we should note that Crane's knowledge of psychoanalysis, however slight or simplified, tends to give a dual focus to a psychoanalytic reading of his poetry by raising the possibility that Crane consciously introduced psychoanalytic structures into his poem to shape the biographical material. As a result, a psychoanalytic reading of *The Bridge* inevitably becomes an exercise in the history of ideas as well, which is to say, becomes by implication a study of the influence of psychoanalysis on the work of an American poet of the 1920s. In what follows, the psychoanalytic discourse moves back and forth across three Cranian "texts" that, in their bearing on the poet's relationship with his parents, exhibit a revealing structural continuity—a poetic text (*The Bridge*), a biographical text (Crane's life as reflected in his letters and the biographies of Horton and Unterecker), and a dream text (the two nightmares that Crane recounted to Grunberg which Unterecker includes in his biography). Though the poetic and the dream texts both involve the encryption of personal material, the level of encryption (the force of repression) is obviously greater in the poetry than in the dreams, for not only was the poetic text certain to be seen by Crane's parents but, to judge from the letters to his father and mother citing salient passages from the poem, Crane actively called it to their attention as part of what appears to have been an oblique form of self-revelation, a veiled exhibition of his deepest feelings about his parents, his personal origin.

The first of Crane's two nightmares, according to Unterecker, seemed to Grunberg clearly about Hart's father and about Hart's own sense of inferiority. Grunberg said he was sure Hart was well aware of its symbolic content. It involved a river, Hart told him. Hart had somehow gotten into a little boat—a rowboat or a canoe—and was floating down the center of the river. He could see the shores on either side and far in the distance he could hear a waterfall. Though his boat floated along very peacefully, he began to worry as the noise of the waterfall got louder. Finally he became frightened. The boat had picked up speed. At it was swept closer and closer to the waterfall, he suddenly saw, standing on the shore just above the falls, an enormous naked Negro. Hart could not keep his eyes off the Negro's huge penis. Even though the noise of the falls was deafening and he was thoroughly frightened, he kept watching. Suddenly he realized that he was naked, too. The boat was at the very brink of the falls now and he felt himself covered with shame. His own penis was tiny, he knew, as tiny as a baby's, and he forced himself to look at it. (pp. 566–67)

The resonances of this dream both in Crane's personal life and in his poetry are far-reaching and complex. Grunberg was undoubtedly correct in thinking that the dream was "about Hart's father and about Hart's own sense of inferiority," yet we should avoid reading the figure of the black man in the dream as simply and solely an image of Crane's father. He is that, but he is a great deal more as well. Keep in mind that it was less than six months prior to this dream that Hart, in describing his boat ride on "the great, magnificent Father of Waters" to the elder Crane, pointed out that he had previously depicted this "tragically beautiful . . . scene" of the Mississippi "pouring itself at last into the oblivion of the Gulf" in the "River section of *The Bridge*." The relevant part of "The River"—both to Crane's real boat ride down the Mississippi Delta and to his nightmare boat ride past the naked black man on the bank—is obvious. As the body of the hobo Dan Midland, who has apparently been killed in a confrontation with the sinister "Sheriff, Brakeman and Authority," is floating down the Mississippi, Crane describes the river's progress in terms that prefigure his dream:

You will not hear it as the sea; even stone
Is not more hushed by gravity ... But slow,
As loth to take more tribute—sliding prone
Like one whose eyes were buried long ago

The River, spreading, flows—and spends your dream.
What are you, lost within this tideless spell?
You are your father's father, and the stream—
A liquid theme that floating niggers swell.

Damp tonnage and alluvial march of days—
Nights turbid, vascular with silted shale
And roots surrendered down of morraine clays;
The Mississippi drinks the farthest dale.

O quarrying passion, undertowed sunlight!
The basalt surface drags a jungle grace
Ochreous and lynx-barred in lengthening might;
Patience! and you shall reach the biding place!

Over De Soto's bones the freighted floors
Throb past the City storied of three thrones.
Down two more turns the Mississippi pours
(Anon tall ironsides up from salt lagoons)

And flows within itself, heaps itself free.
All fades but one thin skyline 'round ... Ahead
No embrace opens but the stinging sea;
The River lifts itself from its long bed,

Poised wholly on its dream, a mustard glow
Tortured with history, its one will—flow!
—The Passion spreads in wide tongues, choked and slow,
Meeting the Gulf, hosannas silently below.[4]

That passion is the subject of these lines seems certain, in-deed they could be said to represent a double dream of passion consistent with a double identification with father and mother. At the climax, the male Father of Waters "lifts itself from its long bed" to pour into the female Gulf. Crane had enclosed an earlier version of these seven stanzas in a letter to his mother dated June 18, 1927, saying that he hoped she would "enjoy the epic sweep of the thing—like a great river of time that takes everything and pours it into a great abyss" (*LF*, 584). But prior to this union of male and female, there is a union of male and male as the poetic quester, imaginatively identified with Dan Midland's corpse, enters the Father of Waters. (This same structure—a union, an imaginative identification, of male and male preceding a union of male and female—governs the quester's subsequent fantasized participation in the sacred marriage of Maquokeeta and Pocahontas, to which "The River" leads.)

One of the obvious similarities between Crane's description of the quester's entry into the Father of Waters and his own nightmare of a boat ride down river is that the river in each case is associated with the figure of a black man. In the poem the Mississippi is described as "a liquid theme that floating niggers swell," while in the dream Crane sees on the river bank a naked black man with a "huge penis." Indeed, the image of a huge penis seems to be implicit in the passage from the poem as well: the floating blacks "swell" the paternal stream whose dark "basalt surface drags a jungle grace / Ochreous and lynx-barred in *lengthening might*" [italics mine] as it moves toward the climactic union with the Gulf. The association of the muddy, brown Mississippi with the figure of a powerful black man is easily understood, and Crane would have found a particularly striking example of this association in a popular Broadway musical of the day. *Show Boat* had opened in New York on December 27, 1927, and one of the high points of the musical was the song "Ol' Man River." (The Mississippi had been much in the news during the spring and summer of 1927 when *Show Boat* was being readied for Broadway. Its spring flood had been one of the worst in modern times, making that year memorable in the lore of the river. One recalls the opening of "The Old Man" section of Faulkner's *The Wild Palms*, "Once [it was in Mississippi in May in the flood year 1927]. . . .") Jerome Kern and Oscar Hammerstein had written "Ol' Man River" with Crane's friend the black singer and actor Paul Robeson in mind. The show's producer, Florenz Ziegfeld, had announced the signing of Robeson for the role of Joe as early as December 1926, but because of delays in getting *Show Boat* into rehearsal, Robeson accepted other engagements and as a result did not appear in the New York production,[5] though he recorded "Ol' Man River" for

Victor Records on March 1, 1928, with Paul Whiteman's Concert Orchestra[6] and starred in the London production of *Show Boat* which opened in early May 1928. Charles Morgan, commenting on Robeson's version of "Ol' Man River" in *The New York Times* for May 27, 1928, predicted that his "hymning of the Mississippi" was sure to "become popular."[7] "Ol' Man River" became identified with Robeson, and in turn Robeson's image as the archetypal noble black man of the 1920s struggling against the white man's oppressive paternalism became associated with the song. Crane's nightmare about the enormous naked black man on the river bank occurred in October or November 1928, and on November 30, 1928, Crane's friend Herbert Wise took him to see a performance of *Show Boat* in New York (*L*, 331), though Crane had undoubtedly heard the record of "Ol' Man River" and knew of its dramatic context long before this. In late December, Crane saw *Show Boat* again in London, visited Robeson backstage, and later spent time with Robeson and his wife in their London home (*L*, 333). Crane had first met Robeson in 1924 when the actor starred in Eugene O'Neill's *All God's Chillun Got Wings*, a play "about a negro who marries a white woman," as Crane wrote his mother in March 1924 (*LF*, 287). To judge from another letter to his mother two months later, the black singer had assumed heroic stature for Crane: "Robeson is one of the most superb sort of people. Very black, a deep resonance to his voice and actor eyes, Phi Beta Kappa, half-back on Walter Camps all-star eleven, and a very fine mind and nature" (*LF*, 315).

Given the popular practice of imaging the Father of Waters as a powerful black man, it requires no great imaginative leap to read the black man by the river in Crane's nightmare as an encrypted image of Crane's father, which is to say, as an image of the threatening aspect of the father. Yet to understand the full significance of the figure of the black man in Crane's dream, we must consider a crucial passage from his life in which he apparently felt that his father had treated him like a Negro. In January 1920, Hart, honoring his father's wish that he enter the family business, went to work for the Crane Chocolate Company in Cleveland and remained in his father's employ for the next fourteen months. Near the end of February 1921, the elder Crane assigned Hart to supervise a basement storeroom in a Cleveland restaurant that the company owned. Unterecker describes the surroundings:

> Across a basement corridor from him were the restaurant kitchens, where Hart delighted in the relaxed, free, good times of the Negro cooks and dishwashers. Grace, when Hart wrote her of his transfer, felt that C. A.'s assigning Hart to this job in this place—particularly because Hart had replaced a discharged Negro handyman—was a deliberate effort to humiliate son and mother; but Hart, lacking Grace's prejudices, managed to thrive on the underground life. For the first time in months he set to work on a poem and in the leisure of his storeroom turned out the first drafts of "Black Tambourine," a study of the store's porter, who, "forlorn in the cellar," seemed caught between two unavailable worlds: lost Africa nothing more than racial memory, and the white, smiling world of the restaurant upstairs barred to him by the world's closed door. (p. 188)

Commenting on the poem in a letter to Gorham Munson, Crane says that "in the popular mind" the Negro has been "sentimentally or brutally 'placed'" in a "midkingdom ... somewhere between man and beast" (*L*, 58). Crane introduces the figure of Aesop into the poem not only to evoke through Aesop's animal fables this world midway "between man and beast" but also to suggest the way in which the slave Aesop transfigured and thus redeemed the condition of slavery, in which men are treated like animals, by the poetic art of fables in which animals behave like men:

> Aesop, driven to pondering, found
> Heaven with the tortoise and the hare;
> Fox brush and sow ear top his grave
> And mingling incantations on the air. (p. 4)

On the morning of April 19, 1921, Crane's father paid a surprise visit to the restaurant where his son worked. Hart had left the storeroom and was having a late breakfast with his black friends in the kitchen. As Unterecker recounts it, "their jokes and stories filled the big kitchen with good-natured laughter, and none of them saw Hart's father descend the basement stairs." The elder Crane "reprimanded Hart, ordered him to return to the storeroom, and, as Hart turned to go, added that since Hart was again living

with his mother, he could eat his meals with her, too. Hart interpreted the remark as an attack both on himself and on Grace. He
whirled to face his father, threw the storeroom keys on the floor,
and, in front of the other help, yelled that he was through with
C. A. for good. C. A., by now as angry as his son, turned white with
rage, shouting that if Hart didn't apologize he would be disinher-
ited. Hart climaxed the scene by screaming curses on his father
and his father's money and rushing blindly from the store" (p.
198). The following day Crane wrote to Gorham Munson that he
had quit his father's employ for good after having "been treated
like a dog now for two years" (*L*, 55). And later he complained
that he had "thrown away" two years "at the feet" of his father performing "peon duties" (Unterecker, p. 200). In view of Crane's evocation of the black's mid-kingdom "somewhere between man and
beast" in "Black Tambourine," it seems clear that Crane felt his father had kept him in economic slavery, had treated the poet
(Aesop) "like a dog" by placing him among, and equating him
with, the descendants of black slaves who depended on the elder
Crane's paternal care.

This early equation of the images of son, poet, slave, and black
man in Crane's mind helps explain the later association in "The
River" of the poetic quester and the blacks as singers. In the passage that immediately precedes the quester's imagined descent
into the Father of Waters, Crane evokes the image of the Mississippi in the context of a black spiritual:

> Oh, lean from the window, if the train slows down,
> As though you touched hands with some ancient clown,
> —A little while gaze absently below
> And hum *Deep River* with them while they go. (p. 68)

The opening line of "Deep River" ("Deep river, my heart lies over
Jordan") is echoed a few lines later in the description of those
who, feeding the river timelessly, "win no frontier by their way-
ward plight, / But drift in stillness, as from Jordan's brow" (p.
68). (The Mississippi and the Jordan are also associated in the
verse of "Ol' Man River": the black man says, "Let me go 'way from
de Mississippi, / Let me go 'way from de white men boss, /
Show me dat stream called de river Jordan, / Dat's de ol'
stream dat I long to cross.") It is worth noting that Paul Robeson

recorded "Deep River" for Victor Records on May 10, 1927,[8] and that Crane, though he began jotting down lines for "The River" as early as July 1926, wrote the bulk of the poem in mid-June 1927 (Unterecker, p. 490). We should also recall that according to an early outline of *The Bridge*, which he included in a letter to Otto Kahn dated March 18, 1926, Crane planned to make the dramatic speaker of one section of the poem a "Negro porter" on the "Calgary Express ... singing to himself (a jazz form for this) of his sweetheart and the death of John Brown alternately" (*L*, 241). The section, which was intended to take "in the whole racial history of the Negro in America,"[9] as Crane noted in a synopsis, was never written, but traces of it can perhaps be seen in "The River" with its reference to "Pullman breakfasters" (p. 68) and its image of someone leaning from the train to hum "Deep River." At any rate the association of the Mississippi with the song of a black singer is clearly present in the poem even before the crucial stanza in which river, song, and singer merge, as, "lost within this tideless spell," you become "your father's father, and the stream— / A liquid theme that floating niggers swell." The river is an unending stream of song, a "tideless spell," which is to say, a timeless (magical) spell (incantation, verse, charm [Latin *carmina*, song]) in which the quester immerses himself and to which he joins his own song. And what the river-song is to the black singer, the bridge-song is to the poetic quester, as Crane makes clear when he echoes this passage from "The River" in the concluding "Atlantis" section: Having addressed the symbolic bridge of the poem as "O River-throated," the quester exhorts his poetic vision: "Atlantis,— hold thy floating singer late!" (p. 116). As the "liquid theme" of the river holds the "floating niggers," so the visionary submerged continent, the mythic land bridge between East and West, is meant to hold the "floating singer." Significantly, the words "niggers" and "singer" are anagrams of one another, an encrypted association that Crane, who describes in "O Carib Isle!" how the temporal erosions of nature "shift, subvert, / And anagrammatize your name" (p. 156), clearly intended. For this anagram, this hidden equation of names, expresses Crane's sense (dating from at least the time of "Black Tambourine") that for white, paternal, commercial America the "singer" (poet) is a "nigger" (slave). The "niggers" and the "singer" are both described as "floating" not only because they expect, in trusting themselves to their songs as a swimmer trusts himself to the water, to be buoyed up and sustained by the creative stream, but also because blacks and poets were considered by commercial America to be economically unstable, to be floaters or drifters. And it is in this regard that the "niggers" and the "singer" are associated with the hoboes in "The River," who are in turn presented as singers:

> Strange bird-wit, like the elemental gist
> Of unwalled winds they offer, singing low
> *My Old Kentucky Home* and *Casey Jones,*
> *Some Sunny Day.* I heard a road-gang chanting so. (p.64)

What these associations ultimately suggest is the extent to which Crane in his self-embraced role of son-poet-slave identified himself with the Negro and thus the extent to which the figure of the naked black man in his dream is not just an image of Crane's father but of Crane as well. Indeed, I would suggest that the black man in Crane's dream is the son's idealized image of the union of father and son, a figure that combines in one person the powerful Father of Waters and the floating black singer, the paternal master and the filial poet-slave. If the black is a dual figure who represents the son's idealized attempt to assume the father's power and authority without directly combatting the father (a combat that would involve the son's risking either his own destruction or the destruction of the paternal authority to recognize and acknowledge), then we can understand why, in describing the quester's union with the Father of Waters, Crane says that, "lost within this tideless spell," you become not your father but "your father's father"; for if the father is himself a son (as this image of the "father's father" implies), if he is not his own origin but merely a predecessor caught in the same generational series in which the son finds himself, then a paternal authority based on the father's temporal priority to the son is thereby shown to be circumscribed: Father Time is represented as being encompassed (circularized) by the timeless (m)other. It is this timeless mother, the muse, who has the power to circularize time, to confer generational earliness, paternal authority, and originality through the tideless spell of song.

Which brings us to the other dream that Crane recounted to Grunberg.

In contrast to the dream in which the father appears in the symbolic form of a black man, the other nightmare of Crane's that Unterecker records is explicitly about Crane's mother. The dream was so vivid, Unterecker notes, that Crane

> had the feeling, long after he was awake, that it was something he had actually experienced. He had gone to bed exhausted, and when he woke up, he was in his old room on 115th Street. He got up, remembering that he had to hunt for something in the attic, and as he stumbled through the dusty attic—half awake—he kept trying to remember what he was looking for. Whatever it was, it was in a trunk. He was sure of that. It was very dark in the attic, but when he found the trunk, there was enough light for him to see that it was full of this mother's clothes. He started rummaging through them, looking for whatever it was he was looking for, pulling out dresses, shoes, stockings, underclothing. But the trunk was so full, it seemed he would never find what he was after. There was so much to look at that when he found the hand, he hardly realized it was a human hand; but when he found another hand and a piece of an arm, he knew there was a body in the trunk. He kept pulling out piece after piece of it, all mixed in with the clothing. The clothing was covered with blood. It was not until he had almost emptied the trunk that he realized he was unpacking the dismembered body of his mother. (p. 567)

I would suggest that this dream expresses, in a series of redundant symbols, the son's desire for a total return to the womb, indeed expresses that desire with a vengeance in its symbolic reduction of the mother's body to a trunk (which is to say, a torso) containing a body that has itself been violently reduced in size in order to fit in this container. Awakening from an exhausted sleep with its suggestion of the amniotic state, Crane finds himself in "his old room" at his maternal grandparents' house on East 115th Street in Cleveland. As an adult, Crane always thought of the house on 115th Street, where he lived from the ages of eight to seventeen, as his family home, and he referred to his bedroom in the north tower of the old Victorian structure as his "ivory tower" (Unterecker, p. 21) and "sanctum de la tour" (Unterecker, photo following p. 48). In a July 1923 letter to Charlotte Rychtarik, Crane reminisced,

> When I think of that room, it is almost to give way to tears, be-
> cause I shall never find my way back to it. It is not necessary, of
> course, that I should, but just the same it was the center and be-
> ginning of all that I am and ever will be, the center of such pain
> as would tear me to pieces to tell you about, and equally the cen-
> ter of great joys! *The Bridge* seems to me so beautiful—and it was
> there that I first thought about it, and it was there that I wrote
> "Faustus and Helen." . . . And all this is, of course, connected very
> intimately with my Mother, my beautiful mother whom I am so
> glad you love and speak about (*L*, 140).

This dream of the son's return to the home of his mother's mother resembles the structure we noted in "The River" in which the quester, entering the river of time that leads back to the oblivion of the gulf, becomes his father's father. The son attempts to circumvent his parents' generation and its conflicts between mother and father and between parent and child by identifying himself with his grandparents' generation, that prior authority to which his parents were subject, the doting grandparents who are the grandchild's natural ally and his court of higher appeal. In the lyric "My Grandmother's Love Letters" (1920), Crane memorialized his maternal grandmother Elizabeth Belden Hart in a scenario that anticipates details of his dream. On a rainy night the poet sits in an attic reading "the letters of my mother's mother, / Elizabeth, / That have been pressed so long / Into a corner of the roof / That they are brown and soft / And liable to melt as snow" (p. 6). (One wonders if the letters had been kept in a trunk in the attic?) As he reads these letters that seem as fragile as the snows of yester-year, the poet attempts to journey back through his grandparents' written memories to the world before his birth. Looking at this intimate exchange of correspondence, this written intercourse be-tween his grandmother and grandfather, the poet seems to be imaginatively present at a scene of origin which is, if not more primal than, certainly prior to that of parental intercourse and clearly more comforting to the poet since these letters attest to a love between his grandparents that Crane had begun to feel was originally absent between his own parents, an original absence that seemed to call into question his personal origin.

In the closing lines of "My Grandmother's Love Letters" Crane raises the same question that concerns him in the sections of *The Bridge* that follow the primal scene of origin in "The Dance": whether, if one is able to journey back imaginatively to the origin, one can then return to the present with that vision of origin intact. The poet asks himself,

> "Are your fingers long enough to play
> Old keys that are but echoes:
> Is the silence strong enough
> To carry back the music to its source
> And back to you again
> As though to her?"

> Yet I would lead my grandmother by the hand
> Through much of what she would not understand;
> And so I stumble. And the rain continues on the roof
> With such a sound of gently pitying laughter. (p. 6)

The image used to evoke the return to origin—carrying "back the music to its source"—suggests the stream of song flowing to the gulf at the end of "The River"—origin and end, source and abyss coinciding in this circular journey.

It is significant that in the months immediately preceding this dream of finding his mother's dismembered body in a trunk Crane was much concerned with establishing a home of his own. His childhood home on 115th Street in Cleveland (the setting of the dream) had been sold in 1925, and his break with his mother three years later seems to have reawakened and intensified his feelings of homelessness. In early July 1928—some two weeks after his letter describing the boat ride on the "great, magnificent Father of Waters"—Crane wrote his father again, asking for a loan to buy a small farmhouse near Patterson, New York, where he was then living, and offering as collateral the $5,000 bequest from his maternal grandfather that was being held in trust for him until his grandmother's death. Clarence Crane replied that business difficulties made it impossible for him to advance Hart the money at that time. By the end of the month Hart wrote his father that he hadn't "enough cash to even get into New York" and that "at present I haven't a place to lay my head": "I've never felt quite as humiliated. I can't ask you for anything more, and I'm not" (*LF*, 626–27). Six weeks later, however, Crane's maternal grandmother died, and suddenly, with his financial worries temporarily at an end, it seemed that he would be able to have a place of his own. But at this point his mother intervened. Trying to coerce Hart into returning to California for a reconciliation, Grace refused to sign the papers needed by the bank to release the $5,000 legacy from his grandfather. In November, Crane sent his mother a telegram threatening her with legal action. Grace replied by telegram that she had signed the papers, but threatened in turn to ask Hart's father "to use his influence with the bank against paying him his inheritance on the grounds of his drinking habits" (Horton, pp. 249–50). Interpreting this as a veiled threat to tell his father about his homosexuality, Hart used his inheritance to leave immediately for Europe, feeling that his mother not only had tried to keep him from having a home of his own but also, as he wrote his friends the Rychtariks, had made it impossible for him to live in his own country. Crane subsequently memorialized this conflict with Grace over his grandfather's legacy in "Quaker Hill" where, faced with the sweeping historical question "Where are my kinsmen and the patriarch race?", the quester has to

> Shoulder the curse of sundered parentage,
> Wait for the postman driving from Birch Hill
> With birthright by blackmail, the arrant page
> That unfolds a new destiny to fill. . . . (p. 105)

The curse of sundered parentage—in the sense both of his parents' divorce and of his break with his mother and his previous estrangement from his father—was much on Crane's mind during the months he spent writing the final sections of *The Bridge*, for the condition of sundered parentage had come to seem an image of the state of the modern American suffering the effects of a spiritual divorce that had shattered an original union between man and nature in the pre-Columbian "nature-world" of the Indians. Because of that divorce of man and nature, the modern American is a son estranged from the maternal body of the virgin continent, a body which, in his frustration, he violates in search of wealth rather than cultivating and making fruitful. Following immediately on the quester's vision of the nature world of the Indians in "The Dance," "Indiana" depicts a characteristic moment in the historical disintegration of that union of man and nature: the deracinating effect that a farmer's abandoning his land to join the Colorado gold rush has on his son who, years later, runs away to sea. The farmer, baffled in his search for gold, died on the way back from Colorado, and the poem's dramatic speaker, the farmer's wife, tells her son the story of his origin as he prepares to leave their Indiana farm.

There can be little doubt that the events of 1928—Crane's break with his mother, his flight and her pursuit through letters, his rapprochement with his father, the battle with his mother over his grandfather's legacy, and his unsuccessful attempt to buy his own home—significantly shaped "Indiana," and these events— along with the nightmares that Unterecker records and what they reveal of Crane's feelings about his father and mother during this period—shed light on Crane's most important alteration of the poem: the reversal that occurred in the roles originally planned for the father and mother in the poem as outlined in the 1927 letter to Kahn. Perhaps the best way to understand the full meaning of this reversal is to recall critics' standard objection to "Indiana." From the first reviews of *The Bridge*, "Indiana" was singled out as the weakest section of the poem because of what critics felt was its cloying sentimentality. That opinion has generally persisted, supported by the knowledge that "Indiana" was one of the last sections completed and the sense that *The Bridge* was finished not out of the force of its original inspiration but under the pressure of bringing to an end a project that had gone on for seven years. That the tone of "Indiana" is sentimental cannot be denied, but what critics have tended to ignore in attributing the poem's tonal lapses either to a momentary failure of Crane's art or to his loss of belief in the project as a whole is that unlike nearly all the other sections of *The Bridge*, "Indiana" is spoken not by Crane's surrogate, the poetic quester, but by another persona. And, to judge from the other major instance of this device in the poem ("Ave Maria"), one of the purposes of these sections is to characterize their speakers by the form and quality of the poetry they are given to speak. Thus in "Ave Maria" Columbus uses dramatic blank verse of an almost Elizabethan grandeur, while in "Indiana" the mother speaks in the mawkish quatrains of a nineteenth-century popular ballad. In each case the verse form evokes a cultural moment personified by its speaker. Crane uses a similar device in "Virginia," where, as Susan Jenkins Brown has pointed out, he parodies a popular song of the 1920s "What Do You Do Sunday, Mary?" from the musical *Poppy* to characterize "a little Five-and-Ten salesgirl-virgin letting down her hair from her Cathedral tower [the pseudo-Gothic Woolworth Building on lower Broadway]—but only for her true suitor on her free Saturday."[10] And just as "Virginia" alludes to one popular song, so "Indiana" evokes another, the 1917 ballad "Indiana" (better known by its first line as "Back Home Again in Indiana"), with its imagery of nostalgic longing for a rural childhood home ("The new mown hay—sends all its fragrance / From the fields I used to roam,— / When I dream about the moonlight on the Wabash, / Then I long for my Indiana home"), as if the twentieth-century ballad expressed the feelings of the runaway son grown older.

In his 1927 letter to Otto Kahn, Crane said that he planned in "Indiana" to allude to the mother "in a way which implies her succession to the nature-symbolism of Pocahontas" (*L*, 307), but this was at the time when he still thought of the poem as "a lyrical summary of the period of conquest" and still planned for its dramatic speaker to be the farmer whose wife had "died on the way back from the gold-rush" (*L*, 307). When the roles of the father and mother were reversed, the mother retained her succession to the nature-symbolism of Pocahontas, but this succession was now presented in what, for American literature, has traditionally been an image of generational decline—the figure of the half-breed. Returning from the gold fields, the mother sees "passing on a stumbling jade / A homeless squaw— / / Perhaps a halfbreed. On her back / She cradled a babe's body" (p. 78). In a moment of maternal mirroring the white mother holds up her own son for the squaw to see, knowing "that mere words could not have brought us nearer. / She nodded—and that smile across her shoulder / Will still endear her / / As long as Jim, your father's memory, is warm" (p. 78). One senses that the pioneer mother recognizes in the homeless wandering of the squaw the same rootlessness that sent her husband to the gold fields and will send her son to sea.

It seems clear that in imagining the mother in "Indiana" Crane was influenced by his feelings about his own mother. The scenario of a mother's self-pitying appeal to her son to write her from overseas and to return home before it is too late parallels Crane's own situation at the time too closely for us to doubt this. It also seems clear that the major factor in Crane's decision to reverse the roles originally planned for the father and mother in this section was his break with his mother and the reversal in his feelings toward her. Had Crane kept to his original plan for "Indiana," it would have been virtually impossible for the father as the poem's speaker to present a negative picture of his dead wife as part of his farewell to his departing son. And if much of the point of "Indiana" is the negative characterization of the white mother who symbolizes the degraded maternal landscape of modern America, then the reversal of Crane's earliest feelings about his own mother (which parallels the movement from the mythic dark [m]other in "The Dance" to the historical white mother in "Indiana") left him with the difficult task of preserving the maternal archetype in its original power and reverence while presenting the white mother as a decadent instance of this archetype. Not uncommonly, this kind of ambivalence is handled by splitting the maternal image into a good and a bad half, each separately embodied, and the final version of "Indiana" shows the traces of such splitting. On the one hand, the structure of the poem, considered in the abstract, suggests an idealized version of the womb fantasy: the father is dead without the son's having to kill him, and the mother pleads with the son to return home. No doubt we are meant to see this structure as completing the epicycle of desire begun by "Ave Maria," the poem that leads into "Powhatan's Daughter." There, Columbus at mid-ocean prays to the Virgin Mother to grant him safe return home, and in the final poem of "Powhatan's Daughter," the mother, as if in reply to that earlier episode, pleads with her son, who is running away to sea, to "come back to Indiana." Yet it is equally clear that the pioneer mother envisions the son's return as occurring entirely on her own terms, not a return that grants the son access to original power but one that keeps him forever subservient. From the first stanza of "Indiana," the mother tries to prevent the son's departure or at least to hasten his return by undermining the notion of original power. During the fantasized primal scene of origin in "The Dance," the poetic quester had entreated Maquokeeta, "Medicine-man, relent, restore— / Lie to us,—dance us back the tribal morn" (p. 73), but the mother in "Indiana" begins her song by evoking the loss of that original earliness:

> The morning glory, climbing the morning long
>   Over the lintel on its wiry vine,
> Closes before the dusk, furls in its song
>   As I close mine . . . (p. 76)

The mother's story opens with an image of closure that is clearly meant to be experienced by her son as a kind of foreclosure: the glory of the morning has past, here in the dusk there is only the fated repetition of unoriginal action. On that disabling note the mother recounts the son's personal origin, the circumstances that led up to his birth on the trail back from the gold fields. The thrust of this account is to show her son the unoriginality of his leaving the farm to go adventuring, to show "How we, too, Prodigal, once rode off, too— / Waved Seminary Hill a gay good-bye." In addressing her son as "Prodigal," the mother implies that, like the son in the parable, he will return home one day defeated by his own irresponsibility and seeking parental succor, and in so doing confirm his unoriginality in the repetition of his parents' failure. We should keep in mind that Crane was writing "Quaker Hill" with its allusion to the threatened lawsuit against his mother over his grandfather's legacy ("birthright by blackmail") at the same time that he was working on "Indiana" in which the mother tries to act as the mediatrix (or perhaps we should say executrix) of her son's birthright by telling him where he comes from, who his people are, and thus where he belongs and what belongs to him:

> You were the first—before Ned and this farm,—
>   First born, remember—
>
> And since then—all that's left to me of Jim
>   Whose folks, like mine, came out of Arrowhead.
> And you're the only one with eyes like him—
>   Kentucky bred!
>
> I'm standing still, I'm old, I'm half of stone!
>   Oh, hold me in those eyes' engaging blue;

> There's where the stubborn years gleam and atone,—
> Where gold is true! (pp. 78–79)

These lines, filled with an irony unperceived by their speaker, undermine the thing they argue for. The mother tells her son what belongs to him as the "first born," that is, she invokes on his behalf the prerogative of generational earliness, after she has just finished describing the loss of original earliness in the closing of the frontier, the loss of any possibility of being first. The promise of America, of the endless frontier, was the golden promise of an inexhaustible access to the original world. But that was not what the farmer and his wife found in Colorado in 1859 when they arrived at a mining town ("A dream called Eldorado" [The Golden]) that had "no charter but a promised crown / Of claims to stake":

> But we,—too late, too early, howsoever—
> Won nothing out of fifty-nine—those years—
> But gilded promise, yielded to us never,
> And barren tears ... (p. 78)

Though she professes uncertainty as to whether their failure resulted from being too early or too late, everything else in the poem points to her sense of belatedness. And it is consistent with her misunderstanding of her son that she apparently considers this tale of belatedness, of parents' dreams foreclosed by the closing of the frontier, to be in some way an effective argument for the son's remaining on the farm rather than searching for a new frontier on the sea or in some other land. In "Indiana," then, the mother in mediating a birthright that consists of an absent paternal origin, a lost earliness, functions as a kind of disabling antimuse—neither the origin herself nor the means to a lost original power. And yet it would be a mistake to paint too black a picture of her (particularly since in Crane's color coding the good mother is the dark [m]other). The pioneer woman may be foolish and possessive but she is not intentionally evil, which is to say that Crane's portrait of her, no matter how much it may reflect his personal feelings about Grace Crane at the time, is not intended to discredit the maternal archetype. In terms of Crane's own psychic economy in writing *The Bridge*, "Indiana" serves in part to separate the image of his own mother (the white woman of materialist America) from that of the Great Mother, the dark woman of the triple aspect (mother-lover-muse) whom he calls Pocahontas, the poet's true mother. What Crane objects to in the pioneer woman is not the excessive character of maternal love, but rather that this mother offers her love only on her own terms, terms that, because they are ultimately self-pitying and self-regarding, reduce the son to being her mirror.

In a letter Crane wrote to his friend William Wright in November 1930, he confessed to being "considerably jolted at the charge of sentimentality continually leveled" at "Indiana." Noting that he "approved of a certain amount of sentiment," he added "Since 'race' is the principal motivation of 'Indiana,' I can't help thinking that, observed in the proper perspective, and judged in relation to the argument or theme of the Pocahontas section as a whole, the pioneer woman's maternalism isn't excessive" (*L*, 357–58). One suspects that Crane was surprised less by the charge of sentimentality than by the fact that it was leveled at the poet rather than the persona. Yet there is no reason to doubt the sincerity of Crane's remark that the pioneer woman's maternalism was not excessive within the overall context of his fantasized portrait of the muse-mother and the vision of a total return. Indeed, for the poet-son, the more intense and narrowly focused the muse's love is the better, as long as that love is given wholly on the son's terms. It is in light of this split in Crane's feelings about the figure of the mother that we should interpret his puzzling remark about race being "the principal motivation of 'Indiana.'"

Granting that the poem's implicit comparison of the pioneer woman and Pocahontas as mother figures tends to evoke the maternal difference between them as being in some sense a racial difference, I would argue that in *The Bridge* race functions in regard to the image of the mother in much the same way that it does in relation to the image of the father in Crane's nightmare of the black man on the river bank. Which is to say that since the black and the Indian represented for the white America of Crane's day the world of animal nature as opposed to that of human culture, and since one of the traditional principles of differentiation between nature and culture, between animal and human, is the incest taboo, Crane's symbolic translation of the white father and mother into a black and an Indian respectively circumvents this taboo by placing the objects of desire in an original nature-world where incest does not exist. As the Negro in Crane's dream represents the fantasized incestuous union of father and son, so the Indian maiden Pocahontas in *The Bridge* represents that of mother and son. And since in each case the idealized figure is drawn from a race that is considered by white America to be subservient or inferior (a subservience that evokes for Crane the child's subjection to his parents), their use as symbols of the union of father and son and of mother and son, that is, their elevation to the status of ideals, represents the triumph of the son: it marks these fantasized unions as occurring on the son's terms.

Yet obviously Crane is neither black nor an Indian, and so, as one would expect, in the very process of symbolizing his forbidden desires in these dark figures he obliquely reaffirms the prohibition that gives those desires their significance within a differential system. Here one finds perhaps a further, not to say deeper, significance to that reversal in the roles originally planned for the father and mother in "Indiana." In 1927, when Crane was close to Grace and at odds with his father, it was his incestuous feelings for his mother that had to be repressed (the estrangement from his father served as a sufficient defense against forbidden desires in that quarter), while at the same period it was the ideal of paternal affection and esteem that had to be reaffirmed. Consequently in the version of "Indiana" that he described to Kahn, the mother is absent from the scene (psychically cancelled by death), and the father speaks to the son, presumably to express his love. But in 1929, when Crane was no longer speaking to his mother and had become closer to his father, it was his incestuous feelings for the latter that had now to be repressed (the estrangement from the other parent serving once again as a sufficient defense in that quarter), while it was the ideal of maternal love that had to be reaffirmed. Consequently, in the finished version of the poem the father is absent, and the mother speaks to the son. In this version, however, although Crane projects the son's ideal of maternal love in the abstract form of the poem—that is, in the scenario of a mother pleading with her son to return home in the father's absence—he evokes in the possessiveness of the pioneer woman the real maternal love that he has known.

It may seem that we have spent more time on "Indiana" than its poetic merit warrants. Yet both because of its formal importance as the closing section of "Powhatan's Daughter" and because of the insight that it provides into Crane's juxtaposition of personal and national history in *The Bridge* as a whole this degree of attention is justified. Indeed, in the latter regard we can see that the autobiographical material which Crane incorporates into the poem is meant to convey his sense of how much this vision, indeed any vision, of a return to national origin depends for its emotional force on the concepts of fatherland and motherland, concepts whose collective force is, in one degree or another, a function of each individual's personal relationship to his parents. That patriotism ultimately derives from the way one feels about one's father, or that the love of the native land, the physical nature of the nation ("native," "nature," and "nation" are all from the Latin *natus*, "to be born") takes its basic emotional tone from the feeling for one's mother simply means that the most powerful trope for binding individuals to a place and thus to each other has always been the parental image, and that to deal with national feelings about the native land inevitably means dealing with personal feelings about one's parents. For this reason Crane's complex, shifting relationship with his father and mother is part of the very fabric of the poem, both as direct thematic motif and as indirect shaping force. Indeed, inasmuch as Crane had cast himself in the role of the prototypical twentieth-century American poet through his surrogate the poetic quester, he had come to view his successful, overbearing father—the millionaire candy manufacturer who invented the Life Saver and who considered his son's poetic career as a rejection of his own life's work in creating the patrimony of a family business—and his disabling, possessive mother, with her virulent midwestern blend of Christian Science mysticism and Chatauqua artiness, as the prototypical parents of the modern American poet in that they seemed to represent between them virtually every obstacle that the serious practice of poetry would have to confront in this country in this century.

NOTES

1. Hart Crane, *The Letters of Hart Crane, 1916–1932*, ed. Brom Weber (Berkeley and Los Angeles: University of California Press, 1952), p. 307. All subsequent quotations from this volume will be indicated in the text by the letter *L* and page number.

2. John Unterecker, *Voyager: A Life of Hart Crane* (New York: Farrar, Straus and Giroux, 1969), p. 534. See also Philip Horton, *Hart Crane: The Life of an American Poet* (New York: The Viking Press, 1957).

3. *Letters of Hart Crane and His Family*, ed. Thomas S. W. Lewis (New York: Columbia University Press, 1974), pp. 619–20. All subsequent quotations from this volume will be indicated in the text by the letters *LF* and page number.

4. Hart Crane, *The Complete Poems and Selected Letters and Prose of Hart Crane*, ed. Brom Weber (New York: Liveright, 1966), pp. 68–69.

5. Gerald Bordman, *Jerome Kern: His Life and Music* (New York: Oxford University Press, 1980), pp. 267–77 and 299.

6. Brian Rust, *The Complete Entertainment Discography from the Mid-1890s to 1942* (New Rochelle, N.Y.: Arlington House, 1973), p. 552.

7. *The New York Times*, May 27, 1928, sect. 8, p. 1.

8. Rust, *Complete Entertainment Discography*, p. 552.

9. Brom Weber, *Hart Crane* (New York: Bodley Press, 1948), p. 261.

10. Susan Jenkins Brown, *Robber Rocks: Letters and Memories of Hart Crane, 1923–1932* (Middletown, Conn.: Wesleyan University Press, 1969), p. 111.

IV

Critical Reflections

Critical Reflections

If reflection is thinking about thought rather than about some external object; if criticism is drawing distinctions in order to discriminate the true from the false, the better from the worse; then the five essays in this section are indeed critical reflections. Despite their diversity, they share a common polemical strategy, taking as their point of departure other theories of Romanticism in order to develop alternative positions from that opposition in thought. The question each asks is: What in the theory is wrong, and why? The answer each offers, however, implies a statement about the nature, purpose, or function of Romanticism.

From the polemical structure of these essays, one might infer that, for contemporary criticism, only critical reflection—thinking about thought—can legitimately lead to a clearer understanding of thought's object, Romanticism; moreover, that understanding can become most incisive only when the mode of thinking is agonistic. In other words, whether their overt stances be political or religious, post-structuralist or empiricist, socialistic or individualistic, the present essays all acknowledge in practice, if not in principle, the essentially dialectic and intersubjective quality of the struggle for truth. In a revolutionary turn, this approach to the question of Romanticism, indebted ultimately to those two stout anti-Romantics, Hegel and Marx, often by way of various French connections, has become the dominant mode of British and American romantic criticism.

Beyond this agreement on the beneficial effects of disagreement, there would seem to be little to tie these essays together. Eschewing the question of earlier generations of scholars—What is Romanticism?—in both its essentialist and its skeptical forms, these critics, like their opponents, challenge the Hegelian thesis that Romanticism is the positing of the object by an autonomous subject. For Samuel Weber, the lesson of Walter Benjamin, as of Paul de Man, is that Romanticism is the name for the awareness of the allegorical character of criticism, for the view that criticism can fulfill its role of completing the work only as a practice of writing. Distinguishing a phenomenological deconstruction from a desubjectivized post-structuralism, Tilottama Rajan recommends that we attend to the intersubjective aspects of narration and reading in Romantic poetry. M. H. Abrams defends his liberal empiricist interpretation of the universal human in Wordsworth against political, specifically neo-Marxist, readings which attempt to take into account what is suppressed as well as what is expressed in the poems. Charles Altieri likewise mounts a counterattack against what he takes to be our contemporary theoretical assumptions of political and psychological demystification by discerning a theological thrust, a pure Augustinian strain, in Wordsworth's attempt to lift his readers to new levels of mental powers, to change their lives. Through his review of recent books by Jonathan Arac and Clifford Siskin, Don Bialostosky also emphasizes the heightened powers involved in reading poetry, but for him this power resides primarily in the reader, or, rather, in the productive activity of reading originally, even violently.

Thus it might be tempting at first glance to interpret this fragmentation and dispersal in current debates about Romanticism as the sign of a loss: only chaos was left after the collapse of the former consensus about the centrality of subjectivism or individualism. A second thought suggests that this kaleidoscopic effect marks instead an awakening, for it is precisely the Romantics who bring to poetry the conviction not only that subjectivity has a history, but also that it is a history, and as such is inevitably tied, for better and for worse, to the conditions of History. Moreover, it is the Romantics who introduce a concrete futurity into poetry as and through a practice of writing.

Weber emphasizes the function of criticism as an eventual *Vollendung* of the work, the completion and dissolution that await it and constitute its destiny. Rajan insists on the temporal dimensions of narrative and reading. Altieri contends that the Wordsworthian sublime prepares the way for the advent of new powers and new attitudes toward the world beyond the text. For Bialostosky, there is a nonacquiescing, cooperating power in read-

ing that does not merely reproduce relationships but makes literature new, that is, produces (literary) history. Even Abrams, while
claiming that "Tintern Abbey" conveys a universal human message
about time and aging rather than a time-bound political ideology
of universality, defends the alterity of Wordsworth's sister in the
poem by pointing out that her imagined, future experience of the
"same" setting will in fact be different, not only because her first
visit will have been made in her brother's company, not only because she will have heard his words (those of the poem) during
that first visit, but because, as a result of these two differences, her
experience of aging will have been transformed.

The essays that follow promise no new critical consensus
about the nature of Romanticism, and that is all the better, for they
testify instead to the fundamentally dispersive force of historicity
and to the possibilities that arise from a heightened awareness that
the end is not in the beginning, that History moves *à la dérive*.
Romanticism thus constitutes, at least for the time being, a revolution in time.

G.D.C.

Criticism Underway
WALTER BENJAMIN'S *ROMANTIC CONCEPT OF CRITICISM*

SAMUEL WEBER

> I wanted to show that words often understand themselves better than those by whom they are used, and also to call attention to the fact that philosophical words are tied to one another in secret orders . . .
>
> —FRIEDRICH SCHLEGEL, "ON UNINTELLIGIBILITY"[1]

When, in the *Introduction* to the *Philosophy of Fine Art*, Hegel surveys the "reawakening" of the philosophical "Idea" and its corollary, the emergence of aesthetics as a rigorous "science of art,"[2] the romantics occupy a conspicuous but also equivocal place. In the never indifferent sequence of the dialectical exposition, the discussion of "irony," under which Hegel here subsumes the romantics, follows that of Kant on the one hand, and Schiller, Winckelmann, and Schelling on the other. The tertiary position thus reserved for romantic irony should by rights mark a culminating turning point in the progress of aesthetics: one in which the residual subjectivism of Kantian aesthetics and the abstract objectivism of Schiller and Schelling move to a higher level of conceptualization at which they are both negated and fulfilled. And yet from the outset it is clear that the romantics, far from constituting a progressive moment in the "reawakening," are for Hegel more like a bad dream. From his opening characterization, Hegel's tone is disparaging and even contemptuous:

> In the neighborhood now of the reawakening of the philosophical Idea (to touch briefly upon the course of further developments), August Wilhelm and Friedrich von Schlegel, avid of novelty in their craving for the distinctive and the unusual, appropriated as much of the philosophical Idea as their otherwise utterly unphilosophical, essentially critical natures were capable of absorbing.[3]

The romantics, essentially "critical natures" and "unphilosophical," are thus to be considered dangerous "neighbors" for a "philosophical Idea" in the process of "reawakening." Their "craving" (*Sucht*) for the new and the different finds no adequate counterweight in a theory consisting of "impoverished (*dürftigen*) philosophical ingredients." "To be sure" (*allerdings*), Hegel concedes, the romantics have introduced "new criteria of evaluation and points of view" into the "different branches of art." But these achievements, he insists, are marred by the deleterious consequences of those inferior philosophical ingredients—that is, by their adaptation of the Fichtean notion of an "all-positing, all-dissolving I" and their application of it to the "ego of the Artist." As a result, romantic theory and practice of art are based on the "most unartistic" of attitudes, irony. The latter, Hegel argues, is ultimately incompatible with artistic "seriousness" and "substance." Romantic irony treats substantial content (*Gehalt*) as a mere reflex of the positing genius of the individual artist; it thereby tends inevitably toward "blissful self-indulgence" and even to "dishonesty and hypocrisy" in its attempts to impress its audience.

For Hegel, then, romantic irony, understood as the consequence of a "principle of absolute subjectivity,"[4] appears as a movement that parodies and ultimately betrays the dialectical progression of aesthetics rather than enacting it. And yet when, at the conclusion of the *Introduction*, Hegel articulates what he takes to be the authentic *Aufhebung* of aesthetics, the term to which he resorts in order to mark the passage from art to philosophy suggests that the relation of the dialectic to romanticism is far from closed or settled: "But precisely on this highest level art now rises above itself in forsaking the element of reconciled sensualization of the spirit, and steps from the poetry of representation over into the *prose* of thought [emphasis added]."[5] In appealing to the notion of prose to describe the discourse in which "art rises above itself," Hegel invokes a line of thought elaborated programmatically by the German romantics. All the more reason, then, for Hegel forcefully—but also forcibly—to seek to demarcate the authentically *philosophical* "prose of thought" from its romantic homonymy. And yet the strident and strenuous character of his efforts to put the romantics in their place suggests that the issue is far from settled. It is as though the romantics' lack of seriousness, a point on which Hegel places such emphasis, tended to contaminate his own treatment of them, preventing him from taking them as seriously as their position would seem to require. As a result, what is left open is precisely the question of this position: Is it that of a *precursor* or of a *usurper*? Or could it be both? And if both, how should the "prose" of the romantics be related to the "prose of thought"?

To be sure, our understanding of romanticism has made great strides in the century and a half since Hegel situated "irony" at the culmination of modern aesthetical theory while at the same time seeking to relegate it to the margins of his lectures on aesthetics. And yet even today, the ambivalence of this gesture is never far away when the effort is made to put the romantics in their proper place historically, artistically, and politically. A more recent case in point is furnished by Paul de Man. In an essay first published (in French) in 1960, "The Intentional Structure of the Romantic Image," de Man attacks "'naturalistic' or even pantheistic" readings of the romantics, arguing that Hölderlin, Rousseau, and Wordsworth are among "the first modern writers to have put into question, in the language of poetry, the ontological priority of the sensory object."[6] That such a "priority" could be ascribed to romanticism at all indicates the complex differences that cohabit, more or less uneasily, this single term. For if a "naturalistic" or "primitivistic" perspective could acquire a certain plausibility in English literary histories, it is virtually unthinkable with regard to German romanticism. Thus, viewed from a comparatist vantage point, de Man's essay can be described as an attempt to (re)-introduce the perspective of German romanticism into English-language literary criticism.

And yet if this is so, why does de Man go to Hölderlin rather than to Novalis or Friedrich Schlegel to find his exemplary text? The "intentional structure of the image" de Man is seeking to elaborate is no more identical with 'irony' (particularly in the Hegelian sense of a "principle of absolute subjectivity") than it is with 'nature'. Rather, its iterative movement undoes the founding of subjective self-consciousness, however ironical, no less than that of the natural object: "Poetic language can do nothing but originate anew over and over again; it is always constitutive, able to posit regardless of presence but, by the same token, unable to give a foundation to what it posits except as an intent of consciousness."[7] Through its intentional structure, consciousness, qua language, is essentially incapable of founding itself and hence can never become fully *self*-conscious, however ironic it may seek to be. It is this unfulfillable but also unavoidable striving toward self-identity that defines the discontinuous relation of language to "the natural object": "For it is in the essence of language to be capable of origination, but of never achieving the absolute identity with itself that exists in the natural object."[8]

As "the first modern writers to have put into question, in the language of poetry, the ontological priority of the sensory object," what the romantics have thus problematized is ultimately the principle of self-identity attributed in "absolute" form to "the natural object," which also defines, in a less absolute, more relative form, subjective self-consciousness. This questioning of self-identity, however, also affects or infects the very generic term which ostensibly defines the nonnatural object and field of de Man's attention: *romanticism*. For despite his use of the word in the title of his essay, de Man is not talking so much about romanticism proper as certain of its "precursors" writing prior to the consolidation of a full-fledged, self-conscious movement. Thus, the *place* of the romantics, far from being fixed once and for all, is strangely in motion—strangely because what it is moving *toward* is anything but clear: "The works of the early romantics . . . are at most *under-way* toward renewed insights and inhabit the mixed and self-contradictory regions that we encountered in the three passages."[9] Thus, what the "early romantics" are "underway" toward is not romanticism proper, but something which has yet to be thought and which in some sense romanticism, at least in its familiar forms, has obscured rather than articulated. The necessity of rereading romanticism is thus clearly stated at the conclusion of this essay.

In 1983, when, in the preface to the *Rhetoric of Romanticism*, de Man attempts to sum up the results of that rereading, his conclusion is that a conclusion, a summing up, is precisely what is missing. Originally "part of a project that was itself historical," the essays collected in the volume fail to "coalesce" into a coherent whole, with the result that "as far as the general question of romanticism is concerned, . . . the task of its historical definition [must be left] to others."[10]

The relation of romanticism to history thus remains an open, unsettled question. The only place, de Man remarks, where he "comes close to facing some of these questions about history and fragmentation" is his essay on Shelley's *Triumph of Life*, "Shelley Disfigured." Despite the distance separating this text from the 1960 essay, the decisive question of romanticism is still articulated with respect to the problem of the self. Having retraced how Shelley's poem, left incomplete by the poet's death, is marked both thematically and formally by radical randomness, de Man concludes by meditating the way such fragmentation elicits and affects the process of reading and reception. The lethal materiality of the mutilated text is "monumentalized into historical and aesthetic objects" by literary scholars and critics. The evaluation of this gesture, however, is anything but simple: "Such monumentalization is by no means necessarily a naive or evasive gesture, and it certainly is not a gesture that anyone can pretend to avoid making. It does not have to be naive, since it does not have to be *the repression of a self-threatening knowledge* [emphasis added]."[11] The challenge of certain romantic texts, then, is to retrace just how such "self-threatening knowledge" can be articulated without being simply "repressed." To "state the full power of this threat in all its negativity," as *The Triumph of Life* does in de Man's reading, "does not prevent Shelley from allegorizing his own negative assurance, thus awakening the suspicion that the negation is a *Verneinung*, an intended exorcism." Through such allegorization, "self-threatening knowledge" is neither simply "repressed" nor simply affirmed (as "negative assurance"), but, rather, *inscribed* in a way that elicits *suspicion* and demands to be read. But how is such an *allegorization* to be "read," if not as part of what de Man describes here as "the endless prosopopoeia by which the dead are made to have a face and a voice which tells the allegory of their demise and allows us to apostrophize them in our turn"?[12] De Man's later writings are the attempt, if not to respond simply to this question, then at least to delineate some of its implications. For our purposes, however, it is enough to note that the dislocation of the romantic work, and perhaps of romanticism itself, depends on a process of allegorization for which the problematization of self and the process of reading are inseparably linked. This link, so powerfully at work in de Man's later texts, continues a line of thought first elaborated by Walter Benjamin. Although Benjamin's theory of allegory, developed in his study of *The Origins of the German Mourning Play* (1925), is well known, less familiar is the fact that this work in many ways builds on the work Benjamin had written a few years earlier on German romanticism. It is a work that casts considerable light on the role of romanticism in the development of contemporary critical theory and as such deserves a wider reception than it has received.

The text to which I am referring bears the title *The Concept of Criticism in German Romanticism* and was written during the First World War. Benjamin was a twenty-seven-year-old graduate student at the time, and the monograph was submitted by him as a dissertation to the University of Bern, from which he received the doctorate *summa cum laude*. It was to be Benjamin's first academic success and also his last. Since this text has not yet been translated into English and will therefore be unfamiliar to most English-language readers, it may be useful to begin with a few preliminary terminological clarifications. These clarifications will have to be preliminary, not least of all because the very notion of terminology touches on the most significant and enigmatic aspects of romanticism as Benjamin sees it. In a letter written in November 1918 to his friend Gershom Scholem, Benjamin remarks that although it is "out of the romantic concept of criticism that the modern notion has emerged,"[13] nevertheless the romantics used the term in a way very different from that familiar today, namely, as "an entirely esoteric concept (one of the most hidden), based on mystical presuppositions insofar as knowledge is concerned."

Before I comment on what Benjamin here refers to as the "esoteric" and "mystical" aspect of romanticism, it should be understood that the romanticism referred to in this book is identified almost exclusively with the writings of Friedrich Schlegel and Novalis. Moreover, the work of Schlegel's held to be exemplary by Benjamin is largely limited to that published during the period from 1797 to 1801, centered around the short life of the periodical the *Athenaeum* (1798–1800).[14] If, then, one of the most insistent motifs that will emerge from this study of German romanticism can be described as the problem of self-delimitation (*Selbstbeschränkung*), then Benjamin's book itself provides an exemplary instance of such self-limiting—not merely in limiting its source materials, both primary and secondary, to a minuscule fraction of German romantic writings on the notion of criticism, but also in defining its own scope and style. The result is what one scholar has certified to be "a professionally done dissertation,"[15] although precisely as such it stopped just short of what Benjamin considered to be the essential issues at stake. The latter are inscribed both in his letters of the period and also in the margins of the thesis itself. Benjamin describes his study as an attempt not "to present (*darzustellen*) the historical essence of romanticism" as such, but, rather, to collect "materials" which might lead to such a definition. That essence itself, he adds in a footnote, "should presumably be sought after in the ... Messianism" of the romantics, which he characterizes by citing the following brief passage from a contemporary critic: "The thought of an ideal humanity perfecting itself ad infinitum is rejected; instead, what is demanded is the 'realm of God' now, in time and on earth ... an ideal realised at every level of life—out of this categorical demand grows Schlegel's new religion."[16] Benjamin's "professionally done dissertation" is thus one intended to lead its readers to the limits of its subject matter and point them in an "esoteric" direction that transcends the purview of scholarly discourse. All the more interesting, then, is the fact that the "subject matter" which is to perform this function is held by Benjamin, and not without reason, to be the antecedent of what today, in the English-speaking world, has come to be known as criticism and its theory.[17] But the esoteric, even mystical genealogy that Benjamin begins to elaborate in this study works to render the familiarity of modern critical theory strange, if not downright uncanny. For what turns out to be peculiar to this subject matter is that, ultimately, it is neither *subject* nor *matter*—or, rather, that it only "matters" by virtue of a certain *subjection* to which it owes its start and gets *underway*. In what follows I attempt to retrace the emergence of this line of thinking in Benjamin's dissertation.

What distinguishes romantic critical theory from its predecessors, as well as from its contemporaries, above all Goethe, is that it conceives criticism to be an integral and essential part of the artistic process, of no less importance or dignity than the work of art itself. Benjamin sums up the distinctive specificity of romantic critical theory in two tenets: first, the individual work of art has an intrinsically coherent structure and, second, an essential characteristic of this structure, and hence of the individual work, is that it is "criticizable"—that is, it requires critical reflection in order to fulfill its artistic function. Criticism, so conceived, does not involve primarily the evaluation of an individual work—this might be called the classical or neoclassical conception—but, rather, its fulfillment or, as Novalis writes, its "Vollendung." This word, Benjamin emphasizes, must be read in its double sense, entailing on the one hand the completion or consummation of the work and, on the other, its consumption or dissolution in the discourse of criticism. This double aspect of romantic critical theory—the elevation of the individual work to a highly organized, autonomous structure with its own intrinsic laws and the elevation of the critical process as the culmination and continuation of those laws, above and beyond the original work—allows Schlegel and Novalis to be considered the founders of modern criticism. And it would not be difficult to extend Benjamin's analysis to criticism today, whether in its formalist tradition, focusing on the immanent analysis of the individual work or, in its more pragmatic versions, construing the literary text to be an artifact that consumes or fulfills itself in the reception or readings it receives. In this respect, little has changed in the seventy years since Benjamin wrote his dissertation, except that the problem of the subject occupied a more prominent place in the neo-Kantian aesthetics that dominated Germany in the twenties than it is does today, when it is often concealed in categories such as "implicit reader" or "community of interpretation."

Nevertheless, whether conscious or unconscious, it is precisely such subjectivism, so Benjamin argues, that renders present-day critics incapable of grasping what is at stake in romanticism. "These romantics"—Benjamin cites Erwin Kircher[18]—"sought precisely to distance themselves from what was then called romanticism, and what still is today" (*Concept*, 107). "What modern critics fail to see," Benjamin asserts, "is the importance of the notion of *work*," which for Schlegel and Novalis is not "the mere by-product of subjectivity, as often misunderstood by modern authors," but, rather, the result of "the laws of the spirit (*Geist*)." The "determinate, immanent structure" attributed by the early romantics to the individual work is no longer conceived in neoclassical categories such as "harmony or organization"; instead, the relative autonomy of the individual work and its structure now depends on "a general notion of art as a reflective medium and of the work as a center of reflection" (71). It is this notion of art as medium of reflection that leads Benjamin to assert that romantic critical theory is not in essence subjective,[19] that it "has to do exclusively with the objective structure of art—as idea, [and] with its manifestations (*Gebilde*)—as works" (13). And again: "Criticism, which today is grasped as the most subjective of activities, was for the romantics a regulative of subjectivity; contingency and arbitrariness in the emergence of works" (80).

What is at stake, then, in Benjamin's account of German romantic critical theory is nothing less unusual, idiosyncratic, or, if you prefer, original than the effort to elaborate a notion or practice of "reflexivity" that would not ultimately be rooted in the premise of a constitutive subject. His first move in this direction is to define the way in which the romantic use of reflection both depends on and diverges from its most immediate philosophical antecedent, Fichte. Schlegel's conception of reflection, as Benjamin describes it, consists of three moments or "levels": first, is thought in its immediate form as thought of an object, what Schlegel calls "meaning" (*Sinn*); second, is what he calls "reason," the thinking which takes as its object the *Sinn*, or first, immediate thought. This level could also be called reflection proper. The distinctive specificity of the romantics in regard to Fichte emerges in the way in which this second level of reflection is interpreted. For Fichte, such reflection only makes sense, only "exists correlative to an act of posing (*Setzen*)" which in turn implies an I (*Ich*) as its origin and agent": "Fichtean reflection resides in the absolute thesis . . . outside of which it means nothing, because it leads into emptiness." "With Fichte reflection relates to the I, with the romantics it relates to pure thinking," unbounded, as it were, by any being or entity such as an I: "Romantic thinking dissolves (*hebt. . .auf*) being and positing into reflection." This is why for the romantics the essence of thought as reflection is not limited by the positional act of an I to its second form of reflection proper, but instead entails necessarily and structurally a third and far more ambivalent level: "the thinking of thinking of thinking (and so on)." In short, without the self-positing I to limit and contain reflection, the latter initiates a movement involving the "decomposition" (*Zersetzung*) of what Benjamin calls the "archetypal, canonical form of reflection" (30) into a "peculiar ambiguity" (*eigentümliche Doppeldeutigkeit*): reflection proper finds itself split, as it were, into either an object or a subject, or, rather, into both: the "thinking of thinking" functions both as an object (of third-level thought) and as a subject—the thinking of thinking—which has "thinking," in its initial form, as its object. This equivocation or ambiguity is what leads philosophers, from Fichte to Hegel, to search for a way of transcending mere reflection in order to avoid the regressus ad infinitum that reflection in its "pure" and unadulterated form would entail. The romantics, as Benjamin describes them, do not draw back before this danger; on the contrary, even before Hegel, Schlegel sees Fichte's attempt to, as it were, "enclose" reflection within the opposition of a self-positing I and a counterposited Not-I, precisely as falling prey to the regressus ad infinitum: "Whenever the thought of the I is not at one with the concept of the world, such pure thinking of the thought of the I leads only to eternal self-mirroring, to an infinite series of mirror-images that contain only the same and never anything new" (35). The response of the romantics is to construe reflection not as the act of an I, but as the process of a Self that can no longer be contained or comprehended in terms of the opposition of Being and Positing, I and Not-I, subject and object, but in terms of the Absolute: "Reflection expands itself without limit and the thinking thus formed in reflection becomes a formless thought, which is directed towards the Absolute" (31). This Absolute, un-

like that of Fichte, however, is determined "not as the consciousness of an I, but as reflection in the medium of art" (39). Such reflection has two manifestations: the first is the individual work of
art itself; the second, criticism. Criticism is second logically and
chronologically, since it addresses already existing works, but its
very secondariness makes it the exemplary manifestation of art as
a "medium of absolute reflection," since the individuation of reflection in the work arrests the process at the same time it determines
it. If criticism arises (*entsteht*) out of the work and in this sense
depends on it, the work in turn refers to an idea of absolute reflection which, however, it restricts and dissimulates precisely by giving it shape. This restriction is lifted and reflection reinstated
through the process of criticism.

The problems that emerge from such an account are obvious
and determine the course of Benjamin's investigation, which focuses on the question of self-limitation. Citing a remark of Novalis,
Benjamin demonstrates that the romantics themselves were well
aware of the difficulty: "The possibility of self-limitation is the possibility of all synthesis, of all miracle. And the world began with
a miracle" (35). Everything depends on the way in which art, as
the medium of absolute reflection, limits itself in this account. The
key term here is the notion of *context, coherence,* or *structure,*
all of which are attempts at translating the romantic notion of
Zusammenhang; in calling attention to the systematic character
of romantic thought in general, Benjamin emphasizes that the notion of the Absolute as artistic reflection is essentially synchronic,
not diachronic, despite Schlegel's famous definition of romantic
poetry as "progressive universal poetry" (91). This definition, Benjamin argues, has nothing to do with the notion of a temporal
progress or *becoming*—a notion sharply criticized by Schlegel
(93); instead, it seeks to articulate the essentially unfinished process by which the reflective medium differentiates itself: "What is
essential is rather that the task of progressive universal poetry is
given in the most determinate way in a medium of forms, as the
latter's progressively more exact, more pervasive organization and
ordering (*dessen fortschreitend genauere Durchwaltung und
Ordnung*)" (92). What the absolute infinitude of art then involves
is not the progressive realization of a self-identical ideal or entity,
but the articulation of a medium understood to consist of a "con-

tinuum of forms." This medium can be said to "unfold" in the individual work, qua "system" or "*Zusammenhang*," and criticism, as an "experiment" performed on the work, continues this process of "unfolding." The question now becomes how such an unfolding is to be conceived?

To be sure this response is not explicitly given by Benjamin in this text, since it would inevitably lead him to address directly the issue which exceeds the bounds he has set himself for his thesis. Not surprisingly, however, it is implicit in his reflections on the romantic approach to the question of form: "Practical, i.e. determinate reflection, self-limitation comprise the individuality and form of the work" (73). Form is conceived not as a means of exhibiting or representing (*darstellen*) content, but as "a peculiar modification of reflection limiting itself" (76). Criticism reflects and thereby delimits—that is, dissolves—the "positive" form of the individual work by exposing its appurtenance to the more general medium of reflection which for the romantics comprises the determining idea of art itself. The problem remains, however, of explaining just how such a general idea of reflection can *limit itself* in individual works and still remain pure reflection. The problem is clear to the romantics, as the following remark of Novalis, cited by Benjamin, indicates: "A work is formed when it is sharply limited everywhere, but within its limits limitless . . . everywhere the same and yet sublimely beyond itself" (76). As individuation of the general medium of reflection, the individual work can fulfill its function only insofar as it is driven out of and beyond itself, and thus comes to be dissolved in—and into—the critical process. The "value" of the work can thus be measured by the degree to which it allows this process (that is, criticism) to take place—by the degree to which it is "criticizable" (78). Such criticism, Benjamin remarks, "is not primarily bent on judging (*beurteilend*) the individual work, but rather on exposing its relations to all other works and finally to the idea of art" (78). Precisely how the exposure (*Darstellung*) of such "relations" is to lead to "the idea of art" as general medium of absolute reflection remains an open question in Benjamin's account of the romantics. And yet, the possibility of a response can be glimpsed in his discussion of romantic irony.

Benjamin distinguishes between two kinds of irony: the more

familiar irony, felt to demonstrate the sovereignty of the author—Hegel's "principle of absolute subjectivity"—who thereby takes himself to be free of all material constraint. This irony Benjamin designates as "material irony" in order to distinguish it from a second variety, which he finds both more "positive" in character and also less subjective; the "irony of form." Unlike material irony, that of form cannot be identified with the sheer freedom of the subject, since all art is "subordinated" to the "objective lawfulness" of a certain formality (83). This irony thus "attacks" the "illusoriness" of the form of a work without, however, utterly abandoning it. In thus undermining the integrity of the individual work, formal irony resembles criticism, which also tends ultimately to annihilate the work. All the more telling, then, the difference brought out by Benjamin when he compares the two, formal irony and criticism:

> How does irony's destruction of illusion in artistic form relate to the destruction of the work through criticism? Criticism sacrifices the work utterly to the will of the One Coherent Context (*um des Einen Zusammenhanges willen*). [Formal irony] on the contrary, does not merely not destroy the work that it attacks, it tends to render it indestructible. ... Formal irony is not, like fortitude or rectitude, an intentional behavior of an author. It can not, as is usually done, be considered the index of a subjective lack of limits; rather it must be valued as an objective moment in the work itself. It represents the paradoxical attempt (*Versuch*) to continue building a structure even through demolition (*Sie stellt den paradoxen Versuch dar, am Gebilde noch durch Abbruch zu bauen*): through the effort to demonstrate the work's relation to the idea in the work itself. (86–87)

Benjamin's description here of the romantic "ironising of form" marks a decisive point in his interpretation of romantic critical theory, for his subsequent work no less than for current efforts to rethink that status of reading and interpretation, whether "literary" or other. With respect to Benjamin's later work, this discussion of formal irony foreshadows the theory of allegory that he will articulate some six years later in his second, and this time definitively unsuccessful, attempt at academic writing (and an academic career), *The Origins of the German Mourning Play*. In terms of the dissertation itself, the account of formal irony con-

tains the germs of an alternative to the impasse of romantic critical
theory, which Benjamin in no uncertain terms locates in the tendency to conflate "the profane with the symbolic form ... Only
at the cost of such imprecise demarcations can all the concepts
of critical theory be integrated into the realm of the Absolute, as
the romantics intended" (98). The critique of such a confusion
will be the point of departure of his theory of allegory in the *Origins*. Although Benjamin himself does not say so explicitly, what
he calls here the "profane" form may be identified with the "positive" form of the individualized work, a form which can never be
adequately interpreted if it is understood merely as the manifestation of the self-delimitation of the absolute, that is, of reflection
itself.[20] To distinguish between a "profane" and a "symbolic" form
is to acknowledge that no positive or profane aesthetic reflection
is capable of "containing" the Absolute within its borders or of
leading to it by any continuous path. In contrast to the immanence
of the symbol (which, as Benjamin will state later in his discussion
of allegory, is legitimate only in theology, not in aesthetics), the
profane form of the individual work of art involves a process of
delimitation which can never, as such, be assimilated to the Absolute, whether as reflection or in any other guise. The romantic attempt to define criticism precisely in such terms is thus forced to
rely ultimately on an "axiomatic presupposition" that sidesteps
rather than addresses the decisive question, that of the relation of
reflection and form, by advancing, as an article of belief, "that reflection is in itself substantial and fulfilled, and does not run off
into an empty infinity" (31). This is why the "formal irony" to
which Benjamin refers is not part of romantic critical *theory* in
the "proper sense," but of a literary *practice* identified with the
dramatic writing of Tieck rather than with Schlegel or Novalis. The
unmistakable implication is that the only way out of the impasse
of romantic criticism—which is perhaps that of criticism *tout
court*—lies not in the effort to dissolve the work in an absolute
and ultimately self-identical critical reflection, but in a *practice of
writing* which, precisely by undermining the integrity of the
individual form, at the same time allows the singular "work" to
"survive."

It survives, however, as a different kind of writing. Such writing would be "critical" insofar as it "reflects"—and, hence, alters—

an already "given," "positive" form or set of delimitations. But this alteration would not be the transformation of a "profane" form into a symbolic one, understood by the romantics as "the pure expression of reflective self-limitation" since the "ironization of form" remains no less "profane" than the form it "survives" (the verb here to be understood both transitively and intransitively). To insist, as does Benjamin, discreetly but firmly, on the necessary distinction between profane and symbolic form is to emphasize that the reflective delimitations which constitute form can never be grasped entirely or essentially in terms of "self." The romantics sought to disengage reflection from the subject by replacing the Fichtean opposition of I and Not-I by an Absolute Self. Benjamin seeks to demonstrate how this movement cannot and does not leave this "axiomatic presupposition" untouched or in force. Thus, although in their theoretical pronouncements the romantics insist that the general medium of reflection constituting the determining idea of art must be conceived as a "continuum of forms," when they set about analyzing the kind of language and writing that most powerfully exemplifies "the highest of all symbolic forms" and "the romantic Idea of poetry itself" (99), the prosaic writing of the novel, they describe it precisely as discontinuous: "The writing style of the novel should not form a continuum, it must be a structure articulated in each of its periods. Each small piece must be detached, limited, its own whole" (99). Such a discontinuous style of writing culminates in the notion of prose as the highest "idea of poetry": in prose, "poetry expands itself ... by contracting, abandoning its incandescence (*Feuerstoff*), congealing," and thus "assuming a prosaic appearance" in which its components "no longer form the same intimate community" as in poetry, but are therefore all the more capable of "presenting the limited." The movement of phrase becomes "simpler, more monotonous, quieter," the context "more flexible," the expression "more transparent and colorless" (Novalis, quoted p. 101). Thus, the entire romantic "philosophy of art" is determined by an "idea of Poetry as Prose," which in turn leads to a concept that for Benjamin marks both the culmination and the limits of romanticism: that of the *Nüchternheit* or "sobriety of art" (103). This proposition, which is "the essentially new and fundamental thought of the romantic philosophy of art," is most fully articulated outside of romanticism proper, in the writings of Hölderlin. The notion of sobriety, which, Benjamin affirms, is "even today powerfully at work with unforeseeable consequences," goes beyond the scope of his study; he therefore merely points to Hölderlin's emphasis on the "calculability" and, hence, the element of repetition at work in the procedures of poetry. It is such calculable repetition that explains the effect of formal irony in assuring a certain "survival" of the work: "What disintegrates in the ironic ray is strictly the illusion, what remains indestructible, however, is the nucleus of the work, consisting not in ecstasy, which can be decomposed, but in the inviolate (*unantastbar*) prosaic figure" (106). Everything depends, we see, on the way in which the "calculable laws" and rhythms of a certain repetitive language—both prosaic and poetic—are to be conceived and, even more, to be practiced. Here, this question will bring Benjamin to a term that defines the horizon of his "thesis" but also opens the way to his major work on the Mourning Play and on Allegory. That term is *Darstellung*—usually translated as "presentation" or "exposition." Here, however, toward the conclusion of the book, it is used in a different sense to describe the function of criticism in the light of the "sobriety of art." Since Benjamin will define the word himself, I will cite it in German:

> Criticism is the "Darstellung" of the prosaic nucleus in each work. The concept "Darstellung" is thereby to be understood in the chemical sense, as the generation of one substance (*Erzeugung eines Stoffes*) through a determinate process to which others are *subjected*. This is what Schlegel meant when he said of Wilhelm Meister that the work does not merely judge itself, it also sets itself forth (*stellt sich dar*). (109, emphasis added)

The romantic idea of criticism thus turns out to consist in a process of "subjection": "others" are subjected so that something can *matter*. As a result of this subjection to the other, criticism "stellt sich dar," *sets itself forth*, sets forth, departing from itself to become something else, something lacking a proper name and which Benjamin, and after him de Man, will call "allegory."

Might not romanticism, then, turn out to be the name under which the awareness of its allegorical character has imposed itself on contemporary criticism? And through this imposition, is the indication of criticism *underway?*

NOTES

1. Friedrich Schlegel, *Schriften zur Literatur* (Munich, 1972), p. 333.
2. G. W. F. Hegel, *The Philosophy of Fine Art*, trans. T. M. Knox (Oxford, 1979), 1:56.
3. Ibid., p. 61.
4. Ibid., p. 67.
5. Ibid., p. 91. Hegel is referring to literary discourse, in which "sensuous appearance" has already been reduced to the arbitrary materiality of the sign, in turn understood by Hegel as a mere vehicle for meaning. Hence, the "prosaic" element of literature prepares the way to the "prose of thought," that is, philosophy.
6. Paul de Man, *The Rhetoric of Romanticism* (New York, 1983), p. 16.
7. Ibid., p. 6.
8. Ibid.
9 Ibid., p. 16.
10. *The Rhetoric of Romanticism*, pp. vii-viii.
11. Ibid., p. 121.
12. Ibid., p. 122.
13. Walter Benjamin, *Gesammelte Schriften* (Frankfurt, 1980), 1.3:801.
14. Benjamin also makes use of a later series of lectures, dating from 1804, the so-called Windischmann lectures (named after their editor) in order to supplement his study of Schlegel's "system." He considered this source "secondary," however, insofar as in it Schlegel had already renounced what might be called the aesthetic radicalism of his earlier period, which for Benjamin is constitutive of the romantic concept of criticism.
15. Peter Demetz, in his introduction to Benjamin's *Reflections* (New York, 1986), p. xii.
16. From a Munich dissertation submitted four years earlier, in 1915: Charlotte Pingaud, *Grundlinien der ästhetischen Doktrin Fr. Schlegels* (Stuttgart, 1914), pp. 12–13.
17. The literal translation of Benjamin's title would be: "The Concept of Art-Criticism in German Romanticism." Art Criticism, of course, in English refers to the plastic arts; "Kunst," for Schlegel and Novalis, however, as Benjamin notes, means primarily, if not exclusively, what we call "literature." At the same time, "literature" (Dichtung, Poesie) is understood by the early German romantics as the exemplary instance of all art, and, indeed, Benjamin explicitly points to the problem of this exemplification, which does not sufficiently articulate the difference between individual art forms. ("A fundamental deficiency of Romantic the-

ory of art is that 'poetry' and 'art' are not sufficiently distinguished," p. 14.) This tendency to conflate art in general with literature in particular is also responsible for the current use of the terms "criticism" and "critical theory" to designate both the interpretation of literature and at the same time aesthetics and hermeneutics in general. Hence, the most economical and accurate English translation of "Kunstkritik" today is simply "criticism."

18. Erwin Kircher, *Philosophie der Romantik* (Jena, 1906), cited by Benjamin, p. 107.

19. I have elsewhere tried to demonstrate how such a concept informs the theories of two of the most popular of recent "reader-oriented" critics, Stanley Fish and Wolfgang Iser. See "Caught in the Act of Reading," in *Demarcating the Disciplines* (Minneapolis, 1986), and "The Debts of Criticism," in *Interpretation and Institution* (Minneapolis, 1987).

20. "The fundamental property of symbolic form consists ... in the purity of the form of representation, so that this becomes the exclusive expression of the self-limitation of reflection." (97).

On Political Readings of
Lyrical Ballads

M. H. ABRAMS

Why this is ideology, nor am I out of it.

The criticism of Wordsworth, which took a linguistic turn in the New Criticism of the 1930s, and more sharply in the semiotics and the deconstructive criticism of the 1970s, has in the present decade taken a decidedly political turn. This sudden left-face in the march of Wordsworth studies, especially of the earlier poetry, is indicated by the prevalence of the term "politics" in the titles of books and essays, such as "The Politics of 'Tintern Abbey,'" "Criticism, Politics, and Style in Wordsworth's Poetry," *Wordsworth's Second Nature: A Study of the Poetry and Politics.* Three books, all published between 1983 and 1986, although they do not feature the word in their titles, are drastically political in their treatment of Wordsworth—Heather Glen's *Vision and Disenchantment*, Jerome McGann's *The Romantic Ideology*, and Marjorie Levinson's *Wordsworth's Great Period Poems*. I want to address two questions with respect to this recent critical direction: What are the premises and procedures of a radically political criticism? And what does such criticism make of the poems in the *Lyrical Ballads* of 1798, but especially of "Tintern Abbey"?

My discussion is not intended to apply overall to the current movement called the "new historicism." That term covers a broad range of overlapping critical enterprises. One wing (its practitioners tend to identify themselves as "new historicists" and to use "power" as their critical leitmotif) is mainly in the lineage of Michel Foucault; the other wing (its exemplars are apt to call what they do "political criticism" and to use "ideology" as their leitmotif) is more distinctly in the lineage of Karl Marx. My concern is with the Sons of Karl rather than with the sons (and daughters) of Michel and, of these, primarily with some radical, or all-out representatives of that critical mode.

At first view, political criticism seems merely an intensified form of a prominent feature in earlier Wordsworth studies. For no other major poet has been more persistently treated from the vantage of his politics than has Wordsworth, in his shift from revolutionary radicalism to Tory conservatism, by a line of critics from his contemporaries to such distinguished recent commentators as Carl Woodring, David Erdman, and E. P. Thompson. Closer inspection, however, reveals an important shift in focus, assumptions, and methods among recent political critics. It seems to me misleading to claim flatly, as Stephen Greenblatt does, that "the traditional historical approach to literature ... finds history to lie outside the texts, to function in effect as the object to which signs in the text point."[1] This description doesn't do justice to many historical critics, all the way back from Leslie Stephen to Ian Watt and David Erdman, who not only advert to social and political history as circumstances that shape a literary work, but also identify implicit social and political structures and values that are inscribed within the literary works themselves. But Greenblatt is revealing when he goes on to specify a newer approach that finds history "in the artworks themselves, as enabling condition, shaping force, forger of meaning." The view that history, not the author, shapes a literary work and forges its meaning is indeed the crucial feature in the shift from traditional historical criticism both to the new historicism and to the new politicalism.

To explore this difference further, we can say in the first place that political criticism, despite its frequent claims to the contrary, moves entirely with the critical current of the present, which is emphatically an Age of Reading. Like many of their critical contemporaries, political critics undertake to read a text so as to make out, whatever it seems to say, what it really means. They often, it is true, set themselves expressly to counter the apolitical close-reading of New Critics, who analyzed a poem as an isolated and autonomous verbal construct, as well as what Paul de Man suggested was the still closer reading of apolitical deconstructive critics, who interpreted the text both as self-referential and as self-disseminative into an open set of undecidable meanings. In opposition to these precursors, new political critics announce what seems to me a laudable intention to salvage a literary work as a determinably meaningful human product, rooted in the biographical circumstances of its author and the social particularities of its time and place, and consequential to us in our present circumstances. They do so, however, by appropriating the modes and devices of close reading that they undertake to displace, but adapting them to a "political"—which is primarily a new-Marxist—way of reading. "Marxism," Irving Howe has ruefully noted, now "finds an old-age home in American universities."[2] We can add that political critics in the universities have modulated Marx's aim to change the world into changing the way we read poems.

Marjorie Levinson defines clearly the shift from earlier historical criticism, whether or not it was Marxist, to the kind she practices. "What [E. P.] Thompson and his fellow workers [she mentions Erdman and Woodring] could not, given their critical moment, address, were the subtler languages of politics in Wordsworth's poetry, and the way these languages inform and inflect the manifest doctrine of the poetry. . . ." Her own procedure is to use historical material expressly "for the purposes of textual intervention" in such a way as "to explain the poem's transformational grammar" and to produce "a closer reading of it"—a closer reading that discovers "new meanings" and, it turns out, "discredits" or "dismantles" a poem's "manifest statement," or "contradicts its expressed doctrine."[3] Political criticism is thus not only a mode of reading; it is also what I have elsewhere called a mode of "Newreading." That is, exactly like the various critical "theories" of recent decades that it sets out to replace, political criticism is designed to subvert what a poet undertook to say, what his text seems to say, and what other readers have taken him to say, in order to convert manifest meanings into a mask, or displacement, or (another of Levinson's terms) an "allegory" for the real meaning—in this case, a political meaning—whose discovery has been reserved for the proponent of the theory.

I

What, on analysis, turns out to be the logical structure of a political theory and practice of reading literature? This structure is both most clear and most rigorous in explicitly principled critics like Jerome McGann and Marjorie Levinson—who invoke frequently both Marx and recent neo-Marxist theorists such as Macherey, Eagleton, and Jameson—but it controls in varying degree the reading of other political critics as well.

(1) The basic premise, to cite Jerome McGann's version, is that "poems are social and historical products"—products "at the ideological level" of social functions, which he describes as in complex interrelation with the "political" and the "economic" levels. That is, the ideology of a particular time and place processes whatever authors undertake to say into representations that McGann calls "concrete forms" of ideology, or an "artistic reproduction" that "historicizes the ideological materials, gives a local habitation and a name to various kinds of abstractions." It follows "that the critical study of such products must be grounded in a socio-historical analytic," and that all more "specialized studies"— such as stylistic, rhetorical, formal—"must find their *raison d'être* in the socio-historical ground." Like other current theories of Newreading, then, a radically political criticism is a "must-be," or necessitarian theory: it brings to the reading of any literary work a predetermination of the kind of meaning—in this instance, an ideological meaning—that the act of reading will necessarily discover.[4]

(2) Upon this must-be—that any literary work must be, and must be treated as, a historicized and concretized ideology—there follows another. In McGann's rendering: "In my view ideology will necessarily be seen as false consciousness when observed from any *critical* vantage, and particularly from the point of view of a materialist and historical criticism. Since this book assumes that a critical vantage can and must be taken toward its subject, the ideology represented through Romantic works is *a fortiori* seen as a body of illusions." In McGann's theory, as in that of most current Marxists, to identify the deflection of an ideological literary product from historical reality is complicated by the awareness

that the materialist critic has no option but to interpret that product through the ideology of the critic's own historical moment. Nonetheless, McGann is able to carry out his critical project with no lack of assurance. Of Wordsworth's "Intimations of Immortality," for example, he says: "The poem generalizes—we now like to say mythologizes—all its conflicts, or rather resituates these conflicts out of a socio-historical context and into an ideological one."[5] Whatever the epistemological problems posed by a radical historicist relativism, the political critic is reasonably confident that he possesses the key to all Romantic ideologies.

(3) In the practice of critical reading, it follows from these linked premises that the first and essential task (whatever the critic may in addition undertake) must be to identify and expose the covert ideology implicated in a work's manifest or ostensible meanings, and so to unravel, or penetrate through, the web of illusions generated by that ideology that disguise, when they do not entirely displace, the social and political realities of its time and place.

In applied political readings, we find an ever-recurrent vocabulary of operative terms for undoing what a work ostensibly signifies and transforming it into its historic meanings. These terms are the reciprocal, in a "critical" reading, of what Levinson calls the "transformational grammar" imposed on the writing of a work by its author's unconscious ideology. Conspicuous in this transformative lexicon are "suppression," "sublimation," "substitution," "displacement," "dislocation," "occlusion." These of course are Freud's terms for the unconscious mechanisms that distort the latent, or true, meaning of dreams, but as Levinson, echoing Jameson, remarks of the paradoxical procedures for uncovering the "ideological subtext" for Wordsworth's poetic texts, "Freud worked out its psychic economy and Marx produced its political logic." Other operative terms often encountered in political readings, such as "absence," "elision," "erasure," "effacement," are imported from deconstructive criticism. As Levinson says, with her usual awareness of her interpretive procedures: to determine in Wordsworth's "Peele Castle" what it is that "works with a cruel perseverance to discredit the manifest themes of the elegy," one "must read the poem closely and deconstructively," but only as preliminary to "reconstructing the contemporary environment" in order that "one might explain the strangely redundant energy of the poem in terms of social contradiction and ideological necessity." To such a fusion of Derrida with Marx, Levinson applies the name "deconstructive materialism."[6]

Especially efficacious is a mechanism for transforming what a text does not say at all into what it most deeply means. As McGann puts it, citing Pierre Macherey on necessary silences in a text, "From Wordsworth's vantage, an ideology is born out of things which (literally) *cannot* be spoken of." And Levinson cites approvingly a long list of political theorists and critics who, "at once materialist and deconstructive, represent the literary work as that which speaks of one thing because it cannot articulate another—presenting formally a sort of allegory by absence, where the signified is indicated by an identifiably absented signifier."[7] In the practice of a determined political reader, it seems clear, a poet's silence can be made to speak louder than his words, and what that silence speaks, the critic knows in advance, must be an ideological necessity and a suppressed historical reality.

It seems to me that something like this set of assumptions and interpretive operations, if appropriately formulated and applied, can yield—in some critics have yielded—credible political discoveries about a literary work. If, that is, the premises are formulated in terms of may-bes instead of must-bes (in other words, as a working hypothesis instead of a ruling hypothesis) and if they are applied in a way that permits the author's text some empirical possibility of countering a proposed political reading so as to adjudge it, say, probable, or forced, or even dead wrong. But the risk in an all-out, must-be theory and practice of political reading is obvious. The critic, bringing to any text an a priori knowledge of the kind of meaning that he or she must of necessity find, and possessed of a can't-fail set of devices for transforming anything whatever that a text says—or doesn't mention—into the predetermined subtext, will infallibly, given some biographical and historical information and sufficient ingenuity, be able to produce a political reading. But such a reading is in effect self-confirming because empirically incorrigible; it is the product of a discovery procedure that prepossesses the political meanings it triumphantly finds. The risk, in other words, is of a critical authoritarianism that brooks no opposition, since no particulars of a text, no indications of what a poet undertook to say, and no appeal to able critics who read the text otherwise, can possibly resist conversion, by this apparatus, into an unconscious ideological cover-up, or displacement, or rationalization of political or social reality.[8] Nor have political Newreaders avoided the further risk of cancelling the imaginative delights that works of literature, in their diversity, have yielded to readers of all eras. For a rigorously political reading is not only a closed, monothematic reading; it is also joyless, casting a critical twilight in which all poems are gray.

II

Recent political readers of Wordsworth have concerned themselves not with his late conservative poems, but with his early, reputedly radical poems, especially the *Lyrical Ballads*. I shall comment only briefly on readings of Wordsworth's narrative ballads in order to focus on "Tintern Abbey," the longest and most notable of what Wordsworth in his title to *Lyrical Ballads* called "A Few Other Poems."

The many political treatments of the narrative ballads are mainly concerned to lay bare their covert evidences of Wordsworth's built-in social ideology, and especially of his upper-class consciousness. As Michael Friedman puts the critical assumption, Wordsworth's "adult consciousness of his class status"—for he was inescapably "a gentleman"—"created a gulf between him and the common folk he observed," although he was incapable of recognizing his assumptions of superiority because they are part of the "historical constraints that limit his consciousness, as they limit the consciousness of all those subject to history."[9] Revelations of Wordsworth's unconscious social presuppositions and attitudes strike me as plausible to the degree that the political point of view functions as a heuristic position rather than an authoritarian imposition—to the degree, therefore, that what Wordsworth wrote is given a fair chance to resist the interpretation. Roger Sales differs from other political critics in his downright dismissal of the early narratives: "Wordsworth's travelling circus of freakish outcasts may appear to offer a critique of the unacceptable face of rural society, yet they merely endorse the same propagandist interpretation of social change as 'Michael' tries to sell us."[10] What I find troubling, however, in even qualified and empirical-minded readings for ideology is that they derogate Wordsworth's ballads by ignoring their innovativeness and artistry and, in effect, canceling their distinction from the flood of contemporary magazine verses which, as Robert Mayo showed in a pioneering article more than three decades ago, dealt with similar subjects and in similar ballad-meters.[11]

It is only when described in general terms, however, that Wordsworth's ballads seem to approximate the popular narratives of the time. To put a Wordsworth ballad next to a magazine poem it seems to resemble is to reveal sharp differences in idiom, artistry, and tone. The magazine verses condescend to their lowly subjects, are self-consciously simple in manner, are cliché-ridden, and exploit a pathos in the plight of the down-trodden and the social outcast that is tinged with a complacent sense of the author's own moral sensibility. In recent decades a number of excellent commentators have revealed the extent to which Wordsworth's seemingly simple ballads are in fact technically innovative; complex, and sometimes self-ironic, in the control of tone (that is, in the implicit expression of the social relations between narrator, subject, and reader); and reliant on implication and indirection, instead of direct assertion, in making their social and political as well as moral points. What I want to stress, in addition, is that in these poems, as Wordsworth himself tells us, he explicitly undertook to engage with and to reform what we now call the "ideology" of the reading public of his time.

In a remarkable essay of 1825, William Hazlitt proposed a political interpretation of Wordsworth's "innovations" in the *Lyrical Ballads* and other early poems: "It partakes of, and is carried along with, the revolutionary movement of our age: the political changes of the day were the model on which he formed and conducted his poetical experiments. His Muse ... is a leveling one. It proceeds on a principle of equality, and strives to reduce all things to the same standard."[12] What Hazlitt, I believe, had in mind was that, in his ballads and early narratives, and in the essays he wrote to explain and justify his poetic aims, Wordsworth had in effect subverted the official theory of poetry which had been dominant in European culture since the Renaissance and was still evident among conservative critics of the late eighteenth century and early nineteenth century. This theory had posited a hierarchy of poetic genres, modeled on the hierarchy of social classes, in which the ruling principle of decorum had fitted the social status of the protagonists, and the social level of the poetic language, to the rank of the genre. As Hazlitt says, Wordsworth's "popular style . . . gets rid of all the high places of poetry," while "the distinctions of rank, birth, wealth, power . . . are not to be found here." What Hazlitt recognized was that Wordsworth had leveled this built-in social hierarchy, and in doing so had translated the egalitarianism of French revolutionary politics into the egalitarianism of a revolutionary poetics.

But we can say more than this about the politics of Wordsworth's enterprise in *Lyrical Ballads*. In his "Advertisement" of 1798, he asserted that most of his poems were "experiments" that needed to overcome what he described, ironically, as "that most dreadful enemy to our pleasures, our own pre-established codes of decision." When he elaborated on this claim in his later prefaces, he made it apparent that these "pre-established codes" are built-in determinants of what we now call "reading" but Wordsworth, in the critical parlance of his time, called "taste"; also that the reading-codes which his poems were designed to overcome consisted of a tacit upper class consciousness, governing the way his contemporaries understood and re-sponded to poetry, that, again in contemporary parlance, he called "pride." Wordsworth also indicated that in his view, the ways in which poetry is read and responded to are interdependent with revolutionary changes in the structure of society. He said in the *Preface* of 1800 that, to provide a "systematic defence of the the-ory" on which he had written poems "so materially different" from those now generally approved would necessitate "a full account of the present state of the public taste," which would in turn re-quire "retracing the revolutions not of literature alone but likewise of society itself."[13] Fifteen years later, in the *Essay, Supplementary to the Preface* of 1815, Wordsworth returned to the subject of the social determinants of reading poetry in dealing with the difficulty faced by himself, as an original poet, in "*creating* the taste by which he is to be enjoyed." There he raised the question of the extent to which that difficulty lies in "breaking the bonds of custom" and "overcoming the prejudices of false refinement," and especially, given the poetic object "which here and elsewhere I have proposed to myself," the extent to which it lies

> in divesting the Reader of the pride that induces him to dwell upon those points wherein Men differ from each other, to the exclusion of those in which all Men are alike, or the same; and in making him ashamed of the vanity that renders him insensible of the appropriate excellence which civil arrangements, less unjust than might appear, and Nature illimitable in her bounty, have conferred on Men who stand below him in the scale of society.[14]

Neither Wordsworth's qualification in this passage of his earlier radicalism, nor the critical idiom of his period, should conceal the fact that he viewed the prevailing mode of reading by the poetic public of his time as informed by upper-class social "codes" that constitute what political readers now call "ideology." Even in 1815, Wordsworth described his poetry as involving "emotions of the pathetic ... that are complex and revolutionary," against which the heart of the reader "struggles with pride."[15] If political readers now find that even Wordsworth's early poems, which he said were intended to revolutionize the built-in politics of his readers' sensibility, were in fact covertly conservative in their ideology, it seems an act of historical justice to recognize that in doing so, political readers apply to Wordsworth a theory of the class-determined writing and reading of poetry of which Wordsworth was himself a pre-Marxian innovator.

III

For an example of the radically transformative power of political readings, we need to turn from Wordsworth's spare narratives about the lowly and the down-and-out to that other poem in *Lyrical Ballads* that we conventionally call, by a convenient but misleading shorthand, "Tintern Abbey." To the uninitiated it might seem that a meditation in a natural setting on the course of the lyric speaker's life would be immune from a passage-by-passage political interpretation. From the ruling principle, however, that all Wordsworth's poems must be an ideological representation, it follows that the personal subject of "Tintern Abbey" must be an evasion of a political and public subject, and that its very silences bespeak what, by ideological necessity, it can neither know nor say, yet can't help revealing. As Marjorie Levinson sums up this way of reading the poem, "The primary poetic action is the suppression of the social. 'Tintern Abbey' achieves its fiercely private vision by directing a continuous energy toward the nonrepresentation of objects and point of view expressive of a public—we would say, ideological—dimension." Kenneth Johnston, in "The Politics of 'Tintern Abbey,'" is more guarded: "It may well be, in light of these interpretive possibilities, one of the most powerfully *de*politicized poems in the language—and, by that token, a uniquely political one."[16]

What makes such readings of "Tintern Abbey" especially interesting, and challenging, to an Oldreader like myself is that—unlike their procedure with other descriptive-meditative poems by Wordsworth—critics in this instance put forward an explicit textual ground for postulating an occluded political subtext. This ground, however, is not in "Tintern Abbey" but in William Gilpin's travel book *Tour of the Wye*, which had been first published in 1771 and was often reprinted. As early as 1957, Mary Moorman had remarked that, on their tour of the Wye valley during which the poem was composed, William and Dorothy Wordsworth "seem to have taken with them" Gilpin's book. Moorman pointed out that, by Gilpin's account, the ruined abbey itself "was a dwelling-place of beggars and the wretchedly poor," and that "the river was then full of shipping, carrying coal and timber from the Forest of Dean." In a footnote, she also cited a passage from Gilpin: "Many of the furnaces, on the banks of the river, consume charcoal, which is manufactured on the spot; and the smoke, which is frequently seen issuing from the side of the hills, and spreading its thin veil over them, beautifully breaks their lines, and unites them with the sky."[17] As Moorman suggests, this passage was probably echoed in the opening description in Wordsworth's poem, where the charcoal smoke is aestheticized, as in Gilpin, into "wreathes of smoke." It can be added that Wordsworth may also have mentioned the poor people in the vicinity of the abbey, although in the mode of a conjecture, in the lines that follow the reference to the smoke:

> wreathes of smoke
> Sent up, in silence, from among the trees,
> With some uncertain notice, as might seem,
> Of vagrant dwellers in the houseless woods. . . .

For a quarter century this land mine remained buried in Moorman's *Wordsworth* until detonated by political readers, who added to Moorman's account the fact, mentioned by Gilpin and other travelers, that the ironmaking furnaces along its lower banks made the river, however pristine in its upper reaches, "ouzy, and discolored" in the tidal section downstream from the Abbey.[18] What these critics take to be Wordsworth's brief and unfeeling adversion to the wretched social realities in and near the ruined abbey seems to have made them especially severe in their reading of the poem as a whole. The stance at times verges on the prosecutorial, with the verdict "guilty as charged," though palliated by assertions that "Tintern Abbey" nonetheless remains, for reasons not clearly specified, a great poem.

Marjorie Levinson's analysis—paralleled by that of Jerome McGann—takes off from a detailed inquisition of what she calls its "snake of a title," whose length and particularity provide tacit evidence that it functions, although unconsciously, as an ideological cover-up for Wordsworth's true subject. (No matter, presumably, that such elaborate titles, specifying a locale, occasion, and even date—establishing, that is, the precise vantage point from which the poet views the prospect, and the time of the viewing—had long been standard in eighteenth-century local poems, the immediate precursors of "Tintern Abbey"; a convention that was continued by Coleridge and other writers of the extended Romantic lyric of description and meditation.[19]) In Levinson's view, that Wordsworth in his title should call attention to the abbey but "then studiously ignore it" indicates his suppression of the socioeconomic facts of the miserably poor who populated the area. In the date of composition Wordsworth cites, July 13, 1798, what gets noted yet "overlooked" is its significance as marking "almost to the day the nine-year anniversary of the original Bastille Day, the eight-year anniversary of Wordsworth's first visit to France, and the five-year anniversary of the murder of Marat." By substituting "above Tintern Abbey" for "below Tintern Abbey," Wordsworth evades the fact that, downstream from the abbey, the river was polluted by effluents from the iron furnaces.[20] Then she proceeds through the text of the poem, intent always on exposing its "transformational grammar" and the ways in which its author "excludes from his field certain conflictual sights and meanings"—an "exclusion," she says, which "is, I believe, the poem's 'wherefore.'"[21]

These interpretive tactics and findings leave me unpersuaded; but also, I confess, somewhat nonplused. For radical political readers preempt the high ground from which they can look down on critical gainsayers as not only politically laggard and intellectually naive, but also as morally insensitive to social woes. According to Jerome McGann, for example, the "priests and clerics of Romanticism"—that is, scholars and critics who, like himself before his critical enlightenment, read Romantic poems for what they say, without exposing them as ideological "dramas of displacement and idealization"—serve to "perpetuate and maintain older ideas and attitudes," hence "typically serve only the most reactionary purposes of their societies"; although, he charitably adds, "they may not be aware of this."[22]

But I must risk confirming my status as a cleric of Romanticism, and at least inadvertently reactionary, by proposing, in place of the authoritarian must-bes of sternly political readers, some principles of a more open—in political terms, a liberal—way of reading poetry.

(1) First, as Coleridge in his radical youth wrote to his even more radical friend, "Citizen Thelwall": "Do not let us introduce an act of Uniformity against Poets."[23] Consequently, a poet is free to write a political poem, but also any kind of nonpolitical poem he or she may choose to write. As against the political version of the prevailing hermeneutics of suspicion, this principle entails that we respect a poet's chosen and manifest subject matter, without the theoretical predetermination that it must be an evasion or cover-up of socio-historic realities that the poet could not or would not confront. And as against the closed political mono-reading, the principle requires that we keep our reading adaptive to the variousness of poetic possibilities, in subject as well as rendering; it is a reading open to surprises.

(2) Let us grant a poet also his *données*—that is, the concep-

tual frame of reference, or the belief system, that he may use to account for and to support, or may represent as following from, the modes of experience that the poem articulates. What traditional critics call Wordsworth's "philosophy" or "myth" of nature, as put forward in "Tintern Abbey," is entitled to the suspension of disbelief for the poetic moment that we yield to Homer, Dante, Milton, and the great preponderance of poets who write in accordance with postulates and beliefs that we do not share. Wordsworth suggests, for example, that in trance states like the one induced in him by remembrance of the Wye valley, "We see into the life of things"; that he has felt in nature "a presence" that "rolls through all things"; and that the remembered scenes, and "nature and the language of the sense" in general, have profoundly influenced his moral life.[24] For the scholar and critic to expound such passages, and for any reader to yield to them a pro tempore imaginative consent, is not, as McGann proposes, to be seduced into accepting and propagating an outworn ideology. It is, instead, to make possible an adequate experience of the poem, part of whose value, in fact, is that it widens the limits of responsiveness imposed by our own beliefs.

The requisite for our imaginative consent to Wordsworth's myth of nature is the feature that he later proposed in order to justify his using, in the "Intimations Ode," the concept of the preexistence of the soul. His subject in that poem, he says, is the experience of a lost "vividness and splendour" in the perceptions of a child to which "every one, I believe, if he would look back, could bear testimony." The sole requisite for employing the concept of preexistence as a way of accounting for this general human experience is that it have "sufficient foundation in humanity for authorizing me to make for my purpose the best use of it I could as a Poet."[25] Furthermore, in "Tintern Abbey," if we attend to the syntax of the passages in question, it is notable how carefully Wordsworth distinguishes between the belief or creed he postulates and the actual experiences that the creed would serve to explain: "such, perhaps, / As may have had no trivial influence"; "Nor less, I trust, / To them I may have owed another gift"; and not "I have known," but "I have *felt* / A presence." Wordsworth's distinction between experiential fact and explanatory concept is especially obvious when, having proposed that in a trance-state "We see into the life of things," he immediately qualifies the proposal as possibly mistaken—"If this / Be but a vain belief'—in order to reassert the experience itself:

> If this
> Be but a vain belief, yet, oh! how oft, . . .
> How oft, in spirit, have I turned to thee
> O sylvan Wye! Thou wanderer through the woods,
> How often has my spirit turned to thee![26]

(3) A third principle of an open reading is that it take into account, and take delight in, the artistry of the poet in articulating and structuring the component parts of a poem, from its beginning to its end. When a strong political reader takes note of Wordsworth's artistry, it is by way of acknowledging his skill (albeit unconscious) at deploying what Levinson calls "disarming discursive strategies," and McGann terms "a strategy of displacement," to disguise or evade the real political subject.[27]

When read in this open and adaptive way, and read in its entirety, "Tintern Abbey," I believe, is recognized to be about a subject that rigorous political readers, by their preestablished code of decision—that is, by imposing their critical ideology—have veiled, displaced, and in important aspects totally occluded. Put briefly, hence reductively: the poem that Wordsworth composed is a sustained lyric meditation, in a natural setting, about what it is to be mortally human, to grow older, and to grow up, through vicissitudes and disappointments, into the broader, sadder knowledge of maturity; about what in this temporal process is inevitably lost, but also what may be gained, and for another person as well as the lyric speaker himself.

In such a reading, the opening description of the natural scene is not interpreted as, of necessity, an elaborate evasion of painful social realities. On social injustices and the sufferings of the dispossessed—what in another of the *Lyrical Ballads* he decries as "What man has made of man"—Wordsworth had just written a number of other poems. In the course of the poem the setting functions in various ways, but an emphatic initiating function, since it is a scene revisited after a five-year absence, is to trigger in the lyric speaker a meditation, continued through all the poem, on the import of such a passage of time at a critical stage of his life and experience. "Five years have passed...." The opening phrase, with its repetitions, announces the theme which resonates throughout, especially in the deployment of the adverbs, "again" (again I hear . . . behold . . . repose . . . see), "when," "while," "still," and above all in the recurrent opposition of "now" and "then," with their shifting references. These are all temporal adverbs, and Wordsworth's manifest, reiterated, and sustained lyric subject is time—time present, past, and future. Not time, however, as an abstract concept, but (in a way that inaugurates a basic concern of Wordsworth's later poems, and also of much modern literature through Proust to the present) *erlebte Zeit*—concretely lived time and its significance to us, in whom time is of the human essence, and for whom time involves, for better or worse, change, on the way to the point at which our lived time must have its stop. And this, dramatically, against the backdrop of a nature unchanging through time—unchanging, that is, as measured by a human rather than a geological temporal scale.

Our principles of reading, adaptive to the text the author chose to write, do not take the allusion to "Tintern Abbey" in the title to be an unconscious revelation of the true social subject of the poem. Instead they enable the recognition that the function of the reference, as in the titles of many local poems, is simply to locate the descriptive vantage point by reference to a recognizable landmark. And that point is "a few miles above Tintern Abbey" because, as the text makes clear, this is the precise place (line 10, "Here, under this dark sycamore") where the lyric speaker had been positioned five years before, and from which he "once again" sees (the text will soon reveal the functional importance of this fact) exactly the same objects, "these steep and lofty cliffs," "these plots," "these orchard-tufts," "these hedgerows." Our principles also grant the poet his representation of the scene again before his eyes as imbued with peace, harmony, and relationship—a relationship that incorporates the wild scene and quiet sky, woods and cottage grounds, and yes (tough-minded judgment for a liberal reader!), even the wreathes of smoke in line 18, despite our knowledge of Gilpin, and whether or not the notice they seem to give is of vagrants who have not chosen their lot of being houseless. The observed landscape serves the speaker—as God, or the cosmic order, had served earlier poets—as an objectified norm for the connection and harmony he struggled to achieve in the disconnection and distresses of the experiences he goes on to describe.

Traditional scholars have their own critical predispositions, including a tendency to focus on the conceptual and philosophical elements of a work of literature. In the second verse-paragraph of "Tintern Abbey," scholarly interest in the creed of nature that Wordsworth puts forward has diverted attention from the no less compelling way in which he expresses his experiences of remembering the scene of the Wye amid the alien and anguished circumstances of the intervening five years. In a way without close precedent, Wordsworth represents his emotional states and feelings as modes of internal sensation, more than eight decades before William James propounded the theory that what we experience as moods and emotions is constituted by a complex of internal and organic sensations.[28] The lyric speaker has experienced

> In hours of weariness, sensations sweet,
> Felt in the blood, and felt along the heart;

and also

> that blessed mood,
> In which the burthen of the mystery,
> In which the heavy and the weary weight
> Of all this unintelligible world
> Is lighten'd;

as well as times

> when the fretful stir
> Unprofitable, and the fever of the world,
> Have hung upon the beatings of my heart.

In such passages Wordsworth does what only the great poets do: by transforming inherited descriptive categories, he makes us realize anew our shared, or sharable, human experiences.

"And now . . . / The picture of the mind revives again: / While here I stand." Both Levinson and McGann, having predetermined that the poem must be about an absented social subject, gloss "the picture of the mind" as a spiritual displacement for what Levinson calls "the picture of the place"—that is, the ruined abbey with its beggars and vagrants. What the lyric speaker asserts, however, is that now, as he stands at the precise spot on the upper Wye where he had stood five years before, the landscape he had pictured in his memory "revives again," in the landscape before his eyes.[29]

Wordsworth uses here a poetic tactic he had found in earlier local poems about a revisitation (including Gray's "Ode on a Distant Prospect of Eton College"), but in a way that he makes distinctively his own and will go on to exploit, with variants, in his later poems on the human significance of passing time, the "Intimations Ode" and "Peele Castle." The banks of the Wye, as the title announces, are revisited, and reposing once again "under this dark sycamore," he sees again the former prospect. This is the Wordsworthian *déjà vu*; the scene on the Wye is twice-seen. But as "the picture of the mind revives again," it is with "somewhat of a sad perplexity (line 61)." For while the scene as he remembers it and the scene now present are similar (there are "many recognitions dim and faint"), they nonetheless differ. And to account for, as well as to evaluate, that difference, the speaker reviews the course of his life. For he recognizes that although the scene-as-now-perceived has changed, it is not because the visual givens have changed, but because the mind perceiving the scene has changed, as a result of its experiences during the intervening five years— "changed, no doubt, from what I was, when first / I came among these hills."

Wordsworth exploits here, as in later poems, his insight that an apparently integral perception involves what professional psychologists, decades later, were to call "apperception"; that is, *ad*-perception. What seems simply to be perceived is in fact apperceived—invested with aspects and a penumbra that are the product of prior experiences of the perceiving mind. Elsewhere Wordsworth often represents this alteration by the figure of the mind projecting light and color on the objects that it seemingly mirrors. At the end of the "Intimations Ode," for example, he represents the altered perception of a sunset that is effected by a matured mind in terms of a sober coloring projected on the visual radiance:

> The clouds that gather round the setting sun
> Do take a sober coloring from an eye
> That hath kept watch o'er man's mortality.

In a parallel way in "Tintern Abbey" the scene which, when first visited in his "thoughtless youth," had been perceived passionately, but without "any interest / Unborrowed from the eye," is now apperceived differently by a mind that has been matured by experience. In this passage, however, Wordsworth represents the change not in optical terms, but in the great alternative figure of a somber musical accompaniment to the visual phenomena:

> For I have learned
> To look on nature, not as in the hour
> Of thoughtless youth, but hearing oftentimes
> The still, sad music of humanity,
> Not harsh nor grating, though of ample power
> To chasten and subdue.

How the speaker, five years older, perceives the former prospect implicates his intervening experiences, summarized in the preceding two verse-paragraphs, of loneliness amid the din of towns and cities, of the heavy and weary weight of a world that has become unintelligible, and of the occasions, often, whether in darkness or joyless daylight, when the fret and fever of the world have hung upon the beatings of his heart.

Political readers ascribe a drastic evasiveness to these allusions to the formative five years, 1793–98, between Wordsworth's first and second visit to the Wye. "We are not permitted," McGann says, "to remember 1793 and the turmoil of the French Revolution, neither its 1793 hopes nor—what is more to the point for Wordsworth—the subsequent ruin of those hopes." Kenneth Johnston, who recognizes, I think justly, the central function of the lines on "the still sad music of humanity," asserts that Wordsworth represents therein his process of learning "as smooth, continuous, and unbroken" instead of "disruptive, violent, uncertain, or threatening," because "harsh, grating music" might "open up the gaps in the fabric of thought, or society, such as those that [Wordsworth] could only anticipate with dread." The critical assumption underlying such claims is made patent in James K. Chandler's comment on the "skewed treatment of the revolutionary period in

'Tintern Abbey.'" "The more," he says, "one looks at 'Tintern Abbey' as autobiography, the more the poem seems an evasion of what [Wordsworth] had actually stood for in 1793."[30] The assumption is that "Tintern Abbey" is not only a political poem, but a political autobiography as well, and as such commits the author to tell the truth, the explicit truth, and nothing but the truth about his political experiences. For their own knowledge of these experiences, political readers rely almost entirely on Wordsworth's expressly autobiographical poem *The Prelude*, parts of which he had already written in 1798 and in which, as completed seven years later, he details his inordinate revolutionary hopes, his disillusionment, and his consequent intellectual and emotional collapse. It seems an odd move to use the political experiences that Wordsworth narrates in one poem as the ground for charging him with unconsciously evading or disguising those facts in another, earlier poem.

The main point, however, is that to an open and adaptive rather than a peremptory reading, the poem that Wordsworth undertook in "Tintern Abbey" is different from his narrative autobiography, *The Prelude*, both in kind and in organizing principle. Its artistic intention is not to represent what is personal and unique about Wordsworth's experiences in France and with the Revolution, but to be a lyric meditation on what it generally is for a human being to grow older and, inevitably, to experience vicissitude, disappointment, and dismay. Consequently the "I" who utters the poem is recognizably Wordsworth, but Wordsworth in the literary agency that Coleridge calls "the I-representative." To the lyric speaker, that is, the poet attributes experiences other men and women can be expected to share, of isolation and fevered depression in a world that seems unintelligible; he trusted that they might also share something of his speaker's consolation at achieving a mature identity that has been informed and tempered by exposure to what is recognizably the modern world of all of us.

The lyric speaker, of course, conducts his account, and accounting, of the changes effected by time in the elected terms of his changing relations to the natural world. "That time is past" (lines 84 following) of his youthful, passionately unreflective responses to nature, and that change is indubitably a loss. But the process of time has also brought a chastened maturity (signified by his hearing often the still, sad music of humanity), as well as the feeling of a pervasive "presence" that binds the mind of man with the enduring natural world. These constitute time's "other gifts ... for such loss, I would believe, / Abundant recompense." This claim of abundant recompense in growing older is not an easy nor an unqualified optimism. "For such loss, I *would* believe" suggests a sought, or willed, belief; whatever the possible gain, time effects loss as we go our mortal way. Many readers of the poem have been sensitive to the elegiac tone in its seeming assurance. The sadness deepens in Wordsworth's later poems on what it means to grow older—the "Intimations Ode" and, still later, after an experience of tragic loss, the "Elegiac Stanzas on a Picture of Peele Castle."

A remarkably acute and sensitive contemporary, John Keats, did not read the wherefore of "Tintern Abbey" as an evasion of a harsh social reality or as the asseveration of a creed of nature, but as a meditation on growing up into the knowledge of a world of suffering. While nursing his dying younger brother in May 1818, Keats wrote, in a letter that repeatedly echoes the phrases of "Tintern Abbey," that "an extensive knowledge is needful to thinking people—it takes away the heat and fever; and helps, by widening speculation, to ease the Burden of the Mystery."[31] He went on to assert that "in his hintings at good and evil in the Paradise Lost," Milton "did not think into the human heart, as Wordsworth has done"; that is, Milton retained the religious creed of a heavenly recompense for earthly suffering, whereas Wordsworth proposes a rationale solely in terms of our temporal life in this world.[32] Keats sketches his own rationale, or "recompense," for suffering in what he calls a "simile of human life" as a "Mansion of Many Apartments," obviously modeled on the sequential stages of his life represented by Wordsworth in his fourth paragraph. From "the infant or thoughtless Chamber" (Wordsworth's "thoughtless youth," line 91), we move into "the second Chamber," where gradually we convince our nerves "that the World is full of Misery and Heartbreak, Pain, Sickness and oppression. . . ."

> We see not the ballance of good and evil. . . . We feel the "burden of the Mystery." To this point was Wordsworth come, as far as I

can conceive when he wrote "Tintern Abbey" and it seems to me
that his Genius is explorative of those dark Passages.

Keats, I think, identified rightly the central concern of "Tintern
Abbey," in its first four verse paragraphs.

But at this point we are not much more than two-thirds of
the way through the poem. And at the beginning of the long last
paragraph comes a lyric surprise. The speaker is not alone, "For
thou art with me, here. . . ." Abruptly, what we had taken to be an
interior monologue is revealed to have been overt speech addressed to an auditor, "My dear, dear Sister," who is not even, as
the reference to hearing her voice in lines 117–18 shows, a silent
auditor. And in this turn to his sister, the focus of the poem shifts
from what it has meant for the speaker alone to what it means to
share with a loved other person, the experience of a life in time.

Political readers give remarkably short shrift to Dorothy and
her role in the poem. "Dorothy," McGann declares, "is, of course,
the reader's surrogate," which I take to be a laconic way of saying
that she serves as a device for manipulating the reader into sharing
with her the displacement of the actual abbey by "the abbey of
the mind." Heather Glen reads the last section of the poem as affirming Wordsworth's "beleaguered subjective individualism." In
his attempt to realize his own self "not in interaction with other
men, but in isolation from them," any other person "can only be
seen as a threat"—unless, that is, the other is "in some sense (as
Dorothy is here) identified with the self" in a mode that Glen calls
"an *égoïsme-à-deux.*" In a similar vein Marjorie Levinson, proposing that "the primary poetic action is the suppression of the social," or the "public," dimension so as to achieve a "fiercely private
vision," says that while the role of Dorothy is to serve the poet
as an audience, that "audience consists of one person, the poet's
'second self', and even she is admitted into the process a third of
the way through, a decidedly feeble gesture toward externality."[33]

Such readings demonstrate the potency of a political *parti-
pris* to override all evidence to the contrary. Of course "Tintern
Abbey" is "subjective" or "private" in its point of view; inescapably
so, because the first-person lyric establishes the lyric speaker as

its center of consciousness. But within this constraint of the genre, it is hard to imagine how Wordsworth could have made it more patent that, in the poem, Dorothy is both a real and crucially functional "other." He startles us into awareness of her presence, devotes the last fifty lines to her, and gives her the salient role of concluding the poem. He prefaces his address to her by asserting (lines 112–14) that, even if the course of his life hitherto had not provided the recompense he has described, the fact of her presence with him might in itself be enough to sustain his "genial spirits"—his vital strength of mind. He even risks seeming sacrilegious, in suggesting her importance to him by an echo from the best-known of the psalms, the twenty-third—"For thou art with me"—which, in the context of a meditation on a life in time, may carry with it some resonance of the sentence that precedes it: "Yea, though I walk through the valley of the shadow of death, I will fear no evil." Furthermore it is by the act of turning from himself to identify, in imagination, with the consciousness of the other person that the lyric speaker moves, with quiet artistry, from the present to the future, but a future that turns out to comprehend both the present and the past, until the discourse rounds back, in an echo of the lyric beginning, to an inclusive close.

I can only sketch briefly the flow of the speaker's memory and imagination—the human faculties that alone free us from the tyranny of time—as he identifies with the conjectured process of his younger sister's life, memory, and imagination. She is now, on her first visit to the Wye, at that stage of her life at which he had been on his first visit, for he detects in her voice and eyes the repetition of his earlier responsiveness to the natural scene:

> in thy voice I catch
> The language of my former heart, and read
> My former pleasures in the shooting lights
> Of thy wild eyes. Oh! yet a little while
> May I behold in thee what I was once,
> My dear, dear sister!

His wish is that the procession of time might in her instance make a pause. But time and aging he knows are inexorable, and he goes on at once to consider his sister's future life, in his elected terms of the interaction of her altering mind with the natural scene, whose normative stability and harmony will be able to counteract for her the experiences, inescapable even in a domestic life (lines 129–32), of evil tongues, rash judgments, selfish sneers, social hypocrisy, and the dreariness of the daily routine.

"Therefore let the moon / Shine on thee. . . ." In the traditional rhetorical cadence of a blessing by an older brother, he anticipates her "after years" when—in exact parallel with the change in him from the "dizzy raptures" of his youth to hearing "the still sad music of humanity"—her "wild ecstasies shall be matured / Into a sober pleasure." "When . . . when . . . Oh! then. . . ." The temporal drama is managed by the adverbial shifters—the "whens" and "thens," which in the preceding paragraph had referred to his past visit, now refer to her conjectured future. "Oh! then, / If solitude, or fear, or pain, or grief, / Should be thy portion. . ." But such sufferings, though expressed as conditional, are for all lives inescapable. And if then "I should be, where I no more can hear / Thy voice"—a suggestion, left inexplicit, that time is capable of removing him by more than physical distance. Her recourse then, like his now, will be to the memory of her earlier visit to the Wye, but with a crucial difference. What he now remembers is a visit when he had stood alone; what she will then remember, however, is that, at her first visit, "on the banks of this delightful stream / We stood together." And her remembrance will include also what he has been saying as they stand together . . . "me, / And these my exhortations."

"Nor wilt thou then forget. . . ." Thus, by way of her remembering in the future the discourse that constitutes the entire poem, the speaker rounds back to those aspects of the scene that he had described at the beginning, namely (ll. 158–159),

> these steep woods and lofty cliffs
> And this green pastoral landscape. . . .

But what she will then remember about these natural objects is what he now tells her, that they

> were to me
> More dear, both for themselves, and for thy sake.

"For thy sake": more dear to him because now, on his second but her first visit, they stand on the banks of the Wye together.

The effect of the lyric closure is only heightened by our

awareness that this affirmation to another was uttered by the poet exemplifying what Keats, between admiration and exasperation, called "the wordsworthian or egotistical sublime." But as Keats recognized, the poet of the egotistical sublime had also thought "into the human heart."[34]

IV

In presenting the course of life in terms of an interplay between nature and the observer's altering mind, in the way it conceptualizes that nature, and in its idiom and rhetoric, "Tintern Abbey" is not only distinctively Wordsworthian, but distinctly a poem of the Romantic age in England. Insofar, I agree with political readers who assert that the poem is, in Jerome McGann's terms, "time and place specific," even though I disagree with the further claim that this specificity must be an ideological rationalization of the contemporary economic and social reality. And as so obviously a poem of its time and place, "Tintern Abbey" poses the cardinal critical question: "What's in it for us readers now?"

Political critics, and new historicists generally, are united in opposing the concept that literature and art can either represent or appeal to what Stephen Greenblatt calls "a timeless, cultureless, universal human essence."[35] "The idea that poetry deals with universal and transcendent human themes and subjects," McGann says, is itself "a culturally specific one."[36] The radical conclusion sometimes drawn from such claims is that the relevance and power of a literary work such as "Tintern Abbey" are confined to the form of consciousness specific to the poet and his moment, or to reactionary revivals of that ideology at a later time, or to a refashioning of the work in terms of the reader's own ideology. The only "trans-historical" value that McGann specifically recognizes is in fact trans-ideological: a critical determination of the ideology particular to an earlier work helps make us aware of the ideology particular to our own time and place: "The importance of ancient or culturally removed works lies precisely in this fact: that they themselves, as culturally alienated products, confront present readers with ideological differentials that help to define the limits and special functions of those current ideological practices."[37]

In despite of such strictures, however, an open reader of "Tintern Abbey" finds that it speaks now, as it has spoken for almost two centuries, and will continue to speak. Not because of transcendent and universal features (metaphysical essences of which I am no less wary than McGann), but for entirely empirical reasons. That is, the poem articulates and orders—although in time-and-place-specific ways that enhance its historical interest and invite imaginative participation beyond our parochial limits—modes of experience that we share with the poet, and that people will continue to share in any predictable future. Should the political and social conditions prophesied by Marx come to pass, it is beyond peradventure that even in a classless society men and women will continue to live a mortal life in time; will suffer, as Wordsworth put it (line 144), "solitude, or fear, or pain, or grief"; will as a result surely become sadder, but may also, provided they are both strong and fortunate, become more comprehensively and sensitively human; and will find support in the awareness that they are not alone, but share their lot with those they love. From such readers "Tintern Abbey" will continue to evoke a deep response because it speaks, in its innovative, ordered, and compelling way, to enduring constants amid the ever-changing conditions of what it is to be human.

NOTES

1. Stephen Greenblatt, ed. *Representing the English Renaissance* (Berkeley and Los Angeles, 1988), introduction, p. viii.

2. Irving Howe, *Politics and the Novel* (New York, 1987), p. 253.

3. Marjorie Levinson, *Wordsworth's Great Period Poems* (Cambridge, 1986), pp. 6, 18, 2, 101, 107, 113.

4. Jerome McGann, *The Romantic Ideology: A Critical Investigation* (Chicago, 1983), pp. 3, 11.

5. Ibid., pp. 12, 89; see also p. 134.

6. Levinson, *Wordsworth's Great Period Poems*, pp. 130, 103, 10.

7. McGann, *Romantic Ideology*, p. 91; Levinson, *Wordsworth's Great Period Poems*, pp. 8–9.

8. The impossibility of countering a predetermined political reading is exemplified on a small scale by McGann's treatment (pp. 68–69) of Wordsworth's eight-line poem "A Slumber Did My Spirit Seal" and by Levinson's divergent interpretation of the same poem, p. 125.

9. Michael H. Friedman, *The Making of a Tory Humanist* (New York, 1979), pp. 191–92.

10. Roger Sales, *English Literature in History, 1780–1830: Pastoral and Politics* (New York, 1983), p. 63. Even Heather Glen, who illuminates what was distinctive in Wordsworth's ballads in their time, nonetheless finds, in contrast to Blake's *Songs of Innocence*, "an implicit affirmation of the primacy of the polite point of view." Wordsworth's portrayal of Simon Lee, for example, is "never entirely free of condescension," and the blow of the mattock with which the narrator severs the root at which the old man has been vainly hacking—which, Glen remarks, "in its violence seems almost like castration"—"completes that belittlement of him which has been implicitly present in the tone throughout," and so serves as an "image for the unwitting ease of the paternalistic 'pity' which diminishes that which is to the suffering other impossible" (*Vision and Disenchantment: Blake's "Songs" and Wordsworth's "Lyrical Ballads"* [Cambridge, 1983], pp. 236–37).

11. Robert Mayo, "The Contemporaneity of the *Lyrical Ballads*, "*PMLA* 69 (1954), pp. 486–522.

12. "Mr. Wordsworth," in *The Spirit of the Age: The Complete Works of William Hazlitt*, ed. P. P. Howe (London, 1932), 11:87. Although Hazlitt couldn't have known it, his political analysis of Wordsworth's early poetry paralleled what Wordsworth himself had asserted in *The Prelude* of 1805—that he had discovered that his vocation as an original poet lay in a shift of his revolutionary and democratic creed from the realm of politics into that of poetry. See *The Prelude* (1805), 12:45–312.

13. *Literary Criticism of William Wordsworth*, ed. Paul M. Zall (Lincoln, Neb., 1966), pp. 10, 16–17.

14. Ibid., pages 182–83. In this passage and its context, both Wordsworth's argument and his syntax are tortuous. He poses the question, "Where lies the real difficulty of creating the taste by which a truly original Poet is to be relished?" then proceeds to answer this question by a series of rhetorical questions, each of which proposes a difficulty in altering his readers' taste, although not "the *real*" (that is, the supreme, most demanding) difficulty. Wordsworth then asserts the principle that a reader's taste for poetry is not simply a passive responsiveness to proffered knowledge; hence, the supreme difficulty for a writer is to evoke an active cooperation, or "power," on the part of a reader, adapted to the originality of his poetry: "Therefore to create taste is to call forth and bestow power, of which knowledge is the effect; and *there* lies the true difficulty" (p. 184).

15. Ibid., p. 185.

16. Levinson, *Wordsworth's Great Period Poems*, pp. 37–38; Kenneth R. Johnston, "The Politics of 'Tintern Abbey,'" *The Wordsworth Circle* 14 (1983), 13. In reading Wordsworth, Johnston does not apply the neo-Marxist hypothesis that all Wordsworth's poems are ideological representations; instead he applies to Wordsworth's early nature poems the hypothesis that they are troubled attempts "to satisfactorily establish the connection between landscape viewing and social responsibility" (p. 9; see also p. 7).

17. Mary Moorman, *William Wordsworth: A Biography*, I (Oxford, 1957), 1:402–403.

18. See the quotations in Levinson, *Wordsworth's Great Period Poems*, pp. 29–32.

19. A few examples of eighteenth-century titles of prospect-poems: Lady Mary Wortley Montagu, "Verses written in the Chiask at Pera, overlooking Constantinople, December 26, 1718"; Thomas Gibbons, "A View from Hay-Cliff near Dover, June, 1749"; Henry James Pye, "Ode, Written at Eaglehurst, which commands a View of Spithead, October 10, 1790." For the continuation of such titular specifications in the Romantic era, see M. H. Abrams, "Structure and Style in the Greater Romantic Lyric," in *The Correspondent Breeze: Essays on English Romanticism* (New York, 1984), pp. 83–89.

20. Levinson, *Wordsworth's Great Period Poems*, pp. 15–16, 55. Kenneth Johnston, giving reasons for conjecturing that Wordsworth may have completed the poem one day later than the title specifies, proposes that Wordsworth may have "turned its clock back twenty-four hours, to avoid setting off the powerful buried charges that would be exploded," if the poem had been dated July 14, the *quatorze juillet* ("Politics of 'Tintern Abbey,'" p. 13). It should be remarked, by the way, that July 14 was not adopted as the official anniversary of the French Revolution until the end of the 1870s; see Pierre Nora, ed., *Les Lieux de mémoire* (Paris, 1988).

21. Levinson, *Wordsworth's Great Period Poems*, pp. 18, 25. David Simpson's political reading of "Tintern Abbey" as an "example of displacement rather than of the Wordsworthian affirmation of nature and imaginative memory" parallels that of Levinson and McGann. See his *Wordsworth's Historical Imagination: The Poetry of Displacement* (New York, 1987), pp. 109–13.

22. McGann, *Romantic Ideology*, pp. 1–2; see also p. 13.

23. Coleridge to John Thelwall, December 17, 1796, *Collected Letters*, ed. E. L. Griggs (Oxford, 1956), 1:279. On May 13 of that year Coleridge had written to Thelwall, "Why pass an act of *Uniformity* against Poets?—I received a letter from a very sensible friend abusing Love-verses—another blaming the introduction of Politics. . . . *Some for each*—is my Motto. That Poetry pleases which interests . . ." (ibid., p. 215).

24. Lines 36–50; 94–103; 31–36; and 108-112. I cite throughout the text of "Tintern Abbey" as Wordsworth published it in *Lyrical Ballads*, 1798. The passage on the "presence . . . that rolls through all things," by the way, if it is a Romantic ideological representation, nonetheless echoes the description of the *spiritus mundi* in Wordsworth's revered predecessor Vergil, in *Aeneid*, 6:724 ff.

25. Wordsworth to Isabella Fenwick, in *The Poetical Works*, ed. E. de Selincourt and Helen Darbishire (Oxford, 1947), 4:463–64.

26. Lines 50–58. In accord with his ruling political hypothesis, McGann (*Romantic Ideology*, p. 88) reads "If this be a vain belief" not as a reference to the immediately preceding assertion that "We see into the life of things," but as one of the moves whereby Wordsworth "displaces" unpleasant socioeconomic facts and his ruined political hopes "into a spiritual economy where disaster is self-consciously transformed into the threat of disaster...."

27. Levinson, *Wordsworth's Great Period Poems*, p. 41; McGann, *Romantic Ideology*, p. 90. Both these readers apparently attribute the artistic greatness of "Tintern Abbey" to the remarkable intricacy and efficacy of its tactics of displacement and evasion. As McGann says with reference to the process by which Wordsworth "displaces" political disaster first into a threat and then a hope, and also converts political loss into seeming spiritual gain: "The greatness of this great poem lies in the clarity and candor with which it dramatizes not merely this event, but the structure of this event" (p. 88). And Levinson: the poem's "identity, or peculiar virtue, in Pater's sense, resides in its particular patterns of displacement" (p. 56).

28. William James, *Principles of Psychology*, 2 vols. (New York, 1890), vol. 2, chap. 25.

29. Levinson, *Wordsworth's Great Period Poems*, pp. 5–6, 24–25. McGann comments on "The picture of the mind revives again": "The abbey associated with 1793 fades ... and in its disappearing outlines we begin to discern not a material reality" but by an act of "spiritual displacement," the "landscape of Wordsworth's emotional needs" (*Romantic Ideology*, p. 87).

30. McGann, *Romantic Ideology*, p. 88; Johnston, "The Politics of 'Tintern Abbey,'" p. 12 (see also p. 7); James K. Chandler, *Wordsworth's Second Nature: A Study of the Poetry and Politics* (Chicago, 1984), pp. 8–9.

31. To J. H. Reynolds, May 3, 1818, *The Letters of John Keats*, ed. Hyder Edward Rollins, 2 vols. (Cambridge, Mass., 1958), 1:277–82.

32. Keats's comparison of Wordsworth to Milton, in their treatment of human suffering, is clarified in his later letter of April 15, 1819; see *Letters*, 2:101–103. In that letter Keats also replaced the simile of life as a sequence of chambers by the simile of the world as "The vale of Soul-Making," and (still in parallel with Wordsworth's theme in "Tintern Abbey") justified the human experience of "a World of Pains and Troubles" as "necessary ... to school an Intelligence and make it a Soul," and thus to give it "the sense of Identity."

33. McGann, *Romantic Ideology*, pp. 87–88; Heather Glen, *Vision and Disenchantment*, pp. 257–58; Levinson, *Wordsworth's Great Period Poems*, pp. 37–38. And pp. 45–46—"the turn to Dorothy, then, is a move toward otherness, or toward a social reality," by making her "a kind of alienated *tabula rasa*"; also, p. 49. David Simpson, *Wordsworth's Historical Imagination*, p. 110: the poem acknowledges "access to a community.... But it is a self-reflecting community, for what he sees in Dorothy is an image of his former self"; and p. 113: his final

turn is toward "the desperately limited version of the social world represented by Dorothy."

34. *The Letters of John Keats*, 1:387 and 282.

35. Stephen Greenblatt, *Renaissance Self-Fashioning: From More to Shakespeare* (Chicago, 1980), p. 4.

36. McGann, *Romantic Ideology*, p. 71; see also 69, 134.

37. Jerome J. McGann, *The Beauty of Inflections: Literary Investigations in Historical Method and Theory* (Oxford, 1985), p. 158; see also *Romantic Ideology*, p. 13. Similarly, Levinson, *Wordsworth's Great Period Poems*, p. 57, voices the need for an "enabling, alienated purchase on the poems we study," and on page 129 says: "It is precisely the contradictions and the formal ruptures ... beneath that smooth surface that endear ['Peele Castle'] to readers who thereby know it *as* a work, a work profoundly of its time, and one which therefore and thereby, criticizes our work and our time."

The Erasure of Narrative in Post-Structuralist Representations of Wordsworth

TILOTTAMA RAJAN

More than any other Romantic poet, Wordsworth has been at the center of theoretical revolutions that have only later been worked out with reference to Keats and Shelley, and that have until recently left Blake untouched. Among these movements deconstruction has had an unusually complex history, which we can only touch on here. In general it has challenged the logocentric authority of the text by exploring "hidden articulations and fragmentations" of voice and intention,[1] and by treating "representation" as an equivocal process that cannot make meanings present without also displacing them. But there are at least two phases in deconstruction, though the term *phases* is a schematic convenience given the brief time-span involved. Drawing on de Man's early and somewhat phenomenological essays on the Romantics,[2] first-generation deconstruction explored the fissures in textual identity without giving up the idea of a consciousness enmeshed in its representation, and thus without abandoning the description of literature in expressive or affective terms. I would include in this group people like myself and Helen Reguiero.[3] Strongly influenced by the de Man of *Allegories of Reading*, a second generation of deconstructive critics including his students Cynthia Chase and Timothy Bahti see constructs like *self* as figures produced by language, and thus place rhetoric in a relation of supposed undecidability but actual priority to psychology. The styles of these two groups are very different. The first still writes books on literary history if not individual authors. The second group, profoundly antinarrative in its commitments, writes chapters on single episodes microscopically isolated from the texts in which they occur at a narrative level, although intertextually displaced by other passages at a rhetorical level. The assumptions of the first group are post-organicist rather than post-structuralist. Without attributing a fixed identity to texts, they nevertheless assume that literary forms are expressive: that the very absence of an organic fusion between signifier and signified can be contextualized in literary history. The second group is rigorously rhetorical in its approach. Because it is this second group we now equate with a deconstruction that is said to be ahistorical and asocial, the object of criticism from traditionalists and leftists alike, I have suggested elsewhere that we see post-structuralism as simply one form taken by a deconstruction that preceded it and may yet develop beyond it.[4] The term *post-structuralism* should itself be understood as what Blake calls a "state" and not as a reification of the critics who temporarily pass through that state. But because post-structuralism has dominated the deconstructive study of Wordsworth as it has not in the case of other Romantics, this paper focuses on what distinguishes it from its precursors, and more briefly on how we might shift the deconstructive study of Wordsworth by shifting deconstruction itself.

Although my subject is the erasure of narrative in post-structuralism, I begin by alluding to the history of deconstruction in Romantic studies in order to raise a question about the rewriting that has produced and unsettles that erasure. That the Yale School rewrites both earlier deconstruction and the phenomenological criticism that precedes it is made quite explicit by Timothy Bahti. Bahti reads Geoffrey Hartman's distinction between apocalypse and *akedah* ("bonding") against the grain so as to make it a shadowy type of the current aporia between the figural and the referential. As figures find their fulfillment in reality, so the tendencies of an earlier, more phenomenological criticism are fulfilled in the tropological analyses of the Yale School. The use of reading

against the grain as a kind of typological reading is curiously escha-
tological, given that Bahti's essay is itself a deconstruction of typological reading as Wordsworth uses it.[5]

In de Man's own career this typological progression from the
old to the new deconstruction is less explicit but just as prevalent.
In the "Intentional Structure of the Romantic Image" (1960) he
draws attention to a typically Wordsworthian aporia: the coexis-
tence of natural imagery with a language that marks nature as
image, as in the phrase from "Tintern Abbey," "nature and the language of the sense" (1.109). In "Symbolic Landscape in Wordsworth and Yeats," written two years later, the paradox of images
that are intents of consciousness but crave the objectivity of the
natural world resurfaces as the aporia of a desired state of mind,
tranquillity, that the text keeps displacing between landscape and
emblem, immanence and transcendence, and thus presence and
absence.[6] In the later essays, however, the pair transcendence/
immanence or allegory/symbol increasingly becomes the pair
figure/reference. The interior or transcendent (a "transcendence
of nothingness," as Lukács might say)[7] becomes the figural; immanence or presence becomes that to which we can refer. As it was
earlier unclear whether the experience named in the text was objective or subjective, so its status as reference or figure, outside
or inside, is now undecidable. That there is this pattern of "rewriting" allows us to pose a question about the anxious purgation of
psycho-phenomenological terminology from post-structuralist
criticism. If what de Man now dismisses as a thematics of consciousness is palimpsestically rewritten in linguistic terminology,
can one not retrace in the texts of rhetorical post-structuralism
a subtextual phenomenology of the signifier? Yale post-
structuralism in the past ten years has created a rhetoric that impedes such retracing, and this paper will isolate some of its features. The Yale School,[8] to borrow the terms of Bahti's
chiasmically entitled essay "Figures of Interpretation: The Interpretation of Figures," has shown us that narrative structures are
always crossed and suspended by the rhetorical structures that
bring them into being. But if I may be chiasmic myself and use
chiasmus as the figure of balance rather than of self-cancellation:
If narrative structures must be returned to the rhetorical structures they efface, do not rhetorical structures inevitably contain

narratives which they efface, which it is also the task of deconstruction to recover?

This essay focuses on the erasure of narrative from poststructuralist criticism—narrative both as a dimension of the text and in the sense of critical narrative. For some time now narrative has been the object of considerable criticism. Foucault has sought to replace genetic or narrativized intellectual history with a genealogical history that sees discourses as constructed by power formations. Critics like Teresa de Lauretis see narrative as logocentric or even phallogocentric.[9] From a different perspective Jerome McGann has reminded us of the insidious way in which critical narrative naturalizes an argument as something that actually happened, as something which has a beginning, a middle, and an end.[10] But Yale post-structuralism, while abandoning narrative for being a metaphysical mode, practices a different kind of hypostasis in which the critical argument claims the authority not of mimesis but of logic. Positioning itself at the fulcrum of an aporia, the post-structuralist analysis maps the disruption of the text's logic with a philosophical rigor to which we are unused, in a language so apparently free of metaphor that we cannot argue with its fictions. Obviously this rigor produces a certain representation of the reading experience, one that is open to challenge from what it excludes. To reintroduce narrative is not to supplant one rhetoric by another, but to raise the question of what narrative might be after deconstruction.

My own definition of narrative is different from the one under attack and seeks to disengage the term from that resistance to difference with which it is associated. Current critiques of narrative almost always identify the term with plot or associate it with a narratology in which character is a schematic function of plot. But the fact that *plot* and *narrative* are two different terms in Aristotle enables us to suggest that plot is only one aspect of the more complex mode called narrative. To elaborate a theory of narrative is beyond the scope of this essay. Restricting my focus to the subjective narrative characteristic of Romanticism, I suggest only that in narrative considered as the process of telling, identity emerges through a series of diacritical relationships with others and with events that both place and displace the subject. This kind of narrative (of which *Jerusalem* and *Alastor* as well as *The Prelude* are examples) can be distinguished at the level of intentionality from the objective narrative characteristic of the realist novel and from the lyric. Where narrative includes characters as well as an author or narrator, lyric is a purely subjective form whose desire is shaped by the exclusion of the other through whom we become aware of the difference of the self from itself. The lyrical subject aims to be what Sartre calls a "shut imaginary consciousness" without the dimension of being-in-the-world.[11] At the other end of the spectrum objective narrative simulates a world of pure referents, and by omitting a narrating subject who expresses himself in relations of affinity or opposition to other characters it elides the status of its "world" as a network of signs. Subjective narrative occupies a position somewhere in between. Generated by the subject's desire for presence in the world, in other words, for reference, it also forgoes the self-identity of the pure lyrical *cogito*. Such narrative is both structurally and psychologically a mode of difference. It projects the subject through alter egos, like the Visionary in *Alastor* or Los and the specter in *Jerusalem*, who are both inside and outside the narrative voice. Structurally its very length creates complications elided by the brevity of lyric. For narratives contain characters and episodes which are linked to each other in relations of connection and difference. These elements are interimplicated, present within each other, in such a way that no element exists in and of itself. A narrative thus forms an intratextual network of differences much like that of language as Derrida describes it:

> The play of differences supposes, in effect, syntheses and referrals which forbid at any moment, or in any sense, that a simple element be *present* in and of itself, referring only to itself, . . . no element can function like a sign without referring to another element which itself is not simply present.[12]

But as important as the relation between narrative and difference is narrative's claim to represent the subject in the world. The paradoxical entwinement of the two aspects is often ignored, by New Critics who protect an autonomous *cogito* by identifying Romanticism with the lyric and by the critics discussed here who put that *cogito* under erasure but whose focus on the lyric or the de-narrativized textual segment dispossesses Romantic semiology of its existential, historical, or political content.

In short, although plot tends to confirm or impose identity, there are other elements that make telling of the plot a work of difference. Critical narrative is likewise a work of difference, and the dogmatism of its emplotment can be qualified by using plot recursively, by interrupting it or by constructing more than one version of it. What constitutes narrative, if it is not plot, is an attitude very different from that involved in the logical analysis of aporias. Narrative constructs the accidents of disfiguration as happening in a world, whether social or phenomenological. It connects and distinguishes episodes of deconstruction from each other, and it represents them as happening to and between people. If we consider critical narrative as a stance rather than as a hypostatized product, two shifts of terminology follow. In place of character we have personification: the decision to focus analysis around the author as textual subject rather than purely on rhetorical structures. In place of plot we have connection and difference: the nonteleological placing of one episode in relation to others such that they do not simply repeat it along a syntagmatic or paradigmatic axis that makes consideration of other episodes redundant.

Narrative was not always absent from deconstruction, although to find it in de Man may seem surprising. Perhaps the major difference between de Man and Hartman, given their commitment in the sixties to a thematics of consciousness, is that Hartman in his seminal study *Wordsworth's Poetry 1787–1814* locates the impulses toward transcendence and immanence in separate parts of the text, instead of seeing them as palimpsestically present within the same space. The narration of a difference that is synchronically distributed into a diachronic rhythm of oscillation holds out some possibility of movement out of the aporia, even though Hartman's own text withholds a resolution. Though the much later "Shelley Disfigured" is an exception, de Man differs in not ranging across the author's canon and in focusing on one or two passages sundered from any historical or life context and placed in a glass case, like those ruins to which Walter Benjamin compares the allegorical fragments of meaning. Hartman makes Wordsworth's poems tell part of a story. The early de Man's bits of a corpus become the object of an interpretive effort vastly in excess of its conclusions. To return again to Benjamin on allegory, these textual segments are "only a signature, only the monogram of essence, not the essence itself in a mask."[13] In the end the attempt to make their mode of signification into a dimension of what they say does not quite take us inside them or explain why Wordsworth and Hölderlin have been yoked together. Despite their different styles, however, the early de Man does not completely erase critical narrative. Typically his essays focus on an earlier and a later writer: Wordsworth and Yeats, Hölderlin and Wordsworth, or, in a curious reversal, Wordsworth and Hölderlin. The very fact of a temporal distinction between the two parts of the essay signals the possibility of development. It is as though by putting these texts in this order he is trying to make them represent some movement from Romanticism to Modernism or from a naive to a self-conscious Romanticism.[14] Equally interesting is the motif of pairs or trios from different literatures which has now become typical of comparative literature. This motif marks the comparatist project as repeating on the level of desire the attempt of the *Geisteswissenschaften* from Hegel through Boeckh to arrange knowledge as historical narrative rather than alphabetic classification. But for de Man there is no encyclopedia, no *grand récit*. In the essay "Wordsworth and Hölderlin," Wordsworth must represent all of early Romanticism, and Hölderlin must mark some further stage in Romanticism as well as represent synecdochically those absent figures in German Romanticism who are more nearly Wordsworth's onto-linguistic peers. Lacking a sufficiency of figures, he must make one name do the work of several. Thus the two poets, all that are left of the pantheon of world literature, must intimate some pattern that their collocation stands in place of.

In the work of Chase, the external form of the pair signifies redundancy or repetition rather than functioning as the trace of a desire for encyclopedic history. It tells us that the same thing happens over and over again, whether in Athens or nineteenth-century Europe. The later de Man does not use this motif. That it functions so differently in his early work is connected with structural patterns we can approach in terms of a phenomenology of reading. One such pattern is a rhetoric of the threshold that emerges in de Man's most narrative essay, "The Intentional Structure of the Romantic Image." This is one of the few places he posits a historical development from intentionality, which is seen as a uniquely Romantic problem, to a consciousness that has achieved an *Aufhebung* and can exist "entirely by and for itself, independently of all relationship with the outside world."[15] If intentionality anticipates what the later de Man will see as the diacritical entwining of figure and reference, this new consciousness is the impossible dream of a pure figurality released from reference, allowed to be a positive term. The essay divides its citations into two segments. A few lines from Hölderlin, attenuated to a kind of ruin and subjected to elaborate desedimentation, are followed by a rapid succession of passages from Wordsworth, Rousseau, and Hölderlin. Despite its greater concern with ontological issues, the first segment anticipates the tactics of de Man's later work. Suspending the pace of the essay almost to the point of stillness by meditating at length on four lines, he creates an effect of blockage or aporia. Problems of existence and essence, and indeed the entire system of Greek myth, are drawn into this aporia. In contrast to the first segment, the second one is brief and dominated by quotation, creating a stylistic shift that heralds critical movement. The abundance of examples combined with a relative lack of commentary suggests that we are on the threshold of some revelation no longer subject to recursive philosophical critique. It is the brevity of the section that creates the impression of a threshold, both in the sense of a new frontier and of a limit to what can now be said. But it is also this sense of a threshold that mobilizes the pairing of the lines from Hölderlin with the three subsequent passages into a movement: perhaps a shift rather than a development, but not simply a repetition.

It is well to recall the liminal structure of narrative in this essay. De Man does not so much provide a critical narrative as intimate its possibility: the *"possibility* for consciousness to exist . . . by . . . itself." That the three passages must more or less speak for themselves, whereas de Man had spoken at greater length for the four lines at the beginning, gives a speculative quality to what little he does say at the end. The essay resembles those Romantic fragments like Keats's "Hyperion" that take us halfway through a phenomenology of mind and then break off, as if to throw into relief the supplementary quality of narrative desire. Indeed a study of de Man's early essays will suggest that the organicist figure of a growth in consciousness which subtends temporal divisions of careers and periods into early and late phases is constantly being effaced in the spaces between these essays.[16] In this essay Book 4 of *The Prelude* marks Wordsworth as being in a late phase, whereas in the essay on Hölderlin the same passage marks his failure to move beyond himself. And in the essay on Wordsworth and Yeats an 1807 poem that is later than the passages first used to represent Wordsworth as late is used to represent him as early. Sliding between blindness and insight, the figure of Wordsworth erodes the stability of those reference points that might fix cognitive processes on a temporal continuum. A powerful desire to write critical narrative thus coexists in these essays with elements that force this drive back into its own shadows. Indeed it is this tension that makes these essays of interest in a period in which the possibility that figures of genesis may be heuristic constructs renders narrative more a complex of attitudes than a finished product. Almost in recognition of this paradox de Man's essay stops when the fragments it has shored against the ruins of philology seem to be falling into place. The essay's self-arrest is connected with the fact that de Man has always eschewed the mode of the book, with its tendency to hypostatize narrative. What the essay offers is an intentional or open narrative that makes the narrative function critically available but leaves enactment of that function to its readers.

In "Wordsworth and Hölderlin" (1966), narrative has become much more tenuous, though there are still traces absent from the post-structuralism of the last decade. For instance in "The Ring of Gyges and the Coat of Darkness," Chase moves from Rousseau to Wordsworth, but in such a way that the chronological movement does not yield a cognitive movement.[17] Hölderlin is made to sound later in a phenomenology of mind in which a greater interiority is valorized over the desire for a correspondence between inner and outer worlds. "We abandoned Wordsworth as soon as the concept of a correspondence between nature and consciousness seemed to be definitely surpassed. This overcoming—which in Wordsworth ensues at a highly advanced point in his thinking— belongs to Hölderlin's knowledge almost from the beginning."[18] The sleight of hand produced by the fact that Hölderlin is not later than Wordsworth points to de Man's more recent sense that the grand march of intellect simply displaces aporias. In fact he is unable to convey how the German poet is any less fissured than Wordsworth. But the positioning of the two in the temporal space of the essay evinces a desire to write literary history. And although de Man is more concerned with broad movements than with shifts within an author's canon, his use of chronological terms such as *advanced* and *beginning* with reference to Wordsworth posits the same movement in the author's career.

In "Lyric and Modernity"[19] (1969) de Man begins his critique of literary history as genetic narrative and of genesis as a figure through which language arbitrarily constructs identity. Now arguing against the view that modernity brings to fruition those antirepresentational tendencies in Romanticism intimated at the end of "The Intentional Structure," he sees modernity as still caught in the duplicitous project of intentionality and thus as an aporia that occurs throughout history. The importance of this essay is that it dismantles the language of periodization. If modernity has always existed, what is the point of distinguishing it from Romanticism? Moreover, the essay also effaces distinctions of genre, for its alleged subject, lyric, is only an instance of a problem that exceeds generic boundaries. The undoing of literary history through the effacement of its plot (the movement from one period to another) and its characters (different authors, different genres) is at the heart of recent works like Chase's *Decomposing Figures*. Chase does deal with three major genres, or with the deconstruction of the master figures that create generic identity: causality in the case of narrative, voice in lyric, and the construction of a face or self in autobiography. But since each figure occurs in all three genres, the genres are linked in a relation of redundancy rather than difference. They show how the deconstruction of a validating figure happens repeatedly. A similar rhetoric of redundancy stops the book from becoming a narrative enterprise. For it arrests any movement (not necessarily teleological) from text to text or author to author—any movement that might create identity by producing differences between as well as differences within entities.

Yale post-structuralism does not generally produce books on individual authors, partly because doing so risks reinstating the author as phenomenological subject. Nevertheless the fate of narrative in literary history predicts a similar fate for the narrative representation of an author's career or of a single poem like *The Prelude* that constructs a narrative of the self. Moreover the decision to write only chapters and to deal only with single passages is a representation of the author that we can address as a set of exclusions. Books are centered on an author or a theme and are compelled by requirements of unity to tell a story or create an order that produces the sense of an interiority. In resisting the phenomenology of the book by not writing related chapters that place Wordsworth in literary history, *The Prelude* in Wordsworth's canon, or Book 5 in *The Prelude*, Chase dispenses with the figures of connection and difference. Her powerful essay "The Accidents of Disfiguration" is in fact about the representation of Wordsworth, about the effacement of his attempt to give himself a face.[20] The erasure of narrative characteristic of post-structuralism plays a strategic role in creating the effect desired in this chapter: the erasure of Wordsworth's narrative. Briefly, Chase studies how accidents of language—slippages between the literal and the figural—disfigure the figures by which the text legitimates itself. Her subject is paradoxically the figure of figure itself, linked to the text's theme of imagination. Focusing on the episode of the Drowned Man, she shows how the literalism of the passage effaces its own concluding attempt to transform fact into figure by making death into something in a fairy tale. The passage then becomes a *mise-en-abîme* of both the autobiographical and critical projects. For what is effaced is a way of reading crucial both to the face worn by the poem, as the imaginative rereading of experience, and to all criticism that gives the poem an identity by refiguring it as the story of something, be it the story of imagination or its deconstruction. That it is the literal which here disrupts the figurative is incidental. As often, Wordsworth's attempts to make the imaginary seem real are displaced by an awareness of figurality, so that the poem slides between the simple referential poles of pure figure or pure fact.

It would be futile to paraphrase Chase's intricate argument, her point being precisely to avoid the thematic hypostases that result from moving "above" micrological analyses of texture. My concern, rather, is with how the erasure of Wordsworth's narrative is produced through a deferral of critical narrative. Like other essays of its kind, this one uses the New Critical method of close reading against itself, circling around a single passage so as to stall any sense that we can move around its ambiguities or that the larger poem can contain them. Even more radical is de Man's "Autobiography as Defacement," which defers the promise of its title by talking instead about the *Essays on Epitaphs*.[21] By making epitaphs a paradigm for autobiography, de Man detains the latter's narrative desire in the linguistic moment induced by the critical essay, before it even has a chance to happen. The figure that legitimates the avoidance of narrative is paradigmatism: a figure of economy that is obviously antithetical to redundancy. Paradigmatism takes the lyric as an instance of language generally, or the Drowned Man as representative of *The Prelude*, thus dispensing with the need to consider other genres or other passages. As an instance of representation, paradigmatism is necessarily subject to the critique of representation practiced by deconstruction itself. Can a single episode in *The Prelude* be used to represent the poem as a whole? Or is not reading a long poem very different from reading a lyric by Emily Dickinson?

Rhetorical reading alters the phenomenology of interpretive space, making us notice those hidden articulations and fragmentations we too easily skim over, but strategically narrowing the doors of perception in the process. Yet in reading a long poem we also experience an extensiveness that qualifies those displacements which nevertheless unsettle the attribution of too firm an identity to the text. Allen Tate distinguished between in-tension and ex-tension in terms of an opposition between connotative intricacy and denotative argument.[22] But an extensive reading is not simply a linear one because the very length of a poem like *The Prelude* makes it unlikely that we will read it like a detective novel in one sitting, so as to subordinate discourse to the unfolding of a story on a syntagmatic axis. Indeed extensive reading necessarily includes rhetorical moments. But it also involves the hermeneutic experience of living with the text as in a mansion of many apartments, making links between passages that are by no means unidirectional but entail complex movement in which we advance and retrace our steps, or reinscribing the text in the psycho-tropology of its historical or biographical con-text. The reasons why we might choose to read extensively are cultural as well as innate. A rhetorical reading, focused intensively on the slippages within and between words, cannot entirely represent the way we read in a critical culture that is intricately intertextual—a palimpsest not only of successive revolutions in critical practice, but also of the different pedagogical and scholarly audiences for which we write. The reinscription of narrative is just one part of a larger project of making criticism an intertextual practice, in Kristeva's sense of the term as the process by which (critical) texts form and are informed by other texts and discursive practices in the institution.[23]

Timothy Bahti's strategy is incipiently different from other work by the Yale School. His essay on the Arab Dream falls into two parts, marked by a turn he himself signals from Hartman to Wordsworth.[24] It is in the first part that he seems closest to de Man. Here his aim is to isolate as tropological the major structuring operation that keeps the poem in being and whose rhetorical status the poem disguises. This operation, the conversion of figures into literal realities, is similar to the one analyzed by de Man in his deconstruction of the Romantic mind's tendency to convert intentional into natural structures. Drawing on Hartman, Bahti translates the story of a poet who converts apocalypse into *akedah* into the story of a poet who literalizes figures that have no natural authority by writing them into the landscape. I will bracket for the moment the question of how completely one can translate one set of binary oppositions into another. Through Hartman, Bahti finds in *The Prelude* a story in which the passage of time fulfills the figures of imagination as true. He then places this story under erasure by deploying passages from across the poem in a de-narrativized form. Weaving between them rather than moving chronologically through them, he lays bare the rhetorical character of a movement from figure to reference that submission to the poem's narrative would naturalize. Equally as crucial as de-narrativization in the first part is another feature that Bahti himself notes. Like de Man he approaches Wordsworth via criticism of Wordsworth, as if to suspend the very act of narrating an interpretation in an analysis of the figures which sustain interpretation.

In the second part Bahti builds on his identification of the movement from figure to reality as tropological and deconstructs the Arab Dream, in which an apocalyptic vision of the imagination as separate from nature is written into the landscape. Focusing on repetitions of events and doublings of characters, such as Wordsworth having the dream through a friend who is and is not himself, Bahti shows how the dream narrative's identity with itself is constantly displaced. In general his analysis follows the line of the Yale School. In its nuances it is slightly different. Unlike Hillis Miller's essay on the same passage it is concerned with actions and characters, with the disfiguration of Wordsworth's attempt to write his dream as narrative, to use the Arab as a guide who will lead him to the conclusion of his dream. Miller focuses less on the dreamer's desire to narrate than on the symbols of stone and shell and the impersonal processes of substitution that displace them from their identity with themselves. He treats the passage as a symbolic poem caught in a language that disfigures it as verbal icon. Although he uses the name *Wordsworth*, it is always with reference to the biographical author, almost never with reference to Wordsworth as character in the dream.[25] It is as though the subject has been erased from his dream and the dream simply happens. Bahti by contrast constructs Wordsworth as a character in an aborted narrative, using the name even though he has pointed out that Wordsworth is not the dreamer in both versions.[26] Bahti's style, in other words, is more narrative than Miller's.

This nuance allows us to raise certain questions. What would happen if deconstruction pursued more insistently the language of narrative rather than logic, if disfiguration were represented as happening to someone existing in a life-world or historical world? Clearly a psychological and phenomenological emphasis would re-enter an approach that has now purged itself of these elements. Indeed the return of these elements is legitimate even within the terms of deconstruction. For as we have earlier observed, Yale post-structuralism systematically translates phenomenological into linguistic binaries, practicing a typological reading of its own past that is subject to Bahti's critique of typology as Wordsworth uses it. Translation is a metaphoric process of equating one term with another. By using one word for two things, metaphor tries to convert the first thing into the second by fusing them in the same word. But it actually marks the fact that one word represents overlapping and different entities. In less abstract terms, the Yale

School's binaries harbor resonances of those oppositions they translate. One often finds in these rigorously linguistic essays thematic nuances absent from structuralism, which has no historical links with phenomenology. We need to open up post-structuralism to these nuances, to explore the difference between language as an abstract network of substitutions and differences and textuality as the functioning of those differences in a represented world of people and events.

Bahti's essay is of interest because it allows us to ask certain questions. But in itself it does not depart from the post-structuralist pattern. It considers the wider context of Wordsworth's poem only as a preliminary to focusing on one passage, the reading of which produces a paradigm of language as disfiguration which can then be referred back to the whole poem, but only to reduce the poem to the problems raised in this passage. The rhetoric of paradigmatism, which makes part and whole interchangeable in Wordsworth's poem, can be linked to a similar paradigmatism informing the relationship between essay and book in the work of criticism. The essay is made to stand for what a book on the author would do. But it is most unlikely that a book on Wordsworth *would* say the same thing as a single essay. To follow the accidents of disfiguration through several chapters would be to see that the face being effaced is not always the same one. Interrelating the different generic and thematic faces of a poem as complex as *The Prelude* leads to a more specific sense of what is being effaced in this poem that is distinct from what is being deconstructed in Sophocles. One of the curious features of Bahti's essay is that the narrative deconstructed in the second section reverses the one deconstructed in the first, although the tropological operation being deconstructed remains the same. Although the essay consistently deals with the way Wordsworth converts figures into realities by writing them as natural events, what is thus hypothesized is initially a view of imagination connected to nature and then in the dream a view of imagination as separate from nature. We do not need to ask what results from the fact that the content of a tropological process is not always the same, since such a question would take us back over ground covered by Hartman. My point is rather that the language of a book will displace post-structuralism's commitment to the signifier over the signified, although a deconstructive book would still see the signified as existing in a diacritical and not a prior relation to the signifier.

Moreover, in the larger interpretive space of a book, we might well see the return of those literary historical considerations which de Man tells us have disappeared from the work of his students because "the intricacies of close reading" leave "no space or energy . . . to return to historical generality."[27] Insofar as the disappearance of these considerations is an effect of style, their return as part of the rhetoric of the book can have no more than a speculative status. My plea for a return to narrative compatible with deconstruction is based less on an assumption that critical narrative can provide a linear representation of what happens in a text, when that assumption is itself questioned by the text, than on a sense that narrative is a basic, though historically shifting, mental function. I use the word *function* rather than the Kantian term *category* to indicate that narrative is not a fixed way of organizing textual phenomena but, rather, a discursive position that we cannot now occupy in quite the same way we did before. It is nevertheless a discursive position different from "lyric" or "rhetoric." Narrative can no longer be conceived as a metaphysical and teleological form that reveals the nature and cause of events, for within a narrative there are likely to be a number of different subnarratives. For the writer as much as for the critic, narrative is attitude rather than product. A study of *The Prelude* could not now take literally its figures of genesis and memory, which claim to ground Wordsworth's interpretation of his life by attributing causality and factuality to something he himself was always revising. It might well draw on the work of theorists like Ned Lukacher on primal scenes as "constellations of forgotten intertextual events offered in lieu of a demonstrable, unquestionable origin."[28] It might also take into account the influence on Wordsworth of associationist psychology, which suggests that memory is not straightforward recollection but the recalling of an associative and thus intertextual cluster.

Post-structuralist representations of Wordsworth can be questioned from within deconstruction in other ways. The Yale School concentrates on the disfiguration of the self as occurring in the relatively asocial context of temporality and later on language. Correspondingly the canonical text becomes *The Prelude*, considered first from the ontological perspective of the relation between interiority and nature, and then from the rhetorical perspective of figure and reference. Such shorter poems as are discussed are ones that crystallize the concerns associated with *The Prelude*—the Lucy poems, for instance. Missing from this textual inscape are what one might call the social poems, lyrical ballads such as "The Brothers" and "Old Man Travelling," or even poems like the ones so often discussed, but considered in their intertextual play with the other poems in Wordsworth's heteroglossic collection that are not pure lyrics. The lyricization of Wordsworth has a long tradition, beginning with the New Critics and continuing through phenomenology and deconstruction to New Historicism. On some level we are again dealing with the erasure of Wordsworth as a narrative poet. This time it is not a question of a causal-genetic structure that authenticates the self by enacting it, nor is it a question of narrative as a mode which replaces lyrical in-tension with ex-tension, thus producing an effect of something happening as well as being rendered ambiguous. Rather, it is a question of narrative as an intersubjective mode in which the subject is diacritically constructed in relation to others. For one of the primary characteristics of narrative, in addition to its generation of a plot, is its inclusion of characters other than the narrating subject. Neglecting this dimension of Wordsworth, we have neglected Wordsworth as a poet who places himself in a social text.

Lest this sound like a gesture toward the latest revolution in Wordsworth criticism, let me add that the New Historicism has so far tended to perpetuate the lyricization of Wordsworth and the consequent attenuation of the canon. If post-structuralism hollows out the lyrical moment, making its paradoxes into aporias, New Historicism simply accepts the image of Wordsworth it inherits, situating lyric as a socially symbolic act of avoidance. Marjorie Levinson, for instance, deals only with three lyrics and "Michael," which she treats as a lyricized narrative.[29] Following on the New Critics' ontogeneric valorization of lyric as the mode of an autonomous and transcendental self, many New Historicists attack the lyrical self, the egotistically sublime poet who supposedly promotes it, and the deconstructive critics who negatively perpetuate the decontextualization and textualization of the subject. Constructing a similar Wordsworth, though from opposite perspectives, both evade the possibility of a poetry that consciously addresses not just the nonidentity of the subject but also his social (dis)placement. They simplify Wordsworth and efface the possibility of a deconstruction more complex and varied than it has been. One way to open up Wordsworth through deconstruction, I have already suggested, is to return deconstruction to its phenomenological roots while giving up classical phenomenology's desire for an *epoche* that would bracket displacement as an intrusion. Another alternative is to link difference to the dialogic and to the hermeneutic. My own current work on Romantic texts and the hermeneutic tradition is concerned with how Romantic writers inscribe the reader in the text both as a way of referring and applying the text to life and as a way of opening it to interpersonal difference. In thematizing reading in the *Lyrical Ballads*, Wordsworth appeals for a hermeneutics of identity in which we are linked by shared feelings, as he does in a conversation poem like "Tintern Abbey," where the implied reader is figured as a sister. But he also reads his own voice by placing himself in dialogue with characters whose social construction is different, as in the original version of "Old Man Travelling," where the poet's lyrically existential sketch of the old man is abruptly juxtaposed against the latter's baldly factual response so as to suspend conversation across the gap between the discursive and perceptual worlds of different classes. In other words he narrates lyric: he takes the personal voice he was beginning to develop in the Pedlar sections of "The Ruined Cottage" and situates it as one strand in a social text, thereby qualifying the monologic tendencies of lyric by locating lyricism in a heteroglossia of voices and readers.[30] Understanding thus becomes a deconstructive hermeneutic which discloses an otherness within the subject produced by the discourse of the other. The deconstruction of identity can be specified in both social and psychological terms. The point is that either approach would see Wordsworth as sensitive to issues of difference rather than helplessly subject to them, and would trace the disfiguration of his figures in phenomenologically or historically specific ways that would give a face to the process of effacement.

NOTES

1. Paul de Man, *Allegories of Reading: Figural Language in Rousseau, Nietzsche, Rilke, and Proust* (New Haven: Yale University Press, 1979), p. 249.

2. I refer to de Man's enormously influential essays "The Intentional Structure of the Romantic Image" and "The Rhetoric of Temporality" as well as to the less theoretically dense early essays reprinted in *The Rhetoric of Romanticism*. Although some followers of the later de Man do not favor the designation of his early work as phenomenological, I am by no means the only one to have made the point (compare Frank Lentricchia, *After the New Criticism* [Chicago: University of Chicago Press, 1980], pp. 284 ff.). De Man himself does not see his early work as being of a piece with his later work, and refers sheepishly to the uncomfortable intertwining of "proper" rhetorical concerns with the "vocabulary of consciousness and of temporality that was current at the time" (*Blindness and Insight: Essays in the Rhetoric of Contemporary Criticism* [1971; rev. ed., Minneapolis: University of Minnesota Press, 1983], p. xii). But whereas de Man apologizes for the phenomenological commitments of the early work, my own view is that this stage of his work is no mere prelude to the later work but is of autonomous value, and also that it constitutes an original contribution to phenomenology: a turning away from the "positive" phenomenology of Husserl and a development of the "negative" phenomenology of Sartre into a "phenomenological deconstruction." I do not take phenomenology to be a kind of realism that strives to return to the natural object, and doubt that any phenomenologist can be seen as having such yearnings except perhaps Husserl. Rather, I make the more commonly held assumption that phenomenology entered literary study through the criticism of consciousness, acquiring in de Man's work a rhetorical character that focuses on forms of language as modes of awareness. De Man is, of course, innovatively different from the Geneva School in refusing to abstract consciousness from textuality, but this is not the same thing as making consciousness an effect of textuality.

3. Tilottama Rajan, *Dark Interpreter: The Discourse of Romanticism* (Ithaca: Cornell University Press, 1980); Helen Reguiero, *The Limits of Imagination: Wordsworth, Yeats, and Stevens* (Ithaca: Cornell University Press, 1976).

4. See my articles, "Displacing Post-structuralism: Romantic Studies after Paul de Man," *Studies in Romanticism* 24 (Winter 1985), 451–74; "The Future of Deconstruction in Romantic Studies," *Nineteenth-Century Contexts*, vol. 11, no. 2 (1987), 131–47.

5. Eschatology is of course a form of self-legitimation. One therefore needs to point out that the politics of self-legitimation is by no means confined to post-structuralism, though its figures may be different. New Historicism relies on a romance of fact. My own rhetoric makes a humanistic appeal to "experience" and to "people," and thus has to be conjoined to a recognition that experience is already a tissue of metaphors. More than any other school post-structuralism has taught us to look at figures genealogically instead of submitting to them, and

for this reason as well as others my arguments against the Yale School must be understood as differences arising from within deconstruction.

6. Reprinted in de Man, *The Rhetoric of Romanticism* (New York: Columbia University Press, 1984), pp. 1–18, 125–44.

7. Georg Lukács, *The Meaning of Contemporary Realism*, trans. John Mander and Necke Mander (London: Merlin Press, 1963), p. 44.

8. For reasons of convenience, I am using this term more or less interchangeably with "rhetorical post-structuralism" to designate the later work of de Man, that of his students, and some of the work of Hillis Miller, though Miller's approach is more eclectic and varied. I do not include Geoffrey Hartman under the term *Yale School*, since his work is better described as a deconstructive hermeneutic.

9. Teresa de Lauretis, *Alice Doesn't: Feminism Semiotics Cinema* (Bloomington: Indiana University Press, 1984), pp. 103 ff.

10. Jerome McGann, "Some Forms of Critical Discourse," *Critical Inquiry* 11 (1985), 399–417.

11. See my essay "Romanticism and the Death of Lyric Consciousness," *Lyric Poetry: Beyond New Criticism*, ed. Chaviva Hosek and Patricia Parker (Ithaca: Cornell University Press, 1985), pp. 194–207.

12. Jacques Derrida, *Positions*, trans. Alan Bass (Chicago: University of Chicago Press, 1981), p. 26.

13. Walter Benjamin, *The Origin of German Tragic Drama*, trans. John Osborne (London: NLB, 1977), p. 214.

14. De Man himself draws attention to the literary historical tendencies of his early essays in his introduction to the special issue of *Studies in Romanticism* that launched the reputations of writers like Chase and Bahti (18 [Winter 1979], 495–499). He tends to see his interest in literary history as an effect of the time at which he was writing, and to regret his membership in a generation that was historically precluded from writing otherwise. Nonetheless, it is surely significant that he sees the elision of historical concerns from the essays in the special issue as also an effect of a mode of writing (p. 497).

15. De Man, *Rhetoric*, p. 16.

16. De Man himself makes a similar point. He refers to the attempt in his early essays "however ironised, to present a closed and linear argument. This apparent coherence *within* each essay is not matched by a corresponding coherence *between* them ... it seems that they always start again from scratch and their conclusions fail to add up to anything" (*Rhetoric*, p. viii).

17. Chase, *Decomposing Figures: Rhetorical Readings in the Romantic Tradition* (Baltimore: Johns Hopkins University Press, 1986), pp. 32–64.

18. De Man, *Rhetoric*, p. 59.

19. Reprinted in *Blindness and Insight*, pp. 166–86.

20. Chase, *Decomposing Figures*, pp. 13–31.

21. Reprinted in *Rhetoric*, pp. 67–82.

22. Allen Tate, "Tension in Poetry," *The Man of Letters in the Modern World*.

23. Julia Kristeva, *Desire in Language*, ed. Leon S. Roudiez (New York: Columbia University Press, 1980), pp. 64–69.

24. Bahti, "Figures of Interpretation: The Interpretation of Figures: A Reading of Wordsworth's 'Dream of the Arab,'" *Studies in Romanticism* 18 (Winter 1979), 601–27.

25. J. Hillis Miller, "The Stone and the Shell: The Problem of Poetic Form in Wordsworth's Dream of the Arab," in *Untying the Text: A Post-structuralist Reader*, ed. Robert Young (London: Routledge and Kegan Paul, 1981). pp. 245–65. Interestingly, when reprinted in *The Linguistic Moment*, this essay becomes part of the narrative movement of the book.

26. Bahti, pp. 608–609.

27. De Man, "Introduction," *Studies in Romanticism* 18 (Winter 1979), p. 497.

28. Ned Lukacher, *Primal Scenes: Literature, Philosophy, Psychoanalysis* (Ithaca: Cornell University Press, 1985). pp. 24–25.

29. Marjorie Levinson, *Wordsworth's Great Period Poems* (Cambridge: Cambridge University Press, 1986).

30. I refer to *The Supplement of Reading: Figures of Understanding in Romantic Theory and Practice* (forthcoming). The sixth chapter deals with Wordsworth.

Wordsworth's Poetics of Eloquence
A CHALLENGE TO CONTEMPORARY THEORY

CHARLES ALTIERI

> But there is a third, and still higher degree of
> Eloquence, wherein a greater power is ex-
> erted over the human mind; by which we
> are not only convinced, but are interested,
> agitated and carried along with the Speaker;
> our passions are made to rise together with
> his; we enter into all his emotions; we love,
> we detest, we resent, according as he in-
> spires us; and we are prompted to resolve, or
> to act, with vigour and warmth.... The high
> Eloquence ... is always the offspring of pas-
> sion. ... Passion, when in such a degree as to
> rouse and kindle the mind, without throwing
> it out of possession of itself, is universally
> found to exalt the human powers. ... A man
> actuated by strong passion, becomes much
> greater than he is at other times. He is con-
> scious of more strength and force, he utters
> greater sentiments, conceives higher designs
> and executes them with a boldness and felic-
> ity, of which, on other occasions, he could
> not think himself capable.
>
> —HUGH BLAIR[1]

Most contemporary criticism would find in Blair's effusions
a good deal to demystify and to reinterpret in accord with a model
of political or psychological interests that such writing labors to
disguise. But suppose we were to take his argument seriously, that

is, to see it as the effort to provide a passionate rendering about the effects of passion, which then makes sense only if one provisionally adopts the projected state of mind. Or better, since we must remain critics, what if we tried to understand analytically what might be involved in such a shift in both critical and dramatic attitudes? We might begin to appreciate the challenge which Romantic poetry can present to our prevailing theoretical assumptions.

Certainly there is now a vital interplay between the domains. Theory has taught us to value the ironic stances by which Romantic poets manage to grapple with their own passionate ambitions, and it is now teaching us how to appreciate the complexities of the poetry as the production of an ideological discourse at once maintaining and exposing the seams of prevailing social values. Yet the poetry may pay a substantial price for such currency. In the high-status world of "sophisticated" theoretically informed criticism, the only authority that the poetry wields derives from its miming our dominant concerns. At one pole we honor only the poet's efforts at self-demystification; at the other we manage to respect their political sensitivity by continually exposing the gulf between what they see and what they frame within their own interpretive projects. In both cases the same basic model of historical reasoning prevails: the contemporary scene sets the agenda, then we test the hypotheses in relation to examples drawn from the past. As a consequence we have little access to the Romantics' fascination with Shakespeare, Milton, and the Bible, and we leave the poetry precious little otherness for the tasks of helping us demystify our own interpretive ambitions and of exploring ethical ideals which resist current fashions.[2] Therefore an exercise like the one I propose may at the least give us a fresh look at the literature and at ourselves, and it may even lead us to modify the concepts and purposes governing our critical practices.

As the basis for this experiment I shall try to reconstruct what I think was the basic model of poetry taking shape for Wordsworth during the first decade of the nineteenth century. After experimenting with dramatic ballads, Wordsworth found himself increasingly drawn to a personal lyric mode which combined traditional rhetorical ideals of high eloquence like those defined by Blair with a psychology much more responsive to the demands of his own intellectual culture. That project offers two fundamental contributions to contemporary theory: it establishes a model of poetry as direct, passionate personal utterance which has obvious and significant differences from both the dramatic model basic to New Criticism and the models of textuality governing both deconstruction and New Historicist semiotics, and on that basis it makes claims for the social significance of poetry without having to rely on a cult of irony or the languages of demystification.[3] For the display of passions becomes both an index of powers that the reader can identify with and a projected test of their value in engaging the world beyond the text. From this perspective Romantic irony becomes a means rather than an end—it helps clear the stage of the traps inherent in the culture's received versions of eloquence so that the underlying force of those energies can speak as a counter-eloquence, at once different from prevailing taste and responsive to the deeper principles which once were vital sources of that taste.

I

I define the ideal of eloquence as that feature of rhetorical performance which exemplifies the power of the passions rendered to situate the speaker so that a mutual process of amplification takes place: what the speaker attributes to the world as worthy of the passion rendered can be tested only to the degree that it moves the audience to identify with it as a potentially transformative force in their lives. This effort to make ideal states concrete and plausible seemed necessary to Cicero, Longinus, and Augustine because they needed a plausible alternative to those versions of rhetoric content to stress the rules that help one achieve practical success. Without that alternative, both rhetoric and rhetorician are bound to the rules of the marketplace, so there is no way to dignify rhetoric or the rhetorician as capable of rivaling philosophy by opening and testing alternative ethical vistas. But if one could make the case for an eloquence which, in Cicero's terms, can make "visible stamped or rather branded on the advocate himself" "the very feelings" that he is trying to elicit for his audience, it becomes possible to surpass mere philosophical abstraction because one then demonstrates the power simultaneously to define, to test, and to promulgate ideas or models of character.[4] In the place of mere argument we are offered a site where the idealized claims of the soul "on fire with passion and inspired by something very like frenzy" become self-authorizing and compel by the mode of speaking which they display as a plausible human action. And in the place of mere efforts to persuade an audience one can imagine the orator literally offering that audience new possible identities in which to participate and through which to test a stance in terms of the modes of power that it can convey.

Educated in accord with principles like Blair's, yet situated in a culture where such principles seemed little more than masks for the real business of gathering wealth and status, Wordsworth would adapt two basic features of this tradition: its semantics in which qualities exemplified in the speaker's projected character are more important than any descriptive criteria for "truth," and its efforts to make that semantics ground an ethical model in which the poet can claim to articulate values which have a more significant claim on society than those bound to practices of getting and spending.[5] For the practical rhetorician the single end of rhetoric is to be persuasive. The theory of eloquence insists instead that a focus on practical rules or on consequences cannot account for the kind of passion which actually transforms individual speakers by leading them to states that practical judgment cannot compass, nor can they deal adequately with the possibility that such performances can modify an audience's values in ways that both rhetor and audience can take responsibility for. While the rules treat the passions simply as instruments for gaining effects, the eloquent orator uses their properties as heuristic instruments. On the one hand passions are passive. We can pretend to passion, but we cannot easily make our selves engage in them. Instead we attribute the arousal of passion to a source outside the self, a source both testing and extending what we can claim to be our psychological powers. This means that however exalted the passions that the orator claims, there must remain shareable links to his audience and clear indicators of the kind of affections which are the building blocks of such passions. Indeed, Blair insists that true eloquence depends on virtuous affections (1:13). Yet the passion cannot simply be equated with those affections. For in its active mode passion achieves transcendental states that depend on the ways in which those affections become visible powers.

Consequently when we are persuaded by an eloquent performance, we cannot account for it by appealing to the criteria that hold for practical arguments. Rather, eloquence challenges that realm of shared predicates and expectations by making visible and purposive an intensity of will and an expansion of consciousness carrying us much closer to our imaginative ideals than we ever reach in our more calculating moments. Thus for Cicero the eloquent expression of passions enables the speaker to "be such a man as he would desire to seem" (*De Oratore*, 1:63), thereby invoking in the place of concern for true description complex social theaters of shame risked and exemplary dignity achieved (for example, 1:85). And for Augustine that social theater easily opens on to a metaphysical one as the grand style becomes a secular analog for the Incarnation because it literally takes the word into the flesh: "If the beauties of eloquence occur, they are caught up by the force of things discussed and not deliberately assumed for the decoration," so the speakers "make their own those things which they could not compose." Finally, Longinus shows how even these transcendental energies retain their social force by positing eloquence as a force creating an alternative community of models and judges which then affords the social context addressed by the most ambitious orators.[6]

We need to return to Blair for the second feature, a distinction that will enable us to shift our focus from these claims about the idealizing role of passionate utterance to more concrete arguments about the kind of force such presences can exert within a world bound to quotidian principles of judgment. For he insists that these idealizing projections be understood as a mode of the sublime, and then he makes an important distinction between a sublime located in our relation to nature and a sublime specific to writing. Where the natural sublime resides in an uncanny or alien force taking control over a responding subject, the writerly sublime locates that power of transport within the exemplary authorial act as it "elevates the mind above itself, and fills it with high conceptions and a noble pride" (Blair 1:58). Rather than referring to states of affairs which confirm or disconfirm statements, writerly action can rely on principles of purposive self-reference, which in turn make it plausible to claim that eloquent discourse establishes states of passion showing the audience a way beyond their ties to practical motives and empirical results. Thus, as contemporary theorists like Lyotard make clear, the sublime offers a sense of surplus carrying intense negative force: the excess of passion that it invokes simply cannot be justified within prevailing mores, yet its intensity leaves an indelible mark on the desires of its audience. But where contemporaries must be content with this disorienting impulse, classical theorists try to build on that negative force an alternative model of judgment enabling one to see fascination as a principle leading us to attempt provisional identifications with the projected passions. Because the passion suspends the hold of both basic forms of empirical reasoning, truth-functional analysis and the assessment of practical consequences, we must use the passions themselves as exemplary. There we must locate possible surrogates or representatives whose ways of surpassing those empirical pressures must be tested for the powers they might make available for any agent who is moved by them and hence drawn to their possible status as exemplars.

Any other attitude toward the performance of eloquence requires translating what has earned the sublime back into the languages of motives that it may have successfully resisted (a phenomenon we see increasingly at work as young academics attempt their moral diatribes against imaginative projections they show themselves unable to appreciate). And any other approach makes it impossible to use the only norm that makes any sense in relation to such performances—that instead of insisting on their possible truth as description or their manipulation of political interests we ask what kind of powers they confer on those willing to attempt those identifications. Some of these powers are simply self-regarding states. But Cicero and Blair are careful to insist that the specific performative powers can serve as both means and ends. For, as our opening passage indicates, eloquence promises to lead us beyond the condition of passive witnesses so that we test in our own engagement the capacity of those authorial sublimities to serve as mediators giving form to values through the passions that the speaker shows a situation or object can elicit. That is why for Augustine the self-celebratory dimensions of the high style can remain subordinate to the transcendental energies that they mediate, why for Cicero the orator demonstrates the highest possibility of virtue under the true spirit of Roman law (1:135–49), and why for Longinus the individual performer elicits affiliations with the community of heroes whom we all can then imagine inspiring and judging our actions.

II

To move from Longinus' heroes to Wordsworth's "Advertisement" to *Lyrical Ballads* is to enter a very different social theater for the enacting of eloquent speech:

> The majority of the following poems are to be considered as experiments. They were written chiefly with a view to ascertain how far the language of conversation in the middle and lower classes of society is adapted to the purposes of poetic pleasure. Readers accustomed to the gaudiness and inane phraseology of many modern writers ... will perhaps have to struggle with feelings of strangeness and awkwardness: they will look round for poetry, and will be induced to enquire by what species of courtesy these attempts can be permitted to assume that title. It is desireable that such readers, for their own sakes, should not suffer the solitary word Poetry, a word of very disputed meaning, to stand in the way of their gratification; but that, while they are perusing this book, they should ask themselves if it contains a natural delineation of human passions, human characters, and human incidents; and if the answer be favorable to the author's wishes, that they should consent to be pleased in spite of that most dreadful enemy to our pleasures, our own pre-established codes of decision. (Zall, 10)

The high tradition of eloquence has become the worst enemy of genuine passion, syphoning it off into artifice, leaving the majority of people with no alternative to debased popular media and requiring the poet, perhaps for the first time, to stage himself as experimental artist. Yet eloquence is not the problem. The problem is finding a language which can resist the culture's preestablished codes of decision to restore a sense of the pleasure and the awe which will accompany a full rendering of the passions. Therefore Wordsworth finds himself repeating the basic gesture of every am-

bitious rhetorical theorist—proposing a version of "natural" eloquence at odds with prevailing cultural expectations yet responsive to its deepest potentials for passionate life. But in Wordsworth
this sense of counter-eloquence takes on a far more radical cast
than one finds in those theorists, a cast that will dominate the next
two centuries by shaping the logic of art as experiment. For now
the new eloquence is not merely a matter of training new orators.
It will require a new language, a new sense of the social affiliations
and struggles that the poet must wage to gain authority for a new
rhetoric, and a new sense of the psychic economy that will enable
the speaker to demonstrate the value of such struggles.[7]

We are all familiar with Wordsworth's specific claims about
the changes in content and in diction required for this new eloquence. These, however, are in my view the least interesting features of his poetic. For his career makes it evident that he would
soon realize that Coleridge was essentially right in his criticism of
those poems in *Lyrical Ballads* written in the spirit of the Preface's
doctrines of the common life. In retrospect one might say that although Wordsworth was there trying to locate within a mimetic
version of poetry the appropriate grounds for a "more permanent,
and far more philosophical language" for nourishing "the essential
passions of the heart" than he found in his predecessors (Zall, 41),
in fact the strength of the theory and his talents as a poet lay
elsewhere—in his capacity to cross that social milieu with modes
of expressive eloquence best located in first person expression.
Therefore his poetry gradually modulates from imitating the pur-
ported eloquence of others with a privileged relation to nature to
working out his own passionate responses to such possibilities and
the problems they create for one who cannot wholly share those
relationships. Yet the principles governing those modulations
were already there in the theory—not in the specific social content but in the accounts he gives of the specific psychological processes governing the life of the passions set free by content. Therefore I want to examine the principles that these theoretical
resources made available to him so that we can focus attention
on the challenges that they present to contemporary poetics. Then
I shall try to support my claims by offering a reading of "Nutting"
as a paradigm for this poetics.

The ideal of eloquence is for Wordsworth inseparable from

the desire to have his poetry speak this "more permanent, and far more philosophical language." For only such ambition could compose a semantic space allowing "the essential passions of the heart ... a better soil in which they can attain their maturity" (Zall, 41). Once poetry could no longer cast itself as instructing us in a shared set of cultural ideals, the basic alternatives, then and now, leave poetics torn between a cult of discriminating taste that cannot address poetry's capacity to move us by what seem the simplest and most important of human truths and a model of privileged access to certain "original perceptions" whose inadequacies tempt us to prove our authenticity by cultivating a rigorous sense of inescapable and irreducible ironies severely limiting our range of emotional investments in the passions rendered. So it was, and is, necessary to develop a third possibility: suppose that poetry could earn its philosophical status less for what it overtly claimed than for what it displayed as the life of those passions and the fundamental qualities of the soils which nourished them. Rather than concentrating on making descriptive claims about the world, poetics could stress the abilities of language to isolate and intensify those states which "produce or enlarge" the capacity of the mind to be "excited without the application of gross and violent stimulants" (Zall, 43). Philosophical value then would consist in how the activity of the speaking demonstrates certain powers of sensibility so as to put the audience in a position to participate in the states rendered.

In other words, Wordsworth's concern for eloquent passions brings him close to the semantics of exemplification developed in contemporary terms by Nelson Goodman. If we were, however, simply to adapt Goodman's analyses, we would once again give the authority to contemporary culture (as well as ignoring some of the problems that Goodman raises). And, more important, we would let contemporary semantic models deprive us of the central role that Wordsworth attributes to the passions. So I hope instead to remain within the language of traditional poetic theories.[8] Wordsworth's originality consists then in his forging a version of exemplification which manages to synthesize what otherwise remain competing and incomplete models of literary experience. Take, for example, his fundamental statement of purpose—that "all good poetry is the spontaneous overflow of powerful feelings."

There is no more radical distinction between a poetry intended to please and to instruct and one devoted to articulating the exalted states of the speaker. It is no wonder then that Wordsworth is usually characterized as having replaced the prevailing concerns for taste and for moral instruction by an essentially expressivist stance. Wordsworth immediately buttresses his claim about feelings by elaborating the subjective conditions allowing for such eloquence. But if we notice only that move, we blind ourselves to how quickly and how smoothly the passage modulates from the singular sensibility to "our influxes and feelings" and "our thoughts," and then from the expression to be contemplated to the effects which such states have on our capacities for action.

> For all good poetry is the spontaneous overflow of powerful feelings; but though this be true, Poems to which any value can be attached were never produced on any variety of subjects but by a man who, being possessed of more than usual organic sensibility, had also thought long and deeply. For our continual influxes of feeling are modified and directed by our thoughts, which are indeed the representatives of all our past feelings; and, as by contemplating the relation of these general representatives to each other, we discover what is really important to men, so, by the repetition and continuance of this act, our feelings will be connected with important subjects. . . . (Zall, 42)

Clearly we also must bring to bear the general model provided by response theories. Yet contemporary versions of that theory also tend to oversimplify the basic force of this passage. For ours is a hermeneutic age bound to two formulations of response which are incompatible with Wordsworth's concerns. We maintain a sharp dichotomy between those energies and expressions that are deeply subjective and those whose terms can be shared as attributes of an objective world, and we use that opposition within a set of academic practices deeply committed to worries about whether there are single coherent meanings for entire works of art. Consequently if we are to talk about the vitality of subjective life we feel compelled to insist on radically relativist frameworks for constituting the "meaning" of the text. If Wordsworth had to formulate questions our way he might have agreed. But for him, and indeed for most theorists of eloquence, questions of meaning simply drop out in favor of questions of projectible imaginative power. Whether or not we agree on the overall "meaning" is far less important than how we align ourselves to that source of powers that promises not to give us back ourselves but to enlarge us by inviting participation in what matters precisely because it is foreign to our banal quotidian selves. It is those powers we can point to rather than meanings we can explicate that explain why works matter, show how exemplars can define possible attitudes toward the world beyond the text, and set the frame of common references which deepens our sense of community.

Wordsworthian "exemplification" then offers expressive acts eliciting the audience's participation as a means of positioning themselves in accord with the site released by passionate speech and the modes of self-reflection which that allows. By his *Essay, Supplementary to the Preface* of his 1815 collection of poems Wordsworth is clear enough about that site to insist on its distance from the claims posited by cognitive theories of poetry, a distance enabling him to finesse most of the questions about meaning and reference dominating our theoretical discussions: "The appropriate business of poetry (which, nevertheless, if genuine, is as permanent as pure science), her appropriate employment, her privilege and her *duty*, is to treat of things not as they *are* but as they *appear*; not as they exist in themselves, but as they seem to exist to the *senses* and the *passions*" (Zall, 160).[9] This does not mean that poetry is only an aesthetic object, only verbal play that makes nothing happen because it makes no assertions. Rather, it connects the poles of expression and response through the much bolder claim that poetry entails a different theory of language than is necessary for the asserting of propositions. That model of language must be able to handle what agents produce in speaking or writing and how they create effects by those productions.

The theory of language extending this imaginative perspective relies on three basic properties which simply have no place in the aesthetic epistemologies shaped by mimetic principles. There is a radically different account of metaphor; the differences located by that account license an ideal of poetry as testimony, which then replaces the ideal of rendering testable truths that had been the Enlightenment's highest goal of cultural production; and there results a rich theory of pleasure accounting for how these exemplary powers offered as testimony have concrete social force.

The topic of metaphor offers the starkest example of how this Wordsworthian position can assume values different from those dominating contemporary theory. We have moved from the New Critical idealizations of metaphor as the vehicle for nondiscursive truths to a variety of analytic and post-structural myths positing it as the serpent lurking within the garden projected in empiricist theories of language and truth. Derrida, for example, shows that the very idea of "proper sense" is distorted by the metaphors of property and propriety apparently necessary in order to refer to the ideal of an unequivocal relation between word and world. But then the only positive functions given to metaphor become either textualist versions of play (not terribly far from the neoclassical concerns for ornament that so disgusted Wordsworth) or returns like Ricoeur's to quasi-mystical claims for a special kind of truth which cannot be parsed into straightforward referring expressions. Wordsworth can dismiss both positions by focusing not on the world but on the conditions of engaging that world given definition through the eloquent passions of a speaker: "If the poet's subject be judiciously chosen, it will naturally, and upon fit occasion, lead him to passions the language of which, if selected truly and judiciously, must necessarily be dignified and variegated, and alive with metaphors and figures" (Zall, 47–48). Here metaphor does not displace reference. Rather, it clarifies what is at stake in engaging questions of reference in terms of the possible dispositions that a speech act can sanction. Eloquence is quite frankly the sign of an excess that knows it cannot be satisfied by descriptions but seeks impressions of "certain inherent and indestructible qualities of the human mind" and likewise of "certain powers in the great and permanent objects that act upon it, which are equally inherent and indestructible" (Zall, 44).[10]

But how do we know whether the metaphors are judiciously chosen, and how do we know that in yielding to the metaphor we open ourselves to experience that idealized relation between the mind and its dynamic ground? Why is the metaphor, or the entire project of eloquence, not simply an evasion of the empirical realities or of the ironies that deconstruction shows inescapable when we rely on those realities to make judgments regarding human desires? There is no easy answer. Indeed if one stays within empiricist frameworks, there is no possible answer because we can only speak about knowledge where there are clear lines of reference and assessment. But precisely because his version of eloquence can surrender both the desire for particular truths and its enemy twin, the necessity for infinite dissemination, Wordsworth offers concepts of pleasure and of power which I think prove extremely useful in showing the way to other models for assessing speech acts.

Let us begin with Wordsworth's own claims for the philosophical value of poetic utterance:

> Aristotle ... has said, that poetry is the most philosophic of all writing; it is so: its object is truth not individual and local but general, and operative; not standing upon external testimony, but carried alive into the heart by passion; truth which is its own testimony, which gives competence and confidence to the tribunal to which it appeals and receives them from the same tribunal. (Zall, 50)

For those who identify with Enlightenment ideals of philosophical rigor it is difficult not to dismiss such enthusiasm contemptuously. Yet there are three claims here that I think both defensible and suggestive. First it makes sense to speak of "general truth" in this context because the aim is not description but exemplification, not statements about the world but the effort to define labels and models for what might be at stake in a range of those descriptions. That distinction then clarifies Wordsworth's principle of testimony, of "truth" which is confirmed by the immediate passion it elicits. For since the statement does not refer in the usual way, its claims on the world can only be judged by what it makes visible in the particular structure of passionate attention and expression that it makes visible. Wordsworth speaks of testimony because the only relevant criteria are the degree to which the model or label achieves generality by providing a concrete surrogate actually demonstrating the powers it claims. One might say, for example, that a poem like "Tintern Abbey" can only sanction its claims about memory and nature to the degree that it demonstrates how the passions so fostered give the mind certain ways of acting that can be projected as a way of being in the world. In this sense the poem is testimony to a power that it makes visible.

But then we need as our third principle a model of uptake explaining how audiences can use that testimony. This is where the marvelous dialectic of the tribunal in our passage comes into focus. Where propositions and themes stress what lies objectively in the world, testimony bases the burden of the discourse on the powers it exemplifies and the identifications made possible by that exemplification. And there is no better image for that act of identification than Wordsworth's sense of the powers of the tribunal and a deepening sense of the world which they yield as their theater. As we find our relations to the world modified by the poem, we turn back to it with an increasing sense of how that testimony has general claims on us. Response is the locus of value, but the source of value remains in how the work maintains the capacity to modify our sense of identity.

III

But now how do we measure the consequences of those identifications or those attributions of confidence? How do we make transitions between the passions created in the moment of reading and the commitments that can or must stem from those moments? One could answer that at this point we go beyond poetics to ethics and politics: poetics shows how testimony might work, ethics and politics provide different values at different times which determine the relative use of different expressions. But while this is a reasonable position, it may too quickly subordinate the powers of poetic eloquence to those more analytic worldly attitudes. Therefore Wordsworth insists on having the projection of eloquent testimony carry its own ethical force. Within the Preface to *Lyrical Ballads* he turns again and again to projections of the "Poet" as an ideal psychological type in order to illustrate the kinds of powers which such testimony offers for our identification (for example, Zall, 44, 47–49, 51). More generally, it seems reasonable to view Wordsworth's entire poetic career as a set of efforts to give ethical force to idealized bearers of certain kinds of passions and habits of mind sanctioning those habits. In *Lyrical Ballads*, the idealized figure is one who can in effect draw out the latent powers of passion contained within certain countercultural ways of using common language; in *The Prelude* attention shifts to the capacity of a single mind to align itself to what is potential in the forces shaping it, and in the organization of the 1815 *Poems* Wordsworth composes a lyric poet's *Phenomenology of Mind* which defines a range of dispositions "proceeding from, and governed by, a sublime consciousness of the soul in her own mighty and almost divine powers" (Zall, 149). No lesser dream could be consistent with a view of his literary heritage as "grand storehouses of enthusiastic and meditative Imagination, of poetical, as contradistinguished from human and dramatic Imagination" like "the prophetic and lyrical parts of the Holy Scriptures, and the works of Milton" and Spenser (Zall, 149). For our purposes, however, there must remain a substantial gulf between this Longinian effusiveness and a theory sanctioning Longinian effusiveness. Therefore instead of relying directly on those larger models I shall begin with Wordsworth's claim that "The poet writes under one restriction only, namely, the necessity of giving immediate pleasure to a human being possessed of that information which may be expected of him . . . as a Man" (Zall, 50). For it is in his analysis of pleasure that Wordsworth gives the most concrete psychology we have for dwelling on the ways that passionate testimony defines and makes available psychological and ethical powers.

All the ladders start with the peculiar ontological position pleasure occupies. As Aristotle argued, there is no one thing that we can call pleasure. Rather, pleasure is essentially relational—a matter of how we engage in other phenomena rather than something we can pursue in its own right. This means that it makes no sense to ask whether the pleasure lies in the object or in the responder. Rather, the pleasure arrives woven into the event or performance. One might say that the enlargements it brings are not separable from the rendering, from the "how" that can lead attention to the qualities and intensities of the actual moment as well as to the nature of the tribunal responding to such qualities. Such enlargements then serve almost as a natural or immediate principle of amplification, "a homage paid to the native and naked dignity of man" (Zall, 51), at least so long as one can believe that the pleasures also lead us to deeper possibilities of both our own nature and the world which calls that nature forth.

This belief was easier for Wordsworth than it is for us. For him a basic distinction between the gross stimulants that usually govern popular taste and quieter, and hence more natural, modes of attention sanctioned an entire theology (see especially, Zall, 51).[11] If one's pleasures could be freed from such gross impositions, there is a reasonable chance that they could be aligned with both the potential of one's own nature and the ways in which that nature was adapted to participate in its environment. But in our critical climate such appeals to nature carry little suasion. Although Richard Eldridge makes suggestive use of the idea of human nature, and although the associationist aspects of Wordsworth's theory offer intriguing parallels to the materialist psychology of DeLeuze and to Rorty's effort to define a model of political sympathies free of the idealist principles of judgment that pervade post-Kantian thinking, there is little point to making this level of Wordsworth's theory the basis for academic claims. Yet our distance from his metaphysics ought not blind us to the intricacy of his psychology, especially in passages like the following, which tease out a dynamics of pleasure suggesting concrete grounds for believing that eloquence cultivates ethically significant imaginative powers:

> To this knowledge which all men carry about with them, and to these sympathies in which, without any other discipline than that of our daily life, we are fitted to take delight, the Poet principally directs his attention. . . . And thus the poet, prompted by this feeling of pleasure . . . converses with general nature, with affections akin to those, which, through labour and length of time, the Man of science has raised up in himself, by conversing with those particular parts of nature which are the objects of his studies. The knowledge both of the Poet and the Man of science is pleasure; but the knowledge of the one cleaves to us as a necessary part of our existence, our natural and unalienable inheritance; the other is a personal and individual acquisition, slow to come to us, and by no habitual and direct sympathy connecting us with our fellow beings. (Zall, 52)

Poetry begins as self-delight—both in terms of the intense states it makes available and in terms of the confidence it builds in the tribunal that through language comes to feel its own attachments to the world growing more varied and more engaging. Thus the amplification that is eloquent passion is also an amplifying of the terms of self-regard available for our reflective lives. Yet because that passion takes testimonial form in language, its very intimacies are also the terms that make it far more social in orientation than the kind of knowledge developed by the sciences, or, as I prefer to see it, than all disciplinary knowledge. In the case of disciplinary knowledge, our pleasure lies in our coming to master a specific set of practices which serve as instruments leading to a deeper grasp of certain aspects of the world. But in the case of the poet's conversations with general nature, our pleasure lies less in the contents of knowledge than in the state of the subject we come to see as coextensive with our experience of the object. The very terms of the pleasure become features of what we then reflect on as fundamental to our humanity—as conditions of attention and as ways of positioning the psyche which we have grounds to think also engage the affective lives of other persons. Beginning from self-love, Wordsworth develops a psychology in which there is considerable sense to the claim that the "Poet binds together by passion and knowledge the vast empire of human society" (Zall, 52). At least the kind of discourse that the poet makes basic for both identity and identification *can* perform that task because the ecstatic sites it composes have no role other than making us aware of the pleasure potential in powers and possible identities we so easily forget we have.

Giving sense to the claim is not the same thing as giving a clear demonstration of its validity. That Wordsworth's psychology of self-delight cannot accomplish. Nor could any theory, I suspect. We need eloquence in this domain because the entire subject of powers generated through imaginative activity is so bound up with self-reflection and with idealization that it simply resists any more analytic stance. We do not come to believe in these powers because some argument is made on their behalf. Rather we are invited to participate in the states they make available. Our measure of power is simply the degree to which the resulting modes of self-reflection engage us in new dimensions of ourselves and our world. That is why the most Wordsworth can do as a theorist is try out various idealized versions of the character of the poet and the processes which his exemplary acts of mind make possible. And that is why in trying to elaborate his theory I can do little more than recall what he sees at stake in those idealizations, then turn to a representative poem as my illustration of his deepest thinking on the subject.

The wisest rhetorical strategy for dealing with idealizations is to work with contrasts: while it may be impossible to persuade others directly of one's claims about values, it often proves to be the case that by clarifying what one opposes, or what happens when the prevailing values are left in place, one opens the way for one's audience to try out the identifications necessary to support one's own position. For Wordsworth the most compelling contrasts are with the psychological problems that he shows seem inescapable under the assumptions about poetry that he had inherited. The sharpest of these in his critical prose occurs in the last of his essays on epitaphs, where he builds from an attack on ornamental diction in so serious and "sincere" a genre to the following far more radical critique:

> If my notions are right, the epitaphs of Pope cannot well be too severely condemned; for not only are they almost wholly destitute of those universal feelings and simple movements of mind which we have called for as indispensable, but they are little better than a tissue of false thoughts, languid and vague expressions, unmeaning antithesis, and laborious attempts at discrimination. Pope's mind had been employed chiefly in observation upon the vices and follies of men. Now, vice and folly are in contradiction with the moral principle which can never be extinguished in the mind; and therefore, wanting the contrast, are irregular, capricious, and inconsistent with themselves. . . . All this argues an obtuse moral sensibility and a consequent want of knowledge, if applied where virtue ought to be described in the language of affectionate admiration. In the mind of the truly great and good everything that is of importance is at peace with itself; all is stillness, sweetness and stable grandeur. Accordingly the contemplation of virtue is attended with repose. . . . The mind would not be separated from the person who is the object of its thoughts. . . . Whereas when meekness and magnanimity are represented antithetically, the mind is not only carried from the main object, but is compelled to turn to a subject in which quality exists divided from some other as noble, its natural ally: a painful feeling! that checks the

course of love, and repels the sweet thoughts that might be set-
tling around the Author's wish to endear us; but for whom, after
this interruption, we no longer care. If then a man, whose duty
it is to praise departed excellence not without some sense of regret or sadness, to do this or to be silent, should upon all occasions exhibit that mode of connecting thoughts, which is only natural while we are delineating vice under certain relations, we may
be assured that the nobler sympathies are not alive in him; that
he has no clear insight into the internal constitution of virtue; nor
has himself been soothed, cleared, harmonized, by those outward
effects which follow everywhere her goings—declaring the presence of the invisible Deity. (Zall, 120–22)

Ornamental diction is dangerous because it is to style what observation is to the life of values. One achieves mastery, but usually
at the cost of failing to understand fully both what one would master and what that other could bring out in the self if one could
loosen one's oppressive need for control. Pope's epitaphs then represent the limitations of an entire century committed to the public
show of principles of judgment that had become terribly distanced
from two significantly related dispositions—the capacity for empa-
thy and the capacity to offer the kind of praise which ultimately
exalts both the self and the objects that become available to that
self once they are seen in the atmosphere which panegyrics compose. Popean judgment mimes too closely the framework of social
negotiation and self-control basic to the culture whose praise it
seeks, so that it prevents us from making the empathic leaps that
lead us beyond social morality to the grace that is deep virtue at
peace with itself. So the poet's task must emulate the task that Kant
posed for a philosophy that would escape the same eighteenth-
century blinders to idealization, that of making manifest and plausible those powers of spirit which lead beyond the social theater
to other, more sublime principles of self-delight and social related-
ness.

If we remain with Wordsworth's prose it is fairly easy to outline those powers he thought could perform that task. In the Preface to *Lyrical Ballads*, the central psychological traits he cultivates are those that "carry everywhere relationship and love." At
times this means attuning us to the ways in which our associative
processes can be aligned to deep patterns of lawfulness; at times

it takes more closely textured psychological attention to the "accuracy with which similitude in dissimilitude and dissimilitude in similitude are perceived" because on that "depend our taste and moral feelings" (Zall, 57). What takes overt form in the meter of the poem in fact gets played out on several psychological levels—all "imperceptibly" making "up a complex feeling of delight, which is of the most important use in tempering the painful feeling always found intermingled with the powerful descriptions of the deeper passions" (Zall, 58). By the Preface to the edition of 1815, Wordsworth breaks this pursuit of a balanced psychic economy down into three basic powers of imagination, each adding a dimension of synthetic energies enabling a richer sense of how the internal life extends the order of perception. At the simplest level the imagination has the power to confer properties on objects so that the object reacts "upon the mind which hath performed the process like a new existence". If we then envision this faculty elaborating those properties so that they react on one another we begin to see how the play of similitude and dissimilitude balances us between delight in the mobility of our sensations and a comprehensive sense of how the unities that then emerge betoken a higher conjunction of man and nature (Zall, 149). Finally all this admits of a fully self-reflexive mode: "But the imagination also shapes and creates . . . by innumerable processes; and in none does it more delight than in that of consolidating numbers into unity, and dissolving and separating unity into number,—alternations proceeding from, and governed by, a sublime consciousness of the soul in her own mighty and almost divine powers." The most elemental forces brought to attention in rhythmic eloquence serve also to indicate the most sublime delights of the mind becoming conscious of its own processes.

IV

To stay on this prosaic level in our discussion of powers, however, leaves us very much in the position of Popean judgment. The true test of our noblest sympathies, of criticism as epitaph and projection for the future, is the ways in which the powers of eloquence take on imaginative force in the poetry. For this test I have chosen to dwell on "Nutting."[12] Here Wordsworth most intensely spells out the stakes in his quarrel with lyric sensibilities formed by Enlightenment values, and here the contrast with representative contemporary criticism makes all too evident the degree to which such struggles for a mode of plausible idealization must continue. Nothing could make those stakes clearer than the very different hero Wordsworth puts forward for our identification: this "Figure quaint, / Tricked out in proud disguise of cast-off weeds" (ll. 8–9) can base its claims on our lyric sensibilities only on passions banished by high culture into the world of low mimetic situations and filiations. In order to give this sensibility a voice, and in order to evade the ironic bitterness about such marginalization, which would only reinforce the old values without coming to terms with the imaginative energies that alienate this hero from his heritage, Wordsworth must locate spiritual resources that break sharply with the prevailing hierarchy of psychic functions: he must stretch available conditions of representation so that they concentrate attention on a force that cannot be made to appear except in the process of poetic self-reflection, and he must articulate through that reflection a mode of sublimity capable of restoring the ego's sense of connectedness with the natural sources of its energies. Rather than pursue the reflective pathos of "The Castaway" or the exalted contemplative scope of the voice in "Elegy on a Country-Churchyard," this poem demands our working against generalized sentiments and Horatian ideals for poetry in order to focus on close readings of what the compulsion to narrate reveals about the mind's relation to its scenic context.

Given its setting, the poem should be able to rely on pastoral conventions. But within the speaker's narrative these conventions prove a seductive and dangerous form for representing experience. Traditional pastoral expectations seem to leave the mind a frustrating excess that finds its most ready outlet in adolescent violence:

> I heard the murmur and the murmuring sound,
> In that sweet mood when pleasure loves to pay
> Tribute to ease; and, of its joy secure,
> The heart luxuriates with indifferent things,

> Wasting its kindliness on stocks and stones,
> And on the vacant air. Then up I rose
> And dragged to earth both branch and bough, with crash
> And merciless ravage: and the shady nook
> Of hazels, and the green and mossy bower,
> Deformed and sullied, patiently gave up
> Their quiet being: and unless I now
> Confound my present feelings with the past;
> Ere from the mutilated bower I turned
> Exulting, rich beyond the wealth of Kings,
> I felt a sense of pain when I beheld
> The silent trees and saw the intruding sky.-
> Then, dearest maiden, move along these shades
> In gentleness of heart; with gentle hand
> Touch—for there is a spirit in the woods. (ll. 38–56)

Apparently the easy humanism of Romance pastoral which the boy invokes cannot sufficiently handle difference, cannot handle the very sense of personal intensity that it elicits. Therefore, as the heart luxuriates, the mind all too readily slips from its sweet mood to a sense that its objects become indifferent and its kindliness wasted. Given the rhetoric available to it, the mind has no other way to express its increasing sense of its distinctive powers but to set itself violently against a nature that becomes merely its object.

Yet this play on difference and indifference soon reveals another power, another greater difference which becomes intelligible only by the poem's power to compose another rhetoric based on the fusing of psychological narrative with the pastoral setting. Here then we find a different version of constitutive subjective energies able to compose a more capacious lyrical theater. Cast out of those conventional attitudes initially producing a coherent emotional scenario, the mind's momentary sense of power dissipates and the hero finds himself transformed into a mere object within a scene whose self-sufficiency makes him utterly expendable. Bower yields to silent trees and intruding sky, leaving the ephebe torn on the dualities of "Kindliness" on which the Enlightenment tradition foundered. From the humanist perspective kindliness refers to the appreciation of a distinctively human potential

in the encounter. But this makes nature a little less than kin, reduced to hoping for the subject's kindnesses and hence also a fit
victim for his tirades. And in that reduced state violence produces
another kindliness, linking him to precisely that capacity for disor-
der in nature which probably made the effort to cover over the
differences seem necessary in the first place. From this perspective, consciousness seems to share not nature's depth but the su-
perficiality of its appearances, as if both domains distanced and distorted some deeper possibility of lawfulness.

The logic is pure Augustine: the secular dream of being more
than nature reduces one to being less than one's own nature can
be. Adequate response depends on finding a way of reading one's
experiences so that the awareness of this acculturated blindness
becomes a means of redefining spirit. For Wordsworth, the new
means is confessional narrative, and the new goal a state of sublimity earned by the narrative process of working through lack and
contradiction. In this more dialectical sense of landscape, poetry
cannot be content with describing nature or reflecting on the general truths that nature might illustrate. Rather, poetry must become self-reflexive enough to provoke errors, then test the capacities of the composing voice to spell out new lines of relation
between a mind in excess of nature and a force of nature that reveals its powers only through the collapse of kindliness. Once the
sky can become an intruding presence, the youth must learn how
narrative enables him to take responsibility for both his difference
from nature and the divisions from himself which generated so un-
reasoned and ostensibly spontaneous a destructive act. The result
is a new, non-Burkean form of the sublime which gives moral force
to the state of self-consciousness it presents as testimony. The
rude shock of what one is not—not one with the appearance of
nature and not one with the rhetoric that gives man superiority
over a yielding nature—forces memory and poetry to the constructive work of the concluding lines. There is a spirit in these
woods, but its meaning and force are reserved for those who can
learn to read it as the poem does—through a series of negations
which clear the way for this particular poetic naming to resist a
history of false associations. Then it requires the dialectic of narrative memory to show why there must be a spirit and why it must

remain on the margins of human experience, beyond the control of an interpretive violence which most ephebes in the culture never outgrow.

Wordsworth's great achievement here is to have his sublime romance and to moralize it too, while making the conjunction testimony to the powers of passion become eloquent about its enabling conditions. On one level, then, it makes sense to cast these Wordsworthian moments in the frame of Freudian instruction scenes. By casting this spirit in the woods as a surrogate father punishing the son for raping his sister-mother and thus composing (or imposing) nature as a super-ego figure, "Nutting" overdetermines the poem's resolution just as it had the violent act. Yet Freudian language (or Lacanian twists on that language) will not suffice because this overdetermination is quite deliberate. The scene instructs because of its overt properties *as* scene, as a mode of presentation that can undo the received model of interpretive authority and make the specific process of unfolding which the poem enacts necessary to define what spirit can be. Rather than limit Spirit to something we find in the unconscious, we are invited to envision it as the active force to which narrative can testify once it comes to understand how the mind is capable of modes of attention and memory more sensitive and more capacious than the models of man the poem seeks to displace.

V

If such testimony is to earn its modernity, that is, its resistance to dominant cultural ideals, it must possess two concrete means of extending and testing the powers that Wordsworth's prose attributes to it—it must show how the expansive passion opens us to new grounds of value, and it must give that testimony an immediacy and force which for traditional theorists of eloquence could derive in large part from the invocation of high cultural traditions. The second is the easier to describe because what Wordsworth inaugurated is now close to being a cultural cliché to which we presently seek alternatives. Poetry as testimony need not seek authority from an idealized cultural heritage to the degree that the artifact itself maintains a system of internal relations sufficient to lead the reader to and through the projected powers of spirit. But this vision of poetic means puts an enormous burden on poetic ends: what possible ground of values could provide a countercultural force simply on the basis of self-reflexive intricacy and the narrative control of shifting investments? Wordsworth's response is to attempt shifting the terms of valuation so that the priority of civic space yields to the priority of autobiographical measures of value. Such values need not be solipsistic or individualist, but they must gain their authority from the relation they allow a person to maintain toward his or her formative experiences.

Establishing those priorities entails developing a model of the resources, the commitments, and the contradictions basic to poetic activity which could overturn the interwoven ideals of judgment, of nobility, and of eloquence that had taken form under the aegis of both Christian Humanism and Enlightenment rationalism. These frameworks cast the noble self as one whose judgment and will managed to subordinate individual interests and passions to some more general categorical frameworks. Selves inherit traditions and through them develop powers of assessment enabling them to align themselves with those ideas and images which define a life worthy of respect. Under those dispensations the role of judgment and imagination is to subordinate the particular to the generalized model, at least in those domains where there are clear public ideals. But Wordsworth was obsessed by the problem of what authorizes those ideals. For him idealization had to remain connected to formative events and influences in particular lives, so that the idealizing would in effect be inseparable from a condition of remembering and the qualities of the remembering could then be subject to public scrutiny against the backdrop of a common world. The result is what might be called a scenic logic which redefines the dynamics of judgment and thus requires shifting from the Miltonic model of public eloquence to a version of eloquence that could take responsibility for its origins in an essentially domestic imaginative theater.

In this Wordsworthian scenic model for the formation of selves the central terms for value derive from persons' capacities to define their own distinctive relationship to the sources of their most intense powers. Because the formation of selves thus involves the dialectical force of all that the intruding sky symbolizes, this scenic logic has affinities with Idealist thought (as Meyer Abrams's *Natural Supernaturalism* magisterially demonstrates). But in order to accommodate his own empiricist values, Wordsworth develops models of reflection and of judgment that do not lead to Kant's and Hegel's synthetic rational processes, and that thereby do not require any specific teleological or transcendental claims. Judgment becomes what Schlegel called a form of "spiritual sensuality" that must locate its generalizing principles within the scene that it composes. No longer confined by abstract ideas or social norms of taste, Wordsworthian judgment depends on a concrete history of negotiations with an environment. The self is scenic, then, because its investments derive from the scenes that it has been attached to and the traces which those leave in its memory. Scenes are not mere instances passively awaiting the forming influence of the mind. Instead they serve as metonyms for behavioral complexes that spread out over time and into a range of repeated habits and related social practices. Because the self neither creates meanings nor can trust dominant cultural generalizations, its deepest powers and most intimate loyalties are shaped by the history of the adjustments it makes to those environmental forces. And because these adjustments involve the measure of time—of repeated connections to nature and other people as well as a history of rewards and instructive failures—the energies they engage can be much more comprehensive and more immediately compelling and flexible than anything generalized principles can afford. The expansive life of scenic consciousness both elicits and rewards a temperament gradually developing patterns of attention and care binding it to its surrounding community. Thus, Wordsworthian versions of testimony, of expansive passion, and of identification enable us to replace Horatian generalization by an ideal of representativeness based simply on the capacity of a work to exemplify certain powers that help an audience adapt itself to similar numinous forces. Because the spirit in the woods can become the spirit defined by the field of energies the poem's narrative act composes, the narrated recognition scene becomes available for the entire society. There can be a spirit in a personal narrative's self-critical activity that can engage the spirit in the woods and can make its contribution to the community the exemplary modes of reflection that it affords for such engagements. Ultimately that engagement even makes it possible to transform the rape of feminine nature into the making visible of imaginative resources that the poet can hope to share with his maiden interlocutor.

VI

My own diction here, and my uneasiness about Wordsworth's treatment of women, make all too visible the problem that still remains for this essay—how is Wordsworth's eloquence still empowering for us? Why should we make the imaginative effort necessary to identify with it, and how can we be reasonably certain that in pursuing such identifications we are not repeating the initial efforts of the boy in "Nutting" to engage a changing world under the aegis of outmoded fictions? I have tried to cast the values at stake in general enough terms that their application to contemporary culture is clear. But that generality could be considered part of the problem, since our literary culture is becoming adamantly historicist and "materialist." Consequently the only way I know to bring out the force of Wordsworth's position is to borrow the strategy he used against Pope, that is, to draw contrasts between the powers that he pursues and the attitudes toward eloquence which now dominate what Frank Lentricchia calls "advanced" positions in contemporary literary criticism. For this experiment I have chosen a reading of "Nutting" posed by Jonathan Arac's recent book *Critical Genealogies*.[13] If I can show that readings like Arac's fail to account for the probable depth and the possible uses of the poet's intelligence, then there is at least a beginning for the case that these gestures of sophisticated critical intelligence often mask what remains a reactionary submission to academic fashion and to the banal forms of self-congratulation sustained by Enlightenment mythologies of an heroic demystifying lucidity. Not to challenge such readings is to submit to a critical climate in which there is simply no possible positive role for poetic eloquence, and hence little use for the lyric imagination except as a repository of symptoms or of approved revolutionary emotions.

Arac and I pose almost exactly the same question: for him the issue is how "Nutting" can be said to present "the psycho-sexual construction of literary authority" (49), and for me it is how the poem presents one plausible way of handling perceived crises in the possibility of wielding literary authority under post-Enlightenment intellectual values. But Arac also wants the reading of "Nutting" to illustrate a critical stance capable of combining the close reading techniques developed by various modern formalisms with a historical perspective that both situates texts as determinate actions in the past and shows how they help produce strata of assumptions and values which limit our powers as social agents in the present. Therefore rather than identifying provisionally with such eloquence we must learn to dismantle it by means of "a new kind of history writing" (2). This model, perhaps this new version of eloquence committed to the interpreter's activity, can expose the ways in which Wordsworth is instrumental in developing a model of literary autonomy that was "accompanied both by the exclusion of women from the experience that makes literature possible and by the assumption of universality that fetishistically treats sexual differences as 'indifferent things'":

> Once poetic authority was lost, once the previously existing social demand for poetry had been transformed, once the writer was no longer producing on direct demand by patrons, or even subscribers, but was isolated in the marketplace producing for unknown readers whose taste could not be predicted but might with luck be formed, once, in other words, a certain condition of alienation prevailed, then the possibility of literary autonomy also came into existence. The process of internalization by which Wordsworth not only defended but also formed a new literary human nature—the human nature that makes psychoanalysis possible—cannot be understood apart from such externalities. The example of "Nutting" has suggested, moreover, that this literary possibility came only at the cost of reasserting an inequality between the sexes, a form of domination even more fundamental than those of social class and cultural tradition. (49)

I agree that Wordsworth's achievement cannot be understood apart from "such externalities." I doubt, however, that we will learn much about those historical forces if we rely as heavily as Arac does on common contemporary understandings of concepts like autonomy and women's interests, or if one allows oneself to translate Wordsworthian language so quickly into the available psychoanalytic analogies. For then our examination of the construction of literary authority proves false both to the history in which the labor took place and to the present possibilities of locating within the poet's engagements with those historical forces a form of authority which has the power to challenge dominant contemporary modes of lyrical sensibility or critical intelligence. These difficulties become most pronounced in Arac's reading precisely at the moment when "Nutting" has the speaker turn on eighteenth-century models of pastoral in order to tease out an alternative source of genius and a corresponding model of attention. Once again Arac and I (and almost everyone else) agree that the moment of crisis in the poem is the turn to "indifferent things." But rather than stay within the poem's projected reasons for that shift in focus, Arac struts his post-structuralist sensibility. He wants to show that this poem is a particularly tense crossing of Wordsworthian themes because it occupies a social position in which it does not "lay claim to the traditional elevation of ode and thereby has more difficulty assimilating epic and tragedy" (39). Forced to a make much ado about a homely act like nutting, Wordsworth finds his language for attributing significance subject to three basic strains: Wordsworth must reject his usual lyrical use of "thing" to transcend differences rather than admit indifference; he finds his dialectical sense of spots of time reduced to a narrative that must be content to reproduce a previous experience, with its own beginning suspended within the mimesis until in the last lines it is rationalized by the address to the maiden; and he must also rely on that address to negotiate the specific terms for confronting indifference, in the process revealing the problematic links between autonomy and a disturbing sense of sexual difference.

In order to create the desired scandal Arac must show that Wordsworth's way of handling the problem of indifference is of a piece with the assertion of authority over the maiden which concludes the poem. Arac begins cogently by noting that the boy's action "restored the otherness of things and rescued the boy from fiction. It was an "act of modernity" because it "stripped away old clothes" and restored us to earth (43). But this allusion to modernity soon opens the floodgates by warranting a turn to "certain resources of psychoanalysis," enabling the critic to expose the narrative as fiction and requiring us to examine the feelings at work. "Clearly" we have a case of screen memories, and we are thus led to discover a "shocking scene":

> For if the feminized landscape is also phallic, as theorists of the pre-Oedipal suggest that in that stage we attribute both sexes to the mother, then the boy's action could be read as castrating the mother. This does not actually define Wordsworth's boyish feelings, only exposes the degree of linguistic figuration that arose from them in his writing. Representation here is not mimetic but allegorical. . . .
>
> The fantastic act of castrating the mother, moreover is originative. By it the father establishes his dominion over what Lacan called the realm of the symbolic . . . in founding by violence the difference between the sexes. The poet thus put himself in the father's place, made himself truly modern, revenging himself on the frugal dame, usurping the law as his own. . . . Rich beyond the wealth of kings by having textually achieved an impossible desire, the speaker has the power to lay down the law to the "dearest maiden." . . . He and he alone has had the experience, but his modernity becomes her tradition. She must believe on faith alone that there is a spirit in the woods, and not find out for herself. (45–46)

The move from "could read" to "the poet thus put himself in the father's place" exposes the kind of thinking we confront here. Possibilities become facts; the presence of a feminized landscape seems to warrant treating what is staged as an anxiety-ridden rape as if it were an empowering castration; resources of psychoanalysis are invoked at a point where the poem suggests clear dramatic and historical reasons for its shift in focus (which is not away from fiction but from one rhetorical frame to another); and the distinction between actual feelings linked to historical externalities and figural language is immediately ignored in order to claim that the figural possibilities constitute historically effective realities even though they do not define anyone's feelings. Finally, in so collapsing the poem's imaginative movement into allegorical translation, this critical perspective simply ignores the most important feature of the dramatic turn. What begins in frustration over the indifference of things leads to a course of action which over time establishes the possibility of a different relation to nature, to poetry, and to gender relations. To speak of castrating nature is to ignore its recovering authority by propagating a complex third term—the sense of guilt and the resulting awareness of a genius in the woods which is presented as transforming the basic dichotomies between fictions and representations enforced by the old poetic dictions.

Thus the poem's modernity is less its insistence on an autonomy that resists history than on finding a presentational mode which can function as the intruding sky does—that is, first to show us our lacks, then to suggest another way to dispose our psychic energies. This can be done if one can correlate a source of authority outside the poem, the genius in the woods, with resources of eloquence within the poem that the poet can invoke as alternative modes of engaging the temporality of experience. But for Arac the only genius lies in the resources of contemporary criticism, so he is left only with his oppositions between narrative and fictionality, or mimesis and allegory. For Wordsworth, however, there is the possibility of so disposing memory that it at once recovers possible force in past experience and proposes the kinds of intensities that those experiences can maintain for poetic reflection in the present. In "Nutting" those intensities are evoked to transform what begins as rape into particular modes of attention that the poet can share with women, who are thereby released from the figurative identification with a maternal nature. Memory mediates between indifferent nature and the projected fictions of the pastoral imagination. If its force can be rendered by a poetry concerned to project, not to imitate or to displace, there is no need to force the maiden to believe what the poet offers. Rather, she is asked to replace his violence by an act of touch which can test the possible force of genius proposed by the poem's manipulation of imaginative scenes. This is still a patronizing attitude toward the woman, but it does offer the chance to get beyond the culture's all too well-established categories—poetry offers sites where those with different social positions can try to understand and share the forces which can modify our emotional lives.

Providing such information and staging such tests of possible accommodations is the role of a new, "modern" emphasis on the internal complexity of poetic elements. And understanding that is a prelude to seeing why Arac's reliance on Freud is so reductive a gesture. It in no way responds to the concern of Romantic thinkers to make the concept of autonomy link poetic and personal states. And, more important, it displaces attention from the capacity of this specific poem to develop a psychic economy different from Freud's version of interior life. The subject projected by "Nutting" does not insist on extending the event into other autobiographical contexts, and it does not impose discursive expectations on what must retain the specificity and the otherness of an imaginative scenario. Poetry must be allowed its sense of excess if we are not to castrate it. To impose Freud's concept of the subject in the self-righteous moralizing mode of critical historicism allows ourselves no intruding sky, no pressures defining our own limitations, reduced terms for understanding the problems that both beset and enable contemporary poetry, and only the most embarrassing theaters in which to attempt to replace the genius in the woods with its critical counterparts.

VII

Any doubts that I have about allowing myself this outburst get resolved whenever I remind myself of the remarks that conclude Arac's discussion: "A new literary history must heed the warning of Walter Benjamin, written just after the outbreak of the Second World War, and acknowledge that our 'cultural treasures' are documents not only of civilization but also of barbarism; to the extent that we revere those treasures we carry on the barbarism" (49). Even though Arac does qualify this assertion by warning us not therefore to lose the "live" elements of past texts, his way of reading defines what he can take those live elements to be. And such construals obviously will not suffice. Therefore one cannot but wonder where the greater barbarism lies—in the blindness lurking in the acts of genius that survive from the past, or in the arrogance that assumes that so transforming that past into our own banalities and so denying the space of idealization that eloquence attempts to construct will improve the political and moral features of contemporary life. And as one wonders, perhaps as one begins to doubt there is any escape from those critical stances, the ancient desire for an exemplary eloquence begins to take on perhaps all too much contemporary currency.[14]

NOTES

1. Hugh Blair, *Lectures on Rhetoric and Belles Lettres*, 1783, ed. Harold Harding (Carbondale: Southern Illinois University Press, 1965), 2:6.

2. I obviously oversimplify, especially with respect to historicist work not as tied to a specific political project and with respect to those like Stanley Cavell, Don Bialostosky, and Richard Eldridge, who are committed to recovering the imaginative force of Wordsworth's poetry in contemporary terms. But the best historical work does not come from the most ambitious theoretical minds, and all three in their different ways may be too quick to allegorize the work in terms of contemporary thinking without letting its own emphases take conceptual form.

3. Several years ago I tried a variant of this argument by defending Wordsworth's claims about the immediacy of poetry against Paul de Man. That essay, "Wordsworth's 'Preface' as Literary Theory," *Criticism* 10 (1976), 122–46, was an effort to reconstruct the concept of event as its model for a Whiteheadian sense of immediacy, but I did not find a good practical correlate for those metaphysical claims. Here I return to many of those arguments, but this time I try to avoid naturalizing poetic language in order to deal with it simply as a form of eloquence inviting us to assume whatever imaginative world is necessary to participate provisionally in the relevant passions. I shall argue that the point is not to locate some privileged moment of insight but to explain how we can become the kinds of persons for whom the states presented by the speech acts can matter. This does not resolve the problem of deciding whether that eloquent self is a person or a stage construct. But the question can be finessed by insisting that the fundamental rule of this rhetorical theater is that all reference is proleptic: the conditions claimed within the rhetorical construct have reality to the degree that we can live our own lives in their terms. In order to mark the distinction between empirical and proleptic reference, theorists like Blair had to develop a distinction between a descriptive sublime and a writerly one.

4. All quotations in this paragraph are from Antonius' speech in Cicero's *De Oratore*, ed. E. W. Sutton and H. Rackham (Cambridge: Harvard University Press, 1948), 1:325–39.

5. There is also a third aspect of this tradition which impinges only indirectly on Wordsworth. Under the pressure of their pragmatic and skeptical oppo-

nents, the best theorists of eloquence are excrutiatingly conscious of the difficulties involved in maintaining so idealized an image of their own practice, in much the same way that the best Romantics maintain ironies sufficient to acknowledge their sense of the limitations involved in having to idealize what remain intensely personal positions. As my colleague Alan Fisher shows in an unpublished manuscript, that situation leads humanist thought to its own version of dialogical principles because thinkers like Plato, Cicero, and Valla realize that they must grapple with issues and with psyches too complex to be treated from any one perspective. For the Romantics that sense of limits requires the very different, more slippery and often more sublime endless dialogue with oneself—not because the ideals sought are impossibly riven with infinite ironies, but because the only way to make them plausible is to win them against a background constantly acknowledging the complex tensions one must negotiate and offering qualitative contrasts demonstrating there are powers of mind and emotion capable of such tasks.

The first problem resides in the appeal of pure idealization, which then is haunted by the possibility of having simply ignored or evaded the practical realm that authors tell themselves they have surpassed. On the most concrete level this becomes a matter of the relation of eloquence to the demands of practical rhetorical theory—with every idealizing Crassus complemented by a figure like Antonius who continually points out how much the orator misses because he reads human powers in terms only of his own extraordinary abilities. Other versions of that dichotomy entail a constant tension between the art of rhetoric and the claim to overcome that art by sincere and truthful passion: how can one tell that the passion is not itself only a higher artifice, yet how can one be sure that the intense state, however achieved, does not lead to new conditions of full belief? The only test is the audience's reaction, but that is complicated by the fact that the art of rhetoric is precisely the manipulation of the audience's response so its belief may be evidence that the speaker's passion does not transcend its own theatricality.

Other problems with the audience prove even more perplexing. Every rhetor who dreams of changing the values of his audience must also rely sufficiently on those values to win the hearts of those shaped by them. How new then are the orator's visions? Perhaps they are little more than self-congratulatory versions of the old system. Since most effective rhetoric must stage itself as counter-eloquence to some more debased form, every audience one persuades becomes a possible sign that in fact one is no different from the old order, one only shares its illusions of difference. And given all these inducements to self-congratulatory delusion, the rhetor is the last person who should generalize about rhetoric, since all of his skills may have no end but to cast spells. But who knows that temptation better than the rhetor, who must make that knowledge visible if there is to be any hope of escaping its confines?

6. For Augustine, see *On Christian Doctrine*, trans. W. D. Robertson, Jr. (Indianapolis: Bobbs Merrill, 1958), pp. 150, 168. For Longinus see "On the Sublime," in Hazard Adams, ed., *Critical Theory since Plato* (New York: Harcourt Brace Jovanovich, 1971), sects. 13–14. The sense of passion and momentary

identity which we find in both thinkers allows Blair a lovely moment of looking down at the world of the rule-governed and artificial rhetoricians as that of fallen creatures: "The emotion occasioned in the mind by some great or noble object, raises it considerably above its ordinary pitch. A sort of enthusiasm is produced, extremely agreeable while it lasts; but from which the mind is tending every moment to fall down into its ordinary situation. Now, when an author . . . throws in any one decoration that sinks in the least below the capital image, that moment he alters the key; he relaxes the tension of the mind; the strength of the feeling is emasculated; the beautiful may remain, but the sublime is gone" (1:66). Although Wordsworth has his quarrels with the cultivation of taste that is basic to theorists like Blair, his writing on the effects of artifice in epitaphs stresses exactly the same sense that artifice disfigures sincere emotion (compare Paul M. Zall, ed. *Literary Criticism of William Wordsworth* [Lincoln: University of Nebraska Press, 1966], p. 113).

7. Coleridge attempts a different and (perhaps unfortunately) more influential recasting of traditional eloquence. Also committed to a poetry capable of expressing the passions at their fullest, Coleridge defines that fullness by distinguishing between eloquence, which impels to a particular act, and poetry, which tries to give the character of a universal to a particular. Where the orator treats a thing of business as if it were an affair of imagination, the poet "treats a thing of fancy as if it were a matter of business." On this basis "the continuous state of excitement" that the poet generates comes to depend on an internal set of relations rather than on its continuity with the languages of social intercourse, and we are on our way to modernist poetics and contemporary textualism. See Coleridge's *Lectures 1808–1819: On Literature*, ed. R. H. Foakes (Princeton: Bollingen Press, 1987), 1:115, 471). I cannot argue that Coleridge is wrong, since clearly internal patterns are crucial to any eloquence; I can only ask whether his is the most useful way to conceive the matter.

8. I feel free to indulge in this exercise because I have discussed the value of Goodman's specific ideas elsewhere and tried to work out what I think are the problems that it raises, especially in my *Act and Quality* (Amherst: University of Massachusetts Press, 1981) and my forthcoming *Infinite Incantations of Ourselves: Painterly Abstraction in Modernist American Poetry* (New York: Cambridge University Press, 1989).

9. In simply taking this statement at face value I provide a good example of theoretical argument suppressing the author's interest in teasing out the related field of complex tensions, which he then manipulates in order to earn the authority that the assertion presumes. Thus I am not fair to Wordsworth here, but because I weaken the sense of the agent, not because I distort the argument that he ultimately supports.

10. In proposing this view of metaphor Wordsworth is entirely consistent with classical theorists of eloquence, adding only his characteristic demand that the excess has its sanction in the way we relate to nature (whereas for classical theory the excess is more likely to stem from our engagement with social exemplars). For the stress on sublime writing leads beyond descriptive criteria to a

concern for how we understand and engage the most ample stagings of human passions, and figuration is central because it replaces the concern for truth with an interest in making visible the terms of passionate engagement that can extend description into the domain of values. In such passion, Longinus tells us, the figure escapes detection as a figure because it becomes folded into the excess of light created by the sublime state: "For just as all dim lights are extinguished in the blaze of the sun, so do the artifices of rhetoric fade from view when bathed in the pervading splendor of sublimity" (89). Such sentiments are often used now to insist that even sublime passion is theatrical and hence a displacing of any claim on the empirical world. But to invoke that attitude with regard to Longinus, or to Wordsworth, is probably to let oneself fall victim to the half-heartedness that Longinus complains of in his concluding paragraph. In Longinian terms such ironic gestures simply refuse to entertain his overall desire to imagine how passion and the desire for fame can compose selves worthy of competing with the great writers of the past. Augustine would make the same charge on different grounds—that to suspect figures is to confine ourselves to a narrow interpretive framework. It is precisely the force of figures that clarifies the limitations in any simple sign theory of language because that force requires us to supplement description with hermeneutics: "There is a miserable servitude of the spirit in this habit of taking signs for things, so that one is not able to raise the eye of the mind above things that are corporal and created to drink in eternal light" (84).

11. Perhaps the most interesting feature of that theology is the way Wordsworth insists on extending the thematics of pleasure to all three temporal dimensions—as if pleasure were power in its most concrete material manifestation and, at the same time, as if the amplifications worked by pleasure were the best measure of how other aspects of the psyche might be deployed. Pleasure in the present tense is a simple measure of intensity and of the possible harmonious relations to nature which that intensity could release by spreading "everywhere relationship and love" (Zall, 52). But relying on the present lacks the qualitative measures necessary if we are to avoid getting caught in dramas of repression and violent supplementation like those which Wordsworth attributes to the flattering self-love addicting readers to the poetry of extravagant and absurd diction (Zall, 63–64). Those qualitative measures depend on our testing the working of pleasure over time. Pleasure both forms and tests character. On the one hand the history of our pleasure shapes the patterns of memory and habit governing our dispositions (Zall, 50); on the other it is only by the tensions between our pleasures and the demands of nature within and without that we learn to contour our desires more fully to deeper rhythms within the natural and social orders. When we turn from the past to the future it proves precisely this dynamic which makes it feasible for the poet to hope that eloquence in the imaginary sphere will create intensities and sympathies modifying our desires and attaching our feelings to important subjects (Zall, 42).

12. I have used a somewhat different version of my discussion of this poem and of Jonathan Arac's criticism of it in my "Wordsworth and the Options for Contemporary American Poetry," forthcoming in Gene Ruoff, ed., *The Romantics*

and Us (Newark, N.J.: Rutgers University Press, 1989). There is also a version in my *Painterly Abstraction in Modernist American Poetry*.

13. *Critical Genealogies* (New York: Columbia University Press, 1987).

14. Had I the space I would have taken up one more aspect of imaginative power—the concern for how the poet can influence the future by shaping taste—because this version of Arac's fear of barbarism became by the *Essay, Supplementary to the Preface* a constant obsession for Wordsworth, and because I think the terms of his hope both plausible and probably necessary for the culture that I see represented in Arac. In essence Wordsworth posits for eloquent poetry the capacity to engage its readers in a dialectic much like the one we have been tracking in "Nutting" with the capacity of

> divesting the reader of the pride that induces him to dwell upon those points wherein men differ form each other, to the exclusion of those in which all men are alike, or the same; and in making him ashamed of the vanity that renders him insensible of the appropriate excellence which civil arrangements, less unjust than may appear, and Nature illimitable in her bounty, have conferred on men who may stand below him in the scale of society? Finally, does it lie in establishing that dominion over the spirits of readers by which they are to be humbled and humanised, in order that they may be purified and exalted. (Zall, 183)

Thus poetry can maintain hope in its capacity to affect the future to the degree that its intensities can on the one hand get us to call into question the interpretive languages we use and, on the other, provide testimony of an internal and external effort with the promise of establishing a plausible alternative, for example, to readerly attitudes devoted to the measuring of vices and virtues. I ask the reader to consider the entire passage (Zall 183–85), perhaps in conjunction with the idea of antithetical models of authorial activity developed in Hazard Adams, "Canons: Literary Criteria/Power Criteria," *Critical Inquiry* 14 (1988), 748–64. Although I think Adams needs a more concrete model of how the ideal of antithetical projection is constructed by authors and used by audiences, he is good at reminding us of how ultimately the value in those authorial projections is their ability constantly to challenge the discursive terms we elaborate for those models.

Wordsworth, New Literary Histories, and the Constitution of Literature

DON H. BIALOSTOSKY

The exhibit "William Wordsworth and the Age of English Romanticism" arrived in the United States just as the country's celebration of the bicentennial of the Constitution concluded, and visitors at the exhibit might well have wondered whether the exhibit continued the celebration. The topic of revolution was familiar; the Declaration of Independence in two different printed versions was displayed among the opening documents of the exhibit; styles of portraiture, printing, and handwriting belonged to the same period; and the mounting and magnitude of the exhibit bespoke matters of comparable importance. Visitors looking closer would have noticed images of an unfamiliar revolution and portraits of unfamiliar founders, but they might nevertheless have held to their sense of connection between the events and wondered what *these* Romantic revolutions were about, what constitution followed them, what roles their celebrated founders played, what treasured documents embodied them, what institutions of interpretation perpetuated those documents, and what controversies embroiled them.

Two recent critics would see merit in such questions and might offer some preliminary answers. Clifford Siskin might reply that "the society that places Literature at its center" (95) was constituted by the Romantic revolution, and Jonathan Arac might add

that "Wordsworth did more than anyone else to establish the vocation of literature in relation to which Coleridge's, and our own culture's, idea of the literary critic took shape" (*Genealogies* 3). Siskin actually juxtaposes Wordsworth and Jefferson in terms drawn
from Garry Wills's *Inventing America*. Arac contrasts Wordsworth and Coleridge in terms that some have used to contrast
Jefferson and Madison, the populist democrat and the intellectual
conservative. Both critics focus on Matthew Arnold as a major
early interpreter of Romanticism whose version of the constitution of literature was as consequential as Lincoln's revisionary
interpretations of the Declaration of Independence and the
Constitution.

Siskin and Arac thus share Jerome McGann's interest in how
modern American critics of Romanticism and of literature generally have adopted their critical forms, stances, words, and authori-
zations from the Romantics themselves, but both identify their
projects with Ralph Cohen's "New Literary History" instead of
with McGann's "New Historicism." While most recent New Historicist writers on Wordsworth have followed McGann's primary interest in reinserting Wordsworth's writing in Wordsworth's historical context, Arac and Siskin develop his secondary theme by
showing how the historical situation of contemporary American
literary culture is constituted: for Arac by the Romantic founders
and for Siskin by Romantic formal innovations.

Siskin argues that a "Romantic Discourse" typified by Wordsworth continues to exert "extraordinary power over our professional and personal behaviors" (13), and he attempts to historicize
that discourse in order to change our relationship to it, diminish
some of its power over us, and permit us to "break our own critical
habits" (190) of "dependence upon" (183) it. Though Siskin
historicizes the discourse-of-addiction as one powerful innovation
of Romantic discourse, he nevertheless relies on it to characterize
the way modern "literary professional[s have] addictively returned" (186) to Romantic genres even in their recent revisionary
attempts to demystify visionary Romanticism. Sensitized to what
he reads as a compulsive repetition of the past by today's doctors
of literature, Siskin attempts to make others aware of the power
of the Romantic canon in order to avoid "the political mistake of
being blind to that power, and of thus facing the inevitable pros-

pect of reproducing ... Romantic relationships that have not yet been written to an end" (14).

"Literature" with a self-conscious capital "L" is one of the principal Romantic inventions Siskin tries to attenuate. "Like America," he writes, "Literature ... is an invention that has obscured its own origins ... [and] dehistoricized a version of the human" that serves coercive political functions (85–86). Dedicated to the Wordsworthian/Arnoldian imperative to "make us feel," Literature prescribes an order in which "every individual ... is supposed to identify sympathetically with the [literary] work" and conform to the psychological norm it establishes (84). Those who fail to do so are doubly damned as lacking the "healthful state of association" Wordsworth required of his readers and as failing to exercise the capacity of being excited "without the application of gross and violent stimulants," whose exercise elevates one being above another (Wordsworth, Preface to *Lyrical Ballads*). They are, in other words, sick and inferior—at once needing the cure of literary education because of their illness and deserving their degradation because of their failure to exert themselves. In response to his own presentation of this version of human needs, Siskin claims, Wordsworth "sets up the writer as the doctor who can cure [his readers'] 'savage torpor'" (81). At the same time he founds the apparatus of Literature that has proliferated into a system of "creative writers, analytic critics, developing students, and loving readers who have helped to form academic departments, publishing houses, foundations, and governmental bureaucracies" (84) that control us not by imposing direct moral prohibitions but by stimulating our desires for literary works, treating our unhealthy failures to appreciate them, and grading our degrees of appreciation.

This vision of the constitution of Literature and its subjects threatens, as Siskin recognizes, "our assumptions about what we study and why" (67). It presents us and our founding father Wordsworth as addicts, pushers, and quack doctors, our object of study as a controlled and controlling substance, and our function (if not our conscious purpose) as the enforcement of conformity and the naturalization of social inequality. To historicize Literature in this way is to produce an effect of alienation that demoralizes our professional identities without reconstituting them. Siskin acknowledges the need to "provide an alternative" (6) to Romantic discourse. What alternatives does he provide?

Siskin offers two alternatives, one explicit and one implied. Explicitly he offers the practice of new literary history his book exemplifies. That practice addresses our current situation "of conceptual and thus generic transition" (4) by enabling an understanding of change, but it offers no "'cure' for our Romantic addictions." In effect, new literary history enrolls critics addicted to Romanticism in something like a Romantics Anonymous where they will hear over and over the "tale of [their] need to be cured" and recognize at each hearing the "ongoing power" of Romantic discourse. Siskin does not posit any other power that could supplant the insidious and ongoing power of Romantic discourse, and it is not at all certain that his new literary history has the power to fulfill his desire "to classify [the Romantic] self as a construct— to put it in the past" (194). At best, it would seem that it might help us become, in the language of Alcoholics Anonymous, "recovering Romantics."

The second, implicit alternative Siskin offers is the late eighteenth-century discourse that he reconstructs in contrast to Romantic discourse. Characterized by sharp differences of social and literary kinds in place of Romantic differences of degree, personified powers in place of mystified individual power, and didactic directness in place of masked Romantic didacticism, this eighteenth-century discourse provides Siskin's instruments of generic analysis and underwrites his direct didactic style. Though presumably this cultural form has been "put . . . in the past," Siskin brings it back and effectively identifies himself with it instead of with the Romanticism he deplores. His repeated insistence on the reassertion of kinds against Wordsworthian reductions of kind to degree sounds like a neoclassic correction of Romantic aberration. Like the personifications he analyzes in the poetry of Collins, Gray, and Goldsmith, Siskin's personified figures of Literature, Power, and Romantic discourse make "the self . . . the subject of their authoritative activities and not an active, authoritative subject" (75). In effect, Siskin recapitulates in his own stance the position of what he calls the helpless self of the poetry of Sensibility even as he reinvests the personified Power(s) that dominated that self. *This* domination of the self by discourse is the reality that makes the active Romantic self seem illusory to Siskin. For him, the absolute powers of the Old Regime still rule from underground in the new.

Arac shares some of Siskin's understanding of the Romantic constitution of literature, but he finds more alternatives and more active power within Romanticism. Arac holds with Siskin that "only around 1800 did there come into being the notion of 'literature' as we have since known it," and that this notion of literature "formed a new, literary human nature . . . that makes psychoanalysis possible" (*Genealogies* 48–49), underwriting "psychological" at the expense of social criticism (56). Following Foucault, as does Siskin, Arac sees the "production of 'literature' as a particular social and linguistic space in the nineteenth century, achieved through a series of separations and purifications" as part of "an increasing differentiation of social functions" (*Genealogies* 264). Arac also sees "the history of criticism [as] . . . part of the history of literature" (3); he questions the social uses which "literary criticism" has served and urges connection of the concerns once enclosed within "literature" to the "larger concerns of state and economy" (307–308). Finally, like Siskin, he wishes to "end [the] cycle of repetition" (93) in which modern critics uncritically read Romantic texts in Romantic terms.

Arac opposes such disciplinary repetition, but instead of repeatedly documenting it, he appeals to an alternative mode of cultural reproduction—the activity of exclusion. He calls attention to those authors, texts, and elements of texts that repetitive emphasis overlooks instead of dwelling on the scandal of repetition itself (81). This emphasis draws Arac's focus from the centers created by repetition to the excluded margins, from texts to contexts, from dominant precursors to recessive predecessors (see Stempel 89). Indeed Arac locates literature itself on the margin of a society in which "other technical skills have proved more socially powerful than the mastery of words as codified in rhetoric" (*Genealogies* 7), whereas Siskin envisions "the society that places Literature at its center" (95). Arac also sees Wordsworth not as Siskin's (and McGann's) "normative and, in every sense, exemplary" figure for the Romantic constitution of literature (196 n.15) but as an alternative to the still dominant figure of Coleridge. Whereas Siskin exaggerates the power and centrality of Romantic discourse in order to compel an alienating recognition of contemporary Romantic practices, Arac attempts to displace powerful Romantic figures with other figures that enable other practices. Arac does not try to put a monolithic Romantic past behind us but to "excavate the past that is necessary to account for how we got here and the past that is useful for conceiving alternatives to our present condition" (*Genealogies* 2).

That present condition for Arac is not Siskin's time of change or transition but, rather, an "impasse" that requires us to discover alternative routes, discipline our powers to enable us to take those routes, and rouse our wills to determine us to exercise those powers. In search of alternative routes he reviews the history of the constitution of literature, from the Romantic founding to the recent critical revolutions, to find what both Bakhtin and the legal profession would call loopholes—unexploited texts and passages, alternative interpretations of familiar texts and passages, underused authorities and fresh contextualizations of well-used authorities. For discipline, he looks to a "more resolute focus on rhetoric" (75) to provide alternative strategies of interpretation that can "repluralize the figures" (78) of rhetoric in the wake of New Critical and deconstructive reductions of those figures. And for inspiration he looks above all to Walter Benjamin, who undertook literary history "as a task for human agency, 'a revolutionary chance in the fight for the oppressed past'" (22).

As one alternative constitutional route, Arac takes Wordsworth around the obstacles to productive criticism posed by "Coleridge's romantic metaphysics of symbol and imagination" (3). This alternative route is difficult, because so much of our Wordsworth has been shaped to fit the Coleridgean mold (even by Wordsworth himself) that some, like Siskin and McGann, make no effective distinction between them and others, like Abrams and McFarland, exclude and repeat their Wordsworth on Coleridgean premises.[1] Arac attempts to renew the Wordsworthian alternative by selecting Wordsworthian texts that have not commonly been taken as constitutionally significant. He chooses "Nutting" instead of "Tintern Abbey," for example, but he might have gone further afield, as those of us have done who have tried to redeem neglected experimental poems and works of the later Wordsworth from the "oppressed past." Siskin, for one, advocates attention to neglected Wordsworthian poetry outside the "Great Decade," especially the plentiful sonnets, but he holds Wordsworth at least as responsible as Coleridge and Arnold for the "myth of creativity" (8) that has justified the exclusion of most of Wordsworth's work from the canon.

Arac finds Arnold less of a roadblock than Coleridge. He discovers more in Arnold's work than the "proverbs of criticism" (Trilling 73) Siskin identifies him with—the tribute to Wordsworth's ability to "make us feel" and the reduction of Wordsworth's poetic work to the selections from the "Great Decade." Arac reads Arnold's biblical criticism, studies his career in the schools, and appreciates his importance in the history of the constitution of literature: "Arnold achieved what Johnson and Coleridge, those earlier geniuses of English criticism, did not do: he established the terms of a continuing cultural discipline" (*Genealogies* 129).

Arac seeks different goals and different means (138) for that discipline than Arnold's, but he affirms the productive, empowering, affirmative aspect of the discipline as such even as he acknowledges the subjected social roles it imposes and the exclusions it necessarily brings into being (126). Arac cites the later Foucault and through him Arnold's contemporary Nietzsche as the source of this affirmation of discipline; Siskin cites the same Foucault, but he reads Foucault's substitution of productive disciplinary power for repressive state power as the exposure of a more subtle domination, not as what Arac calls an empowering self-subjection (126).

Arac's view of a contemporary impasse in literary history leads him to seek ways around our prominent contemporary constitutional interpreters as well, but his way around them is through them. He extensively criticizes half a dozen living judges on today's literary supreme court, including two important Wordsworthian interpreters—Geoffrey Hartman, who refuses to decide cases but writes ingenious opinions, and M. H. Abrams, who deprecates "'ingenious exegetic[s]'" (*Genealogies* 65) and decides cases without enough difficulty. Arac offers his own combination of ingenious exegesis and confident decision as an alternative to both of them and makes himself a strong candidate for a seat on the bench, which, after all, has an open number of seats. Though his involvement with the controlled substance of Romanticism might disqualify him in the eyes of those who distrust its power, Arac seems to me to have made that power productive of knowledge without being compulsively dominated by it.

Arac's model for this productive relation between power and knowledge, however, is more Romantic than he acknowledges. He is not just a disciple of the late Foucault but also of the mid-career Wordsworth. Arac alludes repeatedly to the figure of "Hannibal among the Alps" and to the distinction between the "Public" and the "People" from Wordsworth's 1815 *Essay Supplementary to the Preface*, but he never cites the text by name. Nevertheless, the key terms of his argument are also the key terms of Wordsworth's *Essay*, and the critical role he assumes and the critical discipline he advocates are authorized by it. Without offering an interpretation of the *Essay Supplementary*, Arac writes in the spirit of this marginal constitutional text and draws from it a source of power for criticism understood as the active production of knowledge in response to the enduring power of literature.

That source of critical power has been obscured, however, not just by Arac's allusiveness but by the most important constitutional reading the *Essay Supplementary* has received. M. H. Abrams's much reprinted reading, which appears in both his introductory essay to his 1972 collection of critical essays on Wordsworth, "Two Roads to Wordsworth,"[2] and in a late section of *Natural Supernaturalism* entitled "Transvaluations" (390–99), has canonized a "liberal, comforting," (Klancher 148) and orthodox Wordsworth in a text in which Arac and I find a more liberating, demanding, and radical author. In "Two Roads to Wordsworth," Abrams makes the Preface to *Lyrical Ballads* typify the first road to Wordsworth, the road of simplicity and natural feeling in the language of Enlightenment humanism. Abrams himself took this road to Wordsworth in *The Mirror and the Lamp*. The *Essay Supplementary*, however, typifies the second road to Wordsworth, the road Abrams takes in *Natural Supernaturalism.*

The *Essay Supplementary*, he writes, "reiterates in sober prose the claims [Wordsworth] had made years before, in the verse 'Prospectus' to *The Recluse* . . . and in the opening and closing passages of *The Prelude*: claims that it is his task to confront and find consolation in human suffering" ("Roads" 1). In addition, the *Essay Supplementary* abandons the language of humanism, according to Abrams, to adopt the theological language of Christian paradox, "for Wordsworth claims in this essay that there are 'affinities between religion and poetry', 'a community of nature', so that poetry shares the distinctive quality of Christianity, which is to confound 'the calculating understanding' by its contradictions" (2). Abrams goes so far as to claim that Wordsworth's "chief enterprise as a poet is expressed [in the *Essay Supplementary*] in a Christian paradox—he must cast his readers down in order to raise them up: their spirits 'are to be humbled and humanized in order that they may be purified and exalted'" ("Roads" 2).

Abrams, however, makes the *Essay Supplementary* stand for something that it explicitly rejects, subordinates, and transcends. Wordsworth does indeed write that religious readers of poetry "resort to poetry, as to religion, . . . as a consolation for the afflictions of life" (*Prose* 3.62) and he does note an "affinity between religion and poetry" and a "community of nature" (*Prose* 3.65) between them. But Wordsworth notes these commonalities only in order to warn against the kind of reading they produce and to reject the religious reader as a reliable judge of poetry: "In this community may be perceived also the lurking incitements to kindred error;— so that we shall find . . . no lovers of the art [of poetry] have gone farther astray than the pious and the devout" (*Prose* 3:65–66; see Johnston 339). Wordsworth looks for adequate judgments of poetry not to these religious readers but to "those and those only, who, never having suffered their youthful love of poetry to remit much of its force, have applied to the consideration of the laws of this art the best power of their understandings" (*Prose* 3:66), to those who read poetry not as a source of consolation but "*as a study*" (*Prose* 3:62).

Furthermore, Wordsworth does not say that the poetic imagination resembles religion by confounding the calculating understanding with its contradictions; rather, he says that certain religionists (the Unitarians)[3] confound themselves when they base their religion on the "proudest faculty of our nature" (*Prose* 3:65), the calculating understanding itself. Finally, the poet's difficulty in creating taste does not "lie in establishing that dominion over the spirits of readers by which they may be humbled and humanized, in order that they may be purified and exalted" (*Prose* 3:80–81). Wordsworth does ask whether the problem lies there, but he rejects this alternative and finds the poet's real problem in inspiring the reader to "the exertion of a co-operating *power*" (*Prose* 3:81). The poet's problem is not to subdue the reader's spirit but to invigorate it, not to humble it before the dominion of his own power "by the mere communication of *knowledge*" but to "call forth and bestow *power*, of which knowledge is the effect" (*Prose* 3:81–82).

Arac quotes a passage from Foucault that envisions remarkably similar relations between knowledge and power: "'What gives power its hold ... [is that] it does not simply weigh like a force that says no, but that it runs through and produces things, it induces pleasure, it forms knowledge, it produces discourse; it must be considered as a productive network which runs through the entire social body'" ("Function of Foucault" 78). Power for both Wordsworth and Foucault is thus a precondition of knowledge and pleasure. Wordsworth, however, envisions this knowledge-producing power as a sign and a function of his own genius, whereas Foucault identifies the source of this power with disciplined experts rather than with "the 'writer of genius'" (*Knowledge/Power* 129), but the difference may be less consequential than it first appears. For one thing, Wordsworth insists on his works of genius as a contribution to a cultivated "intellectual universe," a recognizable "advance" which widens "the sphere of human sensibility" (*Prose* 3:82) in the domain of poetic art, and he further insists, as we have seen, that readers qualify themselves as judges not just through the corresponding exercise of their imaginative powers but through study of the laws of the art. "Wordsworth bases his faith in the ultimate triumph of his work," I have argued elsewhere, "not in the fateful tides of taste or even in the enduring powers of love or the human heart alone but in the disciplined activities of the human mind in the enterprise of literary study" (*Making Tales* 7). Wordsworth's personification of "the great Spirit of human knowledge" (*Prose* 3:84), in which both the poet's work and the people's active appreciation participate, manifests itself in those disciplined activities just as Foucault's personified power manifests itself in the various intellectual disciplines and produces knowledge and pleasure and discourse through them.

Arac contrasts this knowledge-, pleasure-, and discourse-producing power to "Foucault's polemical redefinition [of a humanism] that elides any difference between humanism and Christianity." Humanism by that definition is "everything that restricts the desire for power in our ways of teaching, learning, and living" (*Genealogies* 78). This definition encompasses the humanism of both of Abrams's roads to Wordsworth, for Wordsworth's desire for productive power can be found down neither of them. Pleasure and joy can at least be found down what Abrams calls Wordsworth's humanist road, but they are oversimplified, idealized, and vulnerable to irony and to political critique. Down the Christian road, the quest for "consolation in human suffering" presumes the frustration of desire and the sense of powerlessness in the face of disappointments that humble and humanize us. Arac shows that Abrams identifies the historical disappointments of his own generation with the historical disappointments to which Wordsworth responds (*Genealogies* 79), and we might add that Abrams exaggerates the importance of Wordsworth's consoling Christian moments as balm for his generation's suffering those disappointments.

But in the *Essay Supplementary*, Wordsworth finds even in "*suffering*" not a call for consolation but a "connection . . . with effort, with exertion, and *action* . . . To be moved . . . by a passion, is to be excited, often to external and always to internal, effort" (*Prose* 3:81–82). In communicating passion and power, the poet arouses such effort, provokes a response always to the internal effort of maintaining or restoring pleasure and sometimes to the external effort of producing critical discourse, making new poems, discovering literary historical knowledge, or committing political acts. Even the production of consoling discourse may be an active response to suffering, a work of desire, but the acceptance of consoling discourse can easily become an excuse for passivity and a circumscription of desire. Like the complacency of taste against which Wordsworth struggles, the complacency of accepted consolation limits the sphere of human possibilities and rationalizes the acceptance of limitations and the cessation of effort. Such complacency occludes our powers instead of provoking them and erects fixed images of what we and our authors are and can be.

In the spirit of the *Essay Supplementary*, Arac's project at its best moments opposes such complacent humanism and claims the sphere of active power for disciplined writers and readers alike. "Writing solicits from us our interpretive power," he writes, "the stones we critics and readers throw to shatter the old, fixed images and startle new life again. The sublime inheres not only in the text, but also in the reader's activity of fixing upon passages, highlighting them in ways that disrupt any equability of composition in favor of intensity of attention, the means by which literary history prolongs itself" (*Genealogies* 155–56). The exercise of power Arac here envisions seems less cooperative and more disruptive than the power Wordsworth hopes to call up in his readers, for the readers here are doing what the poet does there—violating commonplace expectations, disrupting textual continuities, shattering old images and bringing new ones to life.

But there is just no telling in general when poets will be the retailers of commonplaces and when they will be the instruments of liberation, just as there is no way of knowing in principle when readers will be the standardizers and regularizers of poetic novelties and when they will be the stone-throwing shatterers of old, fixed images. The exercise of the power Arac, Foucault, and Wordsworth call for is an act (Foucault calls it an event), not a role or a capacity, and we discover it only in being acted on and acting in response. It can be informed and cultivated by the disciplines of writing and reading we teach and practice, but it cannot be reproduced by them or regularized in a constitutional distribution of powers to specified functionaries. The exercise of such power is the good for the sake of which we organize disciplines and arrange constitutional functions, but precisely because it is not identical with those arrangements and functions we resist them when they thwart it or exclude us from it. We thus resist not power itself but in the name of and for the sake of power, and we discover power not only in resisting oppressive arrangements and debilitating functions but also in cooperating with interesting arrangements and in serving demanding functions.

Siskin resists Wordsworth's call to the reader to exercise a "co-operating *power*" because he reads that call as an inducement to "the sympathetic participation of [the reader] in the supposedly liberating act of 'making' the poem" (55). For Siskin, the reader is deluded into believing he helps create what in fact he reproduces; he has the illusion of mastery that was the object of Foucault's earlier critique of humanism as "everything . . . which told us that 'acquiescence' made 'mastery' possible" (*Genealogies* 126). But Arac's later Foucault rejects this vision of mystified sovereignty for a vision of productive power. As Arac puts it, "the disciplines extend power to us, and through us to our students, and through our students to us, in the mode of pleasure. Power is productive" ("Function of Foucault" 77).

The reader's exercise of a "co-operating *power*" with Wordsworth's literary power, then, even on Foucault's authority, need not be an acquiescent repetition but may also be a counteraction, and the poet's exercise of literary power need not only be a coercive imposition but may also be a provocation, even a demand, for productive questions and responses. The constitution of literature need not impose the work of the author or teacher as a norm by which to discipline the sensibility of the reader or student; it may, rather, cultivate the disciplines through which poets and readers, teachers and students may recognize and exercise the powers of literature and secure their blessings not only to themselves and their posterity but "in widest commonalty spread" (Wordsworth, Prospectus to *The Recluse*, l. 18).

Both Siskin and Arac block my temptation to conclude with these uninterpreted and uncriticized echoes of the Preamble to the U.S. Constitution and Wordsworth's Prospectus to the *Recluse*, but only Arac would permit me to affirm and elaborate their power. The passages I repeat are not, after all, concluding gestures but preambulatory declarations, and they do not settle the difficult constitutional questions of how to institute the goods they celebrate. The power they would secure and distribute—the textual power Robert Scholes identifies as the ultimate subject of literary studies (20)—comes into being within the disciplinary forms not only of language and literature in general but of specific curricular, canonical, pedagogical, and institutional arrangements as well— what Scholes calls "the English Apparatus" (1–17).[4] What follows the eloquent Preamble to a constitution is the determination of those arrangements in some particular form that both enables and limits the realization of the Preamble's aims. The subsequent history of the constitution is a struggle both to fulfill its enabling provisions and to change those arrangements that disable and disenfranchise. Arac holds, and I affirm, that in the struggle over the constitution of literature, Romantic discourse and Wordsworth's contributions to it should not be dismissed as a seductive regime that disables us with its addictive and complacent consolation. Wordsworth's vision of a democracy of active and disciplined sensibilities, inspired by its poets but not overawed by them, still retains the power to inform our practices and underwrite our institutions, but the struggle to realize that vision is only now coming to maturity. It would be premature and unwise to put this regime in the past when we have not yet seen what we might make of it and what it might make of us.

WORKS CITED

Abrams, M. H. *The Correspondent Breeze: Essays on English Romanticism*. New York: Norton, 1984.

———. "Introduction: Two Roads to Wordsworth." *Wordsworth: A Collection of Critical Essays*. Edited by M. H. Abrams. Englewood Cliffs, N.J.: Prentice Hall, 1972.

———. *Natural Supernaturalism*. New York: Norton, 1971.

Arac, Jonathan. *Critical Genealogies: Historical Situations for Postmodern Literary Studies*. New York: Columbia University Press, 1987.

———. "The Function of Foucault at the Present Time." *Humanities and Society*. 3 (1980): 73–85.

Bialostosky, Don H. "Coleridge's Interpretation of Wordsworth's Preface to *Lyrical Ballads*." *PMLA* 93 (October 1978), 912–24.

———. *Making Tales: The Poetics of Wordsworth's Narrative Experiments*. Chicago: University of Chicago Press, 1984.

Bloom, Harold, editor. *Modern Critical Views: William Wordsworth*. New York: Chelsea House, 1985.

Foucault, Michel. *Power/Knowledge: Selected Interviews and Other Writings 1972–1977*. New York: Pantheon, 1980.

Johnston, Kenneth R. *Wordsworth and* The Recluse. New Haven: Yale University Press, 1984.

Klancher, Jon P. *The Making of English Reading Audiences, 1790–1832*. Madison: University of Wisconsin Press, 1987.

Scholes, Robert. *Textual Power: Literary Theory and the Teaching of English*. New Haven: Yale University Press, 1985.

Siskin, Clifford. *The Historicity of Romantic Discourse*. New York: Oxford, 1988.

Stempel, Daniel. "History and Postmodern Literary Theory." In *Tracing Literary*

Theory, edited by Joseph Natoli. Urbana: University of Illinois Press, 1987.

Trilling, Lionel. "The Fate of Pleasure: Wordsworth to Dostoevsky." In *Romanticism Reconsidered*. Edited by Northrop Frye. New York: Columbia University Press, 1963.

Wills, Garry. *Inventing America*. New York: Doubleday, 1978.

Wordsworth, Jonathan, Michael C. Jaye, and Robert Woof, editors. *William Wordsworth and the Age of English Romanticism*. New Brunswick, N.J.: Rutgers University Press, 1987.

Wordsworth, William, *Wordsworth's Literary Criticism*. Edited by W. J. B. Owen. London: Routledge, 1974.

———. *The Prose Works of William Wordsworth*. 3 vols. Edited by W. J. B. Owen and Jane Worthington Smyser. Oxford: Clarendon Press, 1974.

NOTES

I am grateful to the Graduate School of the University of Toledo for a Faculty Research Award that supported revision of this paper for publication.

1. I have tried in my own work on Wordsworth to clear this alternative route by distinguishing Wordsworth from Coleridge's version of him and by discovering neglected Wordsworthian poetic premises that diminish the dominance of the unifying imagination. See *Making Tales*, chap. 1 and "Coleridge's Interpretation of Wordsworth's Preface".

2. It appears in Abrams's recent collection of essays *The Correspondent Breeze* and in Harold Bloom's 1985 Chelsea series collection of critical essays on Wordsworth.

3. Abrams inserts "the imagination" in brackets to gloss the following passage: "For when Christianity, the religion of humility, is founded upon the proudest faculty of our nature [the imagination], what can be expected but contradictions?" ("Roads" 2). But this passage immediately follows a sentence that complains of the "excesses . . . of those sects whose religion, being from the calculating understanding, is cold and formal" (*Prose* 3:65). In a letter to Catherine Clarkson, January 15, 1815, Wordsworth identifies these religionists as the Unitarians. He writes, "One of the main efforts of the Recluse is, to reduce the calculating understanding to its proper level among the human faculties—Therefore my book is disliked by the Unitarians, as their religion rests entirely on that basis" (*Wordsworth's Literary Criticism* 221). Though Wordsworth later in the *Essay Supplementary* calls the imagination "perhaps the noblest [faculty] of our nature" (*Prose* 3:81), it is not the proudest.

4. Though Scholes holds Romantic aestheticism responsible for some of the current problems of the English Apparatus, his book and its related *Text Book* come closer than any other work I am familiar with to giving practical shape to the program I have been admiring in Wordsworth, Foucault, and Arac.

CONTRIBUTORS

M. H. ABRAMS is Class of 1916 Professor of English Emeritus at Cornell University. He is author of *The Mirror and the Lamp: Romantic Theory and the Critical Tradition, Natural Supernaturalism: Tradition and Revolution in Romantic Literature, The Correspondent Breeze: Essays on English Romanticism*, and of numerous critical essays, including the forthcoming collection *Doing Things with Texts*. He is general editor of *The Norton Anthology of English Literature*.

CHARLES ALTIERI is Professor of English at the University of Washington. He is author of *Act and Quality: A Theory of Literary Meaning, Self and Sensibility in Contemporary American Poetry*, and *Enlarging the Temple: New Directions in American Poetry*. His *Painterly Abstraction in Modernist American Poetry* was published by Cambridge University Press in 1989.

DON H. BIALOSTOSKY is Professor of English at the University of Toledo. He is author of *Making Tales: The Poetics of Wordsworth's Narrative Experiments*.

DAVID BROMWICH is Professor of English at Yale University. He is author of *Hazlitt: The Mind of a Critic* and editor of *Romantic Critical Essays*. His *A Choice of Inheritance: Self and Community from Edmund Burke to Robert Frost*, was published by Harvard University Press in 1989.

MARILYN BUTLER is King Edward VII Professor of English at Cambridge University and author of *Maria Edgeworth, Jane Austen and the War of Ideas, Peacock Displayed: A Satirist in His Context*, and *Romantics, Rebels and Reactionaries: English Literature and Its Background, 1760–1830*. She has also edited *Burke, Paine, Godwin, and the Revolution Controversy*.

STANLEY CAVELL is Walter M. Cabot Professor of Aesthetics and the General Theory of Value at Harvard University. He is author of several books of philosophy, as well as literary and cultural studies, including *Must We Mean What We Say?, The Senses of "Walden," The Claim of Reason*, and

In Quest of the Ordinary: Lines in Skepticism and Romanticism.

GILBERT D. CHAITIN is Professor of French and of Comparative Literature at Indiana University. He is author of *The Unhappy Few*, a study of Stendhal's novels, and of essays on Stendhal, Hugo, Zola, Lacan, and narrative theory.

JAMES K. CHANDLER is Professor of English at the University of Chicago. He is author of *Wordsworth's Second Nature: A Study of the Poetry and Politics* and of various essays on literature and history in the Romantic period. He is currently completing a book to be called *England in 1819*.

CYNTHIA CHASE is Associate Professor of English at Cornell University. She is author of *Decomposing Figures: Rhetorical Readings in the Romantic Tradition* and of articles on literary theory and psychoanalysis.

KAREN HANSON is Associate Professor of Philosophy at Indiana University. She is the author of *The Self Imagined: Philosophical Reflections on the Social Character of Psyche* and of articles on a variety of topics in aesthetics and ethics, American philosophy, and philosophy of mind.

GEOFFREY H. HARTMAN is Karl Young Professor of English and Comparative Literature at Yale University. He is the author of many books on Romanticism and on critical theory, including *The Unmediated Vision, Wordsworth's Poetry, 1787–1814, The Fate of Reading, Saving the Text,* and *The Unremarkable Wordsworth*.

JOHN T. IRWIN is Decker Professor in the Humanities and Director of the Writing Seminars at the Johns Hopkins University. He is the author of *Doubling and Incest/Repetition and Revenge* and of *American Hieroglyphics*. He is presently completing books on Poe and Borges, and on Hart Crane.

KENNETH R. JOHNSTON is Professor of English at Indiana University. He is author of *Wordsworth and "The Recluse,"* and editor (with Gene W. Ruoff) of *The Age of William Wordsworth: Critical Essays on the Romantic Tradition*. He is currently writing a critical biography, *Young Wordsworth: Creation of a Poet*.

GARY KELLY is Professor of English at the University of Alberta. He is author of *The English Jacobin Novel, English Fiction of the Romantic Period,* and *Mary Wollstonecraft and Revolutionary Feminism* (forthcoming). He has edited Wollstonecraft's two novels, *Mary* and *The Wrongs of Woman*.

HERBERT MARKS is Associate Professor of Comparative Literature and English at Indiana University. He has written on American, English, and European poetry, and on biblical literature.

DONALD G. MARSHALL is Professor of English at the University of Iowa. He is the author of essays on Heidegger, Blanchot, and Derrida, and editor of *The Unremarkable Wordsworth*. With Joel Weinsheimer, he has prepared the revised English translation of Hans-Georg Gadamer's *Truth and Method* (forthcoming).

JOHN MURDOCH is Keeper of Prints, Drawings, Photographs and Paintings at the Victoria & Albert Museum. He is the author of *David Cox, Byron, English Watercolours, The English Miniature, The Discovery of the English Lake District* (with Robert Woof), *Painters and the Derby China Works*, and the forthcoming *Seventeenth-Century Limners*, together with numerous articles on British literary and visual culture from the sixteenth to the twentieth century.

BARBARA PACKER is Associate Professor of English at UCLA. She is author of *Emerson's Fall* and of articles on nineteenth-century American authors in the *Cambridge History of American Literature.*

TILOTTAMA RAJAN is Professor of English at the University of Wisconsin. She is author of *The Dark Interpreter: The Discourse of Romanticism, The Supplement of Reading: Figures of Understanding in Romantic Theory and Literature* (forthcoming), and of various articles on aspects of Romanticism and critical theory. She is currently at work on a study of Romantic narrative.

ANDRZEJ WARMINSKI is Associate Professor of Comparative Literature at the University of California, Irvine. He is author of *Readings in Interpretation: Hölderlin, Hegel, Heidegger* and editor of Paul de Man's *Aesthetic Ideology* (forthcoming). At present, he is completing a book on allegory centered on Wordsworth and American narratives.

SAMUEL WEBER is Professor of English and Comparative Literature at UCLA. He is author of *Institution and Interpretation, The Legend of Freud*, and is preparing a book on Walter Benjamin.

INDEX

Numbers in italics indicate an illustration.